# THE LIFE AND AFTER-LIFE OF

# PÁDRAIC MAC PIARAIS: SAOL AGUS OIDHREACHT

The Editors and Publishers gratefully acknowledge the support of Foras na Gaeilge, the Pearse Museum and the Office of Public Works in the production of this book.

# THE LIFE
## AND AFTER-LIFE OF
# P. H. PEARSE

# PÁDRAIC MAC PIARAIS:
# SAOL AGUS OIDHREACHT

Editors
# ROISÍN HIGGINS
# REGINA UÍ CHOLLATÁIN

IRISH ACADEMIC PRESS
DUBLIN • PORTLAND, OR

*First published in 2009 by Irish Academic Press*

2 Brookside,
Dundrum Road,
Dublin 14, Ireland

920 NE 58th Avenue, Suite 300
Portland, Oregon,
97213-3786, USA

This Edition © 2009 Irish Academic Press
Individual Chapters © Contributors

**www.iap.ie**

British Library Cataloguing-in-Publication Data
An entry can be found on request

978 0 7165 3011 4  (cloth)
978 0 7165 3012 1 (paper)

Library of Congress Cataloging-in-Publication Data
An entry can be found on request

Printed by Antony Rowe Ltd, Chippenham, Wiltshire

# Contents/Clár

# Notes on Contributors
## Scríbhneoirí

**Joost Augusteijn** lectures at Leiden University. He is author of *From Public Defiance to Guerrilla Warfare: The experience of ordinary Volunteers in the Irish War of Independence 1916–1921* (1996) and editor of several volumes, including *The Irish Revolution, 1913–1923* (2002). He is currently completing an intellectual biography of Patrick Pearse.

**Angela Bourke** is author or editor of several books and many articles on aspects of Irish tradition, including the award-winning *The Burning of Bridget Cleary: A True Story* (1999). She is Professor of Irish-Langauge Studies and Head of Modern Irish at UCD.

**Caoimhín Breatnach** is a Senior Lecturer in the School of Irish, Celtic Studies, Irish Folklore and Linguistics, UCD. His area of specialisation is Irish language and literature in the period 1200–1900. He was awarded an IRCHSS senior research fellowship in 2007–8.

**Pat Cooke** (formerly Curator of both the Pearse Museum and Kilmainham Gaol) was recently appointed director of the MA programme in Cultural Policy and Arts Management at UCD. He has written on heritage policy and produced major exhibitions on Irish nationalism and the story of the Great Blasket island. As a heritage sector manager, he pioneered the use of museums and heritage buildings as sites for major arts projects.

**Brian Crowley** is the Curator of the Pearse Museum in Rathfarnham, Dublin.

**Thomas Hennessey** is a Reader in History at Canterbury Christ Church University and a Fellow of the Royal Historical Society. He is the author of *The Evolution of the Troubles 1970–72* (2007),

*Northern Ireland: The Origin of the Troubles* (2005), *The Northern Ireland Peace Process: Ending the Troubles?* (2000), *Dividing Ireland: World War One and Partition* (1998) and *A History of Northern Ireland 1920–1996* (1997).

**Roisín Higgins** is a Research Fellow in Boston College-Ireland. She is working on the Irish Sporting Heritage Project funded by the Department of Arts, Sport and Tourism. She is completing her book on the fiftieth anniversary of the Easter Rising, which will be published by Cork University Press.

**Declan Kiberd** is Professor of Anglo-Irish Literature at University College Dublin. He is the author of *Inventing Ireland*, which won the *Irish Times* Literature Prize for 1997, and of *Irish Classics*, which won the Truman Capote Award for the best work of literary criticism published in 2002. He was Parnell Visiting Fellow at Magdalene College, Cambridge for 2003 and Visiting Professor of Irish Studies at Duke University in 2004. His most recent book, *The Irish Writer and the World*, was published in 2005 by Cambridge University Press.

**Róisín Ní Ghairbhí** Is as Ráth Caola in Iarthar Luimnigh do Róisín Ní Ghairbhí. Dhírigh a tráchtas PhD, a baineadh amach in Ollscoil na hÉireann, Gaillimh ar na scríbhneoirí dátheangacha Michael Hartnett agus Eoghan Ó Tuairisc. Tá sí ag obair mar léachtóir i Roinn na Gaeilge, Coláiste Phádraig, Droim Conrach. Tá ailt agus aistí foilsithe aici ar ghnéithe éagsúla de nualitríocht na Gaeilge agus an Bhéarla agus tá suim ar leith aici sa drámaíocht, i gcritic an aistriúcháin agus i léann an iarchoilíneachais. Foilseoidh Cló Iarchonnachta leabhar uaithi ar bheatha agus ar shaothar Mhichíl Uí Airtnéide i bhFómhar na bliana 2009. Léirmheastóir rialta í leis an nuachtán *Foinse*.

**English:** Lecturer in the Department of Irish, St Patrick's College, Drumcondra, Dublin. She has published articles and chapters in Irish and English on various aspects of Irish literature. A new book on the poet Michael Hartnett will be published by Cló Iarchonnachta in autumn 2009. Her research interests include Irish theatre, translation studies and post-colonial studies. She writes critical reviews on a regular basis for *Foinse*.

**Eoghan Ó hAnluain** Baile Átha Cliathach, Léirmheastóir agus iar-Léachtóir Sinsearach le Nua-Ghaeilge sa Choláiste hOllscoile, Baile Átha Cliath é agus ailt foilsithe aige in irisí acadúla agus léannta. Chuir sé eagar ar *Máirtín Ó Direáin, Dánta 1939–1979* (1980) agus ar shraith cainteanna ar chúlra a chuid filíochta leis an Direánach *Ón Ulán Ramhar Siar: Máirtín Ó Direáin ag caint ar chúlra saoil cuid dá dhánta* (eag.) (2002).

**English:** Born in Dublin in 1938. He taught in St Patrick's College, Drumcondra, and was Senior Lecturer in Modern Irish at University College Dublin. In collaboration with the poet, he edited the collected poems, *Máirtín Ó Direáin, Dánta, 1939–1979* (1980) and later published a series of recollections and talks on the background to many of his poems recorded from Ó Direáin, *Ón Ulán Ramhar Siar: Máirtín Ó Direáin ag caint ar chúlra saoil cuid dá dhánta* (eag.) (2002).

**Joyce Padbury** was formerly on the senior administrative staff of University College Dublin. She has an MA in History and is now working on a life of Mary Hayden.

**James Quinn** is the Executive Editor of the Royal Irish Academy's Dictionary of Irish Biography. He has published biographies of the United Irishman, Thomas Russell (2002), and of the Young Irelander John Mitchel (2008). He has also published several articles on radicalism and republicanism in eighteenth- and nineteenth-century Ireland. He is currently working on a book on the Young Ireland movement.

**Elaine Sisson** is a cultural historian and IADT Research Fellow at the Graduate School of Creative Arts and Media in Dublin. She published a cultural history of St Enda's school, *Pearse's Patriots*, with Cork University Press in 2004.

**Regina Uí Chollatáin** is a Lecturer in Modern Irish in the School of Irish, Celtic Studies, Irish Folklore and Linguistics, UCD. She is the author of *An Claidheamh Soluis agus Fáinne an Lae 1899–1932* (2004) and *Iriseoirí Pinn na Gaeilge. An Cholúnaíocht Liteartha. Critic Iriseoireachta* (2008).

**Brendan Walsh** is a Lecturer in History of Education, Educational Policy and Advanced Teaching Methodology at the School of Education Studies, Dublin City University. He is the author of *The Pedagogy of Protest: The Educational Thought and Work of P.H. Pearse* (2006) and co-author of the forthcoming *A Guide to Teaching Practice in Ireland* (2009).

# Acknowledgements

The editors have worked closely with the Pearse Museum, Rathfarnham, in preparing this book. We would like to express particular thanks to Brian Crowley, curator, for supplying the photographs and for giving his time and knowledge. His very good-natured involvement has added to the enjoyment of working on the project. A special note of appreciation also to Anne Marie Ryan for her help with the compilation of the images from the Pearse Museum and to Críostóir Mac Cárthaigh, UCD Delargy Centre for Irish Folklore, for his help with the images from the Irish Folklore Collection.

The images for this book have been supplied courtesy of the Pearse Museum, Kilmainham Gaol Museum, the UCD Delargy Centre for Irish Folklore, and the Irish Film Institute.

The original idea for this volume was formed at a conference organised to mark the ninetieth anniversary of the death of Patrick Pearse. We are particularly grateful to Professor Angela Bourke, who was on the organising committee for the conference and continued to give valuable support and much helpful advice in bringing this project to completion.

The Department of Education and Science provided funding for the conference and made it possible to bring together a wide range of the leading academics currently working on Pearse. The Humanities Institute of Ireland at UCD provided the venue for the opening day of the conference and we are grateful to Valerie Norton and Dr Marc Caball for their assistance. The Pearse Museum hosted the rest of the conference and we are extremely grateful to Pat Cooke, then curator, and the staff of the museum for their help in making it such a success. Professor Mary Daly opened the conference and we greatly appreciate her encouragement and support. We would like to acknowledge also the generous support of the former Head of the School of Irish, Celtic Studies, Irish Folklore and Linguistics, UCD, Professor Séamas Ó Catháin. We would particularly like to thank Anna Germaine, who provided administrative assistance and for whom nothing was too much trouble. Carole Holohan and Niamh Ní Shiadhail assisted on the days of the conference and ensured that things ran smoothly and we are very grateful for the work they put into this.

This book received a subvention from Foras na Gaeilge to assist with the inclusion of chapters in the Irish language and we very much appreciate their support, especially that of Deirdre Davitt and Éamonn Ó Hargáin. We are extremely grateful to Professor Liam Mac Mathúna, who acted as a second editor on the Irish language sections, and we greatly appreciate his giving so generously of his time and expertise.

Lisa Hyde of Irish Academic Press was enthusiastic about this book from the outset. We have been very fortunate to work with her and she provided encouragement and gentle pressure at just the right times. Dr Thomas Hennessey made the initial introductions. Aonghus Meaney has been an informed and extremely efficient copyeditor. We would like to thank all the staff at Irish Academic Press for the work they have done in bringing this book to completion.

Special thanks also to our friends, and to our colleagues in the School of Irish, Celtic Studies, Irish Folklore and Linguistics, UCD and in Boston College-Ireland. Of course, the book would not have materialised without the work of the contributors. They have, without exception, responded promptly to all of our queries and accepted advice with good humour. It has been a pleasure to work with them on this project. Finally, we would like to thank our families for their support while the book was being produced and we dedicate the industry involved to them.

Dublin, 2008

# Nótaí Buíochais

D'oibrigh na heagarthóirí go dlúth le hIarsmalann an Phiarsaigh, Ráth Fearnáin ar chur le chéile an leabhair seo. Ba mhaith linn buíochas ar leith a ghabháil le Brian Crowley, Coimeádaí na hiarsmalainne, as na grianghraif a cuireadh ar fáil agus as a chuid ama agus a chuid eolais fhlaithiúil a roinnt linn. Chuir a rannpháirtíocht dhea-chroíoch go mór leis an taitneamh a baineadh as a bheith ag obair ar an togra seo. Tá focal ar leith buíochais tuillte ag Anne Marie Ryan chomh maith as an gcabhair a thug sí le cur le chéile na n-íomhánnna ó Iarsmalann an Phiarsaigh, agus le Críostóir Mac Cárthaigh, a chabhraigh linn leis na híomhánna ó Chnuasach Bhéaloideas Éireann UCD. Soláthraíodh íomhánna an leabhair seo le caoinchead Iarsmalann an Phiarsaigh, Iarsmalann Phríosún Chill Mhaighneann, Chnuasach Bhéaloideas Éireann UCD, agus Institiúid Scannán na hÉireann.

Shíolraigh tuairim bhunaidh an chnuasaigh ó chomhdháil a reachtáladh le comóradh a dhéanamh ar an nóchadú cuimhneachán de bhás Phádraic Mhic Phiarais. Bhí an tOllamh Angela Bourke ar choiste eagrúcháin na comhdhála agus ba mhór againn a comhairle ghaoismhear, luachmhar agus a cuid tacaíochta leanúnaí agus muid ag obair air seo agus é a thabhairt chun críche againn.

Chuir an Roinn Oideachais agus Eolaíochta maoiniú ar fáil don chomhdháil a chuidigh go mór le tarraingt le chéile réimse fairsing phobal acadúil atá ag obair ar an bPiarsach. Cuireadh tús leis an gcomhdháil in Institiúid na hÉireann don Léann Daonna, An Coláiste Ollscoile, Baile Átha Cliath agus táimid buíoch de Valerie Norton agus den Dr Marc Caball as a gcabhair. Reachtáladh an chuid eile den chomhdháil in Iarsmalann an Phiarsaigh agus táimid go mór faoi chomaoin ag Pat Cooke, Iar-Choimeádaí na hiarsmalainne, as a chabhair. Chomh maith leis sin ba mhaith linn aitheantas a thabhairt don obair a rinne foireann na hiarsmalainne i rith an ullmhúcháin agus i rith na comhdhála féin. D'oscail an tOllamh Mary Daly an chomhdháil agus ba mhór againn an tacaíocht a thug sí féin agus an tOllamh Séamas Ó Catháin, Iar-Cheann, Scoil na Gaeilge, an Léinn Cheiltigh, Bhéaloideas

Éireann agus na Teangeolaíochta, UCD, dúinn agus an chomhdháil á réiteach againn. Fuair muid cabhair riaracháin ar leith ó Anna Germaine, Riarthóir na Scoile, a roinn idir am agus shaineolas go fial linn, go háirithe nuair a bhí tréimhsí brú agus easpa ama i gceist. Ba iad Carol Holohan agus Niamh Ní Shiadhail a chinntigh go ndeachaigh imeachtaí na comhdhála de réir mar ar socraíodh iad agus muid an-bhuíoch den bheirt acu dá bharr.

Fuair an leabhar seo urraíocht ó Fhoras na Gaeilge le cabhrú le cur le chéile an ábhair Ghaeilge. Táimid an-bhuíoch d'Fhoras na Gaeilge as an tacaíocht seo agus go háirithe de Dheirdre Davitt agus d'Éamonn Ó Hargáin as an spreagadh a thug siad dúinn sa ghné sin den obair. Chomh maith leis sin táimid an-bhuíoch den Ollamh Liam Mac Mathúna, Ceann, Scoil na Gaeilge, an Léinn Cheiltigh, Bhéaloideas Éireann agus na Teangeolaíochta, UCD a bhí sásta feidhmiú mar an dara heagarthóir ar na sleachta Gaeilge. Is mór againn an t-am agus an dua a chaith sé agus a chuid saineolais á roinnt aige linn.

B'fhoinse inspioráide í Lisa Hyde ón Irish Academic Press ó phointe tosaigh an leabhair agus braithimid gur mhór an tairbhe dúinn a bheith ag obair léi. Ghríosaigh agus spreag sí muid i gcónaí taobh le brú beag a chur orainn nuair a ba ghá leis. Ba é an Dr Thomas Hennessey a chuir in aithne dá chéile muid. Cóip-eagarthóir eolgaiseach, éifeachtúil é Aonghus Meaney leis, agus ba mhaith linn ár mbuíochas a ghabháil le foireann uile Irish Academic Press as an dua atá caite acu le cur i gcrích an fhoilseacháin seo.

Tá buíochas ar leith tuillte ag ár gcairde, agus ag ár gcomhghleacaithe i Scoil na Gaeilge, an Léinn Cheiltigh, Bhéaloideas Éireann agus na Teangeolaíochta, UCD agus ag ár gcomhghleacaithe in Boston College, Éire. Ar ndóigh, ní thiocfadh an leabhar seo chun críche gan ionchur díograiseach na n-údar. D'fhreagair údair na n-aistí na fiosrúcháin uile ar an bpointe agus glacadh le comhairle le dea-thoil. Ba phléisiúr é dúinn comhoibriú leo ar an togra seo. Le críochnú ba mhaith linn ár mbuíochas speisialta a thabhairt dár gclanna as an tacaíocht leanúnach a léirigh siad agus an leabhar seo á réiteach. Tiomnaímid an dua a caitheadh leis an saothar seo dóibh.

Baile Átha Cliath, 2008

# List of Illustrations
# Liosta Léaráidí

# Introduction

## ROISÍN HIGGINS and REGINA UÍ CHOLLATÁIN

Patrick Pearse depicted himself as a wise fool who had 'done never a prudent thing' and, in many ways, the key to assessing Pearse is in weighing the wisdom in his foolishness. In his writing Pearse expressed a strong conviction that history would elevate his actions and vindicate his vision. However, the passing of time has seen Pearse both revered and reviled. Indeed, as the iconic figure of the Irish revolutionary period, he has become one of the most contested figures in Irish history. Pearse's reputation has been determined by the politics of the present rather than the past and this has often helped to obscure aspects of his life. On the ninetieth anniversary of his death it was noted: 'For decades, poor sea-green incorruptible (and conveniently dead) Pearse was the touchstone of all that was right and wrong in changing Ireland.'[1] Indeed, Pearse has become such a politically charged figure that, despite his influence over Irish history and culture, he was largely neglected by academics in the last decades of the twentieth century.

This collection of essays retrieves Pearse from the simplicities of his iconic status and examines his individual life as educationalist, journalist, Irish language advocate and radical republican. Pearse himself wrote: 'With his own individuality, he must contribute to the cause; upon his own individuality will both he and it be judged.'[2] What emerges in this collection is a multi-faceted figure who does not sit easily in a single category. Pearse's life reflects many of the tensions within Irish society at the turn of the nineteenth century: he was both Irish and English, Victorian and modernist, respectable and revolutionary. The diversity of the roles Pearse played within that society means that the study of his life is greatly enriched by an inter-disciplinary approach. The multiplicity of views in this volume mirrors the lack of clear boundaries in the personality of Pearse himself. He is an elusive figure who is not served by being sanitised or categorised. This volume of essays brings together the expertise of academics from across the arts, social sciences and education. Through their inter-disciplinary approach the chapters represent a diversity of academic voices so that no single or partial narrative dominates. The volume brings together those who work in both Irish and English languages, a reflection of the approach fostered and promoted by Pearse himself through his theories on bilingualism.

### 'FEAR BHAILE ÁTHA CLIATH' / 'THE DUBLIN MAN'

In the west of Ireland Pearse was known simply as 'fear Bhaile Átha Cliath', 'the Dublin man'. The opening section of essays addresses his life as part of the Dublin middle class and reveals how Pearse was shaped by personal relationships and by how he was perceived by those with whom he spent time. Joost Augusteijn builds a portrait of the private Pearse with previously unused sources. The chapter pays acute attention to what Pearse said in private and links this to the changing situation in which he found himself. It shows his development from a young boy, who was seen as incapable of breaking a shop window, to the leader of the Easter Rising. Augusteijn charts Pearse's journey toward the General Post Office and demonstrates that it was neither inevitable nor straightforward. He provides a revised explanation for Pearse's political thinking, establishing how it developed and changed.

The myth which grew around Pearse after his death was greatly assisted by his mother and sisters and much previous attention has focused on the significant influence of Pearse's maternal line. Brian Crowley, instead, examines the relationship between Pearse and his father. James, an English ecclesiastical sculptor, autodidact and religious radical, came to Ireland in the mid-nineteenth century to take advantage of the post-Emancipation church-building boom. The chapter offers a rendering of the Pearses' early home life and Crowley explores the influence of James Pearse in creating an atmosphere of independent thought and aesthetic appreciation. The Englishness of Pearse's father had a profound influence on the identity of the son, and Augusteijn, Crowley and Cooke all show that this contributed to Pearse's sense of separateness from his contemporaries.

Joyce Padbury explores the relationship between Pearse and Mary Hayden, the first professor of Irish History in UCD. The two shared a friendship which centred around a common interest in the Irish language and participation in the Gaelic League. This chapter reveals Pearse as a thoughtful and sensitive friend. His closest female friend, Hayden, wrote of Pearse: 'We talk a lot on all sorts of subjects and I find him most companionable, a really nice fellow.' Hayden's letters to Pearse include discussions of Home Rule and the National University Bill. Pearse involved Hayden in St Enda's as a member of its council and as a visiting lecturer. Their political views diverged, however, over military action, and they lost contact in the last years of Pearse's life. The friendship with Hayden, as revealed in this chapter, casts an important light on a personal aspect of Pearse.

Pat Cooke depicts Pearse as a figure who was deeply unsure of his identity. In this chapter, Cooke explores Beckett's theory of the Victorian Gael in the sense of an Irish writer in flight from self-awareness. He argues that most of Pearse's writings derive from English literary romanticism, with very little dependence on a specific 'Gaelic' experience. 'To the Victorian, the martyr represented an exaltation of character above all other virtues', Cooke explains, and for Pearse's generation, 'character represented a kind of archetype that transcended national differences'. In this, Cooke links the notion of the Victorian Gael and Pearse overcoming, or at least coming to terms with, both his background and his sense of nationalism, describing him as 'a typical European of his generation' and less of an 'idiosyncratic Irish Catholic'. The chapter, invoking Beckett's ambivalent formulation, argues that Pearse was an acute instance of cross-cultural tensions and influences, and makes a case for seeing Pearse as one of the most eminent of Irish Victorians.

## HISTORY, POLITICS AND CULTURE

The second section of chapters considers the significance of Pearse within the political and social environment he inhabited. Declan Kiberd offers an important companion piece to the work of Pat Cooke. He sees Pearse not as a vestigial Arts and Crafts late Victorian radical, but rather as a Modernist at home in the company of his contemporaries James Joyce, James Connolly and, later, Samuel Beckett. As were these figures, Pearse was interested in the question of how 'newness' comes into the world and in the technical problem of presenting unprecedented ideas and feelings in a language dense with precedents. Moreover, Kiberd argues, 'Pearse took Irish asceticism out of the monasteries and into the secular world of writing and cultural politics.' This provides a key to Pearse's cultural and political philosophies and language.

One of the vehicles which provided a forum for this presentation of ideas and language was the journalistic platform which Pearse used from an early age with significant authority, as editor of the first Irish-language newspaper between 1903 and 1909, and as a columnist and editor of other significant journals and newspapers throughout his lifetime. This forum is analysed in Regina Uí Chollatáin's chapter. Pearse is rarely examined from a critical journalistic standpoint, although, Uí Chollatáin argues, in light of current understanding and

developments in the area of journalistic conventions and media history, some of Pearse's journalistic writings may well have been significant in allowing him to 'die willingly'. This chapter explores the
notion of Pearse within the journalistic framework in which he
worked, examining the notion of 'brotherhood' and 'imagined community' for a monoglot reading public and in an Anglophone society. Pearse emerges as the pioneering journalist, the editor, the columnist and the political correspondent, culminating in a selection of
writings which attest to the individual vision within a fragmented
society. This places Pearse among the prominent Irish journalists of
the Revival period, ironically serving a dominant elite public.

James Quinn links Pearse's ideological development with the
Young Irelanders' mission of the nineteenth century, which was 'more
anxious to shape the future than accurately chronicle the past'. Quinn
argues that despite his attempts to shape the future, Pearse was driven
by his sense of duty to his nationalist forebears. In his pamphlet
*Ghosts* (1915), Pearse drew on the writings of James Fintan Lalor,
John Mitchel, Thomas Davis and Theobald Wolfe Tone, who had
provided the basic definition of Irish nationality. Their writings (particularly those of the three Young Irelanders) helped shape Pearse's
revolutionary ideology and, Quinn demonstrates, his decision to take
up arms in 1916 was strongly influenced by the wish to appease the
reproaches of these 'ghosts' by bringing their work to fulfilment.

Thomas Hennessey argues that the Easter Rising and Pearse's
republicanism contributed to the partition of Ireland – which was
inevitable – becoming a permanent reality. Hennessey indicates how
nationalist alternatives were available in the leadership of John
Redmond and Arthur Griffith but the Rising, in breaking the link
with the Crown and Empire, began a process of unionist alienation
from their sense of Irishness. Moreover, the blood sacrifice of the
Rising contrasted with Redmond's attempt to create a new sense of
Irishness among Catholics and Protestants based upon a shared sacrifice on the battlefields of France and Belgium; 1916 has become a
pivotal date in Irish history and Hennessey points up its appeal to
unionists and nationalists as a seminal year in the creation of national
myths, and the way in which the events of that year cemented divisions on the island.

Roisín Higgins discusses the after-life of Pearse. The iconic image of
Pearse was constructed as part of the process of party and state building in independent Ireland and came to represent a touchstone of Irish
republicanism. As a mythical figure of the Irish imagination, Pearse
inhabited a semi-religious role and was used as a moral and political
exemplar. His unique position in Irish nationalism is, in part, due to his
connection to the Proclamation which is often seen as the foundation

document of the Republic. Moreover, it is Pearse who is invoked each time the Proclamation is read aloud at commemorative events. By the 1970s Pearse had become a problematic figure and Higgins addresses the relationship between Irish politics and historiography.

## LANGUAGE, LITERATURE AND EDUCATION

The third section of this collection examines Pearse's literary writings and his contribution to Irish language and education, highlighting the influence of Pearse on twenty first century Irish-language literature and criticism. Angela Bourke explores how Pearse used his short stories to counteract images of deficit within the congested districts of the west of Ireland. She argues that Pearse's ten short stories were less 'quiet acts of faith' than a sustained and deliberate use of the print medium to create a sense of common culture, heritage and destiny. Bourke demonstrates how Pearse used his fiction pages to inspire and motivate both the marginally literate Irish speakers of the impoverished western seaboard and the young town- and city-dwellers who were learning Irish in classes run by the Gaelic League with the aim of imagining and creating a new 'Irish Ireland'.

Róisín Ní Ghairbhí's essay draws on post-colonial theory as well as on less frequently cited sources, like Pearse's political paper *An Barr Buadh*, in order to reassess some of Pearse's *oeuvre* in English and in Irish. She argues that his sophisticated appraisal of the domains and structures available (and unavailable) to those who sought a native voice in Irish literature, his warnings against essentialist readings of Irish culture and his incorporation of these insights in the hybrid forms he used in his own writing make Pearse a post-colonial writer *par excellence*.

The profound influence of Pearse on twentieth century Irish-language literature is reviewed by Eoghan Ó hAnluain in his assessment of Pearse's influence on one of the twentieth century's prominent Irish poets, Máirtín Ó Direáin. Ó hAnluain points out that Ó Direáin counts Pearse alongside ancient Irish heroes in his poetry, raising him to the rank of nobility in his poem 'Éire ina bhfuil romhainn' ['Ireland in the coming times']:

> Because you are no longer the spouse of Conn or Eoghan,
> Pearse's spouse or the love of the heroes
> Mar ní tú feasta céile Choinn ná Eoghain,
> Céile an Phiarsaigh ná rún na laoch

Alongside evidence by contemporaries of Pearse, this essay highlights the band of literary writers who were, in their own quiet way, formulating a rhetoric which would mirror the society in which they not only lived but which preceded them, giving rise to a modern literature which would form the basis for much literary thought and criticism in the latter half of the twentieth century.

The evolving study of Irish language and literature has much to gain also from a meticulous approach, revisiting textual analysis in light of present progression in this area, as put forward by Caoimhín Breatnach. The skills used by Pearse in his treatment of two textual items from *fiannaíocht* tradition are wanting in several respects, Breatnach argues, and in the case of *Cath Fionntrágha* in particular, Pearse's edited texts and his interpretation of their significance reflect strong nationalist sentiments on his part. Breatnach studies his edition of the tale *Bruidhean Chaorthainn* [*The Hostel of the Rowan Tree*], published in 1908, and an episode from the tale *Cath Fionntrágha* [*The Battle of Ventry*], published in *An Barr Buadh* in 1912. The influence on Pearse of earlier works on *fiannaíocht* tradition is also discussed and it is argued that the views of Pearse and other commentators on this material are somewhat one-sided and do not adequately reflect its complex nature.

In keeping with Pearse's interest in the Fianna cycle, Elaine Sisson addresses the particular literary and visual influence of the figure of Cúchulainn at St Enda's school for boys. The figure of the boy-hero was borrowed by Pearse from mythology as the foundation for a modern Celtic masculine identity for his pupils. The leadership qualities of the warrior-hero were combined with the scholarly attributes of Celtic Christian masculinity to produce a contemporary prototype of nationalist male identity. Sisson demonstrates the way in which Pearse drew on pre-Christian sources for the model of the warrior-poet, embodied in the character of Cúchulainn, woven into a Christian model of the scholar-saint, exemplified by the life of St Colmcille, to create a modern nationalist figure: the revolutionary boy-citizen.

In the concluding chapter Brendan Walsh explores further this strong nationalist sentiment within an educational environment. Pearse saw education as a political act and, as Walsh argues, the nineteenth century omission of Irish language, literature and history from the school curriculum did represent the 'imposition of a silence, or systematic absence generated by a dominant elite'. Pearse's approach to education was characteristic of later progressive educational thinkers and, Walsh suggests, his conceptualisation of schooling as an agent of political and cultural resistance anticipated the work of later radical thinkers such as Henry Giroux and Paulo Freire, something which has generally remained unacknowledged.

The work in this volume reveals the full complexity of Patrick Pearse. Although he has been employed as a symbol of constancy in

Irish life, Pearse himself was not always consistent or certain. An examination of his life has provided the contributors to this book with the opportunity to reflect upon aspects of society in late Victorian and Edwardian Ireland and to demonstrate the variety of ways in which Pearse's life intersected with developments in areas such as education, journalism and Irish language advocacy. This was a period of high nationalism and Pearse was one of its most articulate exponents. His reputation became bound to the fortunes of republicanism and nationalism in twentieth century Ireland and this led to a sidelining of his broader significance. This collection of essays, therefore, offers an important reassessment almost a century after his death.

# *Réamhrá*

ROISÍN HIGGINS agus REGINA UÍ CHOLLATÁIN

Chuir Pádraic Mac Piarais é féin in iúl mar amadán críonna nach raibh 'a prudent thing' déanta aige riamh, agus ina lán bealaí is é meá na gaoise ina bhaois, an eochair le measúnú a dhéanamh ar an bPiarsach. Chreid an Piarsach go láidir go n-ardódh an stair a ghníomhartha agus go gcosnódh an stair a fhís. Mar sin féin le himeacht ama tugadh idir urraim agus achasán don Phiarsach. Ar ndóigh, mar phearsa shamhailteach de thréimhse réabhlóideach na hÉireann, áirítear é ar na pearsana is conspóidí i stair na hÉireann. Socraíodh cáil an Phiarsaigh de réir pholaitíocht na haimsire láithrí in áit na haimsire caite agus is minic a chuidigh sé seo le neart gnéithe dá shaol a dhéanamh doiléir. Cothrom an nóchadú cuimhneachán dá bhás, tugadh faoi deara: 'For decades, poor sea-green incorruptible (and conveniently dead) Pearse was the touchstone of all that was right and wrong in changing Ireland.'[1] Ar ndóigh, toisc cumhacht pholaitiúil an Phiarsaigh, rinne an pobal acadúil faillí ann i mblianta deiridh an fhichiú haois, ainneoin a thionchair ar stair agus ar chultúr na hÉireann.

Tugann an cnuasach aistí seo an Piarsach ar ais ó shimplíocht a stádais shamhailtigh agus scrúdaítear a shaol aonair mar oideachasóir, mar iriseoir, mar chosantóir na Gaeilge, agus mar phoblachtánach radacach. Scríobh an Piarsach féin: 'With his own individuality, he must contribute to the cause, upon his own individuality will both he and it be judged.'[2] Is éard a thagann as an gcnuasach seo ná pearsa iltaobhach nach suíonn i gceart i gcatagóir ar bith. Déanann saol an Phiarsaigh scáthántacht ar chuid mhaith de na teannais taobh istigh de shochaí na hÉireann ag casadh an naoú haois déag; bhí sé Éireannach agus Sasanach; Victeoireach agus nua-aoiseach, é measúil agus réabhlóideach. Tugann ilghnéitheacht na rólanna a d'imir sé taobh istigh den tsochaí sin le fios gur shaibhride staidéar ar a shaol an cur chuige idirdhisciplíneach. Déanann iomadúlacht na ndearcadh sa chnuasach seo scáthántacht ar easpa teorainneacha soiléire i bpearsantacht an Phiarsaigh féin. Is pearsa éalaitheach é nach ndéanann sláintiú nó rangú freastal air. Bailíonn an cnuasach aistí seo le chéile, saineolas phobail acadúil ó na healaíona, ó na heolaíochtaí sóisialta agus ón oideachas. Tríd an gcur chuige idirdhisciplíneach, léiríonn na haistí ilghnéitheacht guthanna sa tslí nach mbíonn ceannasaíocht ag insint aonair nó ag insint easnamhach. Tugann an cnuasach seo iad siúd a oibríonn i nGaeilge agus i mBéarla le chéile, agus is scáthántacht é seo ar an gcur chuige a chothaigh agus a chuir an Piarsach féin chun cinn trína theoiricí ar an dátheangachas.

## 'FEAR BHAILE ÁTHA CLIATH'

In iarthar na hÉireann aithníodh an Piarsach go simplí mar 'fear Bhaile Átha Cliath'. Téann na haistí tosaigh i ngleic lena shaol mar chuid de mheánaicme Bhaile Átha Cliath agus léirítear conas a cruthaíodh an Piarsach trí chaidrimh phearsanta, agus chomh maith leis sin, conas a tugadh faoi deara é acu siúd ar chaith sé am leo. Tógann Joost Augusteijn portráid den Phiarsach príobháideach le foinsí nár úsáideadh cheana. Tugann an chaibidil aird ghéar ar a raibh le rá go príobháideach ag an bPiarsach agus ceanglaítear é seo leis an suíomh athraitheach ina raibh sé. Léiríonn sé forbairt an Phiarsaigh ó bhuachaill óg ar samhlaíodh leis nach raibh sé ábalta fuinneog shiopa a bhriseadh, go ceannaire an Éirí Amach. Tarraingíonn Augusteijn turas an Phiarsaigh chuig Ard-Oifig an Phoist agus léiríonn sé nach raibh sé seo dosheachanta nó díreach. Soláthraíonn sé míniú athbhreithnithe ar thuairimíocht pholaitiúil an Phiarsaigh, ag daingniú na slí inar fhorbair agus inar athraigh sí.

Chabhraigh máthair agus deirfiúracha an Phiarsaigh go mór leis an miotas a d'fhás timpeall air tar éis a bháis agus díríodh aird ar leith ar thionchar suntasach na líne máthartha roimhe seo. Ina ionad sin, scrúdaíonn Brian Crowley an caidreamh idir an Piarsach agus a athair James, dealbhóir Sasanach eaglaiseach, duine féinmhúinte agus radaicí reiligiúnach, a tháinig go hÉirinn i lár an naoú haois déag le leas a bhaint as tréimhse rathúnais tógála séipéal tar éis Fhuascailt na gCaitliceach. Tairgeann an chaibidil léamh ar shaol teaghlaigh luath na bPiarsach agus iniúchann Crowley tionchar James Pearse i gcruthú atmaisféar an mhachnaimh neamhspleách agus na tuiscena aestéitiúla. Bhí tionchar domhain ag Sasanachas athair an Phiarsaigh ar fhéiniúlacht an mhic, agus taispeánann Augusteijn, Crowley agus Cooke uile gur chuir sé seo le mothú an Phiarsaigh ar an deighilt idir é féin agus lucht a chomhaimsire.

Déanann Joyce Padbury iniúchadh ar an gcaidreamh idir an Piarsach agus Máire Ní Aodáin, an chéad ollamh le Stair na hÉireann sa Choláiste Ollscoile, Baile Átha Cliath. Roinn an bheirt acu caird-

eas, a raibh suim chomónta sa Ghaeilge agus rannpháirtíocht i
gConradh na Gaeilge mar bhunús leis. Tugann an chaibidil seo léargas ar an bPiarsach mar chara machnamhach, goilliúnach. Scríobh an
cara mná a ba chóngaraí dó, Ní Aodáin: 'We talk a lot on all sorts of
subjects and I find him most companionable, a really nice fellow.' Ar
na díospóireachtaí atá i litreacha Ní Aodáin chuig an bPiarsach, tá
rialtas dúchais agus Bille na hOllscoile Náisiúnta. Tharraing an
Piarsach Ní Aodáin isteach i Scoil Naomh Éanna mar bhall de
chomhairle na Scoile agus mar aoiléachtóir. Scar a ndearcaidh pho-
laitíochta ar ghníomhú míleata iad, áfach, agus chaill siad an teagmháil
le chéile i mblianta deiridh shaol an Phiarsaigh. Caitheann an cairdeas
le Ní Aodáin, mar a léirítear sa chaibidil seo é, solas tábhachtach ar
ghné phearsanta den Phiarsach.

Déanann Pat Cooke cur síos ar an bPiarsach mar phearsa a bhí an-
éiginnte dá fhéiniúlacht. Sa chaibidil seo, déanann Cooke iniúchadh
ar theoiric Bheckett ar an nGael Victeoireach mar scríbhneoir Éireannach ar teitheadh ón bhféinaithne. Deir sé go dtagann an chuid is
mó de scríbhinní an Phiarsaigh ó rómánsaíocht liteartha Shasanach,
le fíorbheagán de ag brath ar eispéireas ar leith 'Gaelach'. 'To the
Victorian, the martyr represented an exaltation of character above all
other virtues', a mhíníonn Cooke, agus do ghlúin an Phiarsaigh
'character represented a kind of archetype that transcended national
differences.' Ceanglaíonn Cooke nóisean an Ghaeil Victeoirigh anseo
agus an Piarsach ag sárú, nó ar a laghad ag dul i ngleic lena chúlra
agus lena mhothú ar náisiúnachas araon, ag cur síos air mar 'a typical European of his generation' agus níos lú den 'idiosyncratic Irish
Catholic'. Taispeánann an chaibidil, trí úsáid a bhaint as foirmle
dhéfhiúsach Bheckett, gur shampla géar de theannais agus de thionchair chroschultúrtha é an Piarsach, agus cuirtear cás chun an
Piarsach a áireamh ar na Victeoirigh Éireannacha is ardchéimní.

## STAIR, POLAITÍOCHT AGUS CULTÚR

Pléann an dara cuid de chaibidlí an leabhair tábhacht an Phiarsaigh
taobh istigh den timpeallacht pholaitiúil agus shóisialta a raibh sé ag
maireachtáil inti. Soláthraíonn Declan Kiberd píosa tábhachtach
comhlánach do shaothar Phat Cooke. Aithníonn sé an Piarsach mar
nua-aoisí ar a shuaimhneas i gcuideachta lucht a chomhaimsire,
James Joyce agus James Connolly, agus níos déanaí, Samuel Beckett,
in áit Victeoireach radacach, mall, buntúsach, ealaín-agus-cear-
daíocht. Macasamhail na bpearsan seo, bhí suim ag an bPiarsach i
gceistiú na slí a dtagann an 'úire' isteach sa domhan, agus i bhfadhb
theicniúil chur i láthair tuairimí agus mothúcháin gan réamhshampla,
i dteanga atá tiubh le réamhshamplaí. Ina theannta sin, deir Kiberd,

'Pearse took Irish asceticism out of the monasteries and into the secular world of writing and cultural politics.' Soláthraíonn sé seo eochair d'fhealsúnachtaí cultúrtha agus polaitíochta, agus do theanga an Phiarsaigh.

Bhí an t-ardán iriseoireachta ar na feithiclí a chuir fóram ar fáil do chur i láthair na dtuairimí agus na teanga seo, ardán a d'úsáid an Piarsach le húdarás suntasach, mar eagarthóir ar an gcéad nuachtán Gaeilge idir 1903 agus 1909, agus é fós óg. Ba ardán é a bhí in úsáid aige fosta mar cholúnaí agus mar eagarthóir ar irisí agus ar nuachtáin shuntasacha eile i rith a shaoil. Déantar anailís ar an bhfóram seo i gcaibidil Regina Uí Chollatáin. Is annamh a scrúdaítear an Piarsach i shuíomh criticiúil iriseoireachta, ach deir Uí Chollatáin, i bhfianaise tuiscintí agus forbairtí comhaimseartha ar stair agus ar choinbhinsiúin iriseoireachta, go bhfuil an-seans gur sholáthraigh fóram na hiriseoireachta deis dó 'bás toilteanach' a roghnú. Déanann an chaibidil seo iniúchadh ar choincheap an Phiarsaigh taobh istigh de fhráma tagartha na hiriseoireachta a raibh sé ag obair ann, ag scrúdú an nóisin 'brotherhood' agus 'imagined community' do phobal léitheoireachta aonteangach i sochaí anglafóin. Tagann an Piarsach chun cinn mar iriseoir ceannródaíoch, mar eagarthóir, mar cholúnaí, agus mar chomhfhreagraí polaitiúil, ag bailiú rogha scríbhinní le chéile atá mar theistiméireacht ar an bhfís aonair taobh istigh de shochaí easpach. Lonnaíonn sé seo an Piarsach i measc iriseoirí iomráiteacha thréimhse na hAthbheochana agus go híorónta ag freastal ar scothphobal ceannasach.

Ceanglaíonn James Quinn forbairt ídé-eolaíoch an Phiarsaigh le misean 'Young Irelanders' an naoú haois déag, a bhí 'more anxious to shape the future than accurately chronicle the past'. Deir Quinn, in ainneoin iarrachtaí an Phiarsaigh an todhchaí a chruthú, gur spreag grá an dualgais dá shinsear náisiúnach é. Ina phaimfléad *Ghosts* (1915), tharraing an Piarsach ar scríbhinní James Fintan Lalor, John Mitchel, Thomas Davis agus Theobald Wolfe Tone, a sholáthraigh an sainmhíniú bunúsach ar náisiúntacht Éireannach. Chabhraigh a scríbhinní (go háirithe iad siúd ar leis an triúr Young Irelanders iad) le cruthú ídé-eolaíocht réabhlóideach an Phiarsaigh, agus léiríonn Quinn go raibh an-tionchar ag mian an Phiarsaigh, cáineadh na 'ghosts' seo a shásamh trína gcuid oibre a thabhairt chun críche, ar a chinneadh chun airm a thógáil i 1916.

Deir Thomas Hennessey gur chuir Éirí Amach na Cásca agus poblachtánachas an Phiarsaigh le cur i bhfeidhm chríochdheighilt na hÉireann – rud a bhí dosheachanta – mar réaltacht bhuan. Léiríonn Hennessey an dóigh a raibh roghanna náisiúnacha ar fáil i gceannaireacht John Redmond agus Arthur Griffith, ach nuair a bhris an tÉirí Amach an ceangal leis an gcoróin agus leis an impire, gur

cuireadh tús le próiseas choimhthiú na n-aontachtaithe óna mothú
Éireannach. Thairis sin, bhí codarsnacht idir íobairt fhola an Éirí Amach
agus iarracht Redmond, mothú nua Éireannach a chruthú i measc
Caitliceach agus Protastúnach a bhí bunaithe ar chomhíobairt ármhán-
na na Fraince agus na Beilge. Is dáta maighdeogach é 1916 i stair na
hÉireann agus deimhníonn Hennessey a tarraingt d'aontachtaithe agus
do náisiúnaithe, mar bhliain shuntasach i gcruthú miotais náisiúnta,
agus an tslí inar dhaingnigh eachtraí na bliana sin scoilteanna ar an
oileán.

Déanann Roisín Higgins plé ar oidhreacht an Phiarsaigh.
Cruthaíodh íomhá shamhailteach an Phiarsaigh mar chuid de thógáil
stáit agus páirtí i Saorstát na hÉireann, agus le himeacht ama ba
chomhartha poblachtánachais Éireannaigh é. Mar phearsa mhio-
tasach de chuid na samhlaíochta Éireannaí, ghlac an Piarsach ról
leath-reiligiúnach agus úsáideadh é mar eiseamláir mhorálta agus
polaitíochta. Tá áit leithleach an Phiarsaigh i náisiúnachas na hÉireann bainteach lena cheangal leis an bhForógra, a shamhlaítear go
minic mar cháipéis bhunaidh na Poblachta. Chomh maith leis sin, is
é cabhair an Phiarsaigh a agraítear gach uair a léitear an Forógra ag
ócáidí comórtha. Faoi na seachtóidí ba phearsa achrannach é an
Piarsach agus téann Higgins i ngleic leis an gcaidreamh idir
polaitíocht na hÉireann agus croinicí staire.

## TEANGA, LITRÍOCHT AGUS OIDEACHAS

Scrúdaíonn an tríú cuid den chnuasach seo scríbhinní liteartha an
Phiarsaigh agus an chomaoin a chuir sé ar Ghaeilge agus ar oideachas,
ag cur tionchar an Phiarsaigh ar litríocht agus ar chriticeas na Gaeilge
san fhichiú haois chun suntais. Déanann Angela Bourke iniúchadh ar
conas a d'úsáid an Piarsach a chuid gearrscéalta chun íomhánna an
easnaimh sna ceantair chúnga in Iarthar na hÉireann a chur ó mhaith.
Deir sí gur lúide 'quiet acts of faith' iad deich ngearrscéal an
Phiarsaigh ná úsáid leanúnach, bheartaithe an mheáin chlóite, chun
mothú an chultúir chomónta, na hoidhreachta comónta agus an dáin
chomónta, a chruthú. Taispeánann Bourke conas a d'úsáid an Piarsach
na leathanaigh fhicsin chun cainteoirí imeallacha liteartha Gaeilge
chósta an iarthair agus áitritheoirí óga baile-agus-cathrach a bhí ag
foghlaim Gaeilge i ranganna a reachtáil Conradh na Gaeilge, a spreagadh agus a mhisniú chun 'Irish Ireland' nua a shamhlú agus a
chruthú.

Tarraingíonn aiste Róisín Ní Ghairbhí ar theoiric an iarchoilíneachais mar aon le foinsí nach dtagraítear chomh minic sin
dóibh, páipéar polaitíochta an Phiarsaigh, *An Barr Buadh*, cuir i gcás,
le hathbhreithniú a dhéanamh ar chuid d'*ouevre* an Phiarsaigh i

mBéarla agus i nGaeilge. Deir sí go ndéanann a luacháil shofaisticiúil ar fhearannais agus ar struchtúir infhaighte (agus dhofhaighte) dóibh siúd a lorg an guth dúchais i litríocht na hÉireann, a rabhaidh i gcoinne léamha eisintiúlacha chultúr na hÉireann, agus an tslí a gcuireann sé na léargais seo le chéile i bhfoirmeacha croschineálacha a d'úsáid sé ina chuid scríbhneoireachta féin, go ndéanann siad an Piarsach ina scríbhneoir iar-choilíneach *par excellence*.

Déanann Eoghan Ó hAnluain léirmheas ar thionchar domhain an Phiarsaigh ar litríocht Ghaeilge an fhichiú haois tríd an measúnú a dhéanann sé ar thionchar an Phiarsaigh ar dhuine de mhórfhilí an fhichiú haois, Máirtín Ó Direáin. Taispeánann Ó hAnluain go n-áiríonn Ó Direáin an Piarsach taobh le laochra seanda ina chuid filíochta, á ardú go céim uasal ina dhán 'Éire ina bhfuil romhainn':

> Mar ní tú feasta céile Choinn ná Eoghain,
> Céile an Phiarsaigh ná rún na laoch

Taobh le fianaise lucht comhaimsire an Phiarsaigh, cuireann an aiste seo an bhuíon scríbhneoirí liteartha chun suntais, a bhí, ina mbealach ciúin féin, ag cruthú reitrice a dhéanfadh scáthántacht ar an tsochaí a raibh siad ag maireachtáil inti agus ar an tsochaí a bhí ann rompu, ag cruthú spáis don nualitríocht, a chruthódh bunús do chuid mhaith tuairimíochta liteartha agus critice sa dara leath den fhichiú haois.

Tá neart le foghlaim fosta ó staidéar éabhlóideach na Gaeilge agus na litríochta trí chur chuige mionchúiseach, ag tabhairt athchuairte ar anailís théacsúil i bhfianaise fhorás comhaimseartha sa réimse seo, mar a chuireann Caoimhín Breatnach chun cinn. Deir Breatnach go bhfuil na scileanna a d'úsáid an Piarsach i gcur chuige téacsúil ar dhá théacs ó thraidisiún na fiannaíochta, easnamhach ina lán slite, agus i gcás *Cath Fionntrágha* go háirithe, léiríonn na téacsanna atá curtha in eagar, agus léamh an Phiarsaigh ar thábhacht na dtéacsanna, mothúcháin láidre náisiúnacha. Déanann Breatnach staidéar ar eagrán *Bruidhean Chaorthainn*, a foilsíodh sa bhliain 1908, agus eachtra ón scéal *Cath Fionntrágha*, a foilsíodh in *An Barr Buadh* sa bhliain 1912. Pléitear tionchar eagráin luatha ar thraidisiún na fiannaíochta ar an bPiarsach agus deirtear go bhfuil dearcaidh an Phiarsaigh agus tráchtairí eile ar an ábhar seo leataobhach, agus nach ndéanann siad scáthántacht cheart ar nádúr coimpléascach an ábhair.

Ag coinneáil le suim an Phiarsaigh san fhiannaíocht, pléann Elaine Sisson tionchar liteartha agus radharcach dhealbh Cú Chulainn i scoil Naomh Éanna do bhuachaillí. Thóg an Piarsach íomha an bhuachaill-laoich ar iasacht ón miotaseolaíocht mar bhunús d'fhéiniúlacht fhireann Cheilteach dá dhaltaí. Nascadh tréithe an ghaiscígh le cáilíochtaí scolártha an fhireannachais Cheiltigh Chríostaí chun fréamhshamhail chomhaimseartha na féiniúlachta náisiúnaí fireann a dhéanamh.

Taispeánann Sisson an tslí inar tharraing an Piarsach ar fhoinsí réamh-Chríostaí do shamhail an fhile-ghaiscígh, ionchollaithe i gcarachtar Chú Chulainn, fite i samhail Chríostaí an naoimh-scoláire, bunaithe ar fheabhas shaol Naomh Colm Cille, le pearsa nua-aimseartha, náisiúnach a chruthú: an saoránach buachalla réabhlóideach.

Sa chaibidil dheireanach, déanann Brendan Walsh tuilleadh iniúchta ar an mothú láidir náisiúnach taobh istigh de thimpeallacht oideachais. Ar bhealach, d'fhéach an Piarsach ar an oideachas mar ghníomh polaitiúil agus mar a deir Walsh, b'ionann an fhaillí a rinneadh sa Ghaeilge, sa litríocht agus sa stair i gcuraclam na scoile sa naoú haois déag agus 'imposition of a silence, or systematic absence generated by a dominant elite'. B'ionann tréithe chur chuige oideachais an Phiarsaigh agus a macasamhail i gcás fealsúnaithe oideachasúla, forásacha eile a tháinig ina dhiaidh. Molann Walsh gur réamhtheachtaire é, a choincheapú scolaíochta mar ghníomhaire ar chur i gcoinne polaitiúil agus cultúrtha, ar fhealsúnaithe radacacha eile ar nós Henry Girous agus Paulo Freire, rud nach dtugtar mórán aitheantais dó de ghnáth.

Léiríonn éifeacht iomlán an chnuasaigh seo castacht iomlán Phádraic Mhic Phiarais. Cé gur baineadh úsáid as mar shiombail leanúnachais i saol na hÉireann, ní raibh an Piarsach féin i gcónaí leanúnach nó cinnte. Thug scrúdú a shaoil deis do scríbhneoirí an chnuasaigh seo machnamh a dhéanamh ar ghnéithe sochaí in Éirinn sa chuid dheireanach den ré Victeoireach agus sa ré Éadbhardach. Taispeánadh éagsúlacht na mbealaí ina raibh saol an Phiarsaigh fite fuaite i bhforbairtí i réimsí ar nós oideachais, iriseoireachta agus chur chun cinn na Gaeilge. Ba thréimhse shuntasach náisiúnach í agus bhí an Piarsach ar na mínitheoirí ba shoiléire. Ceanglaíodh a cháil le cinniúintí poblachtánachais agus náisiúnachais san fhichiú haois, rud a threoraigh a thábhacht i measc an phobail ar leataobh. Ar an ábhar sin, tairgeann an bailiúchán aistí seo athbhreithniú tábhachtach beagnach céad bliain tar éis a bháis.

'The Dublin Man'
'Fear Bhaile Átha Cliath'

CHAPTER ONE

# The Road to Rebellion: The Development of Patrick Pearse's Political Thought, 1879–1914

## JOOST AUGUSTEIJN

In traditional descriptions Patrick Pearse is seen as the man who had the genius to show the Irish nation the road to a free Ireland. Although Ruth Dudley Edwards has taken a more nuanced view, essentially the title of her book reveals a similar outlook.[1] Whether or not the 1916 Rising was a necessary step which led to Ireland's independence is a matter of some debate, but the question of how and why Pearse came to believe this is rarely discussed. Due to the fact that little is known about his early years many have accepted Pearse's own claim that he came to his revolutionary thought through the nationalist background of his mother's family. Dudley Edwards concludes in the *Oxford Dictionary of National Biography* that the 'young Pearse was greatly influenced by his maternal aunt Margaret, who stirred his romantic soul with patriotic ballads of death and exile, tales of mythological Irish heroes, and hagiographical accounts of such doomed revolutionary leaders as Wolfe Tone and Robert Emmet'.[2]

However, the fact that this was an experience he shared with a great many of his contemporaries alongside the fact that Pearse's father was English has rarely been taken into account. Many Irish children in the late nineteenth century had an older relative who still spoke some Irish and whose ancestors had some involvement with one of the various radical movements of the nineteenth century. Correspondence to Pearse in 1901 indicates that Irish-language enthusiasts in Carrickmacross, Co. Monaghan collected 200 Irish proverbs even though nobody actively spoke Irish there.[3] Census records also show that a growing number of young men and women received education in Irish by the late nineteenth century.[4] Pearse's background in this regard, therefore, did not in any way predestine him to become a revolutionary republican, and probably only obtained significance because of his role in the Easter Rising of 1916. In this chapter his actual political thought is traced from his early youth to 1914 when he became fully committed to a violent rebellion. An attempt is made to explain this development by connecting the changes in Pearse's thinking to his personality and experiences; particularly in his early years. The availability of much new archive material on this period has made this possible.

### EARLY NATIONALISM

In his short autobiographical piece Pearse describes his grandaunt's stories on Wolfe Tone, Robert Emmet and the Fenians as the root for his militant nationalism.[5] In an open letter to the nationalist MP William O'Brien he also recalled the influence of his maternal family's involvement in Young Ireland and the Fenians, and their hope that Parnell would complete their work. This led the young Pearse to believe 'that Parnell would be King of Ireland' if the Irish Party succeeded, and that Ireland would then 'have her own army and navy'.[6] Pearse claimed retrospectively to have been fully nationalistic when he entered school: 'if any boy should have carried into the school a faith in Ireland and a love for Ireland I was that boy'.[7] Shortly before his execution Pearse made a direct link between this and his involvement in the Rising: 'When I was a child of ten I went down on my bare knees by my bedside one night and promised God that I should devote my life to an effort to free my country.'[8]

All these statements, however, were made at a time when he was fully involved in radical politics and do not necessarily reflect his actual position as a child. To his contemporaries there were no signs of any radical politics when Pearse first entered the Christian Brothers School as an 11-year-old in 1891. One of his classmates states: 'He was not the type to cut down Union Jacks. There were boys in the school who had strong views on politics no doubt reproduced from what they had heard at home, but he was not among them.'[9] Another fellow pupil went further: 'In early youth the two Pearses [Patrick and Willie] were very pro British. I always felt that he might have had another career but I never felt this of Kent or O'Hanrahan, McDermott or Clarke.'[10] In a speech Pearse gave in the USA in 1914 he acknowledged this and laid the responsibility for this lack of overt nationalism at the feet of the school itself:

> The system of education that I was subjected to grappled me insensibly and by degrees. The books that were put into my hands ignored Ireland. They did not attack Ireland; they simply ignored Ireland ... I began to write composition about OUR empire, and OUR fleet, and OUR army and OUR colonies. I

remember reaching the limit in one composition when I said that our empire would weather this storm as she had weathered many storms before.[11]

In light of his own description of the reaction of some of the Brothers this seems an unlikely scenario: 'My teacher, a Christian Brother, took my composition and wrote on it "No marks". He said to me "Do try to be Irish." The teacher saved me in spite of the system. After that I did try to be Irish.'[12] However, Pearse's interpretation of being Irish at this stage certainly did not concur with mainstream nationalism. Another classmate remembers: 'Bro Craven it was who told him to write of an Irish hero and this set him off. The subject "Was Napoleon or Wellington the greater general?" P. spoke for Wellington and praised him qua Irishman.'[13] Although Wellington had an Irish background, he can hardly be seen as representing nationalist Ireland. It is clear that despite his awareness of the deeds of nationalist icons the young Pearse was far from an Irish radical, and seemed to have identified quite strongly with Britain even when he entered the Christian Brothers.

Such identification is not really surprising when looking at Pearse's background. His father, James, was an Englishman who had converted to Catholicism for business purposes, but really was an agnostic.[14] Politically, like Pearse's maternal family, James Pearse was a supporter of Home Rule, even to the extent that he wrote and published a pamphlet on it at his own cost.[15] This did not, however, mean a rejection of the ties with Britain. The family was known for singing *God Save the Queen* after formal dinners and most of the family friends were from England. Partly due to Pearse's accent, which contained many English inflections, some school friends saw him as English. Liam O'Donnell recalled: 'I regarded P[earse] as an odd English rather than Irishman.'[16]

1.1 *Left to right*: Patrick Pearse, William Pearse, Margaret Pearse and Mary Brigid Pearse. Courtesy Pearse Museum.

Pearse thus had a divided background in every aspect of his upbringing. In his younger years he was made aware and may even have identified with the heroics of nationalist figures, but at the same

1.2 *Left to right:*
John Kelly (cousin),
William Pearse and
Mary Brigid Pearse.
Courtesy Pearse
Museum.

time he was raised in a family which celebrated the connection with
Britain. As a young teenager he was seen and acted as someone supporting the Empire, although he was probably also sympathetic to
the idea of Home Rule. Pearse became well aware of the confusing
influence of such a background:

> when my father and mother married there came together two
> very widely remote traditions – English and Puritan and
> mechanic on the one hand, Gaelic and Catholic and peasant on
> the other: freedom loving both, and neither without its strain of
> poetry and its experience of spiritual and other adventure. And
> these two traditions worked in me and fused together by a cer-
> tain fire proper to myself, but nursed by that fostering of which
> I have spoken made me the strange thing I am.[17]

The most important long-term influence on Pearse's political thinking came not from his family but from his involvement with the Irish
language movement. There is no evidence that his grandaunt's teachings made any impact in this regard. The first signs of a special interest in the language came when he was first taught Irish at the
Christian Brothers School. This was one of the few secondary
schools which had put Irish on the intermediate curriculum in the
1880s. Pearse apparently took to the language with great energy. He
spent a lot of time on it, studied grammar and translation while other
boys were playing, and even researched the language in the National
Library. One classmate recalls a lecture by Pearse on 'some Irish
saga', and he also wrote on it for the school paper.[18] His ability in
Irish grew, winning many prizes in his intermediate exams to the
extent that they largely paid for his schooling.[19] In 1896, the year
Pearse finished his exams, his special abilities in this field caused the
Brothers to appoint him as an assistant teacher.

Pearse then became increasingly involved in the language movement. He was sixteen and had to wait two years before he was
allowed to enter university, where he planned to study law and arts.
Apart from the few hours of teaching he did in the CBS, he needed
to find something with which to occupy himself. Thomas Flannery's
*For the tongue of the Gael*, which he had received as a prize in the
final Intermediate exam and which dealt with contemporary Irish
scholars, had caused Pearse to join the Gaelic League. More impor-
tantly however was his decision to set up a debating society together with his classmate and friend Eamon O'Neill. The New Ireland
Literary Society was initiated on 1 December 1896 with Pearse as its
president. It ran weekly meetings in the Star & Garter Hotel in
D'Olier Street, where they read, recited and lectured mostly on
ancient Gaelic literature but non-Irish subjects were also discussed.
One member recalls a debate on the proposition 'Was Kipling a true
poet?', in which Pearse took a purely literary stance, stating: 'He
[Pearse] did not speak as if he were a Gaelic Leaguer, or in any way
interested in things Irish.'[20] The main focus of the society was
ancient Irish literature, and therefore it was not very political. The
reason Pearse and O'Neill gave for setting up the society in the
founding document clearly positioned Dublin within the United
Kingdom: 'It is an inexplicable fact that Dublin, which must necessarily contain many young men of ability and culture, should possess fewer literary and debating societies than any city of equal
importance in Great Britain. In view of this, it is contemplated to
establish a new literary and debating society, of a high-class, yet popular, nature.'[21] One of the incentives for Pearse to set up the society
may well have been his desire to learn to speak in public. He was

known to be particularly shy, but was determined to overcome this. An attendant at one of his first public speeches witnessed this at close quarters:

> He was obviously nervous and shook in every limb, but was so obviously and terribly in earnest, and conquered or disregarded his trembling frame so well that the crowd listened and if not impressed were somewhat edified – at least I was – and I noticed the quavers gradually left his voice though not his legs & he finished forcibly and well.[22]

He was also known to study rhetoric actively, in particular through Yeats, practising speaking in front of a mirror and even changing the pitch of his voice to improve its impact:[23] 'He had definite views on diction, articulation and the varying tempo of an address. He was convinced that soft-oh, very very soft – and very slow speech, with here and there a flash of drama, or of pathos, travelled farther, deeper. In fact, reached not only the ears of the audience, but their hearts.'[24] It may be tempting to see this as a conscious attempt to become an orator in service of the nationalist cause, but considering his ideas and ambitions at this time, it may be more likely he was thinking of his career prospect as a lawyer.

It is a well-established fact that Pearse was known for his extreme dedication to learning the language and, increasingly, also for his dedication to the language movement as a whole. Considering the fact that Pearse's background did not particularly predestine him to this, the source of such a commitment is questionable. It is asserted here that this probably lay in his personality and peculiar background. From all accounts it is clear that Pearse was socially deficient and out of place in the Christian Brothers School. His English accent and the fact that he was the son of an upwardly mobile lower middle class family among a school frequented mostly by working-class children made his life difficult. Most of his classmates felt the Pearse brothers should never have been sent there, as their accent and general demeanour stood out.[25] Their mother's initial attempts to dress them in a kind of public schoolboy outfit consisting of a tight velvet coat and Eton collar also made them potential victims of bullying: 'He wore a big round collar, type now no longer seen. This riled the boys. I remember a rough boy once holding him up – they all mocked his collar – and began to bully him.'[26]

An ability in sports might have provided Pearse with a social position in the school but he had none: 'He was never an athlete. They started a football team, soccer, and he was in it but useless, running up & down the side line.'[27] Pearse was neither seen nor treated as one of the boys. When a shop window was broken by one of the pupils, the shopkeeper came into the school and was asked to pick out the culprit from a line up: 'The irate dauber pointed to Paddy Pearse, as the culprit – upon which all, master & boys laughed in incredulity. Impossible! Everyone said.'[28] The teachers apparently also found it difficult to punish him even for misdeeds for which others were chastised.[29] All this meant that he never felt connected with his classmates: 'No one knew Pearse. I sat beside him for 4 years in Westland Row but knew nothing of him. He was aloof.'[30] Another remembered: 'I was in school with Pearse. He was gentle and quiet and always went home by the rere [sic] way from Westland Row thru [sic] the lane. The boys would go under the railway arch noisily but he seemed to like to be alone.'[31]

This was exacerbated by his physical problems, some of which were in turn probably made worse by this social isolation. He had a squint in one eye of which he was particularly aware, and which in later life he tried to hide from others by looking at people sideways and raising his chin, most notoriously reflected in his insistence on only being photographed from the right.[32] This however made him appear arrogant and sly, not aided by his inability to engage in small talk and repartee.[33] Liam O'Donnell recalled: 'He did not repel you consciously but he never looked at you. I once used the phrase "his half averted eyes".'[34] He also had a stutter, moved awkwardly, and gave a cold clammy handshake, coming across as being shy and nervous.[35] All this reveals a large dose of self-consciousness; he wrote of himself: 'I am not sure whether it is a good thing for a man to possess as fully as I have possessed it the faculty of getting, as it were, outside of himself and of contemplating himself as if from a little distance.'[36] Pearse was also well aware of the effect he had on others, and in an open letter to himself he aired his social isolation: 'I wonder does anyone like you. I am undecided as to whether I like you or not.'[37]

It was clearly not easy to get close to Pearse, he is variably described as aloof, forbidding, unapproachable and dour. His fellow pupils express some admiration for his uncompromising and loyal stance in cases of conflict with the Brothers, but he was never one of them. Being an outsider made it attractive to find something he could dedicate himself to, something to give his school life direction and purpose and which would enable him to maintain himself in an otherwise hostile environment. From early on in his school life this became the Irish language. Eamon O'Neill recalled: 'He never joined in the ordinary games at playtime. He often climbed up on the high window-ledge of the school-room and sat there reading.'[38]

1.3 Patrick Pearse as a young child. Courtesy Pearse Museum.

## CULTURAL NATIONALISM

Despite the success of the New Ireland Literary Society, Pearse became more and more involved with the more prominent Gaelic League. For a shy and introverted young man the League provided a ready-made social circle, with the relatively high social standing of its leading members in Dublin forming an added attraction. A connection with established society was something Pearse, as part of a rising Catholic lower-middle-class family, always valued highly; this was also evidenced in his choice to study law. His father's lifelong desire to show his own family back in Birmingham that he had made it probably played a part in this as well.[39] Pearse joined the Central Branch of the League, where most of the prominent Dublin language enthusiasts were gathered, counting among its members some representatives of the Ascendancy and a number of Catholic and Protestant clergymen. In this branch Pearse soon came to prominence, due to his extreme dedication and, some said, his active self-promotion.[40] Eoghan Ó Neachtain, later editor of *An Claidheamh Soluis agus Fáinne an Lae*, described Pearse's attitude to every aspect of the League's business: 'Interested is not the word: his earnestness was the most notable trait of his work.'[41] At the same time his fellow students at Trinity College still saw him as 'too serious for levity'.[42] After Pearse started his studies, he wound up the society following advice to this effect from Fr Yorke and at Eoin MacNeill's request. He affiliated it to the League, with most members following his example.[43]

Although the League was avowedly apolitical, Pearse quickly became more politicised in it. Its meetings brought him in contact with many active and advanced nationalists who saw the main purpose of the League as to save Ireland; to save the Irish nation. The implicit acceptance of the idea of the existence of two nations would of course ultimately legitimise a political separation. Already in his inaugural address to the 1897–98 session of the New Ireland

Debating Society Pearse made this clear. He described the emancipation of the Gaelic race as the cause most worthy of success. Ireland
was a nation which had suffered, bled and endured agony more than
any nation. The Irish had fought for eight centuries but now they
were 'further off than ever from the goal towards which we have
struggled'. He felt it was a forlorn hope to believe Ireland would ever
achieve independence because the Irish were neither a military nor a
commercial or manufacturing race and its leaders were forever hope-
lessly divided. Instead Pearse believed the Irish should concentrate on
their special role in the intellectual advancement of mankind.[44] The
subject of a lecture he was invited to give on 15 February 1900,
which dealt with the battle of two civilisations, also makes clear that
he accepted the fundamental distinction between Britain and
Ireland.[45]

To Pearse the restoration of the language was the essence of being
Irish; political nationalism should and could only come second. In his
mind an emphasis on political nationalism was only a distraction
from the real struggle. In one of his first political statements in 1899
Pearse made it clear that he had no time for those who did not understand this:

> Apparently the only thing necessary to make a man or an insti-
> tution Irish is a little dab of green displayed now and again to
> relieve the monotony, a little eloquent twaddle about the *'chil-
> dren of the Gael'* or a little meaningless vapouring about some
> unknown quantity termed 'Celtic Glamour'. Take away the dab
> of green, strip off the leafy luxury of words and what have you?
> The man or the institution is as English as Lord Salisbury.
> Newspapers, politicians, literary societies are all but forms of
> one gigantic heresy, that like a poison has eaten its way into the
> vitals of Irish nationality, that has paralysed the nation's energy
> and intellect. That heresy is the idea that there can be an
> Ireland, that there can be an Irish literature, an Irish social life
> whilst the language of Ireland is English.[46]

Fundamentally Pearse always adhered to this belief. In 1904 he stated
that 'Political autonomy can be lost and recovered' and was 'not an
essential of nationality'.[47] A year later in reply to Thomas Kettle, who
had argued the case for the importance of political independence,
Pearse elaborated on this: 'In truth, the language movement is not
merely more important than the political movement, but it is on a different and altogether higher plane ... Political autonomy ... may ... be
necessary to continue existence of the Nation – in the case of Ireland
it probably is – but it is not, in itself, an essential of nationality.'[48] He

1.4 Patrick Pearse.
Courtesy Pearse
Museum.

clearly believed that the restoration of the language was the basis of a truly independent Ireland and that political independence would follow automatically once it had been achieved: 'All phases of a nation's life will most assuredly adjust themselves on national lines as best suited to the national character once that national character is safeguarded by its strongest bulwark [the language].'[49] In this Pearse mirrored the Irish case on how he believed Hungarian and Flemish emancipation had developed: 'The moral of the whole story is that the Hungarian language revival of 1825 laid the foundation of the great, strong and progressive Hungarian nation of 1904. And so it shall fall out in Ireland.'[50] Pearse did not reject political nationalism but simply believed it was subordinate to cultural regeneration. As a result he refused to take sides in the debate, which was heating up early in the twentieth century, between constitutional and revolutionary nationalists, both of whom were trying to get control over the Gaelic League. Pearse made it clear that he stuck to traditional League policy: 'At such a moment it is essential, even at the risk of hurting people, that the Gaelic League should make it absolutely clear that it, as a corporate body, is to be captured by neither one political party nor the other.' Individual members were free to sympathise with whom they liked as much as they liked.[51] Pearse himself attended the founding meeting of Sinn Féin in 1905 but did not join.[52] His focus on the language was so strong that at a meeting of the Celtic Literary Society he objected when one of the participants began to sing *Who fears to speak* and asked whether the man had an Irish song. The singer walked out in disgust and it was subsequently written that Pearse objected to a national song, but it was in fact the language in which it was sung that he had disapproved of.[53] It is therefore not surprising that few people in the first decade of the twentieth century saw Pearse as an advanced nationalist and some even doubted whether he could be described as national.[54]

The concentration on cultural nationalism guided Pearse's attitude well into the Home Rule crisis of 1912–14. As he had clearly stated in 1899, he did not expect a break between Ireland and Britain ever to develop. Through his position first as editor of the League newspaper *An Claidheamh Soluis,* and later as headmaster of St Enda's school, Pearse actively cooperated with the government, seeking reform, redress and support. Although he had decided not to pursue a career in law, Pearse did continue to function within the British system. He was very proud of his titles B.A. and B.L. (causing opponents to nickname him 'Babble'), and in 1905 even applied for a position as assistant Intermediate Examiner in Irish with the Board of Education.[55] The tension which clearly existed between the public career he and his family had desired for him and a rejection of the connection with Britain was solved when he became editor of the League newspaper, which gave a steady income as well as a connection to respectable society. In line with his position on national regeneration Pearse was one of the few nationalists who supported the Irish Council Bill of 1907 which gave Ireland such a limited degree of autonomy that all others rejected it.[56] Pearse realised his isolation when to his surprise even Sinn Féin joined in the chorus of disapproval: 'The very Ishmaelites of Irish politics have come in from the wilderness and are howling in concert with the pack.'[57] Pearse's support was based on the fact that the Bill would give Ireland control over education. He had long deplored the extent of British influence in that area: 'Morally they were no more entitled to dictate what should be taught to children in Connemara than they were to dictate what should be taught to children in Yokohama.'[58] After the fall of the Conservatives in 1905 Pearse had expressed his hope that the new Liberal government would transfer power over education to the Irish, regardless of its ability to grant Ireland Home Rule.[59] When the Irish Council Bill was brought before the House Pearse saw it as a revolution. If it will 'reach the Statute Book, we shall be on the eve of the greatest and most beneficent revolution in the modern history of Ireland. *The schools will be ours.* The shadows of Death and the Nightmare Death-in-Life will have passed away from the Irish landscape.'[60]

The same attitude had been behind his continuous discussions and conflicts with the government institutions concerning the position of Irish in the education system. By 1907, however, Pearse was satisfied with the reforms that had been introduced and declared that there was now no longer the excuse of a hostile Board of Education to prevent the introduction of Irish in those schools which had so far failed to do so.[61] Further improvements, Pearse argued, should not come from the government but from the people themselves: 'Our immediate point of attack must be not the Government, not the National Board, but the recalcitrant schools. In a word, we cannot expect the British Government to thrust Irish down our throats. We must show that we want Irish.'[62] To Pearse it was not enough to teach Irish. What should take place was the 'creation in the schools of an Irish atmosphere, the Irishising of the hearts and minds of the children, the kindling in their souls of the quenchless fire of patriotism, the setting before them of a great and glowing ideal of *Duty*'.[63] Being fairly satisfied with the progress at primary level, it soon became clear to him that such an integral approach would not emerge in the existing secondary schools. The logical conclusion of the primary role Pearse assigned to education was the idea of setting up his own school – which he did in 1908 – showing that in his mind saving the Irish nation was a long-term process in which a totally Irish school could play a pivotal role. Although he believed Ireland should be independent, Pearse clearly still did not believe it was likely to come through political or military means. The Irish Nation should first be grounded solidly before political independence was possible. The somewhat ambiguous attitude to the political connection was also shown in the banner which hung in the dining hall of St Enda's and read 'Fear God & honour the King.'[64]

Pearse was not very active politically after his school opened. However, the few statements he did make show he did not fundamentally change his outlook. He reiterated his belief that there was a battle of two civilisations but that there could only be real progress on the national question if there was a more general recognition of the importance of what he called the essentials of nationality. In schools, he argued that children 'should be constantly reminded of and made to realise the fact that they are a separate race from England and that it is a disgrace and a badge of slavery for a race to use the language of any other in preference to its own'.[65]

## POLITICAL ACTION

The prospect of the introduction of a Home Rule Bill at the end of 1911 seems to have spurred Pearse back into action, suddenly prompting a heave of political activity. An important element within this seems to have been an invitation he received around Christmas 1911 from Cathal O'Shannon to deliver the Emmet Memorial Lecture in Belfast in March 1912.[66] Pearse was a regular attendant at cultural and political meetings and it had become known that he had developed a particular interest in Emmet as a result of the latter's strong personal connection to the grounds of St Enda's. Pearse subsequently initiated the establishment of an Irish-speaking political society, Cumann na Saoirse (The Freedom Association), and associated newspaper *An Barr Buadh* (Trumpet of Victory). The advent of Home Rule had reawakened Pearse's hope that control over Irish education could be obtained through the political system. However he felt that the interests of Irish speakers were not adequately represented in the debates and this made him invite a number of his friends to form Cumann na Saoirse: 'In which Irish-speakers can analyse and express their political sentiments and initiate political action.'[67] Contrary to his approach at the time of the Irish Council Bill, Pearse made clear in his invitation to join the new society that he believed the Home Rule Bill was a matter of make or break: 'If a Home Rule statute is implemented Irish-speaking members will be needed in the Irish Parliament and if Home Rule is not introduced a sustained agitation will be needed, in which we must ensure that the battle cry is not sounded in the foreign tongue.'[68] He was willing to give Home Rule a chance and was, unlike advanced nationalists, willing to appear in public to support it. However, contrary to other supporters Pearse warned of the consequences of a failure to implement Home Rule at a mass-meeting in O'Connell Street on 31 March 1912:

> I think a good measure can be gained if we have enough courage. But if we are tricked again, there is a band in Ireland, and I am one of them, who will advise the Irish people never again to consult with the Gall, but to answer them with violence and the edge of the sword. Let the English understand that if we are again betrayed there shall be red war throughout Ireland.[69]

This was not just platform rhetoric, as Pearse took a similar line at the first meeting of the new society two days later. According to Peter Kearney who attended, Pearse emphasised the need to arm the Irish. Although those present were in principle in favour they were uneasy with Pearse's desire to make force more than just a theoretical notion.[70]

Even if Home Rule was passed Pearse saw it only as a first step. In *An Barr Buadh* he compared it to a prisoner being released from one of his two manacles. To those who opposed the Bill he emphasised that releasing the prisoner of one manacle would 'make it easier for him to escape, and perhaps it would be a weapon in his hand given him by God. It is clear to us that, not only is this a proposal to take a manacle from the Gael, but it is putting into the hands of the Gael a weapon.'[71] In the course of 1912 Pearse became less hopeful that Home Rule would pass and the threat of the consequences became more direct. However he did not yet see a role for himself in fulfilling this threat but looked instead to the younger generation:

> If Home Rule does not come then momentous events may happen soon. The people of Ireland may be called upon sooner than they may expect to make great sacrifices for the country. What will happen if Home Rule does not come can be left to the younger generation to settle and he could assure them that the younger generation would know what to do if the crisis comes.[72]

In June 1912 Pearse was temporarily removed from the political scene by the financial crisis which befell his schools. He only became politically active again in the summer of 1913.[73]

To Pearse the militarisation of Irish society in this period, which had followed the foundation of first the Ulster Volunteers and then the Irish Citizen Army and the Irish Volunteers, was the second phase of a revolution. He started to see the Gaelic League as providing the first phase in which the minds of the Irish had been prepared, and the Irish Volunteers as forming the second generation which was ready to fight for Ireland. He expressed this most clearly in his article 'The Coming Revolution' published in *An Claidheamh Soluis* on 8 November 1913, in which he described the League as a school which had made Irishmen nationalists: now they had graduated they were ready for revolution. To Pearse the League had been a prophet but not the messiah. With the start of this second phase the importance of the passing of Home Rule clearly rescinded:

> Whether Home Rule means a loosening or a tightening of England's grip upon Ireland remains yet to be seen. But the coming of Home Rule, if come it does, will make no material difference in the nature of the work that lies before us: it will affect only the means we are to employ, our plan of campaign. There remains, under Home Rule as in its absence, the substantial task of achieving the Irish Nation.[74]

Pearse had come to accept that the regeneration of the Irish Nation could follow political independence and did not necessarily have to pre-date it. Although it might not be necessary to use force, it was necessary to be armed, as 'Ireland unarmed will attain just as much freedom as it is convenient for England to give her.'[75] The growing importance Pearse assigned to the carrying of arms in the assertion of Irish nationhood had led him to partake in the founding of the Irish Volunteers in October 1913, being one of the original members of the Provisional Committee.

Early in 1914 Pearse still did not clearly conceive of the idea of a rebellion. He believed the year was crucial and would constitute a new and stirring chapter in the Irish struggle for independence, but he did not see an immediate prospect of action.[76] He reiterated this belief in March 1914 during an Emmet Memorial Lecture given in New York. His own generation, Pearse stated, had joined the Gaelic League, the younger generation was in the Volunteers learning about the use of arms while the next generation, now in the Fianna, 'will one day take – or make – an opportunity of putting their [the Fenians] teaching into practice'. He did believe however that a rebellion would not be too far away: 'before this generation has passed the Volunteers will draw the sword of Ireland'.[77]

The final change in his political thinking and his own role in the advancement of Irish independence seems to have been precipitated by the outbreak of the First World War: 'A European war has brought about a crisis which may contain, as yet hidden within it, the moment for which the generations have been waiting.'[78] This apparent call for action may well be linked to his increasing involvement in the IRB. Pearse had come to the attention of its leaders due to his contributions to advanced nationalist politics and his growing public stature since 1912, as witnessed by being asked to give several Emmet and Tone memorial lectures and writing a series of articles for the IRB paper *Irish Freedom*. Although there was considerable hesitancy in making him a member – in particular due to his support for the Home Rule Bill – Pearse was sworn in by Bulmer Hobson in December 1913. Initially this was solely to enable him to raise funds for St Enda's in the USA, but upon his return in May 1914 he became actively involved. At its first meeting after the outbreak of the war the Supreme Council of the IRB decided to have an insurrection.[79] In all Pearse's subsequent statements he made it clear that a rebellion was now on the cards and that he was going to take part in it himself.[80] In November 1914 he sealed this commitment with a letter setting out what should be done in case of his death or incapacitation.[81]

What caused him to see a role for himself in a violent rebellion has been subject of some debate. Dudley Edwards in particular has suggested that it had much to do with the financial difficulties of his school.[82] Some disillusion with the progress of the language movement was also apparent.[83] Other influences have been identified such as a growing obsession with the lives and ideas of Wolfe Tone and Robert Emmet which supposedly developed into a wish to emulate their lives and sacrifice himself for Ireland.[84] His trip to the USA and the need to satisfy an audience there longing for action, has been seen as another contributing factor.[85] It is difficult to apportion the importance of these influences, but it is clear from the above that the development of his thinking in the years before the war was consistent with the progress of the Home Rule Bill, the introduction of Volunteering in Ireland and the advent of the First World War.

## CONCLUSION

Pearse was not predestined to become the leader of the Easter Rising. In his early years he underwent conflicting influences from the distinctly different backgrounds of his parents. As a boy he accepted Ireland as part of the United Kingdom but was also clearly sympathetic to the Home Rule movement, which was supported by both sides of his family. In his early years at the Christian Brothers School he was certainly not seen as a nationalist, however, under the influence of some of the Brothers and his growing immersion in the Irish language he became distinctly more nationalistic. The dominant role the language and later the Gaelic League came to play in his thinking can largely be explained by his particular personality and consequent need to provide himself with an acceptable identity.

The period between secondary school and university seems to have been particularly influential in developing Pearse's peculiar type of nationalism. Through his involvement in the language he came to the conviction that political nationalism was desirable but largely irrelevant and its attainment unrealistic. To him only a regeneration of the Irish nation through the resurrection of the language could ultimately provide Ireland with true independence. Political independence could aid in this but was not a prerequisite. Control over the education system, however, was a vital element in the regeneration of the language, which explains Pearse's willingness to support the Irish Council Bill of 1907 and the Home Rule Bill of 1912. In the period between these two parliamentary bills Pearse showed no particular interest in politics. Instead he attempted to implement his idea to create a truly Irish generation by concentrating on making his secondary school a success.

Pearse's support for the Home Rule Bill of 1912 was no surprise, but the way events unfolded caused him to commit fully to the organisation of a rebellion by the end of 1914. The favourable conditions under which the Home Rule Bill was drafted convinced him that this was the moment at which it should be implemented. If it did not happen this time he believed it would never come voluntarily, and more drastic measures would be necessary. The militarisation of Irish society in reaction to the opposition of unionists to the Home Rule Bill made the threat of force by nationalists a logical step. When even this appeared to be insufficient to force the English to grant Home Rule, and Pearse became more and more closely associated with advanced nationalism through his involvement with the Irish Volunteers and the IRB, the opportunity for a rebellion provided by the outbreak of the First World War became an inescapable necessity.

# CHAPTER TWO

# 'I am the son of a good father'[1]: James and Patrick Pearse

## BRIAN CROWLEY

For the present I have said enough to indicate that when my father and mother married there came together two very widely remote traditions – English and Puritan and mechanic on the one hand, Gaelic and Catholic and peasant on the other; freedom loving both; and neither without its strain of poetry and its experience of spiritual and other adventure. And these two traditions worked in me and fused together by a certain fire proper to myself ... made me the strange thing I am.[2]

This quotation comes from the unfinished autobiography of Patrick Pearse. His maternal background offers no surprises. Pearse was a committed Catholic, one of the leading lights in the Gaelic League and the editor of their journal, *An Claidheamh Soluis agus Fáinne an Lae* from 1903 to 1909. From his writings, both fiction and non-fiction, it is clear that for Pearse the world of the Catholic Gaelic peasant was a prelapserian ideal, the repository of the true spirit of the Irish nation. The surprise for many comes from the reference to his father, James Pearse, whom he described as 'English, Puritan and mechanic' as, since his execution following the 1916 Rising, Patrick Pearse has become the central iconic figure of twentieth-century Irish Republicanism.

Pearse was uneasy at times with his hybrid background. However much he might have rushed to embrace the world of his Gaelic mother, he was always aware that he stood apart as his father's son. This unease was not ameliorated by the fact that his father was an Englishman and moreover a free-thinking radical whose relationship with the Catholic church could be described as ambiguous at best. It is perhaps for this reason that Patrick Pearse's father, James, is so often a shadowy figure in the traditional Pearse narrative. Although Ruth Dudley Edwards writes quite extensively about James Pearse in her biography of Patrick Pearse, she also dismisses his influence on his son:

> Besides providing a good material existence for his family,
> James confined his attention to his family to occasional expen-
> sive presents, and in their reminiscences he is a shadowy figure.
> Dominant though he was intellectually he was too distant from
> Patrick to counter-balance the narrow and often maudlin
> nationalism with which the boy was being fed though maternal
> influences.[3]

While it cannot be denied that Patrick Pearse's relationship with his
mother was more emotional and intense than with his father, this
does not negate entirely the paternal influence. Clearly for Pearse the
circumstance that he felt set him apart, making him the 'strange thing
that I am', was his mixed parentage. Seeing him as 'his father's son'
allows an image of Patrick Pearse to emerge that is more complex
and more radical than the popular myth allows.

James Pearse was born on the 8 December 1839 in Bloomsbury,
London, the son of a poor picture-frame maker. He had one older
brother, William, and a younger brother, Henry (James would later
name two of his sons after them). In his fragment of autobiography,
Patrick described the delight that he, his brother and sisters took listening to his father's tales of his childhood. The family rented two
rooms and a garret. James's mother, Mary, was a Unitarian and the
dominant figure in the home.  Resources were sometimes strained,
but it was a happy home. Years later, James Pearse wrote with some
sadness to his perspective new bride, Margaret Brady:

> It is only when we have lost our home forever that we can fully
> realize its value, for my own part I am sure the happiest part of
> my life was spent with the 'Old Folks at Home'. But that is all
> past and gone...[4]

When James was between the ages of seven and eight, the family
moved from London to Birmingham. His formal education seems to
have been limited and his foray into the local Sunday School was not
a success; apparently his questions led the divine who ran the classes
to regard him as an atheist, which, Patrick adds in his autobiography,
'in due time he became'.[5] His first job was in a chain factory. He
loathed this work and his next position as a printer's devil proved an
equally miserable experience. He left that job following an alterca-
tion with his employer's son. There was, according to Patrick, 'a
deep thing was moving in him, for he had the plastic fingers of his
father with in addition something of fiery vision that called for
expression, he studied art in a local art school and then went as an
apprentice to a sculptor'. Patrick goes on to describe his father,
'working at his craft in the daytime and in the Art School every

evening; he read books by night and came to know most of English literature well and some of it better than most men who have lived in Universities'.[6] James Pearse was part of the group Richard Hoggart has described as the 'earnest minority' within the working class in nineteenth and early twentieth century Britain, which sought to challenge the middle- and upper-class monopoly on learning and knowledge. Their reading, according to Hoggart, was:

> wide, solid and inspiring. They read volume after volume of Morris and Ruskin ... they joined Mutual Improvement Societies and Mechanics Institutes, and attended University Extension lecture-courses or others of the various forms of further education. They bought the volumes in Morely's Universal Library and other cheap series.[7]

Birmingham was a major centre for this movement. Known as 'the city of trades', it specialised in precision engineering and highly skilled manufacture. As a result it had a large working-and lower-middle-class population that was educated, self-confident and anxious for self-improvement. With increased education came a rise in radical thought as working-class men and women began to question the social, political and religious orthodoxies of society. Birmingham became a centre of radicalism and, in 1871, the first Republican club in Britain was set up there.[8] James Pearse was to be influenced by this movement, in particular its 'secularist' or 'freethought' wing, which disputed the central tenets of Judaeo-Christianity and promoted a purely scientific and rational understanding of the universe.

James Pearse's reading was wide-ranging and reflected both his desire for self-improvement and his interest in freethinking. His books, many of which survive in the Pearse Museum collection, reflect a man with a voracious thirst for knowledge. Given his profession, it is hardly surprising that as well as literature he read widely on art and architecture, both contemporary and historic. However, unlike Hoggart's archetypical Victorian autodidact, James did not favour cheap editions. His books are lavishly bound and

2.1 James Pearse. Courtesy Pearse Museum.

2.2 *Seated, left to right*:
Margaret Pearse, Mary
Brigid Pearse, Mrs
Margaret Pearse, Patrick
Pearse.
*Back row, standing left
to right*: William Pearse,
James Pearse. Courtesy
Pearse Museum.

illustrated. His collection also contained several antiquarian volumes. The illustrator, Gustav Doré was a particular favourite of James and of his son, William. Patrick inherited his father's bibliophilic tendencies. Even in a period of severe financial crisis, in which he would deny himself even the smallest luxury, his eye could still be tempted by a particularly fine edition of Shakespeare he saw in a shop window.[9] James Pearse's library shows him to have had an interest in history, both modern and ancient. He owned copies of many standard Irish history texts, such as Thomas D'Arcy Magee's *History of Ireland*,[10] as well as volumes on contemporary world history such as a history of the Franco-Prussian War[11] and a book on the ill-treatment of Native Americans in the United States.[12] Books on religious matters also appear; his collection contained several Bibles, books on theological issues and biblical history. He owned copies of the works of the Jewish historians Josephus[13] and Philo Judaeus,[14] who wrote extensively about the time of Christ. He had a Hebrew grammar,[15] as well as a defence of Judaism by the Jewish writer Carlos Vero, which was written in response to an anti-Jewish sermon preached at an *auto-da-fé* in Lisbon in 1705.[16] There was also a copy of the Koran in the Pearse library.

Surprisingly, there are very few books on specifically freethinking issues in the Pearse Museum collection. One that does survive is a biography of Charles Bradlaugh published by his daughter, Hypathia Bradlaugh Bonner.[17] James Pearse was a follower and admirer of Bradlaugh. He seems to have been personally acquainted with him, as James had written a letter to Hypathia Bonner enquiring after her father's health on the very day of Bradlaugh's death. In this letter he tells her that no man, except his own father, 'ever took the same hold upon my affections as Mr Bradlaugh'.[18] Born in London in 1833, Bradlaugh, like James, came from a working-class background and was largely self-educated. A lifelong supporter of Home Rule, Bradlaugh was also a champion of women's suffrage, birth control, the rights of subject peoples in the British Empire and workers' rights. Although he defended the individual's right to own property,

he advocated the break up and redistribution of the great landed
estates. He was also a confirmed Republican, which for him meant
being against inherited privilege in the form of the monarchy, the
artistocracy and the House of Lords.[19]

James Pearse, radical and atheist, may well have been circumspect
about some of these issues when he first arrived in Ireland c.1857,
shortly after the completion of his apprenticeship as a stone carver. In
the second half of the nineteenth century Ireland was going through
something of a church-building boom. The Catholic Church was anxious to use the new church-buildings to project a confident image of
status and power. The style generally favoured was that of the Gothic
Revival, a great boon to ecclesiastical sculptors, with its requirement
for detailed and intricate carving. Such was the rate of building that
there was a church built in Ireland for every week of the nineteenth
century.[20] This resulted in English craftsmen moving to Dublin, many
of them settling around Great Brunswick Street (now Pearse Street).

Although James may have been working in Dublin in the late
1850s, it is possible that he may not have settled in Ireland perma-
nently at that stage. On 28 April 1863, at the age of twenty-two, he
married an eighteen year-old Birmingham girl, Emily Suzanna Fox, in
St Thomas's Church, Birmingham. The couple had four children. In
1870 James Pearse, his wife and young family converted to
Catholicism, a prudent move for an ambitious ecclesiastical sculptor
while working in Ireland. James's first wife died on 26 July 1876.
According to Patrick's autobiography, his father's first marriage was
not a happy one; James blamed his wife's negligence for the death of
at least one of their children.[21]

In need of a wife and anxious for a secure home life, James began
courting Margaret Brady, a nineteen-year-old working in a newspaper shop around the corner from his premises in 27 Great
Brunswick Street. Margaret was the daughter of a coal-factor and her
grandfather had been a native Irish speaker from Co. Meath who was
evicted during the Great Famine. She was a traditional, pious, well-
mannered girl with limited education. Their letters from this period
suggest genuine affection, although Margaret is considerably more
ardent and complains that she would like James to write his letters
'more affectionately... I don't know if you are so anxious to see me
as I am you'. At times he could be quite playful however, and would
gently tease Margaret about her piety:

> I do not mean to embrace you more than ninety times and kiss
> you a trifle over twice as many times during the whole afternoon,
> I hope it will not rain but that the Gods will shine upon us. And

> I promise you his reverence shall have no cause to chide you
> when next you seek his ghostly presence.[22]

They married in 1877 and set up home in Great Brunswick Street.
Their eldest daughter, Margaret Mary, was born in 1878. She was
followed by Patrick Henry in 1879, William James in 1881 and Mary
Brigid in 1884. Patrick recalls his earliest memories of being a child
in the basement of Great Brunswick St, listening to the 'rhythmic tap-
tapping' which came all day from the workshop. His parents' marriage seems to have been generally happy. James Pearse's affection for
his children is also evident in Patrick's autobiography in which he is
portrayed as a loving, if distant, father:

> My father came up to our room only once or twice in the day,
> and at evening. When he came our games were always hushed.
> Not that we were afraid of him; but by some old convention or
> instinct we never made any noise once his white stone dusty fig-
> ure had come into the room. He was big, with broad shoulders
> that were a little round; he was very silent, and spoke only once
> or twice during the course of a meal, breaking some reverie to
> say something kind to my mother or something funny to one of
> us; Otherwise whether we were by ourselves or one of our rare
> visitors were there, sitting a little abstracted, always a little lone-
> ly we thought, a little sorrowful at times indeed, but these were
> very very seldom, he would in order to please my mother, rouse
> himself to exercise the wonderful social gift that he had, and
> then my mother's face would flush with pleasure, and we would
> laugh in pure happiness or join shyly in the conversation.
> Occasionally at night when he was kissing us, or when going
> away … the deep reserve in his nature would breakdown and he
> would lift one of us and press our face against his rough face
> and put his arm around us and draw us very close against his
> stone-dusty blouse. And these occasions were so few that I
> remember them one by one.[23]

He was a generous father and not only made Patrick a rocking-horse
called 'Dobbin', he also brought a second one back from London.
One very significant purchase for the family was a magic lantern.
According to Mary Brigid Pearse's book about her brother's childhood, Patrick saved up his pocket money to purchase a cheap lantern
which did not work. On Patrick's next birthday, his father presented
him with a proper machine. Thus began Patrick Pearse's career as an
orator, giving illustrated talks to his family, coached and supported
by his father. James also used the machine to give talks to his friends
and family, usually about twice a year.[24]

2.3 Pearse and Sons, 27, Great Brunswick Street (now Pearse Street). Courtesy Pearse Museum.

In 1880 James Pearse went into partnership with another Englishman, Edward Sharp. Professionally, things were going well and some of his finest work dates from this period. In 1882 Pearse and Sharp were awarded a first-class award at the Dublin Exhibition for a High Altar in statuary and coloured marbles.[25] In 1889 he did one of finest secular pieces, the figure of *Erin go Breagh*, commissioned by the National Bank for the roof of 34, College Green.[26] Other notable work from this period includes Enniscorthy Cathedral and the Church of St Michael in Tipperary town.[27] Business was good; James's papers show significant investments by him in bonds from the Borough of Birmingham. In 1889 he took out a lease on 83, Bristol Street, Birmingham, which was being prepared as a business premises for him.[28] In 1890 James went out on his own again, and set up Pearse and Sons. His son from his first marriage, James Vincent, followed him into the stone-carving trade. Willie was later to join the family business, while also attending the Metropolitan School of Art part-time. Patrick, who was concurrently studying for a Bachelor of Arts in modern languages and for the Bar, helped with some administrative work for a while and seems to have been of particular help with his father's last great commission, the Pulpit of the Four

Masters, in St Eunan's Cathedral in Letterkenny, Co. Donegal.[29] The success of James Pearse's business excited some jealousy amongst the Irish stone carvers and sculptors. Despite his conversion and marriage to an Irish woman, a campaign against Pearse and Sharp on religious and racial grounds was started by the son of his former partner, P.J. O'Neill. James mounted a stout defence of his position in a letter to Archdeacon Kinnane of Fethard on 31 January 1883:

> I am bound to admit that we are both guilty of being Englishmen but as God in his wisdom thought fit to call us into existence upon the other side of the water, and as His will was done in the matter, and not ours, we think there needs no apology from us on that head.[30]

He goes on to talk about his conversion to Catholicism and includes the letter from Fr Pius Devine of Mount Argus who had overseen his conversion. In the letter Fr Devine recalls James's

> sensible objections and difficulties, whilst you were under instruction and the clear headed manner in which you saw the answers as soon as they were proposed to you by me. Indeed I don't think I ever received a convert – and I received a good many – with whose disposition before and after reception I was so pleased with as I was with yours [*sic*].[31]

The sincerity of this conversion remains highly suspect. Dependent as he was on the goodwill and favour of the Catholic clergy to earn his bread, it is hardly surprising that James Pearse was reticent, and at times even disingenuous, when it came to issues of his personal faith. Only one year after his letter to Archdeacon Kinnane, he invested a sum of fifty pounds in a debenture with the Freethought Publishing Company headed by Charles Bradlaugh and Annie Besant.[32] This was no disinterested investment, it was a deliberate gesture of support for an organisation which saw as its main function the furtherance of the atheist and agnostic cause. The publications produced by this organisation did not merely challenge religious orthodoxies, they rejected, and at times ridiculed, many of the central tenets of Christianity.

It seems likely that James Pearse also wrote a series of pamphlets in support of the freethought movement  under the pseudonymn 'Humanitas'.[33] These pamphlets include titles such as *The Follies of the Lord's Prayer*,[34] *Socialism, A Curse*,[35] *Is God the First Cause?* [36] and *Against Socialism*.[37] If 'Humanitas' and James Pearse were indeed one and the same person, then these pamphlets reveal him to have been quite extreme in his Freethinking views. It would also mean that he was living an almost Wildean double-life. In Ireland he was a pious purveyor of ecclesiastical statuary while, at the same time, in England he was a free-thinking firebrand, scornful of all forms of religious belief. The only pamphlet James Pearse published under his name is supportive of the Catholic Church. This pamphlet, entitled *A Reply to Professor Maguire's Pamphlet 'England's Duty to Ireland' as it Appears to an Englishman*[38] was written in 1886 in response to a pamphlet by Dr Thomas Maguire, Professor of Moral Philosophy at Trinity College, called *England's Duty to Ireland as Plain to a Loyal Irish Roman Catholic*.[39] Maguire's is an extreme piece of polemic in which he portrays Home Rule as a disaster for Ireland, leading to chaos, bloodshed and pogroms on the Protestant population.

2.4 Maquette for *Erin go Breagh*, 34 College Green, Dublin. From an original magic lantern slide. Courtesy Pearse Museum.

He describes the Home Rule party as being wanting in 'industry, honesty, veracity, self-respect and cleanliness',[40] while their supporters were mere oafish lovers of chaos or to be characterised as 'the unsuccessful man at college', eager to obtain a position for themselves.[41] Maguire also accuses the Church of supporting Home Rule solely in order to gain more power in the schools. Apparently, when James read this pamphlet he turned from his normal quiet persona and cried out: 'I'll teach that bloody fellow a lesson. He ought to rinse out his mouth.'[42] His reply, which is four times as long as Maguire's, takes on his opponent's argument almost phrase by phrase. He quotes from Polybius, Caius Gracchus, Tiberius Sempronius, Addison, the Irish historian Thomas D'arcy Magee, Gladstone and John Bright. While some commentators have felt that James Pearse seems slightly pompous in the pamphlet, it is important to recognise the inequality which existed between the two protagonists and the courage and self-confidence required for James Pearse, a stone carver with no formal education to speak of, to take on a representative of the academic elite.[43] While the central thesis of the pamphlet is a rejection of Maguire's criticisms of the Home Rule and the Parnellites, there is also a sense that James Pearse is angry at Maguire using his position and education to mock those less educated. At one point James Pearse writes: 'Excuse my persistence. I am a humble

2.5 *The Marriage of the Virgin and St Joseph* by James Pearse. From an original magic lantern slide. Courtesy Pearse Museum.

man, but, like yourself, object to being gobbled up either by a "yahoo" or a professor.'[44] Maguire describes female Parnellites as being more 'ferocious than "les Lécheuses"'.[45] James replies that, 'when a man of education goes out of his way to choose a foreign term of the worst meaning, with which to paint the women of those with whom he politically differs, the objectionable word is too good for him'.[46] James Pearse's political views, as laid out in this pamphlet, are those of a committed Parnellite and he displays a particular admiration for Michael Davitt, a fellow self-made and self-educated man.[47]

On 5 September 1900, while staying in his brother's home in Birmingham, James Pearse died suddenly of a cerebral haemorrhage. His family was keen to stress that he had died 'fortified by the rites of the Roman Catholic Faith' in the death notice which appeared in the *Freeman's Journal* two days later.[48] Patrick writes in his autobiography that his father 'groped painfully and pathetically to find by himself such light as he could; and through great darkness he did find light as his life drew to a close'.[49] James Pearse left an estate valued at £1470. 17s. 6d intestate, and Patrick was appointed the sole administrator.[50] While Mary Emily McLoughlin (née Pearse) remained friendly with her father's second family, there is hardly any mention of James Pearse's eldest son, James Vincent, among the family papers, even when he died twelve years later in Dublin, aged forty-three. Initially, Patrick was involved in the running of Pearse and Sons. Willie, who was quite a talented artist, was groomed to take over and did some fine work, including a statue of the Mater Dolorosa for the Mortuary Chapel of St Andrew's Church, Westland Row, Dublin. While the business did seem to take off in the early years, there was a downturn in the market for ecclesiastical sculpture and the business was wound up in 1910. The capital was used to fund Patrick's school, St Enda's, which had recently moved to new premises in The Hermitage, Rathfarnham, a large eighteenth-century villa set in fifty acres of grounds on the perimeter of Dublin City.

James Pearse's legacy to the school was not simply financial. His books formed the nucleus of a library of two thousand volumes, while his engravings and sculptures joined the school's growing art collection. Talks illustrated using his magic lantern slides were a central part of school life. Pearse inherited a highly developed aesthetic appreciation from his father. He placed particular emphasis on the beauty of the surroundings in which the boys in his school were to be educated. He wrote in the school prospectus that

> The internal decoration and furnishing of the School have been carried out in accordance with a carefully-considered scheme of colouring and design. The object held in view has been the encouraging in the boys of a love of comely surroundings and the formation of their taste in art. In the classrooms beautiful pictures, statuary, and plants replace the charts and other paraphernalia of the ordinary schoolroom.[51]

St Enda's was set up to promote bilingual education in English and Irish, but it turned out to be much more than that. In its day it was one of the most educationally innovative schools in the country. When commentators discuss Pearse's educational philosophies and theories, the influence that his father's educational experience may have had on these ideas is often ignored. James Pearse was representative of one of the most remarkable educational movements of the nineteenth century. He overcame the limitations placed on him by his birth and economic situation, to pursue knowledge and culture. It was a similar love and passion for learning which Patrick Pearse sought to create in St Enda's. He saw, through the example of his father, that a true education could only develop through a desire to learn as opposed to the cramming and rote learning which characterised the state-run Intermediate education system which he famously referred to as 'The Murder Machine'.

It is difficult to assess the importance of James Pearse in his son's development as parental influence is nebulous and

2.6 *The Flight into Egypt* by James Pearse. From an original magic lantern slide. Courtesy Pearse Museum.

impossible to quantify. However, it is possible, for example, to see Pearse being influenced, to a degree, by his father's unorthodox religious beliefs. While Patrick Pearse observed his religious duties and had a very strong faith in God (he particularly identified with the self-sacrifice of Christ), he was by no means a conventional Catholic. As editor of the Gaelic League's newspaper, *An Claidheamh Soluis agus Fáinne an Lae*, in 1903 he openly criticised the Catholic bishops of Ireland over, as he perceived it, their lack of support for the language movement.[52] He attacked the bishops again in his short-lived newspaper, *An Barr Buadh,* in 1912.[53] It is also significant that many of the characters in his literary works have religious and spiritual experiences that bypass organised religion, often resulting in a return to faith. While he may have been a man of deep faith and a regular communicant, Patrick Pearse displayed a degree of spiritual autonomy which was in no way characteristic of the oppressive and dogmatic brand of Catholicism present in Ireland in the late nineteenth century. He never rejected organised religion in the way of his father, but he did not see it as something beyond challenge. He was aware that the 1916 Rising would be condemned by the Catholic Church, but he received communion on the Easter Sunday before it began. In his writings it is clear that, for him, personal faith was more important than the dictates of the institutional church.

2.7 Patrick Pearse, 1914. Courtesy Pearse Museum.

Patrick Pearse embraced his various roles as Irish-language revivalist, educator and revolutionary with, as described by David Thornley, 'gusto above the normal'.[54] Although he lived and worked in the repressive, inward-looking, Catholic bourgeois milieu depicted by James Joyce in *Dubliners* and in *The Portrait of the Artist,* he had none of the spiritual paralysis that one associates with Joyce's characters. This could, in part, be attributed to his family background as the son of a self-made man whose motto was 'Self-reliance: Labour conquers all'. Despite Patrick Pearse's deep affection and admiration for his father, he was often uncomfortable with his mixed heritage. It made him 'the strange thing I am' and set him apart. In many ways however, Pearse enjoyed being different; the sense that he was marked out from the crowd. However, this could also give him an unwelcome sense of alienation. In 1912 he wrote an insightful, self-critique in his short-lived newspaper, *An Barr Buadh*:

> I don't know whether I like you or not. I don't know whether anyone does like you. I know full many who hate you ... Pearse, you are too dark in yourself. You don't make friends with Gaels. You avoid their company. When you come among them you bring a dark cloud with you which lies heavily on them ... Is it your English blood that is the cause of that, I wonder? ... I suppose there are two Pearses, the sombre and taciturn Pearse and the gay and sunny Pearse ... I don't like that gloomy Pearse. He gives me the shivers. And the most curious part of the story is that no one knows which is the true Pearse ...[55]

In this piece, he associates his Englishness with the negative aspects of his personality, his melancholia and emotional distance from others. Significantly, in his autobiography, Pearse describes his father as having exactly these negative traits. It is therefore possible to argue that it was Pearse's sense of Englishness and alienation which led him to embrace the Gaelic, Irish world of his mother with such ferocious intensity and that his determination to 'de-anglicise' Ireland was undertaken with the zeal of a convert. It is indeed tempting to see Pearse's very self-conscious adoption of the role of Irish hero as an attempt to secure his identity within the culture and the history of the community around him.

Patrick Pearse is best remembered for his role in the Easter Rising. The language of social equality contained within the Proclamation of the Irish Republic was in tune with the radicalism of James Pearse. Following Pearse's execution it was his relationship with his mother which was emphasised. Pearse wrote two poems for her prior to his death, *To My Mother* and *A Mother Speaks*,[56] in which he adopted the persona of the self-sacrificing Messiah; making clear comparisons between the fate of his mother and that of the Virgin Mary. This iconic image of Mrs Pearse, the mother of two executed sons, inevitably overshadowed Patrick's paternal heritage. Therefore when J.A. Shields wrote in his hagiographical pamphlet of 1937 that 'Pearse the Patriot was his Mother's Son',[57] he was echoing the mythology which deliberately excluded Pearse's father. Mary Brigid, Pearse's younger sister, when reproducing parts of her brother's autobiography in *The Home Life of Patrick Pearse* excluded many of the sections dealing with her father's background and religious beliefs. The booklet to commemorate the handing over of St Enda's to the State in 1970 featured only the section from the Pearse auto-biography that dealt with Patrick's maternal ancestors.[58] A radical, freethinking English father did not fit with the image of Pearse pro-moted by the conservative establishment. He was portrayed as a respectable, church-going schoolteacher and most of his more radical and innovative views were sidelined. In the shadow of the Northern Troubles, Pearse and the revolutionary tradition in Ireland under-went a radical reassessment. The resultant debates about Pearse often lacked subtlety and his reputation 'suffered the extremes of blind defence and debunking assault'.[59] Pearse's mixed heritage suited nei-ther side in these arguments and was rarely explored. However in the years following the Good Friday (Belfast) Agreement and in an increasingly multi-cultural Ireland where notions of 'Irishness' are necessarily more complex, it is time to reassess Pearse. By looking at him as the child of both his parents, as traditionalist and modernist, we may find in Pearse a legacy much more suited to the complexities of twenty first century Ireland than has hitherto been imagined.

# 'A young schoolmaster of great literary talent': Mary Hayden's friend, Patrick Pearse

## JOYCE PADBURY

Ruth Dudley Edwards has described Mary Hayden as Pearse's 'closest woman friend',[1] and according to his sister Mary Brigid, Miss Mary Hayden 'was a great friend of my brother'.[2] There is little documentation of their friendship beyond what Hayden has recorded in her diaries, letters and some other writing. Pearse's letters to Hayden have not survived; however her contributions to their correspondence have been preserved in the Pearse Papers. They are a valuable source because so few letters written by Mary Hayden are extant, and more particularly for what they tell us about her friendship with Patrick Pearse. Although the sources regarding this relationship are not extensive, a study of them provides an impression of a friendship that was mutually and intellectually companionable, warm, relaxed and uncomplicated.

Mary Hayden was seventeen years older than Pearse. She was born in 1862 and grew up in a comfortable middle class Dublin family of the rising Catholic professional class of the later nineteenth century, her father being a medical doctor and a professor in the medical school of the Catholic University of Ireland. Mary was one of the earliest women graduates of the Royal University, gaining the BA and MA degrees in 1885 and 1887.[3] In 1895 she and Katherine Murphy were the first women to win the Junior Fellowship of the Royal University, a prestigious four-year appointment paying £200 a year, a very respectable sum. Mary Hayden was now a well-known figure in the cultural life of Dublin and in 1892 had been a founding member of the National Literary Society, which she regularly attended. She also attended the Contemporary Club and a variety of other cultural gatherings, enjoying the stimulating environment of the literary revival and the friendships she made with many of its leading figures, such as W.B.Yeats, George Sigerson and Douglas Hyde. Though proud to

3.1 Omeath 1905. *Back row, left to right*: Professor Mary Hayden, Mrs Dora Sheridan née Clayton, Edward (Ned) Sheridan, Patrick Pearse. *Front row, left to right*: William Pearse, Éibhlín Nic Niocaill (?), Harry Clifton, Mr and Mrs Geoghegan. Courtesy Pearse Museum.

earn what money she could from teaching and writing, and often short of ready cash, Hayden was fortunate also to have a modest income, inherited from her father, which allowed her an independence not enjoyed by the less fortunate of her women contemporaries.

## THE START OF A FRIENDSHIP

Hayden tells us that she first met Patrick Pearse when he was not yet twenty, which would place the meeting in or around 1898.[4] At that time, Pearse was studying privately for the BA degree of the Royal University, a non-teaching university, preparing for the legal examinations of the King's Inns, and at the same time was highly involved with the Gaelic League. Hayden became friendly with him through their mutual interest in the Irish language and in the activities of the Gaelic League, and it is in this context that he appears in her diaries. Her references to him are not very detailed and the diaries, unfortunately, do not go beyond 1903. Hayden had started to learn Irish towards the end of 1897 and she found it 'rather interesting'.[5] The following year she attended lessons at the Gaelic League with her friend Hester Sigerson (a daughter of Dr George Sigerson). For Hayden, after her intensive studies of German, French, Latin and Greek, the prospect of tackling another language was apparently not too daunting. Though she does not mention it, the fact that the Gaelic League was the first association to admit men and women on equal terms would have been an additional attraction of the League for someone like Hayden, whose latent feminism had already manifested itself in other contexts, such as women's education and women's suffrage. A student at that time, Mary Colum has described how in the Dublin of her young days men and women of all classes and occupations took to the activities of the Gaelic League branches, the language lessons, the native games and dances, and in her words, 'a good time was had by all'.[6] Another student, Mary Macken, recalled how she, with a few other University girls and boys, attended Gaelic League classes in 1899 where the teacher was 'an undergraduate named Pearse, enthusiastic, nervous and shy'.[7] Other students had similar recollections of him.[8]

This also was Mary Hayden's early impression of Pearse. Though Hayden was not then a young student, she too enjoyed the 'camaraderie' of the League, and quite easily became involved in its business. She was co-opted to the Coiste Gnotha (Executive Committee) of the Gaelic League in 1902, and was thereafter elected and re-elected annually, her membership continuing until 1913. Pearse had been a member of the Coiste Gnotha since 1898. In March 1902, Hayden and Pearse were among a party of five men and nine women who went to Cashel, Connemara, to practise the language. She wrote: 'We are to speak Irish always at meals.'[9] She also noted that most of the local people knew English but, 'they knew of our coming, so spoke Irish to us'.[10] After two days there, Hayden recorded that she 'got on with the others all right and induced Mr Pearse to talk – he turns out to be only 22, so I suppose he's just shy'.[11] Later in the week, when the party was going to an American wake, on a black, dark and pouring wet night, Hayden 'took an arm each of Mr Pearse and Mr O'Neill' to walk to the venue. On this expedition there is no more in her diary about Pearse, who returned to Dublin before the rest of the party. In the succeeding months Hayden and Pearse often met at the Gaelic League. After a Council meeting, which ended shortly before midnight, she recorded: 'Mr Pearse insisted on walking home with me, I was sorry for him, but glad of his company.'[12] He similarly accompanied her home after other meetings. The two were also part of a small group which used to meet to talk Irish sometimes, over tea at the home of Agnes O'Farrelly, another member of the Coiste Gnotha and a friend of Hayden's. In May, when Hayden went to hear some of the competitions at the Oireachtas, she 'had lunch in the refreshment room with Mr Pierse [sic] and got him to talk quite a lot'.[13] She was getting to know the shy young man who, for his part, seemed to welcome the friendship of the older woman with whom he could be more at ease, his social skills being weak. She once described herself to him as 'elderly – fast becoming even old'.[14]

They were both again in Connemara in January 1903. Over the preceding Christmas Hayden had been in touch continually with Pearse about arrangements for their accommodation in Connemara where, in her opinion, some of the prices quoted were too high. As she wrote to Pearse: 'Hotel keepers in Ireland are singularly short-sighted in their policy.'[15] She wrote several short notes to him for his opinion about the choices available, and he called to see her. It was she who was making the booking, which was finally concluded with the hotel in Letterfrack. There were to be at least two other members of the party who dropped out. Hayden wrote in her diary:

> Here I am, down at Letterfrack, Co. Galway, trying to get prac-
> tise in Irish speaking. Mr Pearse an enthusiastic Gaelic Leaguer
> (BA, BL) is my companion and there is no one else except a young
> priest at the hotel. Mr Pearse is only 23, young enough, if I had
> married <u>very</u> early indeed, to be my son, yet Hester, and I dare
> say others, didn't think my coming with him over proper; how-
> ever – I came and <u>he</u> at least seems to have no hesitation about
> accepting the situation as a matter of course, which is a blessing.
> We talk a lot on all sorts of subjects and I find him most compan-
> ionable, a really nice fellow. I am enjoying my holiday greatly.[16]

Hayden remained in the west some days longer than Pearse, but on her return to Dublin he met her at the train: 'it was really very good of him'; and he wheeled her laden bicycle right across town.[17] Other brief diary entries show that she had got quite used to Pearse's company, noting: 'such a boy he seemed, with his young fresh face!    I might easily have been his mother'.[18] Her regard for him was not in any sense maternal, however, and, as the friendship developed, it had something of the character of a favourite nephew with a companion-able and compatible aunt.


### AN CLAIDHEAMH SOLUIS AGUS FÁINNE AN LAE

The following month there arose the issue of the editorship of the Gaelic League newspaper *An Claidheamh Soluis agus Fáinne an Lae*, an appointment which Pearse was keen to obtain. Hayden attended a meeting of the Coiste Gnótha which lasted nearly five hours and, as she put it, 'a fine lot of time was wasted in talk. The biggest ques-tion was as to the editor'.[19] There were three candidates for the post (W.P. Ryan, a journalist, Patrick MacSweeney, a native speaker, and Pearse), who, according to Hayden, were voted on considerations of journalistic training, full command of Irish and level-headedness. No decision was taken except that the post would be advertised.[20] In Hayden's view, Pearse should be the choice: 'He would be the man to make the paper succeed, I think'; and she discussed the matter with Agnes O'Farrelly.[21] When the Coiste Gnotha finally met on 2 March to make the appointment, there was a long discussion, which ended with Pearse being elected as editor by a large majority. Hayden wrote to Pearse a few days later to congratulate him: 'I look forward to the Claidheamh flashing out in fine style within the next few weeks.'[22]

Almost immediately controversy surrounded the newspaper when it carried an anonymous article which criticised the bishops' Lenten Pastorals for their lack of reference to the Irish language.[23] According to Ruth Dudley Edwards, it was not clear whether Pearse or his predecessor as editor was responsible for the inclusion of the controversial article in the issue which appeared just five days after Pearse's appointment. However, Pearse stated emphatically that 'the present editor's responsibility begins with the issue dated March 14th', as pointed out by Regina Uí Chollatáin.[24] It therefore was not Pearse who was responsible as editor, although he may have written the article; he was known to be critical of the clergy in *An Claidheamh Soluis*. Hayden was among the moderates in the League who were alarmed by the tone of the article. She wrote in her diary of her concern that the article

> was grossly imprudent and never should have got in. It may do a lot of harm. Many of the Bishops and of the priests would be glad to ruin the Gaelic League; they are jealous of it as an organisation outside themselves. Certainly <u>at present</u>, it does not do to give them a pretext.[25]

Though at the time she did not blame Pearse, shortly afterwards she did criticise him, for either that or another article, when she wrote: 'Still he <u>had</u> put in an article which vexed the priests; and it is best to humour them, even when they are foolish. It is funny how they stand together, against the laiety [*sic*]'.[26]

On another occasion, Hayden was 'rather sorrowful' over *An Claidheamh Soluis* on Pearse's account: 'Your last article was a little bit over defiant in my humble opinion ... though I agree with every word of it'. To soften her criticism of Pearse in this instance, she wrote: 'I here assume the character of the <u>candid friend</u> – and hope you won't be vexed'.[27] She was possibly (depending on the date of this letter) referring to his article on the rejection of the Irish Council Bill, in which Pearse trenchantly defended his role as editor, against the 'spleen of such half-friends and whole enemies' as might make his legitimate, if unpopular, attitude 'an excuse for their own inveterate distrust or hate'.[28] Hayden's comment that, 'we should be the better for trying ourselves a bit in shallow waters; we've had time to forget how to

3.2 Pearse family,
*left to right*: (?),
Patrick Pearse,
Margaret Pearse, Mrs
Margaret Pearse,
William Pearse and
Mary Brigid Pearse.
Courtesy Pearse
Museum.

swim'[29] would suggest that she, like Pearse, favoured acceptance of the
Bill, which was a proposal for minor administrative devolution of eight
departments of the Irish administration. Pearse's acceptance was based
on the fact that education was among the departments to be trans-
ferred to Irish control. Many years later, Hayden tells us that she had
a long argument with Pearse about the Irish Council Bill of 1907,
which, she noted, he thought 'ought to have been accepted'.[30] The
Council Bill was widely condemned in Ireland as an inadequate substitute for Home Rule and was withdrawn. Ruth Dudley Edwards, writing of what she calls Pearse's 'soft line' on the Council Bill, sees him
standing 'to the right of even the parliamentarians'.[31]

## SHARED INTERESTS AND MUTUAL REGARD

By this time, Hayden and Pearse seem to have developed a genuine
warm regard for each other. As she wrote to him: 'I do want some

thought-interchange and some gossip too'.[32] The intellectual content of a friendship had always been important for Hayden who, as a young girl, had not been adept at small talk, which she disliked. The comment by Ruth Dudley Edwards that Hayden and O'Farrelly had 'more pretensions to intellect than personal charm'[33] may well be true. Intelligent conversation enabled Hayden to mix easily with people she met on her travels abroad, and at home in circles like the National Literary Society and the Gaelic League. Pearse's seriousness of purpose attracted her. Furthermore, the sense of exclusion, of which she and other women were conscious in many aspects of public life, was not part of her experience in the Gaelic League, where she could take part in its business on an equal basis with men. Pearse treated her as an intellectual equal; she regarded him similarly, and she could engage in debate with him as between two minds of equal value. He was a stimulating companion whom she found to be also personally estimable. His kindness to her, when she was first getting to know him, was appreciated, as evidenced by the diary entries. He was a sensitive friend.

In Connemara in 1903, Hayden was receiving letters from Arthur Conan, who was dying.[34] Like her other friends, Pearse must have known something of the impending tragedy, which could have added to his solicitude for her. A few years later, two letters to Pearse from Hayden in Manchester (where she had gone to study Old Irish with Dr John Strahan), while covering a variety of subjects, are also in part quite personal and are in reply to letters from Pearse in which he seems to have expressed concern for her well-being. He had apologised for delay in writing, and sent her birthday greetings. In her reply, she is feeling sorry for herself, and seems open to sympathy: 'Most people of my friends do not write for weeks – at least so it seems to me ...Thanks very much for your wishes of <u>returns</u>, but I don't feel as if I wanted many of them.'[35] A short letter written by Hayden from France, also undated and in reply to one from Pearse, includes the words, 'I can't say that I feel in any better spirits', again suggesting that he was a supportive friend.[36]

Pearse wrote to Hayden about practical matters, like the choice of ink for printing *An Claidheamh Soluis*, his own literary projects, and more personally, on his ideas for his own future. It was the latter which provoked her advice to him to marry and have a family:

> No, I don't want you to have such a future as you plan for yourself ... There is a part of human nature that asks for human relationships and human sympathies ... [She hoped to see him] settled as a paterfamilias with children ... Tá tú óg fós.[37]

In another letter, she advised him to be 'often in the company of

young people'.[38] She felt it necessary also to modify his idealised view
of women and to defend the character of men: 'I've got to stand up
for men to you; you are so hard on them. – If there were none, where
would <u>you</u> be?'[39] In this letter, her observations on male and female
characteristics, both admirable and unpleasant, including her
thought 'that the finest type of men have much of the woman about
them as the finest type of women much of the man – which only
means I suppose that they unite the best qualities of both sexes', are
a significant rejection of gender stereotyping, a rejection inherent in
much of the stirrings of her younger life.

Hayden's letters to Pearse gradually became quite chatty. The initial 'Dear Mr Pearse' had became 'A chara', which clearly was more
friendly; and she signs off as 'Mise do fíor chara, Máire Ní Aodáin'
(but never just Máire or Mary). She lent him books, rebuked him for
delay in returning them and then felt guilty:

> Altogether I seem always to be at you about something. I was
> dispirited with myself when I remembered after, how I acted the
> candid friend to you at Lucan.[40]

Writing to Pearse from Washington DC, Hayden asked for news,
wrote that she was collecting postcards for his sister's album, asked
him to send her a *Claidheamh* 'or two, if you have time', and sent
remembrances to his mother. Hayden had previously been in America
around the turn of the century (to visit her brother), and this letter to
Pearse is useful evidence that she visited America again in 1905.[41]

Hayden has told us that until about 1914 she saw a great deal of
Pearse, 'especially in summer when we often went cycling together'.[42]
This friendship had commenced at an opportune time for Hayden,
who, though a strong, busy character, was experiencing a sense of
loneliness compounded by the death of Arthur Conan and the failure
of her application for a Senior Fellowship of the Royal University. As
she wrote in one of her letters to Pearse: 'I've had a lot of partings
from places and still more and worse from people, and every new
one recalls the others, more or less'.[43] The companionship of Pearse,
the long chats and cycle rides with him, and the shared Gaelic League
activities were satisfying, enjoyable, supportive, and without emotional complication. Hayden liked the shy young man, his intelligence, his idealism and his lack of coarseness; as she wrote, 'from a
doubtful story or jest he shrank as from a blow'.[44]

## THE NEW UNIVERSITY

Hayden and Pearse were involved in several contemporary issues. They
participated, according to their particular concerns, in the general

clamour for acceptable provision of university education for Irish catholics; his that the university be truly national, and hers that women be admitted on equal terms with men. Both were members, and Hayden Vice-Chairman, of the Catholic Graduates and Undergraduates Association, which put pressure on the Irish Members of Parliament in their efforts to achieve settlement of the university question.[45] As the Gaelic League intensified its campaign for a favourable place for Irish studies in the new university,[46] Pearse and Hayden were enthusiastic supporters, and both defended, as consistent with normal university requirements, the idea that Irish be an essential criterion for university admission.[47] Both also were members of a deputation from the Coiste Gnotha which pressed the case first to the Commission responsible for the preparation of the initial statutes of the new National University, and then to the University Senate, where Hayden herself was a member.[48] They were both teachers with a keen interest in education. Hayden would later write of Pearse: 'It was through the education of the rising generation that he looked for the regeneration of the country.'[49] For her part, to judge from much of her own writing, Hayden saw education as the

3.3 Patrick Pearse. Courtesy Pearse Museum.

way forward also for women, as a means of finding a release from dependency and the achievement of equal citizenship. Pearse had done some teaching at his old school, Westland Row, at University College when Father Delany, the President, invited him to teach Irish classes in 1901–2,[50] and at Alexandra College,[51] where Pearse succeeded Agnes O'Farrelly, the first teacher of Irish in the school. He was an unsuccessful applicant for the post as lecturer in Irish in 1909 when the foundation appointments were being made in the newly chartered University College Dublin; the appointment went to Agnes O'Farrelly.

Hayden was a vastly more experienced teacher, having taught at matriculation and university level for about twenty years in various schools and colleges for girls in Dublin. In 1909 she was appointed to the foundation staff of the new University College Dublin, and in 1911 she became the first holder of the Chair of Modern Irish History. Pearse, writing

on 'The University Statutes' in *An Claidheamh Soluis* had criticised
the omission of the subject Modern Irish History from the professor-
ships initially established.[52] At the time of his writing, no appointments had yet been made in the new university, so he was not to
know that his friend Mary Hayden would be appointed to the lec-
tureship which was to deal with the subject.  Within two years she
and several other lecturers were raised to the status of professor.
Hayden was an ideal person for Pearse to have associated with St
Enda's, Pearse's bilingual school for Catholic boys. The school
attracted much interest among the cultural intelligentsia, including
many of his Gaelic League associates, whom Pearse involved in the
school in various ways. Mary Hayden is listed in the prospectus as
one of the ten-member Council. Her name is also listed as an Extern
Lecturer; others included Douglas Hyde, Agnes O'Farrelly, Eoin
MacNeill, W.B. Yeats and Padraic Colum. In 1909 Hayden gave a lecture on 'Anglo Saxon Literature', described in the school magazine,
*An Macaomh*, as 'a very animated and animating talk'.[53]

## POLITICAL ISSUES

3.4 Walled gar-
den, St Enda's
School. Courtesy
Pearse Museum.

In her younger years, Hayden had no interest in party politics – on
which she rarely commented – and she seemed to have had no great

objection to the Union with Britain. The years of the literary renaissance and her enthusiasm for the Irish language were to change her
attitude. She wrote, in *An Claidheamh Soluis*,[54] about patriotism as
cultivated in practical ways, to lead to a self-respecting and self-
reliant Ireland.  National pride should be encouraged by the use of
Irish products and the Irish language; the young should be educated
about the native language, history and tradition;  and emigration
when not necessary was to be deplored.  Education had been fundamental to Hayden's attitude on women's rights, and it now also
shaped her outlook on nationalism. She would, in time, become a
convinced nationalist of the constitutional kind and in due course a
supporter of the Home Rule aspiration. The national question does
not seem to have entered to any great degree into Hayden's conversations with Pearse. She later recalled that 'When I knew him best,
he seemed not much interested in actual politics, though his love for
Ireland was then, as always, intense and passionate.' She considered
him an idealist, not interested in 'questions of party intrigue'.[55] Nor
did Hayden ever become strongly committed to party politics. While
she would, in general, be supportive of the Irish Parliamentary Party
on the Home Rule issue, she was also very critical of Redmond and
other members for their lack of support for women's suffrage.

By 1914 Hayden was losing touch with Pearse; but her affection
for him endured.  She seems to have dropped out of active participation in the Gaelic League, perhaps through dislike of the increasingly
political tone of its affairs. In any case she was engaged with the suffrage campaign, as well as with her new role in University College
Dublin as university professor, member of the College Governing
Body and member of the National University Senate. Pearse too was
busy, with St Enda's, the Volunteers and the IRB.  Hayden's remorse
about the decline of the friendship is clear in her letter to his mother
after Pearse's death:

> He is constantly in my mind now especially at night. I see him
> in all sorts of places in which we were together. I regret very
> very much that I saw so little of him lately, but I suppose it could
> not well be helped; he was heart and soul in a cause which,
> deeply as I sympathise with everything done for Ireland, I could
> not in conscience help.  I do wish though that I had seen him
> even once in the last few months.[56]

In deference to the concerns of Denis Coffey, President of University
College, 'not to further identify the College with the rising', Hayden
had not signed her name to a 'kind personal article' on Pearse sent to
his mother, but she seemed willing to see the article published over
her initials.[57]  She did not herself seek a publisher for the article, but

if it had appeared over her initials, the author might easily have been identified.

Hayden was not a pacifist, but she disliked war and violence and, like many others, she did not approve of the 1916 Rising. However, the Easter Proclamation contained wording very acceptable to feminists. Claiming the allegiance of every Irishman and Irishwoman, 'the Republic guarantees religious and civil liberty, equal rights and equal opportunities to all its citizens'. This reassuring statement was frequently recalled by women in the succeeding years when trying to protect women's rights. During the women's campaign in 1937 against certain provisions of the new Constitution, Hayden referred with approval to the civil and religious liberty affirmed in the Easter Proclamation and the Free State Constitution.[58] In her *Short History of the Irish People*, first published in 1921, Hayden referred to Patrick Pearse as 'a young schoolmaster of great literary talent'.[59] This describes the person who was her friend, and it is how she liked to think of him. Writing in the 1930s, she recalled that his 'mind was of a strange and unusual type'.[60] As a pioneer in education for women, and a feminist believing in women's rights, Mary Hayden too was a remarkable person. Her friendship with Pearse had many elements of a meeting of minds. As they diverged in political terms, Hayden continued to esteem the person she had known as a stimulating intellect and a sympathetic companion.

## CHAPTER FOUR

# Patrick Pearse:
# The Victorian Gael

## PAT COOKE

Patrick Pearse was already twenty-one years of age when Queen Victoria's long life ended in 1901. He was the son of an Englishman, James Pearse (1839–1900), a classic Hardyesque stone-carver who had lived and died within the ambit of Victoria's reign. But he was also the son of an Irish mother, Margaret Brady, born in 1857, with roots in the Irish-speaking area of County Meath.

Only once in the substantial corpus of his writings did he ponder these bifurcated origins, and that was in a fragment of unpublished autobiography written towards the end of his life. The hand-written manuscript provides some crucial insights into Pearse's mind, because here, in his exceptionally clear hand, we can see not only what he wrote, but what he crossed out. Summing up the impact upon him of his Anglo-Irish parentage, he writes:

> And these two traditions worked in me and fused together by a certain fire proper to myself, a fire fostered by her whom I have just named [his Irish-speaking aunt, Margaret] made me an Irish Rebel but nursed by that fostering of which I have spoken made me the strange thing I am.[1]

While it is not possible to date the manuscript precisely, internal evidence indicates that it was written sometime in the last sixteen months of his life.[2] Thus here in this unpublished source is a tone that contrasts dramatically with that found in what he was publishing at this time, in such essays, for example, as *Ghosts* (1915) and *The Spiritual Nation* (1916). Here, instead of a prophet uttering adamantine certainties about the destiny of the Gael, we find a man deeply unsure of his identity: a man who finds in himself a peculiar mixture of cultural elements, amounting to a 'strangeness' that transcends his Gaelicism and his unswerving nationalist faith.

In an essay of 1934 entitled 'Recent Irish Poetry', Samuel Beckett used the term 'Victorian Gael' to describe a type of Irish writer 'in flight from self-awareness' and in thrall to a set of literary conventions amounting to a 'correct scenery, where the self is either most happily obliterated or else so improved and enlarged that it can be mistaken for part of the décor'. These 'antiquarians' he accuses of 'delivering with the altitudinous complacency of the Victorian Gael the Ossianic goods'.[3] The usefulness of this neologism for present purposes lies in the way it suggests the syncretic quality of Irish experience in the late nineteenth century. Ireland's claim to cultural and political independence was being asserted by a people exposed to forces of modernisation that prevailed throughout Europe and in the wider, developing world, influences which dialectically sharpened efforts to define nationality in the experimental climate of the Irish Revival.

The era to which the term 'Victorian' applies spanned almost seventy years, from 1837 to 1901. It had no clear internal demarcations, shaded into Edwardianism, and contained many of the roots of twentieth-century modernism. Seen against this background, there are aspects of Pearse that suggest a much wider range of cultural experience than that of an insular Dubliner fixated on language revival. In him are found some of the classic traits of the middle-class Victorian: the tension between respectability and the itch for reckless, foolhardy adventure; the worship of childhood and the *ennui* induced by encroaching age; the belief in discipline and hard work; and the longing for a cause worthy enough to sweep away the pettiness of everyday life in a mission characterised by chivalry, honour, nobility and self-sacrifice. All of these traits Pearse shared not only with contemporary Irishmen but with Englishmen, and more widely with Europeans, of his generation – a word for which he had a particular fondness.[4]

When Robert Wohl undertook a study of pre-war fixation with the idea in *The Generation of 1914*, he could not envisage an exercise confined to a single European country because 'the idea of the generation of 1914 came to imply a unity of experience, feeling and fate that transcended national borders; because different national experiences brought out different aspects of the generational phenomenon'.[5] Pearse was not only of that generation, but quite well travelled as well. As a young and prominent member of the Gaelic League, he attended the Eisteddfod in Wales and Celtic gatherings in Scotland; among middle-class Dubliners he pioneered the holiday home in the west with his house at Rosmuc, to which he travelled by train; in 1904 he travelled to Europe to study bilingualism in the schools of Flanders and to listen to the operas of Wagner at Bayreuth; and he was in America for three months in 1914.

But it was not just travel that would have exposed Pearse to an exceptional range of cultural influences for a young Irishman of his day. The influence of his father James, particularly in the formative years of childhood, was probably deeper than has been appreciated. James Pearse, for whom an uncanny fictional parallel can be found in Hardy's journeyman stonemason Jude in *Jude the Obscure,* was an autodidact and bibliophile. As his business prospered, James put together a substantial and expensive library that displayed a wide interest in history, literature, the visual arts and comparative religion. The young Pearse, a shy and bookish boy, grew up surrounded by this eclectic collection. There is evidence of the ranginess of his child-hood reading in the autobiographical manuscript. He locates the origin of his obsession with the martyr-hero in the reveries of his eight-year-old self:

> This was my way with every book that was read to me, with every picture that I saw, with every story or song that I heard: I saw myself daring or suffering all the things that were dared or suffered in the book or story or song or picture: toiling across deserts in search of lost cities, cast into dungeons by wicked kings, starved and flogged by merciless masters, racked with Guy Fawkes, roasted on a gridiron with St Laurence, deprived of my sight with the good Kent.[6]

Of the three martyrs mentioned here none is Irish. Perhaps the omission of Cúchulainn, with whom he became obsessed in later years, testifies to the authenticity of these childhood recollections. In the December 1909 edition of *An Macaomh*, the school magazine, Pearse observed that 'Wellington is credited with the dictum that the battle of Waterloo was won on the playing fields of Eton. I am certain that when it comes to a question of Ireland winning battles, her main reliance must be on her hurlers'.[7] The English public school was as much an influence on Pearse's educational thinking as the fosterage of St Enda (he sited his school, after all, in two gracious eighteenth-century buildings). His cast of mind was more analogical than perhaps has been credited, and more steeped in English cultural influences than hitherto acknowledged.

### DARK PASTORALISM

As Seamus Deane has noted, Pearse's prophetic effect flows from a high-pitched prose style, biblical in its cadences and resonances, that grows shriller in his last years.[8] But where an examination of Pearse's style in an exclusively Irish context has led some to descry elements of pathological excess, looked at within a broader field of cultural reference it appears more derivative and conventional – indeed quite typical. The Jesuit, Francis Shaw was one of the first to point out how 'aggressively unorthodox' was Pearse's biblical tone; the conflation of

Christian and pagan values, of Cúchulainn with Christ, he concludes, is 'in conflict with the whole Christian tradition'.[9] But Shaw too readily attributes this to Pearse's exotic personality, and fails to see how typical it is of a high-Victorian sensibility. Its eloquent origins can be found in Carlyle, who, as A.O.J Cockshut observed, was setting a fashion which 'many later Victorians were to follow, of trying to use the language and emotional power of Christianity without accepting its doctrines'.[10] There is good evidence for Carlyle's influence on Pearse. One of his former pupils, Kenneth Reddin, recalled in an article of 1945 how Pearse came upon him one day reading in the library. 'Read these books too', advised the headmaster:

> But remember they are a little obvious; they will never harden your mind. One must harden one's mind, harden it to the temper of steel ... He handed me Carlyle's *Sartor Resartus* and the dialogues of Plato, and passed on.[11]

In the library at the Pearse Museum there is also a 1907 edition of Carlyle's *On Heroes, Hero-Worship and The Heroic in History*. Though he was referring to Thomas Mitchel and not to Pearse, Roy Foster is surely correct in his passing remark that Carlyle should be seen as 'that unrecognised founding father of Irish national rhetoric'.[12]

Pearse's notoriously sanguinary sentiment that 'bloodshed is a cleansing and sanctifying thing' and 'the old heart of the heart needed to be warmed by the red wine of the battlefield', found in 'Peace and the Gael', written at Christmas 1915, is frequently given a narrow reading, in which it serves to crystallise the uniquely morbid pitch to which Pearse is said to have taken Irish republican rhetoric. However, few have commented on how it was written barely seven months after the publication of Rupert Brooke's last collection of poems in May 1915, a month after his death while in transit to the Dardanelles. In a collection laden with morbid anticipations, the following lines from 'The Dead' have a particular resonance:

> But, dying, has made us rarer gifts than gold. These laid the world away: poured out the red Sweet wine of youth ...[13]

Is it possible that Pearse's 'sweet wine of the battlefield' is a direct echo of 'the sweet wine of youth'? Wohl picks up on a disposition in Brooke that resonates strongly with the sensibility of his near contemporary (Pearse was eight years older). In 1913, while standing before Niagara Falls, Brooke suddenly realises that he had remained at heart a man of the Victorian age:

> I sit and stare at the thing and have the purest nineteenth century grandiose thoughts, about the Destiny of Man, the

Irreversibility of Fate, the Doom of Nations, the fact that Death awaits us All, and so forth. Wordsworth Redivivus. Oh dear, oh dear![14]

Among Pearse's writings there is an analogous instance of this grandly enacted scene, albeit lacking the irony and literary self-awareness that marks Brooke's moment of realisation. It occurs in an essay he wrote for the Christmas 1910 issue of *An Macaomh*, and is possibly the most complex piece of prose he wrote. The headmaster of St Enda's school is lying in his bed at night, listening to the sound of the waterfall that lay along the River Owendore as it wended its way through the fifty acres of park and woodland surrounding his bedroom on the third floor of the Hermitage:

> When the river is in spate, as now, I hear the roar of the near-est cascade, a quarter of a mile off at night from my bedroom. It reminds me of the life out there in the woods, in the grass, in the river ... Once or twice I have seen the little eager form of an otter gliding behind the sallies where the stream cuts deep. I think it is partly to that freebooter we owe it that the trout are not as numerous now as they were of yore. Yet we will not inter-vene between him and the fish; let them fight on their old war, instinct against instinct. Sometimes rabbits come out and gam-bol under the trees in the evening; and they are happy, in the foolish way of rabbits, till one of the river rats wants his supper. So day and night there is murder in the greenwood and in every greenwood in the world. It is murder and death that makes pos-sible the terrible thing we call physical life. Life springs from death, life lives on death. Why do we loathe worms and vul-tures? We all batten on dead things, even as they do, only we, like most of our fellow creatures, kill on purpose to eat, where-as they eat what has been killed without reference to them. All of which would be terrible were death really an evil thing.[15]

The transitions in this passage have the complexity of a fugue. As with Brooke, it begins in Wordsworthian mode, with echoes of 'Tintern Abbey' as the 'sounding cataract' haunts him 'like a passion'. The benignly pastoral image of the rabbits pre-echoes 'The Wayfarer', one of the last poems he wrote in the hours before his execution ('little rabbits in a field at evening, / Lit by a slanting sun'). But the mood quickly darkens and enters a Darwinian world where the rabbit becomes the rat's supper, and shades into the necrophiliac intensity of 'batten on dead things'. The tone here is distinctly Tennysonian, recalling, for example, the following lines from 'Maud':

> For nature is one with rapine, a harm no preacher can heal;
> The Mayfly is torn by the swallow, the sparrow spear'd by the
>     shrike,
> And the whole little wood where I sit is a world of plunder and
>     prey.[16]

Then we arrive, with a shock, at the premonitory: 'life springs from death, life lives on death'. We have to jump forward five years to August 1915 to find that phrase repeated in the most famous of Pearse's political speeches, the one he gave at O'Donovan Rossa's graveside: 'life springs from death, and from the graves of patriot men and women spring living nations'. But the source of this one phrase of Pearse's may be more complex still. In one of his last political pamphlets, *The Sovereign People*, he quotes the following passage from one of his four evangelists of Irish nationalism, Thomas Mitchel:

> In all nature, spiritual and physical, do you not see that some powers and agents have it for their function to abolish and demolish and derange? But is not the destruction, then, as natural, as needful, as the construction? – Rather tell me, I pray you, which is construction – which destruction? This destruction *is* creation: Death is Birth and 'The quick spring like weeds out of the dead.'[17]

The last line is from the third stanza of Shelley's 'Lines Written on Hearing of the Death of Napoleon':

> And so with living motion all are fed,
> And the quick spring like weeds out of the dead.[18]

So the well-spring of this most memorised of Pearse's political utterances is English literary romanticism, diverted via the rhetoric of Mitchel's Carlylean prose, and modified by evolution's sanguinary implications. It depends hardly at all on a particularly Irish or Gaelic experience, and its dark pastoralism is more easily traced to an English literary sensibility.

The fact that Lewis Carroll's *Alice* books were among Pearse's favourites may not only shed light on his complex attitude to nature but illuminate the roots of his political sensibility. In an essay on 'The Animals of Wonderland', Rose Lovell-Smith explores the impact of Darwinism on Carroll's vision of nature. She observes that Carroll inverts the theme of kindness to animals established in more orthodox children's literature, and speculates that news of evolution, for all its disturbing implications, affected Carroll as 'a kind of mental liberation'. Her argument is that Carroll found in evolution's anarchic implications a release from:

the requirements of moral responsibility and constant self-improvement imposed by mid-Victorian ideals of Christian duty ... the exhilaration of an amoral anti-society in *Alice in Wonderland* may be, therefore, in part the exhilaration of a Darwinist dream, of selfishness without restraint.[19]

Pearse was renowned as a man of extraordinary gentleness to animals – yet, as we have seen, he was capable of dreaming scenes of animal carnage. Was it in this way that the otherwise respectable, diligent Pearse sensed in himself the most dangerous revolutionary of them all, a man for whom 'life springs from death', not merely in the sense of an Irish political tradition of revolt from British Rule, but as the primordial condition of all life? Echoing his cascading reverie of woodland life in Rathfarnham, there is a passage from two years later where he manages, in four dramatic leaps, to bridge the gap between the Darwinian world and the struggle for Irish nationhood. In 'From a Hermitage' in 1913 he wrote:

> The dragonfly among insects is in fact as the tiger among beasts and the hawk among birds, as the lawyer among men, as England among the nations. It is the destroyer, the eater-up, the cannibal.[20]

Paul Fussell has pointed to how a special meaning is attached to the phrase *Et in arcadia ego* in English literary tradition. Instead of construing it as 'I have dwelt in Arcadia,' it is invested with a darker meaning: 'Even in Arcadia I, Death, hold sway'.[21] In Pearse's vision of nature, it is death that at once unifies and unravels the pastoral scene. No wonder 'The Wayfarer' was among the last poems he wrote.

## CHARACTER AND THE MAN

To the Victorian mind, the martyr represented an exaltation of character above all other virtues.[22] Character (typically perceived as a male quality) is a matter of bearing, fortitude and, above all, style. As a mode of action, it finds its sharpest expression in the way a man faces the prospect of death. In *Remembering Sion* Desmond Ryan recalled an occasion sometime around 1912 when Pearse, having had doubts cast upon his capacity for decisive and radical action, explodes with 'Let them talk! I am the most dangerous revolutionary of the whole lot of them!'[23] This apparently hysterical outburst may hold yet another clue to a depth of resolve in Pearse that is at once personal and transcendently conventional. Perhaps in the idea of character we find a key that may help us understand a man who, even as he planned a Rising against British rule, finds his patriotism overborne by his strangeness. For a man of Pearse's generation, character represented a kind of archetype that transcended national differences. His most lyrical vision of martyrdom occurs in a passage that appeared in the school magazine in May 1913:

> I dreamt I saw a pupil of mine, one of our boys at St Enda's, standing alone upon a platform above a mighty sea of people; and I understood that he was about to die there for some august cause, Ireland's or another. He looked extraordinarily proud and joyous, lifting his head with a smile almost of amusement; I remember noticing his bare white throat and the hair on his forehead stirred by the wind, just as I had often noticed them on the hurling field. I felt an inexplicable exhilaration as I looked on him, and this exhilaration was heightened rather than diminished by my consciousness that the great silent crowd regarded the boy with pity and wonder rather than with approval – as a fool who was throwing away his life rather than a martyr that was doing his duty. It would have been so easy to die before a hostile crowd: but to die before that silent, unsympathetic crowd.[24]

It is the boy's profound detachment, his implicit understanding of what the moment requires, that explains his magnificent forbearance. 'Fool' is a complex word as Pearse uses it; it means one who is secretly wise in the face of the crowd's incomprehension. In this intensely realised vision, the ideological motive remains unspecified – the boy is about to die for '*some* august cause, Ireland's or *another*' – but character is all. It is precisely this focus on character that helps explain Pearse's blandly equable reaction to the spectacle of Ulster arming. Though the Orangeman may be 'ridiculous' for believing 'incredible things', he is 'estimable in so far as he is willing and able to fight in defence of what he believes', so that ultimately 'the rifles of the Orangemen give dignity even to their folly'.[25] To Pearse's eye, the Orangeman was a 'Fool' in the exalted rather than the derogatory sense. Character, a man's – or any man's – willingness to fight or die for what he believes in, elevates action over ideology, making Ulster's importation of arms an admirable example to be imitated rather than a betrayal of fellow-Irishmen to be abhorred.

Fittingly, perhaps, it was an Englishman who was to provide testimony to Pearse's apotheosis as the exemplar of the cult of character. The chairman of his court martial, General Blackader, dined with the Countess of Fingall on the evening after he had pronounced sentence of death on Pearse. Blackader was in a dark mood; he confided to his hostess that he had just had to 'condemn to death one of the finest characters I have ever come across. There must be something very wrong in the state of things that makes a man like that a rebel.'[26] In that brief encounter at Arbour Hill Barracks, the officer had recognised one of his own type, cut from the same pan-European mould of self-command and bearing in adversity. The fool had been recognised on at least some of his own terms.

Character was a moral condition that flowed not from talent or grace, but from unrelenting good works. The Victorians devoted enormous energy to the inculcation and sustenance of character. Its primary cultural technology, practically a Victorian invention, was the public school. The public school, observes Girouard, conducted life 'on a plane of constant moral struggle' in which 'the Victorian schoolmaster found it hard to relax'.[27] Pearse the schoolmaster followed typically in the footsteps of his eminent predecessor, Thomas Arnold of Rugby, whom Carlyle had described as 'a man of unhasting, unresting diligence'.[28] In Pearse's transformation from gentle cultural nationalist to radical revolutionary there is a strain of this high-Victorian exhaustion. Its corollary is pleasure and relaxation foresworn. This is the theme of one of his most famous poems, 'Renunciation', whose last stanza runs:

> I have turned my face
> To this road before me,
> To the deed that I see
> And the death I shall die.

The writer Aschenbach, the protagonist of Thomas Mann's *Death in Venice* (1912), is described as having had a childhood foreshortened by the onset of hard work. Aschenbach's vision of the 'new type of hero' echoes Pearse's 'forbearance in the face of fate, beauty constant under torture' are qualities 'true to the spirit of the times', and Aschenbach himself is 'the poet-spokesman of all those who labour at the edge of exhaustion'. He sums up his life as one of 'self-conquest, a life against odds, dour, steadfast, abstinent; he had made it symbolical of the kind of over-strained heroism the time admired'.[29] Pearse's steely renunciation, his 'over-strained heroism', reveals him less as an idiosyncratic Irish Catholic than as a typical European of his generation.

### RESPECTABILITY: P.H. PEARSE, B.A., B.L.

Amid the fervid demands of living up to the high calling of character, there were, even for Pearse, moments of comic-heroic self-understanding. P.H. Pearse had his J.A. Prufrock moments (Eliot's poem was written in 1912). In 1913 he announces, in the last issue of *An Macaomh*, with his 'Commandments of Respectable Society' that, after all, he is no Prince Hamlet. The commandments include:

Thou shalt not be extreme in anything – in wrongdoing lest thou be put in gaol, in rightdoing lest thou be deemed a saint; Thou shalt not give away thy substance lest thou become a pauper; Thou shalt not engage in trade or manufacture lest thy hands become grimy; Thou shalt not carry a brown paper parcel lest thou shock Rathgar; Thou shalt not have an enthusiasm lest solicitors and their clerks call thee a fool; Thou shalt not endanger thy Job.[30]

Yet the habits of the respectable Dubliner were too deeply ingrained in Pearse for him to lend himself fully to the role of the fool. The fool is only apparently so: underneath it all, he is a wise man in drag. His earnestness, in the end, trumps his sense of the ridiculous. With characteristic punctiliousness, he signs the Proclamation 'P.H. Pearse'. In fact, throughout his life he signs most of his letters, even some to his beloved mother, with a starchy 'P.H. Pearse'. Here was a man who subscribed in everything but his darker passions to the mores of respectable society. Ruth Dudley Edwards's description of him in 1899 as a 'respectable Dublin middle-class prig' is just, as is the observation that 'the snobbish house names and the pretentious notepaper which he always affected were symptoms of a personality which clung obdurately to many of the trappings of gentility'.[31] Desmond Ryan, who knew him better than most, corroborates this

4.1 Gaelic League Congress, 1900. Pearse is on the extreme left of the second row from the back, top hat in hand. Eoin MacNeill is standing immediately to his left. Courtesy Pearse Museum.

4.2 Aeridheacht
Gaelic League, Ros
Muc *c.* 1905. Pearse
is front row centre
(in a grey hat).
Courtesy Pearse
Museum.

when he describes him as having 'the narrow outlook of a very
respectable Dubliner'.[32]

   As a young man his sartorial self-possession verged on dandyism.
A group photograph taken at the Gaelic League Congress in 1900
(figure 4.1) shows the twenty-one-year-old in pince-nez and a wing-
collar shirt, set off with a bow-tie; he holds a top-hat delicately in his
hand. Perhaps thinking of this very occasion, his childhood friend
Eamonn O'Neill later recalled Pearse attending an early Gaelic
League Ard Fheis thus accoutred. Pearse thought his exotic finery
demonstrated 'respect for the assembly', but his friend felt that it lost
him votes in the election, and he worried that many would conclude
that 'a man who wore a top hat and frock coat could not be a true
Gael!'[33] Though he soon learned to soften his appearance into something less forbiddingly formal, sartorial gravitas remained one of
Pearse's hallmarks throughout his life. One of his Irish-speaking students at St Enda's, Pádraig Óg Ó Conaire from Connemara, later
recalled the exotic impact of Pearse and his friends on the people of
the Gaeltacht. When these young language enthusiasts from Dublin
'invaded' Connemara in the early years of the century, remembered
Ó Conaire, 'it amazed us to see such well-dressed people speaking
Irish'.[34]

   Another photograph shows Pearse in the company of a young
priest roughly the same age as himself, surrounded by Connemara
people. The only smartly dressed figures in the scene, Pearse and his
companion avert their gaze self-consciously from the camera. But the

4.3 James Pearse and
Mrs Margaret Pearse.
Courtesy Pearse
Museum.

onlookers are transfixed by the lens, staring at it as if it were the source of some magical power. This gap between knowingness and naïvety measures some of the distance between the modernity of the central figures and the rest of the group's fascination with an exotic technology. The orderly arc in which the group is arranged around them embodies a palpable cultural distance which Pearse, for all his passionate love of the Gaeltacht and its people, sensed. Writing in Irish in his short-lived magazine *An Barr Buadh* in 1912, he broods:

I don't know if I like you or not, Pearse ... you are too dark in yourself. You do not make friends with Gaels. You avoid their company. When you come among them you bring a dark cloud with you that lies heavily upon them. Is it your English blood is the cause of that, I wonder?[35]

Is it the shadow of the father, then, that makes him the strange thing he is? In rising from mason to successful businessman, James Pearse had made a journey that lay at the heart of numerous Victorian novels, from lowly man of no means to middle-class respectability. About 1888, James sought to capture his own social arrival in that recently established recorder of social nuance, the family photograph. All of the family are impeccably dressed, Patrick in a classic Victorian variation on the Fauntleroy suit. James himself betrays a hint of yet another Victorian trait: dandyism. More than one photograph was taken on the occasion. James changes hats between shots. In one he wears a straw hat, tilted at a slightly rakish angle; in the other an oriental style fez that conveys a hint of the bohemian (he was, after all, a sculptor and free-thinking follower of John Bright). Perhaps it was the father's influence, then, that lay behind the top hat and bow tie Pearse sported at the Gaelic League Congress in 1901. In time, due maybe to the raillery of friends like O'Neill, he toned down to a dark suit and tie, which he wore throughout his life with little variation. The suit and tie, of course, which prevails to this day, was one of the more enduring innovations of the Victorian age.[36]

### THE LOST BOYHOOD OF P.H. PEARSE

Pearse was born into a golden age of childhood writing. Lewis

Carroll's *Alice in Wonderland* appeared in 1862; Edward Lear's *The Owl and the Pussycat* in 1867; Stephenson's *Treasure Island* in 1883; J.M. Barie's *Peter Pan* in 1904; and Kenneth Grahame's *The Wind in the Willows* in 1908. In *The Home-Life of Patrick Pearse*, his sister Mary-Bridget provides evidence that Pearse was familiar with a wide range of childhood classics. She mentions his having read *Alice in Wonderland, Through the Looking Glass, Sylvia and Bruno, The Wallypug of Why, Prince Boohoo, The Swiss Family Robinson* and *Uncle Tom's Cabin*. She particularly recalls the White Knight in *Through the Looking Glass* as one of his favourite characters.[37] For his English class in St Enda's, the headmaster chose *Treasure Island* as one of his texts. In an essay in *An Macaomh* in May 1913, Pearse cites Barrie's *Peter Pan* as an influence for one of his own plays:

> Mr J.M. Barrie makes his Peter Pan say (and it is finely said) 'To die will be a very big adventure', but, I think, that in making my little boy in *An Rí* offer himself with the words 'let me do this little thing', I am nearer to the spirit of the heroes.[38]

Barrie's play was first produced in 1904, and Pearse's *An Rí* in 1911. Peter Pan's tragedy was that he could never grow old or die. In his own play, Pearse reverses the tragic focus by conjuring up the spirit of a boyhood martyr, a type for whom death is reduced to a 'little thing' – exactly that 'laughing gesture' of the boy on the scaffold cited above. If *Peter Pan* represented a generational fantasy of eternal childhood, of adulthood postponed, Pearse's Cúchulainn represented an alternative way of cheating adulthood: by embracing death from within the bounds of childhood itself. In an earlier article for the school magazine (May 1909) he wrote of 'the knightly tradition of the macradh of Eamhain Macha, dead at the Ford, in the beauty of their boyhood', and goes on to cite the words of Cúchulainn which he had emblazoned over an archway in the school's first home in Ranelagh: 'I care not though I were to live but one day and one night, if only my fame and my deeds live after me'.[39] Contemporaneously, Mann's Aschenbach has a close encounter with the beautiful boy Tadzio in the hotel lift in Venice. He notices the boy's teeth are bad: '"He is delicate, he is sickly," Aschenbach thought. "He is most

4.4 *Standing, left to right*: Patrick Pearse, James Pearse and William Pearse. *Seated, left to right*: Mrs Margaret Pearse, Mary Brigid Pearse and Margaret Pearse. Courtesy Pearse Museum.

likely not to live to grow old." He did not try to account for the pleasure the idea gave him.'[40] Tadzio, like the boy of Pearse's dream, cheats adulthood through death in Venice. But there is also a fundamental difference: Mann's beautiful boy succumbs to fate while Pearse's is master of his. The manliness of Pearse's boy-martyr is the fantasy of disillusioned adulthood, of a capacity for action unadulterated by the weary responsibilities and temporising accommodations of a grown-up world.

For Pearse, like so many of his European contemporaries, was steeped in a newly-invented literary genre that had turned childhood into a golden age, a lost paradise, and adulthood into a doomed condition of inexorable decline. 'To have reached thirty, is to have failed

4.5 Unpublished autobiographical fragment. Courtesy Pearse Museum.

in life,' laments H.H. Munro's protagonist in his story 'Reginald on the Academy' (1904).⁴¹ In a fine phrase, Francis Cornford described his friend Rupert Brooke as 'magnificently unprepared for the long littleness of life'.⁴² Encroaching adulthood brought with it the early onset of *ennui* and world-weariness. When the War arrived, 'it provided an escape from the dreary sleep of middle age and conventional living'.⁴³ In fighting against this fate, only one exasperated strategy seemed possible, one that seemed to mark off a change of mood between a Victorian and a distinctly Edwardian sensibility. As Jackie Wullschlager has succinctly put it: 'where the Victorians had escaped into a fantastical vision of childhood for solace and distraction, the Edwardians went one stage further and attempted to play at childhood in their own adult lives'.⁴⁴ In this sense, it is perhaps more accurate to describe St Enda's, founded in the same year as Baden-Powell's Boy-Scout movement (1908), as the work of an Edwardian rather than a Victorian Gael.

Grieving for a lost childhood as middle age encroached only added to Pearse's desperation. The fragment of autobiography is the ultimate, poignant testament to his inability to fly the nets of childhood into anything resembling contented adulthood. In his own handwriting it comes to forty-five pages, and ends like this:

> That long convalescence is in the retrospect the happiest and at the same time the most important period in my life. In it all the strengths and fealties and right desires that have worked in me, and have given to my life such utility as it can claim, have authentically their roots from that time. They were as yet puny and faltering and inarticulate enough, such strengths and fealties and right desires as a child is capable of, but destined through effort and suffering, with not a few set-backs and deflections to grow with my boyhood and youth and to find at length in my manhood some sort of expression.

The convalescence referred to was a bout of scarlatina, to which he succumbed after the family had moved to Sandymount, sometime in 1884. This places the reminiscence somewhere between his fifth and twelfth years (the family moved back to Great Brunswick Street about 1892). So the fragment ends with the account having failed to leave the shores of childhood. Ahead, lie the dreary years of adulthood, trickling out in the bathos of 'some sort of expression'. When one bears in mind that he was writing this more or less in the same period as those final pamphlets – in a tone that is consistently declamatory and nervelessly free of doubt – the contrast is sharp. Here is how, for example, *The Separatist Idea* (published February 1916) ends:

> That God spoke to Ireland through Tone and through those
> who, after Tone, have taken up his testimony, that Tone's teach-
> ing and theirs is true and great and that no other teaching as to
> Ireland has any truth or worthiness at all, is a thing upon which
> I stake all my mortal and all my immortal hopes. And I ask the
> men and women of my generation to stake their mortal and
> immortal hopes with me.

When Pearse looked in the mirror, what looked back at him was a
shy man with a pronounced squint in the right eye. He overcame the
weakness this might have represented by having all of his formal
photographs taken in profile. Full-on portraits of Pearse are rare, and
do not figure in his iconography. It is as if this full-on Pearse is that
'strange thing', a bewildering composite of two strands of identity
that could not be reconciled within the frame of a unified vision; as
if the consciously posed profile in courage, with its gaze averted
towards posterity, represented a turning away from his own impon-
derable deeps.

Pearse's inability to carry his autobiographical project to a conclusion, then, reveals something of his typically Victorian cast of mind.
In breaking off so abruptly, perhaps he sensed the dangers posed for
decisive action by protracted introspection.

Elizabeth Helsinger has observed that a profound change in the
sense of self took place between Wordsworth and Tennyson. Where
Wordsworth had seen introspection as a positive exercise leading to
visionary knowledge of the self and the world, the Victorians had
come to suspect it as a form of morbidity. 'The Victorians knew what
Wordsworth never quite admitted, she writes, 'that self-discovery has
become not the prelude to an active life but an inadequate substitute
for it.'[45] Pearse undertook his autobiographical fragment at a moment
of maximum peril to his climactic project of self-sacrifice. The diver-
sion into what might have been an extended autobiographical excur-
sus threatened to reduce him to bewilderment. Beckett's characteri-
sation of the Victorian Gael as one 'in flight from self-awareness'
comes close to the mark with Pearse.

His essay at autobiography ends turbulently in a series of bewildered
sentences, of eddying phrases, crossed-out and over-written (see above).
He has looked into the abyss and resolved to look away. Two fears combine to subvert his journey of personal exploration: the prospect of
writing about his own adult years, and lingering too long over the
cracks in his fissured identity. So his exercise in autobiography breaks
down upon a classical Victorian anxiety (as in Tennyson's 'In
Memoriam') about whether one 'can or should pursue an introspective
journey toward a self-revealing vision'.[46] His poem 'Renunciation',

written initially in 1912, is his antidote to the introspective lures of autobiography. It opens in with an image of self-mutilated vision:

> Naked I saw thee,
> O Beauty of Beauty
> And I blinded my eyes,
> For fear I should fail.

Pearse's attempt to write an autobiography comes at the end of a century of Romanticism, during which the modern sense of the self had emerged. Its cultural preconditions were literacy, individuality and a sense of history. But the end of the century was also a crucial transitional moment. Freud had not yet appeared to decode the signposts to the unconscious contained in what people said and wrote about themselves. Pearse could still write with candour and a certain innocence about things which psychoanalysis would soon cast in a new light. As Helsinger notes, the Victorians conceived the confessional mode 'not as intimate speech but public discourse'. The double-take of self-consciousness was not available to Pearse, no more than it was available, for example, to Walter Pater in writing his autobiographical *Praeterita*, where candid and, to modern eyes, embarrassing revelations are made.[47] Against this background, the unconstrained frankness, homoerotic avowals and (to modern eyes) uncomfortably pederastic connotations of his poem 'Little Lad of the Tricks' are more easily understood:

> Raise your comely head
> Till I kiss your mouth:
> If either of us is the better of that
> I am the better of it.
>
> There is a fragrance in your kiss
> That I have not found yet
> In the kisses of women
> Or in the honey of their bodies.

On a close reading, it becomes clear that Pearse is neither confessing to acts of pederasty nor disavowing homoerotic feeling. Instead, the poem contains a self-directed revulsion at the irruption of impure thoughts (that the flush in the lad's cheek would turn 'white with dread of me / Could you read my secrets'). Jackie Wullschlager has commented well upon the delicate balance of desire, temptation and forbearance involved in this mindset. In the case of Lewis Carroll, for example, adult sexual desires were subconsciously directed towards children where strong taboos made them seem safe, and where the child could be 'a focus for emotional satisfaction which never threat-

ened the ideal of chastity'.[48] Elaine Sisson, in her recent book on
Pearse's school, has also commented justly that that Edwardian
homoerotic culture generated erotic imagery that appealed to a sentimental rather than a 'knowing' audience.[49] This is yet another
example of where reading Pearse either exclusively in terms of his
own work or within the narrow confines of an exclusively Irish experience, results in a less complex, if not distorting, interpretation.

CONCLUSION

In *Modern Ireland, 1600–1972*, R.F. Foster declared summarily that 'the
ideology of 1916 is inescapably connected with Pearse'.[50] It is to the
writings of Pearse that most writers turn when seeking to explain the ideological content of that watershed event. Yet the habit of resorting to
Pearse to explain 1916 leads also to the idea that Pearse himself can be
explained by his published pronouncements on Irish culture and history.
However the biographical challenge he poses is more formidable that
that. This short survey has tried to sketch a range of formative influences,
both cultural and familial, that surely make it no exaggeration to describe
Pearse as one of the most complex characters in Ireland's modern history. This well-read, and comparatively well-travelled, son of an English
father and Irish mother was the product of a more complex mix of cultural influences than is summed up in such one-dimensional labels as
'Irish Republican' or 'Irish nationalist'. No doubt, in the prose and poetry of his final years Pearse set out to shape a literary bequest through
which his sacrificial end would be understood on exactly these terms. It
was a project in which he was to prove astonishingly successful: whether
idolised or attacked, Pearse seems consistently to have been judged in
and on the terms of his own pronouncements. But it is possible at least
partially to deconstruct this mythic stereotype and discover a personality that was trying, by declaiming a patriotism simple in its certainties, to
fly the nets of a troubled identity. In this, he was typical of his generation, a generation of whom it is only possible to make sense against the
backdrop a shared European civilisation.

Desmond Ryan who knew Pearse more intimately than most, was
driven to paradox in his attempt to sum up the man he had known
as pupil and secretary. Pearse, he wrote, 'was always a moderate, and
always a revolutionary'.[51] Pearse the 'Victorian Gael' is yet another
paradox, but one, perhaps, that offers a stereoscopic reading of a
man we have become used to seeing as a one-dimensional icon.

History, Politics and Culture
Stair, Polaitíocht agus Cultúr

CHAPTER FIVE

# Patrick Pearse:
# Irish Modernist

## DECLAN KIBERD

The rebels of 1916 were not just rebels – they were revolutionaries. A rebel knows what he is against, but a revolutionary knows what she is <u>for.</u> The drive towards futurity is what marks the writings of Patrick Pearse. He attempts in poems to contemplate a point in the future from which the yet unmade republic might become visible:

> O wise men, riddle me this: what if the dream come true?
> What if the dream come true? and millions unborn shall dwell
> In the house that I shaped in my heart, the noble house of my
> thought.

Today, it seems almost heretical to link Pearse to James Joyce – but there is no fundamental difference between those lines just quoted and the closing determination of another 1916 dissident, Stephen Daedalus in *A Portrait of the Artist as a Young Man*, 'to forge in the smithy of my soul the uncreated conscience of my race'. Those lines have a wholly Pearsean ring.

Both men based their analysis on Oscar Wilde's notion that the future is what artists already are, that art creates environments which only much later can be realised and inhabited by future generations. This is why Ellmann insisted that we are all still learning how to be Joyce's contemporaries.[1] But that is true also of Pearse.

Their view of cultural history operated in much the same way. Joyce juxtaposed Homer and modernity, in order to point out and explore the buried parallels. Pearse's fusion of pagan and Christian ideas of heroism was deeply offensive to pious Christians and to energetic exponents of paganism in the first decade of the twentieth century – so much so that one could even claim that he deliberately used each code to expose the shortcomings of the other. However, the dialectic is even more subtle than that implies. Pearse believed that every civilisation carried within it the hidden lineaments of the next code, at first obvious only to rare, sensitive souls, whose vision

5.1 Patrick
Pearse. Courtesy
Kilmainham
Gaol Museum.

was keen enough to x-ray the outlines beneath the sur-
face, but which, when the code was established, would
be fully clear to all.  Hence his insistence that what
seemed like old pagan sagas of stoically endured pain
really did have an encoded Christian story: 'The story of
Cuchulain symbolises', he said, 'the redemption of men
by a sinless god.'[2] The *Táin* he interpreted as an unconscious retelling (or forecasting?) of the tale of Calvary.
The balancing of retelling against forecasting there was
deliberate: as a scholar, Pearse was well aware of the
possibility that later Christian monks and scribes might
have been tempted to reconfigure certain scenes of the
old tales along more Christian lines, but he preferred to
believe that the ancient pagan tellers truly had fore-
dreamed a Christian element in their narrative.

This is a little like the historian Ernest Bloch's notion
of an 'ideological surplus',[3] to be found in every great
text, which answers less to the needs of its own time
than to those requirements which will emerge only in
the future, but an ideological surplus which provides a
rear-rocket that propels the basic work all the faster
into that opening future.

What unnerved contemporary Catholics and Celticists – say a
Father J.J. Horgan or a W.B. Yeats – was the enthusiasm with which
Pearse mingled references to Colmcille and Cúchulainn, as if they
really were part of a developing continuum.  Colmcille had said, 'If
I die, it shall be from the excess of love that I bear the Gael'.  Pearse
energetically glossed the line:

> A love and a service so excessive that one must give all, must be
> willing always to make the ultimate sacrifice – this is the inspi-
> ration alike of the story of Cúchulainn and the story of
> Colmcille, the inspiration that made the one a hero and the
> other a saint.[4]

Everybody knows how these lines jangled on the nerves of Father
J.J. Horgan, who wrote that the Rising was a sin and Pearse a heretic.[5]
But they also troubled that pagan, W.B. Yeats, at least as much, for he
wrote the key phrase into the closing stanza of 'Easter 1916':

> And what if excess of love
> Bewildered them till they died?

The sheer audacity of the Rising – conducted by a handful of
deeply intelligent and courageous men and women at a moment in
history when the map of the whole world was heavily coloured red

– is matched by the intrepid nature of Pearse's dialectical imagination, as it worked on those 'discrepant' images. British readers at the
time – and Irish too – had enjoyed Augusta Gregory's *Cuchulain of
Muirthemne*, a prose retelling of the Celtic saga, which also noted the
pagan and Christian elements in the death of the hero: the energy
with which he smote his enemies in single combat was pagan, but the
manner of his death, strapped to pillar or rock, with a bird descend-
ing to drink the last drop of his blood – that was a version of Jesus
on the cross.   In the narrative of Augusta Gregory that combination
was a recipe for just the sort of muscular Christian that her son
Robert was trying to emulate at a British public school. In such versions, Cúchulainn was little more than a public schoolboy in the drag
of a Celtic hero.  Imperial theory and Celtic scholarship allowed the
colonised native a disguised version of the British present, but only
on one condition: that the muscular Christians of the natives were
safely confined to a remote historical past. This is the point at which
the explosive nature of Pearse's thinking becomes manifest, for he
takes that fused figure out of the historical cabinet to unleash him as
a force in the actual present. The unused potentials of an image, its
'unfinished business', that ideological surplus which still lay unex-
ploited in its own time, can issue forth as a seemingly new challenge.

Why, then, have Pearse and his comrades been so often treated as
nostalgists, sentimentalists, exponents only of the backward look?
Why has this futuristic element in their thought been lost as much to
their admirers as to their detractors?  Why is the homoerotic element
in his poetry a matter for vengeful arraignment, whereas the same elements are now routinely praised in the lyrics of a Wilde or a Gogarty?
One reason is that the Easter insurgents masked their own modernity,
for they knew that in a society undergoing rapid change, it is wise to
present the very new as a restoration of the very old.   So they invoked
Cúchulainn as a sponsor of their dream of a welfare state. Over three
decades before such a state emerged in Britain or Scandinavia, they
spoke of the need to 'cherish all the children of the nation equally'.
This social-democratic vision was as much the work of Pearse as of
Connolly, for in his final years he had come to conflate his
Christianity with a radical critique of the desk-bound, consumerist
middle class. This he conducted in a corrosive style of Wildean witti-
cism which showed far more humour than he is usually given credit
for. As in his cultural analyses, so in his humour, Pearse delighted to
mingle categories normally kept quite separate in watertight compart-
ments, the better to test the tolerance of all adherents.   In effect, he
uses the blend to disrupt all codes with which the new thinking comes
into contact, as when, in a chemical experiment, two molecules col-
lide and join, releasing a new, unprecedented type of energy:

Our Christianity becomes respectability.  We are not content with
teaching the ten commandments that God spake in thunder and
Christ told us to keep if we would enter into the life and the precepts of the Church which he commanded us to hear: we add
thereto the commandments and precepts of Respectable Society.
And these are chiefly six: Thou shalt not be extreme in anything
– in wrongdoing lest thou be put in gaol, in rightdoing lest thou
be deemed a saint; Thou shalt not engage in trade or manufacture, lest thy hands become grimy; Thou shalt not carry a brown
paper sack lest thou shock Rathgar; Thou shalt not have an
enthusiasm lest solicitors and clerks call thee fool; Thou shalt not
endanger thy Job. One has heard this shocking morality taught in
Christian schools, expounded in Christian newspapers, even
preached from Christian pulpits.  Those things about the lilies in
the field and the birds of the air, and that rebuke to Martha who
was troubled about many things, are thought to have no relevancy
to modern life.   But if that is so, Christianity has no relevancy to
modern life, for these are the essence of Christ's teaching.[6]

The Jesus who emerges from those lines is a sort of bohemian, a precursor of liberation theology with its option for the poor. The
Proclamation of the Irish Republic encodes those values, many of
them rooted in Pearse's earlier writings. The personification that
'Ireland through us summons her children to her flag' derives from his
poem 'Mise Éire', with its call for insurrection as an act of reparation
by children guilty in many past moments of selling their own mother:

Mise Éire
Sine mé ná an Cailleach Béarra.

Mór mo ghlóire
Is mé do rug Cúchulainn cróga.

Mór mo náire
Mo chlann féin do dhíol a máthair.

Mise Éire
Uaigní mé ná an Cailleach Béarra.[7]

[I am Ireland
I am older than the hag of Béarra.

Great my glory
It was I who bore the brave Cúchulainn.

Great my shame
My own children sold their mother.

I am Ireland
I am lonelier than the hag of Béarra. ]

That there was no sexist attempt to project onto Mother Ireland a femininity which the rebels were anxious to deny in themselves is already manifest in the fact that the Proclamation addresses Irishwomen as well as Irishmen and that at a time when women still did not have the vote. Up to seventy women served as soldier-volunteers in the Rising. Had the rebels been successful, Hanna Sheehy-Skeffington would have been appointed the first female government minister anywhere in the world, a year before Alexandra Kollontai won that honour for the Soviets. These radical elements were occluded in subsequent commentaries by conservative nationalists whose greatest aspiration was to live in Rathgar and produce solicitor-sons, and by revisionist historians opposed to the revolutionary tradition in Ireland. But they were occluded also at the time of the Rising itself, because such masking is a longstanding tactic of revolution.

After all, the French rebels of 1789, standing on the edge of a meritocratic modern world, became unnerved by the very openness of the moment which they were creating; and so they presented themselves not as revolutionary businessmen but as resurrected Romans, restoring ancient democratic rights. Some of the French rebels clad themselves in the roman toga for portraits by painters such as David. Even the more intrepid, who were not unnerved, went along with the tactic, knowing that it would help to soothe fears among the wider community that what was afoot was a risky new departure rather than a wise restoration.

5.2 *Fionn: a dramatic spectacle, c.* 1914. Courtesy Pearse Museum.

Much of the writing of the 1916 leaders adopts a similar set of tactics. James Connolly presents *Labour in Irish History* as a conscious contribution to the Irish literary revival, arguing that socialism would simply be a return to the Gaelic system of landholding, with the state now rather than a single ruler retaining the land in the name of all the people. Pearse presented his liberal, child-centred theories of education at St Enda's college as a revival of Gaelic fosterage traditions. The underlying radicalism of that project may be inferred from the fact that Jim Larkin sent his sons to St Enda's, planning a 'finishing school' for them in Moscow. All of these tacticians knew that in a land addicted to rapidly lost traditions, in order to secure a hearing a thinker may have to present the new as a version of the very old. In truth, revolution may need the double sanction of Cúchulainn and Colmcille. But that, of course, is precisely the same technique which was in 1916 being perfected in the experimental city of Zurich by James Joyce, who was learning how to gift-wrap the most subversive narrative of the modernist movement, *Ulysses*, in one of Europe's oldest tales, *The Odyssey* of Homer.

Moreover, viewed from this distance, Joyce's book may be seen to have been just as much a part of the revival movement as Connolly's *Labour in Irish History* or Horace Plunkett's *Ireland in the New Century*. What the Gaelic League, the Agricultural Co-operative Movement, Sinn Féin and the Abbey Theatre all had in common was that, emerging after the failure of Westminster to deliver the promised Home Rule in 1893, they were all exercises in self-help. The League ran the first industrial parades on St Patrick's Day to promote Irish goods, while the Co-op journal *The Irish Homestead*, sought to revitalise Irish farming and industry. Joyce's first short stories appeared in the *Homestead* and their attempt to diagnose the nature of the 'paralysis' afflicting Irish mindsets fitted perfectly with the paper's agenda. Joyce's early stories, like the 'Nestor' episode of *Ulysses*, concern themselves with the frustrated attempt by a boy or youth to learn wisdom from an older man, who turns out to be compromised, broken or simply ridiculous. The underlying trajectory of *Ulysses* is of a self-help narrative of a corrected pedagogy, at the end of which the confused intellectual, Stephen Dedalus, learns how to reconcile theory and practice from Leopold Bloom. Like Pearse's long passage which I quoted, Joyce's book attempts to reconcile a bohemian with a business ethic, producing a climax unique in modernism, during which the bohemian and bourgeois, far from being enemies, make common cause.

The central problem posed by Pearse and Joyce is one and the same; and it is also the problem posed by the Rising itself – how does newness come into the world? As a narrative, *Ulysses* obsesses over such questions as who first distilled whiskey? Who was the first person to eat an oyster? and so on. Joyce knew that he was attempting something without precedent, yet all he had at his disposal was a language and literature dense with precedents. This is why he shared with Pearse a deep interest in that moment in biblical history when Moses comes down Mount Sinai, after his meeting with god concerning the future of the children of Israel, and bearing a new dispensation which is called (in one of the most famous self-describing phrases of *Ulysses*) 'the tables of the law in the language of the outlaw'.

The new contract, negotiated on behalf of a people wandering in the wilderness and seeking to rehearse an absolute liberty, is less a set of old, rigid laws than a freely negotiated relationship. That negotiation happens during a prolonged period of watching and waiting, in which a radical newness might supervene. That is the burden of Pearse in 'The Rebel':

> My mother bore me in bondage, in bondage my mother was born;
> I am the blood of serfs;
> The children with whom I have played, the men and women
> with whom I have eaten,
> Have had masters over them, have been under the lash of masters,
> And, though gentle, have served churls ...
> I am the flesh of the flesh of these lowly ...
> I that have vision and prophecy and the gift of fiery speech,
> I that have spoken with God on the top of His holy hill.[8]

Commentators still marvel at the rhetorical assurance of these lines, whose style owes something to Walt Whitman and something to the Bible, without noticing that beyond the self-dramatising of the prophet who feels himself on a hot-line to God, there is something deeper still – an obsession with the fiery speech, those tongues of Pentecostal fire that portend newness, a new set of laws in the language of outlaws.

Nothing is harder to achieve than such newness. Moses found it for Israel, Whitman for America, and both Pearse and Joyce were trying to do likewise for Ireland. The motive behind the Rising was Pearse's fear, shared with Joseph Plunkett and Desmond FitzGerald, that if something were not done, the very idea of the nation, so arduously articulated in major texts of the previous two decades, might disappear in the trenches of World War One. Joyce created *Ulysses* for much the same reason: as Dante reimagined a Florence which he thought might disappear, so the exile Joyce gave concrete reality to an Ireland which he felt, as early as a 1907 essay in a Triestine newspaper, was in danger of vaporising under the invertebrate Irish Parliamentary Party. 'If she is truly capable of reviving, let her awake', he wrote, 'or let her cover up her head and lie down decently in her grave forever'.[9]

There is a sense in which all those brilliant texts, paintings, art-
works and plays produced in the years before 1916 cried out for
implementation in some form of action, some enactment.

But how does one turn image into event? How but with a wholly
new set of words and forms? Hence the concern in so many writings
of the period with the relationship between an idea and a deed. The
demarcation lines between theory and practice grew blurred in those
years. After all, W.B. Yeats began as a signed-up member of the IRB
and Sean O'Casey served as secretary of the Irish Citizen's Army
before concluding – as activists manqués – that they would seek their
solutions in literature; just as Pearse, Plunkett, MacDonagh and
Connolly all wrote poems and plays, before deciding – as writers
manqués – to embody their ideas in action, but an action which
would, Wilde-like, confine its talent to the writing while unleashing
its true genius in the act as a form of art. The closeness of the worlds
of stage and street in the period suggests a desire to remake the
whole world along the lines of art. Hence the use of Easter symbols
in a consciously theatrical fashion, evoking not only new life from a
dead land, but the very notion of resurrection itself. The deeds of
Cúchulainn, written up by Standish J. O'Grady in his study of the
1870s, were now taking fire in other people's heads. The conditions

5.3 St Enda's *The
Passion Play*, Easter
1911. This was
produced in the
Abbey Theatre
with Willie Pearse
playing the role of
Pontius Pilate.
Courtesy Pearse
Museum.

Ceann an fo[ɼpaɼ]e.
The Captain of the Guard.

píolát.
Pilate.

an táɼn-Saʒaɼt.
The High Priest.

Sʒoil Éanna, Rát Feaɼnáin: Oɼáma na páɼe, Cáiɼʒ 1911.
St. Enda's College, Rathfarnham: The Passion Play, Easter 1911.

for theorising a revolution – say, staging a play like *Cathleen Ní Houlihan* – were scarcely different from those for starting one. That start took a suitably literary form: the reading of the Proclamation in front of the Ionic columns of the General Post Office by a man whom the actress Máire Nic Shiubhlaigh called 'A bit of a pose'.

There is indeed a Wildean element in Pearse, which never gets mentioned when people discuss his obsession with the male body – though Whitman's art could have been seen as providing the clue and the link – and it has to do with his innermost structures of thought and feeling. Wilde was also a product of the Arts and Crafts movement which provided the backdrop to the Pearse family and to the interior designs at St Enda's. In fairy-tales for children such as 'The Star Child' and 'The Happy Prince', Wilde provided a set of models on which Pearse would build his own Irish-language equivalents, 'Íosagán' and 'Eoghainín na nÉan'. The fact that Wilde had taken some of his plots from old Connemara women who 'paid' his doctor-father with a story rather than a fee suggests that Pearse also may have tapped into similar traditions of storytelling heard from men and women in the west. Both men hoped that, in time, their tales would re-enter the anonymity of folk tradition – something that has almost come true. Pearse wrote in his Foreword to *Íosagán agus Scéalta Eile* in 1907: 'Ag cur na scéalta seo in eagar dom, ní ionadh mo smaointe ar mo chairde a d'inis dom iad agus ar an áit uaigneach ar chiumhais na hÉireann a bhfuil a gcónaí' [In putting these stories into order, it's no surprise that I think of my friends who told them to me and of the lonely place on the edge of Ireland where they live].[10] In both Wilde's and Pearse's stories, the child is an agent of redemption, bearing messages to a fallen adult world, whose values of innocence and integrity are in jeopardy until restored, often by the death of a child-figure. For them, as for Peter Pan, to die is an awfully big adventure. Inscribed into both performances is the notion of the triumph of failure, an ancient idea but one given a Christian spin with the proposition that he who loses life may save it.

A separate paper would be needed to demonstrate the ways in which Wilde anticipated Pearse in his blending of the New Paganism of the 1890s with a revised personification of Jesus as the ultimate bohemian dissident – a conjunction framed most potently of all in Wilde's prison letter *De Profundis*. The fact that both men were exponents of the long tradition of Irish prison literature is also worth noting. And Wilde's emphasis on the need for education rather than schooling, for imaginative engagement rather than indoctrination in the classroom, would find many points of contact with the relaxed regime at St Enda's, a 'republic of childhood' in which, for example, the boys were allowed to vote on whether they would play hurling or cricket in the summer term. Wilde was also important as a drama-tist who taught that the conditions of life are plastic and that on the stage, even in a divertissement like *The Importance of Being Earnest*, a play can rehearse revolution, with women acting more like men, servants storing up information against that moment when they will dictate to their masters, and free play replacing work as people choose liberty over routine.

Wilde had indicated how newness might come into the world when he wrote that 'the first duty in life is to adopt a pose – and what the second is nobody has yet found out'. That was the real reason why Pearse needed to be a bit of a pose and why the rebels of 1789 needed to cast themselves as ancient Romans. Like adolescents, they toyed briefly with a role in hopes of learning something new about themselves, much as Pearse played with the idea of being Cúchulainn and Colmcille in one person. In the lead-up to the Rising, he wrote in an essay called *Ghosts* that Robert Emmet should be added to that pantheon. Interestingly, Karl Marx had warned about this lamenta-ble tendency of ghosts to appear on the eve of revolutions and had complained that they often had the effect of smothering those revo-lutions, returning a people once intent on newness to the old agen-das, the old names and dates. Radical innovators needed to mask their newness with an ancient imagery, but this should be but a brief tactic, before the manifest content fell away to reveal the revolution-ary content latent beneath. Otherwise, history would be reduced to costume drama, with people trapped in all the old, familiar narra-tives.

It is clear that Joyce's *Ulysses* passed this test: the Homeric struc-ture was a mere shell that fell away, to reveal the new thing which Joyce had created within it. But what of Pearse? Was his attempt at newness stifled or has it yet to be fully explained? He cannot be held responsible for either the pietistic nonsense or the vitriolic attacks written about his thought after his execution in 1916. A truly revi-sionist method would attempt to restore to his ideas the openness they had when first he shaped them.

Perhaps the most telling clues may be found in his literary criti-cism, for he was a more gifted literary analyst than creative artist. As a literary artist, his emotional range was rather narrow, indicating the somewhat restricted nature of his actual, lived experience. Yet, as early as Joyce and George Moore, he foretold the vital importance of the short story as a literary genre, in which Irish authors might depict the everyday lives of those marginals and 'submerged popula-tion groups' (which Frank O'Connor would later define as the natu-ral subjects of that form). He understood that the narrative style of the story should be terse, rapid and graphic, yet he opposed attempts by an tAthair Peadar Ó Laoghaire and his followers to impose 'caint na ndaoine' because (he said) 'the ordinary speech of the people is never literature, though it is the stuff of which literature is made'.[11] It is hard for us today to realise just how much trouble that modernist stance got him into, especially when he published his own stories. One of the early reviewers, a follower of Ó Laoghaire, memorably opined that 'if Irish is the talk of broad-chested men, this is the language of mincing shop-walkers'.[12] There was already something in Pearse that brought out the homophobe in a certain kind of critic; and the attack on his personality-structure began from within the language movement long before it was taken up by anti-nationalists.

To read Pearse's literary essays in *An Claidheamh Soluis agus Fáinne an Lae* now is to hear one of the clearest of all voices for the modern movement in literature:

> We hold the folk tale to be a beautiful and gracious thing only in its own time and place ... and its time and place are the winter fireside, or the spring sowing time, or the country road at any season. Thus, we lay down the proposition that a living literature <u>cannot</u> (and if it could) should not be built up on the folk tale. The folk tale is an echo of old mythologies: literature is a deliberate criticism of actual life ... why impose the folk attitude of mind, the folk conventions of form, on the makers of literature?  Why set up as a standard of today a standard at which Aonghus Ó Dálaigh and Seathrún Céitinn would have laughed? ... Irish literature, if it is to live and grow, must get into contact on the one hand with its own past and on the other with the mind of contemporary Europe ... This is the twentieth century; and no literature can take root in the twentieth century which is not of the twentieth century. We want no Gothic revival.[13]

In his musical criticism, he likewise insisted that peasant *sean-nós* was not the Irish form of art-music, merely the country person's form, and that musicians should not be afraid to study the modernist techniques of Europe.  In all his criticism, Pearse emphasised the artist as <u>thinker</u>: 'every piece of literature expresses the views of its creator ... it is in this sense a piece of criticism'.[14] Not for nothing had he read and closely studied the thought of Matthew Arnold.

There is no complete description of the *mentalité* of the 1916 Rising or of Pearse himself in any work of literature or of history – though it should be added that Ruth Dudley Edwards's biography comes closer than most. Revolution, of its very nature, is hard to represent in direct form and so are revolutionaries.  Pearse is so potent a figure in O'Casey's drama that he has to be marginalised as a speaker at a window on the edge of things; and in similar fashion the Rising itself in that play happens mainly offstage. Likewise, in *The Dreaming of the Bones* by Yeats, the entire action of the Rising happens else-where. One shouldn't be over-critical of these marginalisations. After all, the poet-soldiers of World War One, also experiencing new-ness, found it all but impossible to narrate their experience in any language comprehensible to the civilians back home. What they had gone through in the trenches remained largely unexpressed, although there are some teasing links between lines of Rupert Brooke and those of Pearse:

> Now God be thanked who matched us with this hour,
> And caught our youth, and wakened us from sleeping.

In general, however, the technical problem of representing Pearse and his newness remained unresolved, even by Pearse himself. As a result, he is often depicted as humourless and dour when in fact he could be very funny; staid and rigid when he might at times be quite the bohemian; repressed and buttoned-down even though he was on many occasions effusive. If revolution is well-nigh unrepresentable on stage or in a text, this may also be true of the revolutionary's person-ality which, by very definition, seeks to elude what Samuel Beckett would later call 'the distortions of intelligibility'. Why should anyone have to have a clear identity, describable on the line of a passport? Pearse was as English as he was Irish, indebted to Wordsworth and Arnold as much as to Ó Dálaigh and Céitinn. Why should a person have to have – as Foucault rather desperately asked – a clear gender? Why should we, in order to narrate ourselves, have to display know-able, believable personalities? Because he disrupted so many of the settled categories with which he came into contact, Pearse was found by most people to be unbelievable, weird, incoherent or just plain odd.  But why shouldn't he have seemed so?

What if we were now to reread him not as a screwed-up neurot-ic, but as a major precursor of Samuel Beckett? To be an artist is to fail, said Beckett, but to fail as no other can do – to fail better.  That sounds a lot like Pearse, who sought a vision of which he could never fully speak, because he could only speak of having sought it. He was, like Beckett, a renouncer of light, music, visual beauty. His anti-*ais-ling* is as bitter as Beckett's, because it is forever negating the very language in which it utters its negations:

> Fornocht a chonac thú
> a áille na háille,
> is dhallas mo shúil
> ar eagla go stánfainn.

Chualas do cheol
a bhinne na binne,
is dhúnas mo chluas
ar eagla go gclisfinn.

Bhlaiseas do bhéal
a mhilse na milse,
is chruas mo chroí
ar eagla mo mhillte.

Dhallas mo shúil,
is mo chluas do dhúnas;
chruas mo chroí
is mo mhian do mhúchas.

Thugas mo chúl
ar an aisling a chumas,
is ar an ród seo romham
m'aghaidh a thugas.

Thugas mo ghnúis
ar an ród seo romham,
ar an ngníomh a chím,
is ar an mbás a gheobhad.[15]

[Naked I saw thee,
o beauty of beauty,
and I blinded my eyes
for fear I should fail.

I heard thy music,
o melody of melody,
and I closed my eyes
for fear I should falter.

I tasted thy mouth
o sweetness of sweetness,
and I hardened my heart
and I smothered my desire.

I turned my back
on the visions I had shaped
and to this road before me

I turned my face.
I have turned my face
to this road before me,
to the deed that I see
and the death I shall die.]

In the traditional *aisling* or vision-poem, the gallant lover liberated
the captive female, but here he turns away. As Beckett would later
do himself, Pearse took Irish asceticism out of the monasteries and
into the secular world of writing and cultural politics. The rebels in
the Post Office, debating the ethics of what they were doing every
day, experienced that same inner loneliness which is known also by
the Protestant mystic exponent of self-election. They were fast
becoming their own priests. Their use of rosary-beads was simply a
way of rejecting the common ecclesiastical view that by opting for
revolution they had placed themselves outside the Catholic Church.
In fact, by virtue of their earnest discussions, they were among the
first Irish exponents of what is now called 'the priesthood of the
laity'; and in their public flaunting of rosaries to satirise the ecclesiocracy, they anticipated the current Latin American exponents of
liberation theology. It is also worth adding that they were among
the gentlest revolutionaries in history, since a major objective was to
take Ireland clean out of a bloody and unnecessary world war.

These things have to be said now because the insurrectionists, for
all their gifts, never managed fully to represent themselves. The broken, fuzzy lettering of the Proclamation, though it makes the document now look like an art-work, seems to symbolise that problem:
the fact that the inner vision which animated the leaders was not
clearly definable in any language. The problem was as old as Moses
– how to express an unknown code in a known language? This was
something that Yeats, operating at the outer limits of words, deeply
understood; and he posed the question again and again by means of
black pigs and rough beasts who portended a future code he could
never directly describe. In his play *The Resurrection*, he stated the
question very well: 'What is there is always something that lies outside knowledge, outside order? What if at the moment when knowledge and order seem complete that something appears?'

The three main poets among the leaders of the Rising, Pearse,
MacDonagh and Plunkett, were all students of mysticism and of the
writings of mystics, as Samuel Beckett would be some years later.
They shared the labour of Beckett's Unnamable. As MacDonagh
wrote in *The Irish Review*, the mystic 'has to express in terms of sense
and wit the things of God that are made known to him in no language'.[16] This is why their poetry has such a devoted following in

India, not just for its political implication, but for harmonising a desire for political freedom with the intuition of a spiritual domain in which union with the godhead might still be possible. That has, of course, nothing to do with the sectarian Catholicism of which Pearse is often accused, since by very nature the mystic bypasses all priests. From Joan of Arc to Thomas Merton, mystics have subverted the institutions of the Church. Indeed, George Bernard Shaw's celebration of national heroism in the mystical utterances of *Joan*, a play written during the later stages of the Civil War in Kerry, might itself be a belated act of homage to Pearse and the rebel poets, whom Shaw in 1916 said should have been treated as prisoners-of-war. Shaw added that they were only doing what any Englishman would do, if he had the misfortune to find his country invaded by a foreign power.

Yeats was by no means the only major student of magic and mysticism in revivalist Ireland. Joyce also joined the Theosophists; Beckett studied eastern philosophy; and the interest taken in mysticism by the 1916 leaders was brought by James Cousins and Margaret Noble to the attention of Indian intellectuals. It is high time that phrases like Pearse's 'áille na háille', 'binne na binne', 'milse na milse', be reread not just in terms of Ó Rathaille's 'gile na gile' but also of mystic philosophy. All oppressed people have produced an intelligentsia whose anger turned outward but whose probing of the meaning of life in such stressful conditions led them also to turn deeply inward. It was, after all, in the name of that despised spiritual domain that the Irish, and later the Indians, stood against empire. They were not nostalgists in this, but seekers of an alternative form of modernisation – what Ashis Nandy, the Indian social psychologist, would now call 'critical traditionalists'.[17] They were trying to apply in life intuitions and ideas which they had previously only imagined. They were not masochists or self-appointed martyrs but shrewd strategists who wagered that they had a chance of winning; and that if they didn't, their children probably would. They were sailing into the unknown, into a future that was exhilarating to them precisely to the extent that it was unknowable.

They chose that unknown, like the first person to eat an oyster, or the first to write a book composed almost entirely of interior monologues. The crisis of their civilisation ran so deep that they felt they had no other choice. Their act could never be wholly their own, because the anxiety which inevitably accompanies doing something new caused them to conjure up ghosts of Cúchulainn, Colmcille, Emmet. These figures were the known vessels into which the unknown potentials of the future might be poured. Every such break with the past invites other breaks, and thereby increases the strain upon everybody. To allay these fears, people constantly summon up ghosts from the past.

That is why 1916 was celebrated and so misrepresented in 1966. The simplified ghosts of Pearse and Connolly were summoned by 'the youngest cabinet in Europe'[18] intent on abandoning the challenge of newness mapped out, however vaguely, by the executed leaders. And that may be why the government needed another celebration in 2006. Intent on bidding goodbye a second time to 1916, its members knew that it must be buried on one last occasion, for though forgotten, it is never quite gone. That celebration is of a piece with the domestication of those rebel modernists, Joyce and Beckett, now converted into heroes of Tiger Ireland. In Tiger Ireland everyone is knowable, narratable, decipherable. Joyce is glasses and a hat; Beckett boots and a bowler; Pearse a military uniform and a twitchy eye. Yet nothing could be further from the spirit of the Irish Renaissance than such simplifications.

Pearse's theory of education was a protest against the fact that everyone was made to read the same books, think the same thoughts, be decidable in an instant. He and Joyce and Beckett – for all the huge differences between them – had one thing in common. They refused the given lesson, and also the idea of imitation. The imitation of any model, however exalted, was the very definition of slavery. Models should be briefly entertained and then kicked away, to allow for the more arduous process of creating a multiple self. To present a revolution as a mere revival for the sake of decipherability was perhaps a mistake, but it was done for a reason: so that the gesture of revolt would not be immediately seen as such. This may, however, have allowed later commentators to cast Pearse as a mere rebel rather than a revolutionary. Yet his spirit and self-image were wholly radical. His comment, once the Rising was under way, that Dublin was now worthy of a place alongside the French Commune was apt, for the communards had been trying to go further than the men and women of 1789. In the words of Richard Sennett:

> Rebellions in mœurs, in manners broadly conceived, fail because they are insufficiently radical in terms of culture. It is still the creation of a believable personality which is the object of a cultural revolt, and, as such, the revolt is still enchained to the bourgeois culture it seeks to overthrow.[19]

Pearse has suffered at the hands of hagiographers and nay-sayers, whose fear of ambiguity is greater than their capacity to cope with the shock of the genuinely new – and because, like so many radicals, he refused to be fully available in the received, approved ways. It may be that he is still light years ahead of us. It may be that he is the man in the macintosh at Paddy Dignam's funeral in Joyce's great book, the mystery man whom everyone has seen but nobody can identify.

CHAPTER SIX

# 'The History of a Century in a Generation'[1]: The Perspective of an Irish Journalist, P.H. Pearse

## REGINA UÍ CHOLLATÁIN

> Gaelicism is the birthright of us all: of Protestant as of Catholic, of Unionist as of Nationalist, of non–native speaker as of native speaker, as of North as of South.[2]

This quote from an editorial by P.H. Pearse in 1904 probably best sums up his journalistic approach. Pearse was an Irish journalist and on examination of these writings, he was generally objective but fearless when it came to revealing 'truth' as he viewed it in a journalistic capacity.[3] His writings are indicative of the fact that truth is an important factor in journalism, but 'Truth is never just "out there". Truths are always in some way created by language, society, individuals or cultures.'[4] Pearse's journalistic writings span many lively and controversial debates on these topics, voicing the public expression of his theories and musings. The many facets of his life are popularly summarised in terms such as nationalist, revolutionary, Irish-language enthusiast, educationalist and writer but, aside from Ruth Dudley Edwards's and Raymond Porter's factual analysis of the 'journalist', where Pearse's writings are considered mainly in terms of their political and historical value, Pearse is rarely examined from a critical journalistic standpoint.[5] Philip O'Leary's comprehensive study of the literary revival covers many issues related to his journalistic exploits,[6] while Proinsias Mac Aonghusa and Donncha Ó Súilleabháin provide insights into his journalistic role in the context of the Language Movement.[7] Liam Mac Uistín's biography, and the author's study of the public organ of the Gaelic League, *An Claidheamh Soluis agus Fáinne an Lae*, deal with his editorial role in literary, language and cultural contexts, but 'Pearse, the journalist' has yet to be examined under journalistic conventions.[8] This provides a framework for the very diverse approaches taken by the public and the private Pearse, views which are often contradictory. The converse is also true, in that a study of Pearse, the journalist, has much to offer in terms of contemporary mainstream and minority language media studies.

As a pioneer of Irish-language journalism, Pearse adhered to journalistic principles with the result that most of these writings can be examined within the framework of journalistic conventions. The absence of in-depth study on the influence of the professional route he chose in the study of law, is of further interest in light of Séamas Ó Buachalla's view that 'the mental training that he received as a lawyer left its mark on Pearse's writing style and on the argumentative method he practised in journalistic affairs in *An Claidheamh Soluis*'.[9]

## THE JOURNALISTIC FRAMEWORK

The lack of material in this area is due firstly to the fact that journalistic criticism in mainstream Irish journalism is relatively new and secondly to the fact that Irish-language journalism is in the very embryonic stages of critique.[10] A third reason for this lack of attention could be attributed to the nationalistic views that these writings seem to portray, views that are more relevant to the historical and political dimension of study on Pearse than to journalism or language. Mid- and late nineteenth-century news publications confirm that nationalistic doctrine was viewed as an integral element of Irish mainstream journalism of this period. These journals, particularly those of the Young Irelanders, had a profound influence on Pearse in later years.[11] Pearse was editor of *An Claidheamh Soluis* between March 1903 and November 1909, the aim of which was to create an Irish-reading public.[12] While Pearse and his contemporaries in the Gaelic League may well have believed in this as a worthy aim for the newspaper, recent research by Liam Mac Mathúna can lead one to conclude that while the Irish Language Revival movement was very productive in many aspects, the purist approach adopted by well-meaning revivalists may in fact have stunted a very integral and progressive element of language evolution, by turning its back on literary code-mixing in Irish and English, throughout this period. Allowing for the influence that this had on Irish literature for 300 years previous to this, in Mac Mathúna's study of English/Irish code-mixing in Irish literature 1600–1900 it is difficult to overlook the gap in language practice after 1900, between the word on the street as it were (or in the Gaeltacht, where Irish language was the first language), and the more intellectual, purist approach.[13] This is particularly relevant in the study of journalism allowing that the journalist is usually telling the story or giving the message to the general public, rather than the select few.

The business of journalism is primarily news and communication. It is well documented that Irish-language literature and the language associated with it may well have foundered were it not for the support of the Irish-language journals of the Revival period, the result of which is a vibrant corpus of literary writings. While this form produced and fostered literary language and criticism, perhaps if journalistic conventions were fully adhered to, focusing on communication primarily, it is possible that the Irish language may have taken its own course and developed as a written and spoken language, regardless of in-depth analysis and argument that dominated the discourse. In hindsight the current trend in Irish-language newspapers would have been more straightforward, working within the framework of journalistic conventions. Pearse's version of this, albeit less polished, may actually have resulted in the desired 'Irish-reading public', allowing the living language to take its own natural course.

6.1 Patrick Pearse in his barrister's robes. Courtesy Pearse Museum.

As a Young Irelander who is recognized as a champion of the Irish language, the (English language) writings of Thomas Davis in *The Nation* of 1843–1845 defending the Irish language show 'the limitations of his own advocacy and, more generally, of the defence of Irish in the paper', argues Jean-Christophe Penet.[14] Were Irish allowed to develop with a more integrated approach, this could have been helpful in the transmission and distribution of the language through new developments in communication and industry. The leaders of the movement may have wanted to create an Irish-reading public but

> There was much between the mind of the *fin-de-siècle* intellectuals of this Revival and the outlook of the ordinary people who were readily accepting English up to that point, almost unknown to themselves.[15]

While Pearse may be considered a 'nativist' in his general tendency, his writings and bilingual policy as editor of *An Claidheamh Soluis* demonstrate a progressive, forward-thinking journalist with a 'genuine interest in and willingness to learn from any culture in contemporary Europe and even farther afield'.[16]

Regarding the links with nation and language, like Davis before him, Pearse throughout his editorship frequently links language, literature and the building of nationhood:

A language is evolved by a nation for the purpose of expressing its thought ... Thus a nation's speech is, in a real sense the creation of that nation ... A literature is the expression in literary form of the mind of a race.[17]

He understands – something that some of us don't yet understand – that Irish is the basis and the strongest authority of Irish Nationality. He understands, if Irish lives, Ireland will survive as a nation.[18]

As we put it a few weeks ago, the speaking of Irish is not an end but a means to an end, the end is Nationality.[19]

This progression on the concept of nation and nation building was the result of the political climate in European nations at the end of the nineteenth and the turn of the twentieth centuries. It is normal to assume therefore that Pearse was very much in line with the journalism of the era in his references to nation and its links with language, culture and literature. It was not unusual either for intellectuals with interests in language revival to use this platform as a vehicle for communication, debate and comradeship. Another example of this type of journalism in a minority language context is the paper *Ar Bobl* founded in Brittany by the poet 'Taldir' in 1904.[20] In his capacity as editor of the main Irish-language newspaper of the Revival period, Pearse can be credited with bringing Irish-language journalism into a more enlightened era.

Pearse may have written, 'acted, and died for a people who did not exist' on one level, and he may even have 'distorted into his own image the ordinary people of Ireland, who lacked his own remarkable qualities, but who had perceptions and complexities of their own that he could never understand'.[21] However, Philip O'Leary has demonstrated how Pearse used this imaginary people in 'a more spiritual Ireland than that in which he lived' in his stories, although the private 'introverted Pearse had little contact with, and perhaps even less empathy with, the great majority of the plain people of Ireland'.[22] In the context of minority language journalism and contemporary theories on nationalism, the public Pearse, despite this perceived lack of understanding, was very much in touch with the need for communication and mutual support in the public arena. He advocated the need for what he refers to as 'brotherhood', in July 1906, in assessing one of the many conflicts within the Language movement.[23] In September 1906 he links this sense of cooperation with the understanding of nationalism, saying that 'the individualism that exalts its selfish demands above the interests of the nation' is negative, but

there is an individuality which shows itself in power of judgement, power of initiation and execution, power of co-operation
and organisation, the individuality which is ready to accept personal responsibility and to utilize its own resources, which pours
out what it has of good rather than wait for a suction pump to
extract it.[24]

Although acknowledging the need for brotherhood, the medium
for giving the message, which was more minority than mainstream
directed, may have been pivotal in allowing Pearse to practise individuality while creating a sense of community. The contrast between the
public and private individual is also revelatory in assessing the journalism of the Revival period, given the prominent roles that some of
these journalists were to fulfil in the future. In the context of a minority language in a community which was both urban and rural, and
which was spread out over the whole island, combined with contemporary theories on nationalism as the nation being an 'imagined political community', it can be said that Pearse conceived the nation as a
common ground, regardless of demographics. This is very evident in
the journalistic writings and raises questions about his reading public.

While addressing the issue of the monoglot mass reading publics
created by capitalism and print, Benedict Anderson outlines three
ways in which print-languages were the foundation blocks for
'national consciousness', focusing on the fact that they created unified fields of communication, gave fixity to language and thirdly, created languages of power. These were 'largely unselfconscious
processes', he argues.[25] In this context, taking Pearse's own motto for
St Enda's with the hope that his 'fame and ... deeds live after me', it
may be prudent to acknowledge the futuristic projection that is often
to the fore in the 'story' and in the 'truth' Pearse conveys. Pearse was
writing for the broader public of his day on a minority forum, but on
further examination of his writings, there are similarities between
Pearse's approach to this understanding of nationalism and the
approach of other journalists of this and the preceding era. This is
not new in the understanding of nationalism and language, but questions the use of the medium itself for the journalists who were giving
the message. Pearse, it can be assumed by his use of bilingualism in
*An Claidheamh Soluis*, was directing the message to a far-reaching
Irish public. However, given the difference between the intellectual
Revivalists and the everyday English- (and Irish-) speaking public, it
is possible that the 'comradeship' referred to by Anderson may,
through the 'unconscious process', only include the upper echelons of
the Gaelic Revival, and the understanding that came with being part
of that community. In this instance the use of the bilingual medium

through which the message was communicated was pivotal, albeit one which is not quite as relevant as it would be for minority language journalism in a contemporary context. This was a community, or as referred to by Pearse, a brotherhood, which was defined by its cultural roots rather than its language. This concept is explored by Anderson in light of the sacrifices posed by comradeship, sacrifices which 'lie in the cultural roots of nationalism':

> Finally, it is imagined as a *community*, because, regardless of the actual inequality and exploitation that may prevail in each, the nation is always conceived as a deep, horizontal comradeship. Ultimately it is this fraternity that makes it possible, over the past two centuries, for so many millions of people, not so much to kill, as willingly to die for such limited imaginings.[26]

This explanation of the nation as an imagined community correlates to the links and to the policies which Pearse, the journalist, implemented in his writings and finally through his death in 1916. In light of the imagined community created by a print culture, these are significant, not in the roots of the 'people who did not exist' in a physical sense but in light of the community which did exist in Pearse's mind and in his writings, his perceived reading public. Traditionally Irish-language journalism has been considered an area for minority language study. However, as linguistic and sociolinguistic elements become more apparent in the area of media history it is important to note that these writings may also be relevant in mainstream media studies leading to greater and broader understanding of the role of media in society.[27] Pearse, as a pioneering journalist, embraced this approach progressively, bringing further understanding to what John Hartley describes as 'the conditions for journalism's existence; where it comes from, what it is for, and how it works'.[28]

## PEARSE, THE PIONEERING JOURNALIST

When making what he refers to as a fair comparison in describing journalists as 'the mediators between us and our information', Ivor Kenny quotes a line in *Jumpers*, by Tom Stoppard: 'The Media. It sounds like a convention of spiritualists'.[29] This, possibly more accurately than any other literary source, describes the journalistic philosophies of P.H. Pearse. Pearse, by default, can lay claim to being the forerunner in the Irish-language contingent of this 'convention', referred to by Stoppard, in that he paved the way and laid the foundation for a 'news' and progressive, idiomatic approach to writing in the Irish language. This play on the word 'convention' can now correspond to journalistic convention. Pearse's literary essays and writing

An ClAIÓEAm. Saṁain 8, 1913.

Saṁain 8, An **CLAIÓEAm** 1913.
·SOLUIS·

## THE COMING REVOLUTION.

I have come to the conclusion that the Gaelic League, as the Gaelic League, is a spent force; and I am glad of it. I do not mean that no work remains for the Gaelic League, or that the Gaelic League is no longer equal to work; I mean that the vital work to be done in the new Ireland will be done not so much by the Gaelic League itself as by men and movements that have sprung from the Gaelic League or have received from the Gaelic League a new baptism and a new breath of grace. The Gaelic League was no reed shaken by the wind, no mere *vox clamantis*: it was a prophet and more than a prophet. But it was not the Messiah. I do not know if the Messiah has yet come, and I am not sure that there will be any visible and personal Messiah in this redemption: the people itself will perhaps be its own Messiah, the people labouring, scourged, crowned with thorns, agonising and dying, to rise again immortal and impassible. For peoples are divine and are the only things that can properly be spoken of under figures drawn from the divine epos.

If we do not believe in the divinity of our people we have had no business, or very little, all these years in the Gaelic League. In fact, we had not believed in the divinity of our people we should in all probability not have gone into the Gaelic League at all. We should have made our peace with the devil, and perhaps might have found him a very decent sort; for the liberally rewards with attorney-generalships, bank balances, villa residences, and so forth, the great and the little who serve him well. Now we did not turn our backs upon all these desirable things for the sake of *is* and *id*. We did it for the sake of Ireland. In other words, we had one and all of us (at least, I had, and I hope that all you had) an ulterior motive in joining the Gaelic League. We never meant to be Gaelic Leaguers and nothing more than Gaelic Leaguers. We meant to do something for Ireland, each in his own way. Our Gaelic League time was to be our tutelage: we had first to learn to know Ireland, to read the lineaments of her face, to understand the accents of her voice; to re-possess ourselves, disinherited as we were, of her spirit and mind, re-enter into our mystical birthright. For this we went to school to the Gaelic League. It was a good school, and we love its name and will champion its fame throughout all the days of our later fighting and striving. But we do not propose to remain schoolboys forever.

I have often said (quoting, I think, Herbert Spencer) that education could be a preparation for complete living; and I say now that our Gaelic League education ought to have been a preparation for our complete living.

### As Irish Nationalists

In proportion as we have been faithful and diligent Gaelic Leaguers, our work as Irish Nationalists (by which term I mean people who accept the ideal of and work for the realisation of an Irish Nation, by whatever means) will be earnest and thorough, a valiant and worthy fighting, not a mere carrying out of a ritual. As to what your work as an Irish Nationalist is to be, I cannot conjecture; I know what mine is to be, and would have you know yours and buckle yourself to it. And it may be, nay, it is! that yours and mine will lead us to a common meeting-place, and that on a certain day we shall stand together, with many more beside us, ready for a greater adventure than any of us has yet had, a trial and a triumph to be endured and achieved in common.

This is what I meant when I said that our work henceforward must done less and less through the Gaelic League and more and more through the groups and the individuals that have arisen, or are arising, out of the Gaelic League. There will be in the Ireland of the next few years a multitudinous activity of Freedom Clubs, Young Republican parties, Labour Organisations, Socialist Groups, and what not; bewildering enterprises undertaken by same persons and insane persons,

### Good Men and Bad Men,

many of them seemingly contradictory, some mutually destructive, yet all tending towards a common objective, and that objective : the Irish.

For if there is one thing that has become plainer than another it is that when the seven men met in O'Connell Street to found the Gaelic League, they were commencing, had there been a Liancourt to there to

make the epigram, not a revolt, but a revolution. The work of the Gaelic League, its appointed work, was that : and the work is done. To every generation its deed. The deed of the generation that has now reached middle life was the Gaelic League : the beginning of the Irish Revolution. Let our generation not shirk *its* deed, which is to accomplish the revolution.

I believe that the national movement of which the Gaelic League has been the soul has reached the point which O'Connell's movement had reached at the close of the series of monster meetings. Indeed, I believe that our movement reached that point a few years ago—say, at the conclusion of the fight for Essential Irish; and I said so at the time. The moment was ripe then for a new Young Ireland Party, with a forward policy; and we have not by our hesitation. I propose in all seriousness that we hesitate no longer—that we push on. I propose that we leave Conciliation Hall behind us and go into the Irish Confederation.

Whenever Dr. Hyde, at a meeting at which I have had a chance of speaking after him, has produced his dove of peace, I have always been careful to produce my sword; and to tantalise him by saying that the Gaelic League has brought into Ireland

### " Not Peace, but a Sword."

But this does not show any fundamental difference of outlook between my leader and me; for while he is thinking of peace between brother-Irishmen, I am thinking of the sword-point between banded Irishmen and the foreign force that occupies Ireland : and his peace is necessary to my war. It is evident that there can be no peace between the body politic and a foreign substance that has intruded itself into its system : between them war only until the foreign substance is expelled or assimilated.

Whether Home Rule means a loosening or a tightening of England's grip upon Ireland remains yet to be seen. But the coming of Home Rule, if come it does, will make no material difference in the nature of the work that lies before us : it will affect only the means we are to employ, our plan of campaign. There remains, under Home Rule as in its absence, the substantial task of achieving the Irish Nation. I do not think it is going to be achieved without stress and trial, without suffering and bloodshed; at any rate, it is not going to be achieved without *work*. Our business here and now is to get ourselves into harness for such work as has to be done.

I hold that before we can do any work, any *men's* work, we must first

### Realise Ourselves as Men.

Whatever comes to Ireland she needs men. And we of this generation are not in any real sense men, for we suffer things that men do not suffer, and we seek to redress grievances by means which men do not employ. We have, for instance, allowed ourselves to be disarmed; and, now that we have the chance of re-arming, we are not seizing it. Professor Eoin Mac Neill pointed out last week that we have at this moment an opportunity of rectifying the capital error we made when we allowed ourselves to be disarmed; and such opportunities, he reminds us, do not always come back to nations.

A thing that stands demonstrable is that nationhood is not achieved otherwise than in arms : in one or two instances there may have been no actual bloodshed, but the arms were there and the ability to use them. Ireland unarmed will attain just as much freedom as it is convenient for England to give her; Ireland armed will attain ultimately just as much freedom as she wants. These are matters which may not concern the Gaelic League as a body; but they concern every member of the Gaelic League, and every man and woman of Ireland. I urged much of this five or six years ago in addresses to the Ard-Chraobh : but the League was

### Too Busy with Resolutions

to think of revolution, and the only resolution that a member of the League could not come to was the resolution to be a man. My fellow-Leaguers had not (and have not) apprehended that the thing which cannot defend itself, even though it may wear trousers, is no man.

I am glad then that the North has " begun." I am glad that the Orangemen have armed, for it is a goodly thing to see arms in Irish hands. I should like to see the A.O.H. armed. I should like to see the Transport Workers armed. I should like to see any and every body of Irish citizens armed. We must accustom ourselves to the thought of arms, to the sight of arms, to the use of arms. We may make mistakes in the beginning and shoot the wrong people; but bloodshed is a cleansing and a sanctifying thing, and the nation which regards it as the final horror has lost its manhood. There are many things more horrible than bloodshed; and slavery is one of them.

P. H. PEARSE.

[Irish-language section at bottom — three columns]

### CÓṀAIRLe.

[Is mian liom beaga gan leanaṁna baile bo ḃ́oṁ́caḃ́ aṙ an ṙClaiḋeaṁ ṙus ḃéiṁiḋ á cúmaċaiṫ móiṙ aṫ iṫéoiriḃ aṙ mian leo léiṫ bo cuṙ óṙ an ṙcuiobaim sin i nSaeḋilṫ. Ió aṫ méaḋ ṫo mian fẏeaṙṫa aṙ toiṁiṁ a cúiṫeann liṫeaḋ i mḃéaṙla ṫáim.]

### Seanṁóiṙeaċt i mḃéaṙla.

Darā, Is mian liom mo ḃeaṙán bo cuṙ le ṫeaṙiaṁ na scuibinnóiṙi siṁ 'sa ṙClaiḋeaṁ ṫṙoaṫ na paṙṫiṫe ṫá ṫá calaṁte aṫ an ṙaeoilṫ ṫ́us na aṫ́aniaṫḃ mó ṫ́eaṫ́ann annóṙ, mó ṫeaṫasc, nó aṫn caiṫṫ aṫn ṙeaṫ.

an ṙaeoilṫ naṫa aṫ ṁiṁeann an ṫoṁnaiṫ iṫ an ṙaeoilṫeaṫce. Cūṫas ṫ́éaṫṁe, i nóiṫeain aeṫa, aṫus aṫ faṙu iṫ 'u ṫonas aṫn nóṫ eúaṫas ṫ́oal ṙaeḃilṫe ó ḃeaṫ na ṫaṫane : ṫ́un i ṫuṫail an ṙaeoilṫ ṫṙom ṫo ṫ́ṙuiṫ an ṙaeoilṫ ṫṙo ṫuṫoṁ́ṁ́i ṫlaṫca aṫ ḃome ṫaṫane a ṫaṫnoṫs teṫ an ḃṙaṫaiṫe. Caṫ ḃome voiṫ́-ṫean maṫ ṫ́éoṁ́uṫoṁṫ onṫa. Ḃo Caṫṫa ṫ́o ṫeas ann ḃeṫ aṫ ṫuṫṙaṫce le sean-ṫeaṫaṙ na ḃeaṫeann uṫa ṫaṫane i venṫai nioṫ eúṫaṫuṫe an an nṫaeoilṫ ṫean an nṫaeoilṫ. [Ba maiṫ liom ṫo ṁḃeaḋ uṫ be sean-ṫeaṫaṫ na ḃeaṫeann uṫa ṫaṫane n-oimiṫeaḋa vo ṫ́ṫ léo. Ḃnuṫ a ṫuḃṙeam beṫ ṫuṫ an ṫaṫane nó ṫuṫn iṫ an ṙé c.] ṫean ṫáiṫ. [Ba maiṫ liom ṫo ṁḃeaḋ mé vo n-oimiṫeaḋa vo ṫuṫ léo. Ḃnuṫ a ṫuḃṙeam beṫ ṫuṫ an aṫṙanaṫ nó ṫuṫni aṫn ṙé c.] an ṫ c.]

### MAC MIC AN ṀISTEALAIĊ

Tá Seán Misteal ina ṁḃaoṙ aṙ New York. Toṫaḋ é Ḃia Luain. Mac Mic ṁ́ṁ Sheán Misteal seo'ṫuinne seaḋ é.

### Céiṙó Móṙ.

Ḃéiḋ céiṙó móṙ i nḊaṙus an Ṗomṁóin. Ḃiṁ Luain, aṫ céṫó tá ḃe ṁí cóm ṫo móṫaṙpṫó i ḃeo 6.—Ṗ. an ċ.]

Even if you can't read Irish you will enjoy our pictures. Become a subscriber.

*6.2 An Claidheamh Soluis agus Fáinne an Lae*, 8 November 1913. Courtesy UCD Delargy Centre for Irish Folklore.

style correlate with more recent studies on the journalistic profession. A love for writing still remains the most common answer as to why journalists chose journalism coupled with 'an enjoyment of reporting, a desire to be involved in current events and history, an interest in politics, and the enjoyment of telling a story'.[30] Pearse's writings mirror the development of a society with a story to tell. Cathal Mac Coille, Pól Ó Muirí and Póilín Ní Chiaráin, all three Irish and English journalists of high acclaim, have drawn the analogy of the role of the witness giving evidence and the role of the journalist.[31] This is not unusual either in light of Pearse's passionate interest in the

6.3 Mrs Margaret Pearse starting the presses on the *Irish Press*, 5 September 1931. (Eamon de Valera can be seen in the background.) Courtesy Pearse Museum.

oral storytelling tradition of the Gaeltacht community, referred to in his introduction to his short stories and upon which some of his stories are founded, correlating with Jean Aitchison's view that 'The oral traditions of previous millennia may be the direct ancestors of modern journalism'.[32]

Pearse's journalistic writings attest to a witness account of a vibrant, changing society, one in which he has a crucial and central role to play.

## PEARSE, THE IRISH LANGUAGE JOURNALIST

Judging from contemporary theories on media studies, to critically analyse Pearse's writings in light of Irish-language journalism alone or to set his Irish journalistic writings apart from the English contributions would not constitute a balanced evaluation of his work. This is particularly true in light of his belief in bilingualism as a tool for promoting the Irish language and an education system on Irish lines:

> At this stage, it may be well to iterate that the object at which the bilingual system aims is the education of the child in two languages … Its object is the teaching of Irish just as much as the teaching of English and the teaching of English just as much as the teaching of Irish; or to be more accurate, its object is not so much the teaching either of Irish or of English, as the education

of the child through the medium of both Irish and English ... Both as written and spoken tongues.[33]

This is also relevant in assessing the profile of a journalist whose writings in both languages still contribute to political thought in twenty first century Ireland. The 'news', the 'truth', the 'story that had to be told' takes precedence over the medium, in this case the language, used to relate the story, highlighting the role of the medium as discussed earlier. This logic applies to journalistic writing in Irish generally, a perspective which, to some extent at least, refutes the link between the Irish language and the cause, as referred to earlier in the understanding of nationality as a concept fostered on the platform of journalism. Curiously, for a political figure in one of the most revolutionary periods in modern Irish history, Pearse's journalistic writings have yet to be examined critically as a corpus of twentieth-century writings. Although his Irish-language writings are poignant and insightful of the volatile but exciting era of which he was part, he has never been assessed as a major journalist in either language.

### PEARSE, THE EDITOR

Ivor Kenny probes the thinking, methodologies, theories, aspirations and *modus operandi* of eighteen editors in light of late twentieth-century editing.[34] Reading these conversations, citing mantras and opinion from editors such as Conor Brady in the *Irish Times*, Vinnie Doyle in the *Irish Independent*, Hugh Lambert in the *Irish Press*, Damien Kiberd in the *Sunday Business Post*, Tom Collins in the *Irish News*, leads one to ponder what Pearse's mantra as an editor of a national bilingual newspaper of the Language movement would have been. If the illusion that a newspaper is merely an account of events, news and opinion, then it is important, as Brian Looney, editor of the *Kerryman* in 1994 states, that 'The editor should not be seen in his paper'.[35] This was clearly the antithesis of what Pearse envisaged as the role of the editor of a public organ:

> We gladly make the statement, adding the explanation that, as we are the editor of this paper, we are not in the habit of consulting with anyone as to what should appear and what should not appear in it, nor is any such condition attached to our appointment. We try as best we can to interpret the spirit of the League and to define what is, in our opinion its true policy, but we should be the veriest serf did we bind ourselves to record here from week to week, not our own views and convictions but the views and convictions of someone else. In final resort, everyone must recognise that an official organ, unless it be edited by a mere machine, can guarantee to

6.4 *An Claidheamh Soluis*, 29 April 1916. Courtesy UCD Delargy Centre for Irish Folklore.

do no more than speak for the individual who is its editor. The measure of its authoritativeness is simply the measure of that individual's grasp of the principles of the organisation. [36]

This framework therefore allowed Pearse the individual input, while still creating the community as referred to earlier. His editorial theory would be at total variance with Brian Looney's philosophy but the similarities between this policy and Hugh Lambert's thinking on the role of the *Irish Press*, a newspaper which stemmed from the political aspirations of another major political figure of twentieth-century Ireland, Éamon de Valera, are starkly similar in sentiment: 'A paper has to say: this is what we stand for, this is what we believe. Not many papers have succeeded in doing that.' [37]

The reading public for *An Macaomh* was very different to that of *An Claidheamh Soluis* and the freedom afforded to Pearse in a journal of this nature is obvious, and in terms of journalistic conventions, extreme. The retrospective value of these writings is important and highlights the need for media criticism and historical review. The writings in *An Claidheamh Soluis* were for the broader public domain, albeit through the use of main and minority language, and survive within this realm. *An Macaomh* was directed at a school community. Although these writings are rightly used in contemporary analysis of Pearse, it is important to recognise the public at which they were directed and assess them in that light alongside general journalistic conventions. In an outburst uncharacteristic of Pearse's writings hitherto, he ruthlessly and recklessly develops this notion of using his journalistic voice as a public platform for his own opinion in *An Macaomh*:

> During the past six or seven years, I have grown so accustomed to having an organ at my disposal for the expression of my views and whims that I have come to look on an organ as some men look on tobacco and others on motor cars and aeroplanes, as among the necessities of life … I have still my organ, and it is a luxury to feel that I can set down here any truth, however obvious, without being called a liar, any piece of wisdom, however sane without being docketed a lunatic. *An Macaomh* is my own, to do as I please; and if through sheer obstinacy in saying in it what I think ought to be said … at least I shall enjoy something of the grim satisfaction which I suppose motorists experience in wrecking their thousand guinea Panhards driving them as they think they ought to be driven.[38]

Pearse saw his role as editor/journalist of this type of journal in a different light. He is not merely acting as a mediator between the reading public and the information, nor as a medium in the process of 'a nation talking to itself' (Arthur Miller),[39] but as, to use his own analogy, a vehicle to put forward his own views and those of the organisation which he served. His early personal philosophies portrayed as editor in *An Claidheamh Soluis* aspire to high moral ground, independent thought and the determination for ultimate perfection, indicating that he understood the duties and obligations of editorship at this level. This could also often be interpreted as a fundamental quest for personal attainment and perfection: 'Everyone is capable of one thing – his best';[40] 'Our reply may take the form of that great reply of Parnell's to one who asked a similar question: "I shall never be the one to say: Thus far and no further."'[41]

## POLITICS AND JOURNALISTIC WRITINGS

The role of print media as an influential and powerful tool in the development of Irish society in the twentieth century is rarely more evident than in the writings of political figures. John Horgan examines how history and politics have shaped the media of Ireland and in turn, media have been shaped by politics and history.[42] The concept of nation is important here also in light of the journalistic period of Pearse's writings. Iarfhlaith Watson links the roles of citizens in a nation who are loyal to one political culture.[43] *The Star* founded in 1929 as a 'semi-official organ' of Cumann na nGaedheal and the *Irish Press* founded in 1932 feature prominently in the theory that the latter years of Cumann na nGaedheal and the first years of the Fianna Fáil government, 'saw the increasing involvement by the State in areas of media policy'.[44] This is also evident in the Censorship of Publications Act 1929–1967. In light of the absence of newspapers claiming to be the 'official organ' of a said political party, with the exception of extreme right- or left-wing publications proclaiming direct allegiance to political ideals and movements, there may be some common ground between the roles of de Valera as the driving force behind the *Irish Press* for Fianna Fáil and the role of Pearse as editor of the official organ of the Gaelic League in 1903–1909. Both political figures used the respective papers as a platform for swaying public opinion and as a vantage point for promoting the views of the organisation to which they were affiliated. However, this is where the similarities end.

6.5 Patrick Pearse as a young boy with gun. Courtesy Pearse Museum.

Firstly, today and during the most prominent years of the *Irish Press* it would be a very rare occurrence for a leader of a political organisation or movement to also be the full-time editor of a weekly newspaper or indeed a full-time journalist covering events and issues as they arise. This usually falls under the remit of the current-day 'Political Correspondent'– the expert in the field. This is why, on examining Pearse's most prolific journalistic writings, it is important to bear in mind that he was not speaking as an 'expert' or even as a 'Political Correspondent' for the most part, but as a member of a very vibrant, evolving society which was still in the embryonic stages of the advancement to a new understanding of independence. The luxury of being able to focus primarily on a specific area of journalism, and the recognition at a professional and societal level which accompanies that, was never afforded to the likes of Pearse and his contemporaries, Eoin Mac Néill, Piaras Béaslaí, Shán Ó Cuív, Dubhghlas de Híde, Seosamh Laoide and many more. Indeed, it was very common in Ireland and Britain for journalists to become politicians and for politicians to work as journalists. In 1908, when the editor of *The Peasant* used the term 'mellow' to describe Pearse's writings on the Irish-language, Pearse described in detail his workload in being not only a full-time editor but also a schoolmaster. Considering that this was a national newspaper of the time, dealing with economic, political and societal controversies apart from Irish-language revival issues, it demonstrates the wide chasm between newspapers of a set political affiliation today and a newspaper devoted to the Irish-language and developing a modern viewpoint towards an egalitarian, open, society which could take its place among the nations of Europe. The viewpoint expressed below, while acknowledging the importance of being an editor of an 'official organ', clearly attests to Pearse's agenda at this time, which, while not entirely apolitical either, is significantly educationally driven:

> It exhorts us to be 'mellow'. Personally we think that we are about as mellow as anyone who at once a schoolmaster and the editor of an 'official organ' can in reason be expected to be ... For ourselves our editorial and sub-editorial work (for we still have a good deal of both to do) is got through either in a crowded classroom where we are supposed to be presiding over study or else after midnight in a certain icy apartment in the lower region of Scoil Éanna, some hours after professors and pupils have gone off on their nightly visit to 'Tír na nÓg'. To be continuously 'mellow' under these circumstances is a height of heroism to which we aspire but which we have not yet attained.[45]

It would appear on further examination of Pearse's writings that his love of learning and pursuit of educational excellence drove his rebellious streak. His role in the fight for compulsory Irish as a subject for matriculation is only one of the examples of the power he invoked through his journalistic writings on education.

## COLUMNIST AND NATIONHOOD

Pearse's journalistic exploits in the years subsequent to his editorship of *An Claidheamh Soluis* (1909–1916) depict a mindset determined to postulate. While he wrote in different journals and dealt with varied topics from education to religion to politics, the journalist portrayed always retains the seal of a person trying to be heard – a voice with a message, with news to tell. His writings from this period include *An Barr Buadh* from 16 March to 25 May 1912; a column in the Irish Republican Brotherhood's monthly publication *Irish Freedom* between June 1913 and February 1914 under the title 'From a Hermitage'; his final writings in *An Claidheamh Soluis*, 'The Coming Revolution', 8 November 1913, and 'Psychology of a Volunteer', 3 January 1914; a weekly column in the *Irish Volunteer* between 9 January and 15 February; and an article in *Spark*, 'Peace and the Gael' on 9 April 1916.[46]

His final pamphlets referring to Tone, Mitchel, Emmet and Lalor deal with his political viewpoint but are not classified here as journalistic writings. The influence of Davis on Pearse, in a journalistic forum traces early indications of Anderson's 'comradeship'. Due to the parallels between Lalor's writings in *The Irish Felon* (1848) and the Young Irelander's *The Nation* (1847), where he advocates the belief in the repossession of lands as a means to national freedom, and Pearse's writings in which he explores the value of the revival of the Irish language as a means to national freedom, it is not surprising that Pearse found 'comradeship' in the sense of fraternity that was being built upon through the avenue of print culture. Clearly, both Pearse and Lalor felt that the political process was not enough to secure their 'imagined' national freedom:

> Ireland demands from you now something more than her present dole of daily food – a mode and system of procuring full food for herself. Political rights are but paper and parchment. It is the social constitution that determines the condition and character of a people, that makes and moulds the life of man. [Lalor][47]

> Intellectual freedom must precede political or national freedom; the first case of every race struggling to maintain their national existence is to educate their people on national lines and through the medium of their own tongue. [Pearse][48]

> If Ireland was completely separated politically from England tomorrow, it would probably be an independent nation, but it would not be an Irish nation, because as long as English is the common language for Irish men and women, Ireland will only ever be a foreign nation regardless of the freedom it has. [Pearse][49]

Pearse's concept of national freedom and its links to the Irish language and the Gaeltacht have much in common with Lalor's concept of the value of the land in the understanding of nationality and heritage. Both viewed the 'peasantry', in Lalor's case the tenants (guardians of the heritage of the land), and in Pearse's case the Gaeltacht native speakers (guardians of the language heritage), as the most valuable assets on the road to freedom. Allowing that anecdotal evidence

6.6
*An Barr Buadh*,
March 1912.
Courtesy Pearse
Museum.

places Pearse reading Lalor's 'Clearing Decks' (*The Irish Felon*, 22 July 1848) on his last visit to the National Library it is difficult to ignore the link between both sets of writings and writers. Robert Mitchel Henry would claim that Lalor was a major influence on the decision taken by James Connolly and Pearse with regard to the 1916 Rising.[50] In the writings between the years of 1912 in *An Barr Buadh* and the articles in *An Claidheamh Soluis* as a correspondent, the frustration of a revolutionary which comes to the fore is at variance with his role as editor. The new role provided the freedom to voice thoughts that had arisen as a result of the frustration of failing to aspire to that highly acclaimed but unattainable perfection. *An Barr*

*Buadh*, founded in March 1912, was considered to be a political Irish-language weekly. The frustration between loyalty to education and the pull towards political activities is very clear in a letter Pearse wrote to himself in the May 11th issue, where he rebuked himself for taking the political path and reminded himself that he should 'do well what [he] set out to do four years ago'.[51] Allowing that the writings on political freedom and language were written in 1908 and 1909, Pearse was on a conflicting path but it is at this point that the 'confessional' element of the writings yield the story. Pearse was still a pacifist and a journalist with a cause, but there is a pronounced change in the internal wrangling of this journalist – the incessant conflict between the need to proclaim and to be the 'witness'. This series of eleven letters that Pearse wrote in *An Barr Buadh* show definite leanings towards the confessional element at a community level in the letters to others, and at a personal level in the letter to himself. Marshall McLuhan has explored the complex relationship between medium, author and audience in terms of the 'confessional character' of the medium:

> Both book and newspaper are confessional in character, creating the effect of inside story by their mere form, regardless of content. As the book page yields the inside story of the author's mental adventures, so the press page yields the inside story of the community in action and interaction.[52]

These later writings demonstrate the 'tremendous difference, a difference in kind, between being editor and being anything else in a newspaper', as described by Conor Brady:

> There is no comparison between any other newspaper job and the commitment of 24-hour, seven-day-a-week, 52 weeks a year responsibility which you have mentally, intellectually, emotionally with the paper when you're the last man down the line.[53]

This also highlights the significant difference between Pearse and a full-time paid editor, which in one way was less complex than that of say, Conor Brady. The era in which he wrote and edited brought with it a certain freedom of speech of its own.

Was this journalism or was it propaganda? Pearse had a journalistic vision – the language was not the issue – it was the key to nationalism rather than the means or the obstacle, and he used it in his journalistic writings as a media component not as an obstacle. In light of the language issue, one has to question whether Pearse's journalism was actually a more realistic approach than what is being done today due to lack of cross journalism – journalists writing in both languages, as Pearse did. As a journalist in both languages but primarily Irish, this is what Pól Ó Muirí has to say:

The truth is that were Irish-speakers offered newspaper columns, op-ed pieces and spots on television on the English-language media on a regular basis, they could transform the cultural debate. There are any number of articulate, interesting and pioneering professionals working in the field of language maintenance who are more global in their outlook, more mature in their thinking, more intelligent in their analysis, than our home-grown Littlejohns. The only problem is they are rarely given the opportunity to express themselves.[54]

## CONCLUSION

For Pearse, journalism was not a means to promote the language – he was a journalist. However, he was a journalist with an agenda of his own which took priority. His own story became more important to tell which was not always negative, as his story was important in an era where leadership and journalism were often intertwined. As Ruth Dudley Edwards points out: 'During his six years as editor of *An Claidheamh Soluis*, he showed more inclination to lead than to follow.'[55] He was not using journalistic writings to promote Irish, he was using Irish and English to promote his understanding of the aims of his journalistic writings – creating the link between language and nationalism, a theory which he explored in his last article in *An Claidheamh Soluis*, 'The Psychology of a Volunteer'.[56]

He did not always succeed in differentiating between his own politics and national politics, and political events. However it is not the duty of a journalist to judge, support or criticise one political party over another – merely to 'witness' and provide objective opinion. As a 'witness' therefore of the 1916 Rising, it is interesting to muse on what line of reporting he would have followed, allowing that he was a political leader also. He may in fact have thrown a clearer perspective on the events of 1916 in the context of nation, language and cultural developments. A burning question in light of Irish-language journalism is whether or not his own, and the 'national story' would have been told in Irish or English, or at all.

The role of the journalist was one which Pearse bore with quiet determination yet displaying a fervent understanding of the necessity of this medium of communication, regardless of the language employed, to 'tell the story', to be the 'witness' or merely to spread the 'news'.

Pearse's journalistic writings attest in many ways to issues of inequality and exploitation, as referred to by Anderson. This created that 'fraternity' or 'brotherhood' in Pearse's terms, which in turn allowed Pearse, as an associate of the fraternity, to die 'willingly'. They also however reveal hope, truth and progressive thought within an evolving Irish society. Time has told its own 'story' however, and perhaps the imaginings were not so imaginary. Pearse wrote in 1904 that 'Gaelicism is the birthright of us all'. We have come a long way in modern Ireland witnessing peace agreements that would not have been 'imagined' in 1916 and prior to it. In the context of present language and cultural developments, Pearse's statement in 1904 may well have more relevance now than it did then. Perhaps the imaginings were not so limited after all.

CHAPTER SEVEN

# Laying the Ghosts:
# Patrick Pearse and the
# Reproach of History

## JAMES QUINN

Patrick Pearse's sense of history, in particular the notion that he owed a sacred debt to his nationalist predecessors, was a key influence in shaping his actions throughout his life. History worked as an inspiration and a legitimisation for Pearse, but it also worked as a reproach, and the desire to appease this reproach became an increasingly pressing concern, particularly in the months leading up to the 1916 Rising. Whether invoking the memory of Cúchulainn or Robert Emmet, mythical and historical events and personalities exercised a great influence over Pearse's thought, and in many ways were more real to him than those of the present.[1]

### YOUNG IRELAND

The historical writers who influenced Pearse were mostly those of Young Ireland. A crucial part of the Young Ireland project set out by Thomas Davis and Charles Gavan Duffy in the *Nation* was the teaching and popularising of Irish history.[2] Chronicling the existence of a separate Irish nation throughout the preceding centuries and its stubborn resistance to conquest would, they believed, help to justify Ireland's claim to self-government. Therefore they devoted much of the *Nation* to historical topics, disseminated hundreds of stirring historical ballads, and published numerous historical works, most notably in their Library of Ireland series. The emphasis in the Library of Ireland was very much on the troubled century from the 1590s to the 1690s, with Irish history portrayed as a continuous struggle against foreign domination. Heroic warriors such as Hugh O'Neill, Owen Roe O'Neill and Patrick Sarsfield were annexed to the nationalist tradition and claimed as the forerunners of Tone and Emmet. The Library of Ireland works were short, accessible and cheap. They sold in great numbers and for the next half-century and beyond formed the basis of historical collections in nationalist homes and reading rooms, popularising a view of Irish history as a series of uprisings, each reinforcing the tradition of resistance.

Young Ireland history was deliberately and unashamedly polemical. The Young Irelanders regarded themselves as patriots with a mission rather than disinterested antiquarians and were more anxious to shape the future than to accurately chronicle the past. They believed that history should provide a clear and compelling narrative that explained the sufferings of the past, justified the struggles of the present, and held out hope of deliverance in the future. Their works aimed primarily to capture the inspirational drama of history and deliberately avoided the dry and colourless style of more academic historians.[3] Among the historians most admired by the Young Irelanders was Thomas Carlyle, who famously regarded history as the biographies of great men.[4] As in Carlyle's works, much Young Ireland history concentrates on drama and declamation, on lauding heroes and excoriating villains.

The Young Irelanders also devoted considerable effort to writing the history of their own times. The most popular and influential accounts of the 1840s were those by Charles Gavan Duffy published in the 1880s, Michael Doheny's *The Felon's Track* (1849), and John Mitchel's *The Last Conquest of Ireland (Perhaps)* (1861).[5] These works differed in many respects, but were at one in their favourable portrayal of the Young Ireland movement and their disparagement of Daniel O'Connell and his followers. O'Connell was portrayed as a flawed figure, who could have commanded the Irish people to do as he pleased, but, fearing the shedding of blood, backed down in the face of British government intimidation at Clontarf in 1843. Clontarf took its place as one of the great lost opportunities of Irish history, when a willing and expectant people had only awaited the word from their leader to rise up and seize their freedom. O'Connell's failure to use the immense power at his disposal led John Mitchel to condemn him as 'Next to the British government ... the worst enemy that Ireland ever had'.[6] O'Connell's followers fared even worse: they were generally portrayed as Catholic bigots and servile place-hunters, who regarded Repeal as a mere bargaining counter rather than a sincere assertion of Irish independence and nationality. In contrast the Young Irelanders were portrayed as selfless idealists, the

7.1 Pearse at Bodenstown 1913. Courtesy Pearse Museum.

non-sectarian advocates of an inclusive nationalism, unwilling to traffic with their country's independence.

The works of the Young Irelanders were avidly read in nationalist homes and reading rooms throughout the second half of the nineteenth century and greatly influenced the nationalist view of the period. Pearse identified strongly with the Young Ireland interpretation of history, and dismissed O'Connell as being 'repudiated by the generation that came after him' because of the timidity of his nationalism.[7] Pearse saw himself and his fellow separatists confronting John Redmond and the Irish Parliamentary Party in the same light as the Young Irelanders confronting O'Connell and his followers.[8] He condemned the constitutionalists of his day as 'mean and shameful', claiming that for the last quarter-century they 'have done evil, and they are bankrupt'.[9] He believed they were bankrupt because they were prepared to negotiate and compromise on the question of independence for Ireland, whereas for Pearse this was something so sacred that it could not be bought or sold.[10] Just as the Young Irelanders condemned O'Connell's alliance with the whigs in the 1840s, so Pearse condemned the home rulers' cooperation with the Liberals, believing that any alliance with British liberalism served only to corrupt and undermine Irish nationality. By engaging in such an alliance he argued that the constitutionalists had proved themselves not the successors of Parnell (as they claimed) but traitors to his separatist legacy, and like all traitors they would be scorned by future generations of nationalists.[11]

## THE FOUR EVANGELISTS

It therefore fell to pure nationalists such as Pearse to carry on the work of their predecessors. Pearse defined patriotism as 'in large part a memory of heroic dead men and a striving to accomplish some task left unfinished by them'.[12] This concern with fulfilling one's duty to the past was most explicitly acknowledged in his pamphlet *Ghosts* (written on Christmas day 1915) and in his subsequent pamphlets *The Separatist Idea*, *The Spiritual Nation* and *The Sovereign People*. He noted that the demand for Irish independence 'has been made by every generation; that we of this generation receive it as a trust from our fathers; that we are bound by it; that we have not the right to alter it or abate it by one jot'.[13] Pearse claimed that this demand was most insistently pressed by those whom he termed 'the four great nationalist evangelists': Theobald Wolfe Tone, Thomas Davis, James Fintan Lalor and John Mitchel. He saw each of them as representing a different aspect of Irish nationalism, but all were at one in calling for their work to be completed.[14] One important name who was not invoked by Pearse in *Ghosts* was Robert Emmet, but this was simply because Emmet had left behind no body of written work that would have qualified him as an evangelist. The ghost of Emmet, however, haunted Pearse's imagination as much as any other: he readily admitted that it was 'the spirit of Emmet' that led him to the Hermitage and inspired him while he was there.[15] Emmet's youth, eloquence, and willingness to sacrifice himself for Ireland endeared him to Pearse. The ringing words of Emmet's speech from the dock were a constant reproach to those who had yet to complete his work, and indeed Pearse claimed that the city of Dublin 'would one day have to wash out in blood' the shame of its quiescence in Emmet's execution. For Pearse, Emmet was clearly another one of 'those voices ... that bid us to be faithful still and to make no peace with England until Ireland is ours'.[16]

## WOLFE TONE

Pearse revered Tone primarily because he had defined with memorable clarity and precision the doctrine of Irish nationalism – the achievement of separation from England through the unity of all Irishmen. For Pearse, Tone was not alone 'the greatest of Irish nationalists' – he was 'the greatest of Irish men'.[17] He avidly read Tone's autobiography, which traced out his career from the optimism of the founding of the United Irishmen in 1791, the disillusionment in the face of government repression in 1794, the loneliness and frustration of his life as a revolutionary agent in Paris, and finally his grim readiness to give up his life in pursuit of Irish independence. It was a work that consoled and inspired Pearse, and he kept it by his side at all times.

## THOMAS DAVIS

But despite Pearse's adulation of Tone, he clearly found something lacking in Tone's definition of Irish nationalism. What it lacked was a spiritual dimension and this Pearse found in Thomas Davis. In his writings and lectures Davis had sought to convince contemporaries of the value and uniqueness of Irish nationality – a spiritual quality based on shared historical experience and an ancient tradition of cultural achievement; because of this Davis attached a particular importance to the writing of history.[18] Davis believed that it was the duty of the historical writer to inspire and nurture this sentiment; reading history should 'lead us into love of self-denial, of justice, of beauty, of valour, of generous life and proud death; and to set up in our souls the memory of great men, who shall then be as models and judges of our actions'.[19] He maintained that a uniquely Irish nationality stretching back into antiquity had been forged over the centuries by Ireland's 'piety, its valour and its sufferings', creating a legacy that formed a common spiritual bond among the generations.[20] Pearse maintained that Davis's great contribution to Irish nationalism was to recognise

> that the thing which makes her one is her history, that all her men and women are the heirs of a common past, a past full of spiritual, emotional, and intellectual experiences, which knits them together indissolubly. The nation is thus not a mere agglomeration of individuals, but a living, organic thing, with a body and a soul.[21]

Davis's appreciation of the spiritual dimension of nationalism was expressed through his love of Irish history and culture, most notably his love of the Irish language. He had argued that

> A people without a language of its own is only half a nation. A nation should guard its language more than its territories ... To lose your native tongue, and to learn that of an alien is the worst badge of conquest – it is the chain on the soul. To have lost entirely the national language is death.[22]

To halt the onward march of English Davis proposed the establishment of a newspaper in Irish and the introduction of a programme of bilingualism similar to that which Pearse would later champion.[23] Such sentiments allowed Pearse to proclaim Davis as 'the lineal ancestor of the spiritual movement embodied in our day in the Gaelic League'.[24]

Davis was also a crucial influence in the importance he attached to education. He believed that a practical programme of education was needed to inculcate a spirit of national consciousness in Irishmen and claimed that education was the only kind of 'moral force' in which he had any faith. A fierce critic of contemporary educational practices, he condemned the schools of his day as learning factories that crammed 'pupils with facts or words, without developing their judgement, taste or invention, or teaching them the application of any knowledge'.[25] He was critical of the new national schools, particularly their neglect of Irish history and the Irish language. In fact he believed they were undermining the sense of Irish nationality and were a backward step when compared with the hedge schools which at least 'kept up something of the romance, history and music of the country'.[26] These were criticisms that Pearse would echo over half a century later.[27]

## JAMES FINTAN LALOR

The third of Pearse's great influences was James Fintan Lalor, who during the Famine had criticised Irish nationalists for their preoccupation with the political formulae of repeal and federalism and their indifference to economic issues, particularly the crucial question of land tenure. In vigorous, straightforward terms Lalor had stated that it was the Irish people who were the true owners of the land and resources of Ireland and that Irish independence would be worthless unless these resources were shared equitably throughout the population. Although Pearse came rather later to Lalor, he proved an important influence in the years immediately before 1916. Increasingly troubled by the distress he saw in Dublin streets, particularly after the great lock-out of 1913, Pearse wondered why a country with so many natural advantages should be so poor, and found his answers in Lalor, concluding that 'separation from England would be valueless unless it put the people ... and not merely certain rich men ... in effectual ownership and possession of the soil of Ireland'.[28] The plebeian radicalism of Lalor formed a convenient bridge towards Connolly's socialism, and it was Pearse's invocation of Lalor that made Connolly praise *Ghosts* as he had praised none of Pearse's earlier writings and claim that it should be circulated by the thousand.[29]

Pearse also admired Lalor's indomitable revolutionary spirit: despite illness and deformity he was to the forefront in calling for action in 1848, and after his release from prison had embarked upon a futile insurrection in County Waterford in September 1849, dying weeks later. In the days leading up to the 1848 insurrection Lalor had written:

> It is never the mass of a people that forms its real and efficient might. It is the men by whom that mass is moved and managed. All the great acts of history have been done by a very few men. ... Remember this – that somewhere and somehow and by somebody a beginning must be made.[30]

Such courage and willingness to seize the initiative led Pearse to praise Lalor as 'a fiery spirit, as of some angelic missionary ... strong with a great spiritual strength'.[31]

## JOHN MITCHEL

Of all the Young Irelanders, the one who most influenced Pearse (at least in the last few years of his life) was John Mitchel. Pearse praised Mitchel as Ireland's 'greatest literary figure', and credited him with reintroducing to Irish writing a power and vehemence not heard since the great Gaelic poets of the past. He described Mitchel's *Jail*

*Journal* as 'one of the holy books of Ireland ... the last gospel of the new testament of Irish nationality'.[32] Seeing the tentacles of British influence in every aspect of Irish life, Pearse concurred with Mitchel that British policy in Ireland was not a series of *ad hoc* actions, but a deliberate and systematic plan to enslave Ireland. Most famously in his *Last Conquest of Ireland*, Mitchel had argued that the Famine was not a natural disaster but an opportunity callously seized by the British government to exterminate Ireland's rural population as part of its plan of conquest.[33]

Mitchel's writings struck a chord with many Irish nationalists, particularly those who recoiled against many of the values of the modern world.[34] Both Pearse and Mitchel shared a serious disenchantment with modern life, especially the materialistic and individualistic society that had emerged from liberal capitalism, and they welcomed war and bloodshed as the price to be paid to sweep away the complacency and materialism of their times. Borrowing Mitchel's Carlylean rhetoric, Pearse wrote: 'One scarcely knows whether modern sentimentalism or modern utilitarianism is the more sure sign of modern decadence. I would boldly preach the antique faith that fighting is the only noble thing, and that he only is at peace with God who is at war with the powers of evil.'[35] The shadow of Mitchel's glorification of war and destruction lies over many of Pearse's later writings: in *The Sovereign People*, for example, he quoted with approval from Mitchel's *Jail Journal*: 'Destruction is creation: Death *is* Birth

7.2 Still from a propaganda film showing Michael Collins signing Irish government bonds outside St Enda's on top of the block on which it was said Robert Emmet was beheaded, *c.* 1919. Courtesy of the Irish Film Institute.

and "The quick spring like weeds out of the dead"'.[36] According to his pupil Desmond Ryan, Pearse's disenchantment with modern life became more extreme as he witnessed tens of thousands of Irishmen join the British army in the early months of the Great War, and he became increasingly convinced 'that the national consciousness of Ireland was on the point of extinction'.[37] Ryan recalled the normally mild-mannered Pearse 'bringing down his clenched fist heavily on the table where we were sitting and declaring: "I would rather see all Dublin in ruins than that we should go living as we are at present."'[38]

Both Pearse and Mitchel believed that, in a sacred cause, violence was ennobling, and for Mitchel there was no more sacred cause than hatred of the British Empire. Pearse adopted Mitchel's Manichean worldview in which British imperialism and Irish nationalism stood at opposite poles. In *The Sovereign People* (written only three weeks before the Easter Rising) Pearse wrote: 'a nation is holy and ... an empire is not holy ... The nation is of god; the empire is of man – if it be not of the devil.'[39] Defending Mitchel against those who claimed that he was a fanatic consumed by hatred, Pearse argued that 'Mitchel's hate was of the English empire, of English commercialism supported by English militarism, a thing wholly evil, perhaps the most evil thing that there has ever been in the world  ... Such hate is not only a good thing, but it is a duty'.[40] By 1914 Pearse was explicitly elevating the writings of Mitchel above those of the more conciliatory Davis, as he decisively committed himself to armed insurrection.[41]

The extremism of much of Pearse's rhetoric at this time may well have been a cover for the doubts and uncertainties that he suffered. There were times when the moral implications of violence seem to have troubled him greatly. Even in his militant writings in the months before Easter 1916 he noted that 'It is a terrible responsibility to be cast upon a man, that of bidding the cannon speak and the grapeshot roar'.[42] Desmond Ryan recalled that towards the end of Easter week as the flames roared around them in the GPO, Pearse suddenly 'turned to me with the very last question that I ever expected to hear from him: "It was the right thing to do, was it not?" he asked curiously.'[43] Similarly, Desmond Fitzgerald recalled that while in the GPO they constantly discussed the morality of what they had done and 'brought forward every theological argument and quotation that justified the rising'.[44]

There was, however, another form of theology that could offer sustenance and sanction, and that was the historical canon in which he was so immersed. Since he owed such an intellectual debt to his nationalist icons, their reproaches (or more precisely, the reproaches that Pearse had chosen to attribute to them) could not be ignored.

Pearse repeatedly refers to their writings as 'gospels', and to him they have all the force and authority of holy scripture. He regularly invoked the heroes of Ireland's past in the manner of a litany of saints, and spoke of his certainty being bolstered by consulting his 'national confessors'.[45] Deviating from their teaching he described as blasphemy.[46] His elevation of secular writings to the level of sacred texts struck some more orthodox Catholic contemporaries as somewhat profane, but Pearse's nationalism seamlessly blended the sacred and the secular. He regarded national freedom as bearing 'the marks … of sanctity, of catholicity, of apostolic succession', and those who sought to bring it about as being engaged in a sacred crusade.[47] Mitchel, for example, he described as 'of the stuff of which the great prophets and estatics have been made. He did really hold converse with God; He did really deliver god's word to man, delivered it fiery-tongued.'[48]

Failure to do the bidding of such prophets was to break faith with the past and sacrifice one's honour in the present. In Pearse's writings there is an almost obsessive concern with manliness and honour. In this too he mirrored his Young Ireland predecessors. Their decision to secede from the Repeal Association in 1846 rather than accept O'Connell's peace resolutions owed much to the fact that a complete repudiation of physical force in all circumstances would have destroyed their honour as men. Similarly their decision to rise in 1848 was largely motivated by a desire to vindicate their honour by living up to the bellicose rhetoric they had used in preceding months, an outlook with which Pearse could readily empathise.[49] No doubt he would have concurred with the words written by Duffy from prison in the last issue of the *Nation* before the attempted rising:

> We fight, because the honour, the interest, the necessity, the very existence of this ancient nation depends upon our valour and devotion at this hour. If we cower, if we flinch, if we falter, the hopes are gone for which our fathers' fathers gave their life's blood. Gone in the stench of dishonour and infamy that will cling to it for ever.[50]

Pearse often argued that modern life had eroded the traditional virility of the Irish people, and sometimes worried that their failure to establish their independence stemmed as much from Irish apathy and cowardice as it did from English oppression and treachery. Noting the readiness of Ulster unionists to arm themselves and the failure of nationalists to do likewise, he noted:

> Men who have ceased to be men cannot claim the rights of men; and men who have suffered themselves to be deprived of

their manhood have suffered the greatest of all indignities and deserved the most shameful of all penalties ... In suffering ourselves to be disarmed, in acquiescing in a perpetual disarmament ... in sneering at those who have taken arms, we in effect abnegate our manhood. Unable to exercise men's rights, we do not deserve men's privileges. We are, in a strict sense, not fit for freedom.[51]

Pearse was acutely aware that in the eighty years preceding his birth there had been four uprisings against British rule, but in his lifetime there had been none. This was a source of genuine shame to him, a shame heightened by his visit to America in 1914 and his meetings with unreconstructed Fenians such as John Devoy, whose revolutionary spirit had not faltered in half a century. It seemed to Pearse, however, that his own generation was in danger of failing to keep faith with Ireland's nationalist past. He recalled how the Fenians had been mocked for their inactivity in recent times: 'A nice figure we cut during the Boer war! We *talked*.'[52] He winced at the memory and was determined that it should not happen again. And it was not just the ghosts of the past that played on Pearse's mind – he was also troubled by the ghosts of the future: Pearse was acutely conscious of his place in history and of how he would be judged by generations to come. Would he be seen as one who talked rebellion but never fired a shot – or would he, like Tone and Emmet, be seen as a man who was prepared to back his words with his life? The famous motto of Cúchulainn prominently displayed at St Enda's – 'I care not though I were to live but one day and one night provided my fame and my deeds live after me' – no doubt worked on the imagination of the school's headmaster just as it did on that of his pupils.

By early 1916 Pearse had employed such extreme revolutionary rhetoric that he had left himself with little choice other than to engage in armed insurrection. He believed that the tradition of sacrifice and suffering in the Irish past had created a moral and spiritual debt that those in the present were duty-bound to repay. He was determined that Easter 1916 would not become his Clontarf. Another such opportunity might not come in his lifetime, and Pearse would be prevented from playing the historical role that he

7.3 *Ghosts.* Courtesy Pearse Museum.

TRACTS FOR THE TIMES, No. 10.

GHOSTS.

BY P. H. PEARSE

DUBLIN: WHELAN & SON, 17 UPPER ORMOND QUAY. 1916.

PRICE ONE PENNY. One Dozen or over, Post Free.

believed was allotted to him. Given the particular set of circumstances in which he found himself in 1914 – an international war, a domestic political vacuum with the suspension of home rule, and a sizeable armed force at the disposal of the IRB – the clamouring of his ghosts became irresistible. When he gave his stirring oration at the funeral of O'Donovan Rossa in August 1915, the most striking image he used was that of the graves of dead Fenians – these very graves were a powerful reproach while Ireland remained under British rule. Similarly the presence of the dead saturates the militant pamphlets he wrote in the months preceding Easter 1916, and when the Rising occurred it was famously invoked by 'God and the dead generations from which [Ireland] receives her old tradition of nationhood'.[53]

Such an attitude contrasts sharply with a more internationalist revolutionary tradition that regarded a sense of obligation to past generations as an encumbrance on the development of a progressive revolutionary consciousness. Thomas Paine, for example, wrote that 'The vanity and presumption of governing beyond the grave is the most ridiculous and insolent of all tyrannies', while Karl Marx complained that 'The tradition of dead generations weighs like a nightmare on the brain of the living.'[54] However, for Pearse, the past was a more benign presence with which he felt a close kinship. His ghosts were not unwelcome visitors, and his attempt to placate them was more an act of affirmation than an act of exorcism.

After the Easter Rising Pearse repeatedly spoke in terms of having fulfilled his life's mission, and on the eve of his execution wrote to his mother:

> You must not grieve for all this. We have preserved Ireland's honour and our own. Our deeds of last week are the most splendid in Ireland's history. People will say hard things of us now, but we shall be remembered by posterity and blessed by unborn generations.[55]

In his final speech to the court martial on 2 May he stated his pride in his actions and his belief that he had done the right thing: 'We have not lost. To refuse to fight would have been to lose; to fight is to win. We have kept faith with the past, and handed on a tradition to the future.'[56] For Pearse every such act fortified the spiritual nation of his imagination and ensured that military failure would never be moral failure.

Pearse prefaced *Ghosts* with the observation that 'Ghosts are troublesome things … The ghosts of a nation sometimes ask very big things; and they must be appeased, whatever the cost.'[57] When the rising had ended many observers commented on Pearse's satisfaction and serenity: his action in 1916 certainly appears to have been successful in laying his personal ghosts. But the story does not end there. Responding to the injunctions of the past creates a new historical context in which the cycle begins again. Pearse's martyrdom and apotheosis placed him firmly in the company of those who had spurred him to action; new voices from beyond the grave now cried out to others. His mother, for example, refused to accept the Treaty in 1922, claiming that, if she did, she feared 'that the ghosts of my sons would haunt me'.[58]

For many who came after him, Pearse would become the most insistent ghost of them all, whose reproach would in turn have to be appeased.

## CHAPTER EIGHT

# Pearse's Legacy: The Partition of Ireland

## THOMAS HENNESSEY

While it is not new to say that the impact of the Easter Rising dramatically altered nationalist Ireland's relationship with Britain, it is perhaps not as well recognised that the rebellion's impact had profound implications for the unity of Ireland. The background to the Rising was the Home Rule crisis of 1912–14, followed by the outbreak of war. It seems certain that Ireland would have been partitioned at some point because of Ulster unionist resistance to Home Rule. This is not to say that, but for the Rising, there would have been a united Ireland; rather that the Rising made sure there would not be one. At the heart of this was the notion of republicanism.

As a cultural nationalist, Patrick Pearse believed that a republic would safeguard the Irish nation from Anglicizing influences. Like many cultural nationalists he perceived the nation in organic terms whose individuality had to be cherished in all its manifestations. Gaelic revivalism took on the characteristics of a religious movement in which Irish names, language, literature, sports and manufactures were to be adopted and their English equivalents renounced. Its goal was the inner regeneration of a spontaneously evolving decentralised community led by an elite of public-spirited men and women. Gaelic revivalists were driven into politics to counter the Anglicizing effects of the state.[1] Pearse was a republican because he believed that a republic offered the greatest security from English cultural influence. He argued that to claim independence as the indefeasible right of Ireland was to claim everything for Ireland, all the spiritual exaltation and all the worldly pomp to which it was entitled. Independence included spiritual and intellectual independence as well as political independence. True political independence required spiritual and intellectual independence as its basis or it tended to become unstable: a thing resting merely on interests which changed with time and circumstance. Pearse made a distinction between spiritual and intellectual independence corresponding to the distinction which existed

8.1 Pearse (centre left with white rosette) at the funeral of O'Donovan Rossa. Courtesy Pearse Museum.

between the intellectual and spiritual parts in Man. The soul was not the mind, he believed, but it acted by way of the mind and it was through the mind that one got glimpses of the soul. It was possible to speak of a national mind and a national soul and to distinguish one from the other. Pearse could not convince himself that there was actually a mystical entity which was the soul of Ireland and expressed itself through the mind of Ireland. However, he believed that there was, indeed, a spiritual tradition which was the soul of Ireland – the thing that made Ireland a living nation – and that there was such a spiritual tradition corresponding to every true nationality. This spiritual thing was distinct from the intellectual facts in which chiefly it made its revelation, and it was distinct from them in a way analogous to that in which a man's soul was distinct from his mind. Like other spiritual things it was independent of the material, whereas the mind, to a large extent, was dependent on the material.

Pearse speculated that spiritually the United States and England were one nation (while intellectually apart), and that spiritually the Austrians were one nation with the Germans. The spiritual thing which was essential to nationality seemed to reside chiefly in the language,

which was understood to include literature and folklore, as well as
sounds and idioms. It also revealed itself in all the arts, institutions,
inner life and actions of the nation. If nationality could be regarded
as the sum of the facts spiritual and intellectual, and freedom as the
condition which allowed these facts full scope and development, it
would be seen, argued Pearse, that both the spiritual and the intellectual facts (nationality) and the physical condition (freedom) entered
into a proper definition of independence or nationhood. Freedom
was a condition which could be lost and won and lost again; but
nationality was a life which, if once lost, could never be recovered. A
nation was a stubborn thing, very difficult to kill; but a dead nation
did not come back to life, any more than a dead man did.[2] For Pearse
there could be no accommodation between the Irish nation and the
British empire:

> The nation is a natural division, as natural as the family and as
> inevitable. That is one reason why a nation is holy and why an
> empire is not holy. A nation is knit together by natural ties, ties
> mystic and spiritual, and ties human and kindly; an empire is at
> best held together by ties of mutual interest and at worst by
> brute force. The nation is the family in large; an empire is a
> commercial corporation in large. The nation is of God; the
> empire is of man – if it be not of the devil.[3]

If John Redmond, the leader of the Home Rule movement, were
to have his way, believed the Fenian newspaper *Irish Freedom*, the loyalty of the Irish people would not be to Ireland but to the British
empire, their allegiance would 'not be to Cathleen Ní Houlihan but
to George V', and their aim would not be to recreate and continue
Irish civilisation but to bolster up England's private empire: to be
loyal to a monarch, not King of Ireland, but usurper of it.[4] Pearse
argued that the Irish Party had done evil and was bankrupt in policy,
credit and words:

> They have conceived of nationality as a material thing, whereas
> it is a spiritual thing. They have made the same mistake that a
> man would if he were to forget that he has an immortal soul.
> They have not recognised in their people the image and likeness
> of God. Hence the nation to them is not all holy, a thing invio-
> late and inviolable, a thing that a man dare not sell or dishonour
> on pain of eternal perdition. They have thought of nationality as
> a thing to be negotiated about as men negotiate about a tariff or
> a trade route, rather than as an immediate jewel to be preserved
> at all peril, a thing so sacred that it may or may not be brought
> into the market places at all or spoken of where men traffic.[5]

Pearse took his model of an Irish state from Wolfe Tone, who in the late 1790s had advocated the creation of an Irish republic. He summarised Tone's republican teachings as:

1. The Irish Nation is One.
2. The Irish Nation, like all Nations, has an indefeasible right to Freedom.
3. Freedom denotes Separation and Sovereignty ...
6. Freedom is necessary to the happiness and prosperity of the Nation.

In the particular case of Ireland, Separation from England is necessary not only to the happiness and prosperity, but almost to the continued existence of Ireland, inasmuch as the interests of Ireland and England are fundamentally at variance, and while the two nations are connected England must necessarily predominate.[6]

Tone, noted Pearse, had taught that there could be no half-way house between Ireland and England as a permanent solution, for there were only two alternatives facing Ireland – enslavement or freedom.[7] With the Proclamation of the Irish Republic, in 1916, Pearse and the other signatories put the idea of a republic on the political agenda in a way it had never been before; immediately prior to the Rising the very idea of taking on the military might of the British Empire appeared, to most nationalists, a fantasy.

### NATIONALIST LOYALTY TO THE CROWN

One of the primary aims of the Rising was to deliver a death blow to the concept of Irishness as advocated by John Redmond. He offered an alternative sense of Irishness: one that was compatible with Britishness. Redmond's strategy for securing Home Rule was to attempt to reassure unionists in Britain and Ireland that a Dublin government and parliament would be loyal to the Crown and Empire. He pointed out that Parnell had accepted that, under an Irish parliament, Irishmen would continue to be subjects within the United Kingdom. The British monarch would still be Ireland's monarch, the link that would still attach Ireland to Great Britain. Peace between the two countries would be established when Ireland was treated as a nation or, at least, as a free colony like the other Dominions such as Canada and Australia.[8] For Redmond the idea of a 'Union of Hearts' between the Irish and British peoples had always been implicit in the Home Rule movement, and he offered a positive Irish commitment to the welfare of Britain, the Union and the Empire. The grant of Home Rule would, it was argued, cultivate a

Britannic loyalty among the nationalist population. In 1912, Willie Redmond, the MP for East Clare and John's brother, compared the position of Irish nationalists with that of the Boers in South Africa, who had not contented themselves with merely denouncing British rule, as Irish nationalists were accused of doing, but who had come out under arms and for three years fought Britain. Who, he asked, was now prepared to say that the Boers had not been entitled to fight for their liberty, and who would now argue that the Boers were not entitled to their liberty and rights? The post-war South African settlement, granting Dominon self-government, had been denounced by British unionists as a dangerous and disastrous thing for the Empire, but Willie Redmond argued that it had been justified by the results. Claiming, in the House of Commons, that the whole empire was in favour of Home Rule, he asked:

> Why is the Empire in favour of Home Rule? For two reasons: in the first place the people of the Empire have seen Home Rule working at home. They have seen in every part of the Empire disturbance, disloyalty, and rivalry give way to unity, brotherhood, and friendship amongst men of all classes ... all religions, once they came to sit together side by side in national and local Parliaments of their own. The Empire, too, is in favour of Home Rule because the Empire has seen what effect Home Rule has upon Irishmen there ... There is no Parliament in Australia ... Canada ... in any part of your Empire, where Irishmen like ourselves of the same flesh and blood, the same sentiments, the same history and traditions, the same deep religious feeling, are not to be found among the most loyal, the most able, the most contented, and the most respected in the British Empire. Why? Because there they find there are no traditions of prejudice against them, either on account of their race or creed.[9]

As Sir Thomas Esmonde, MP for North Wexford, emphasised:

> We Irish people have no rooted antipathy to the Empire. The Empire is quite as much our Empire as yours. As a matter of history Irish brains ... valour, and ... genius have done quite as much to build up this Empire ... [as] either British genius or ... intelligence. But we must be allowed a proper position in the Empire.[10]

Redmond, as leader of the Irish Party, had adopted a conciliatory tone towards the Irish unionist community. In 1898 he declared:

> What has been the real stumbling block in the way of the

English people granting us Home Rule? It has been the fact that Ireland herself has been divided upon this question of Home Rule into two camps, and that many thousands of the Irish people have held aloof from the national movement.[11]

The Ulster crisis demonstrated to Redmond the level of this aloofness. So, when war broke out between Britain and Germany, in August 1914, he seized the opportunity to demonstrate to British and Irish unionists, Irish nationalism's compatability with British imperialism. On the eve of war, Redmond offered the Irish nationalist Volunteer movement to the British government for the defence of Ireland from a German invasion. He then took the unprecedented step, for a nationalist leader, and urged Volunteers to join the British Army and fight against German imperialism and for Home Rule. His vision was to create a new sense of Irish national myth in which nationalists and unionists would bury their domestic differences so that

> As our soldiers are going to fight, to shed their blood, and to die at each other's side, in the same army, against the same enemy, and for the same high purpose, their union in the field may lead to a union in their home, and that their blood may be the seal that will bring all Ireland together in one nation.[12]

### REDMONDITE BLOOD SACRIFICE

Irish Party MPs led the way. Willie Redmond enlisted in the Royal Irish Regiment as a private soldier, rising to the rank of Major; he was killed on the Somme in 1917 and his body was carried to its final resting place by soldiers of the 16th Irish Division and the 36th Ulster Division. Eamon de Valera won the resultant by-election for his seat in East Clare. Stephen Gwynn MP became a Captain in the Connaught Rangers; John Redmond's son William joined the Irish Guards and won an MC; Dr Alan Esmonde, who joined the R.A.M.C., had died at camp; his son, Captain Esmonde, succeeded his father as MP for Tipperary. The former Irish Party MP Tom Kettle also enlisted. His view was that, having mixed with Englishmen and Protestant Ulstermen in the British army's ranks, 'there is no real or abiding reason for the gulfs ... that now dismember the natural alliance of both of them with us Irish Nationalists'.[13] Kettle was killed in action on the Somme in October 1916. He, and Willie Redmond, presented an alternative form of sacrifice for Ireland which the Irish Party and its supporters believed had brought Catholics and Protestants together.

8.2
O'Donovan
Rossa funeral
cortege leav-
ing City Hall.
Courtesy
Pearse
Museum.

One result of this was a southern unionist reassessment of the Irish Party's nationalism and imperialism throughout the war. Consequently, by the time of Willie Redmond's death at the Somme in 1917, J.H. Bernard, the Church of Ireland Archbishop of Dublin, in a memorial address to the fallen Irish Party MP, praised those nationalists who had enlisted: 'all of whom had proved that "their views on questions of Irish domestic policy were fully consistent with loyalty to the Crown"'. All those MPs, said Bernard, represented political views which did not commend themselves fully to many of the speaker's friends, or indeed himself, but 'when it came to fighting for your country, King, and Empire they [the Irish Party MPs] were on their [unionists] side, "and we were on theirs". (Applause)'.[14] This appreciation was followed by an even more extraordinary speech, considering its source, from the Lord Chief Justice of Ireland, Sir James Campbell, a previously implacable die-hard opponent of nationalism, who explained how

> It was not by his former political life and career that Major Redmond had ... laid the foundation of the affection and respect that was entertained throughout the length and breadth of Ireland for his memory. It was for his action since the war. From the day the war broke out Major Willie Redmond never looked back. He at once realised what was the path of honour and duty for all his fellow-countrymen: and from that day he, like many others who found themselves faced with the momentous realities of this dreadful war and its tremendous possibilities, entertained

8.3 Former St Enda's pupils and teachers posing in Volunteer uniforms, Easter Sunday 1916. *Back row, left to right*: Éamonn Bulfin, Conor McGinley, Desmond Ryan, Fintan Murphy, Peter Slattery. *Front row, left to right*: Brian Joyce, Frank Burke, Eunan McGinley, Joseph Sweeney. In 1967 these men re-posed this photograph (see figure 15.3). Courtesy Pearse Museum.

the honest conviction that in their past years, they had spent too much time in accentuating the points on which they differed, while they overlooked the many points of agreement. (Applause).[15]

The *Irish Times* noted that Major Redmond had seen that 'the road to Irish unity and progress led through the narrow gates of sacrifice', and in his three years as a soldier he had done 'more to bring Irishmen together than all our politicians had done in the thirty years before his death'.[16] The results of this could partly be seen in the Irish Convention of 1918 where, for the first time, southern unionists accepted an advanced form of Home Rule for Ireland – something unthinkable before the War.

Yet the opposite affect appeared to be occuring among the Protestants of Ulster. They had experienced their own blood sacrifice in 1916. If any one event might be selected as the crucial moment when any hope that a psychological partition of Ireland would be avoided were dashed, then the impact of the Battle of the Somme upon the Ulster unionist psyche, and the Ulster Protestant community generally, coming as it did so soon after the Easter Rising, was probably it. On 1 July 1916 the 36th (Ulster) Division, the bulk of which had been formed from the UVF, attacked German trenches over a fifteen-mile front of the Somme sector in France. During the next

two days the Ulster Division lost over 5,000 men, killed, wounded
and missing. The impact of these casualties on small towns and vil-
lages, and on whole streets in Belfast, was enormous. The lesson
drawn by many Unionists after the Easter Rising, when they compared their blood sacrifice for King and country, was that of instinc-
tive nationalist disloyalty. In contrasting the Easter Rising with the
Battle of the Somme, the Reverend R.S. Morrison, rector of St
Saviour's, Portadown, told a gathering of Orangemen in July 1916:

> A feeling of profound and heartfelt sorrow held chief place in
> their minds for their gallant and noble brothers who had made
> the supreme sacrifice for King and country ... the bravest of the
> brave – whose splendid deeds and deathless glory would ever
> shine resplendent on the pages of British history, whose names
> would be cherished in the hearts and affections of all loyal
> Ulstermen from generation to generation the world-wide over
> ... Ulster was poor and weaker by their loss, but gloriously rich
> and stronger by the memorial of invaluable service so willingly
> rendered, and involving such costly self-sacrifice to our Empire
> in her hour of greatest need. Whatever the future might hold
> for the Empire their sacrifice had not been made in vain ... The
> Sinn Fein rebellion ... in the midst of such a national crisis ...
> was an irrefutable impeachment of the Nationalist ... party ...
> which no Loyalist Britisher would ever forget ... To talk of a
> future compromise arrived at by the patriotic Irishmen who
> have fought side by side on the banks of the Somme, and whose
> forefathers fought against each other on the banks of the Boyne,
> was the dream of a visionary.[17]

The impact of the war and the Rising made some Ulster unionists
think hard about their identity. Sir James Stronge explained that 'For
myself ... I still believe that the people of the British Isles form one
nation. But, if they should ever become two nations, I prefer to
remain a Briton even at the cost of ceasing to be an Irishman.'[18] He
warned that:

> ... there is serious risk that ... such Irish feeling as remains
> among us may disappear. Many events in recent years have
> tended to weaken our connection with the rest of Ireland, and
> if it becomes clear that the majority of Southern Unionists
> desires our absorption into an Irish 'Nation' our conversion into
> 'West Britons' will be complete.[19]

It was the *rapprochement* between Ireland and the empire that
Pearse and the rebel leadership sought to prevent. But it also did the
same with regard to any *rapprochement* between nationalism and

Ulster unionism. Stephen Gwynn argued in the *Freeman's Journal*:

> Pearse and his followers brought to Ireland, not merely war, but
> civil war and hatred ... like a pestilence. The old ditch which
> divided us is deepened, new blood flows in it, but Willie
> Redmond and those who died like him, gave their bodies to
> bridge that gulf. Their example preached fellowship and broth-
> erhood, not to Ireland only, and not only between Irishmen. It
> is for Ireland to weigh the issue ... to decide a course. Is it to fol-
> low Pearse, who risked and lost his life without hope of imme-
> diate success, in order to revive in Ireland an ancient war? Or
> will it adhere to Willie Redmond, who risked and lost his life in
> the hope that through foreign war Ireland might at least reach
> an honourable peace?[20]

Gwynn attempted to restore the sacrifices of the nationalist soldiers in
the trenches to the forefront of political debate in Ireland. His interest
was chiefly that these soldiers' work for Ireland in Flanders, Gallipoli,
Serbia and Mesopotamia should not be, 'neutralised, cancelled and
blotted out' back home.[21] Gwynn also warned about what the rebels'
demand for an Irish republic, now taken up by de Valera and a
revamped Sinn Féin, would mean; it would only further alienate Irish
unionists from the concept of Irish self-government by severing all
links with the Empire. As Gwynn put it, the demand for freedom

> must then be a freedom which Ireland will accept. To propose
> an Irish Republic is to put forward an ideal to which out of four
> and a quarter million Irishmen at least a million and a half – the
> Irish Protestant Unionists – will have nothing to say.
>
> What is the use in talking about England? It was not England
> who stopped Home Rule coming into being. It was Ulster.
> Ulster is the real difficulty; not England. The core of the resist-
> ance is within our own shores; and our real task is to transform
> Ireland into a true unity from being what she is to-day – thanks
> to Mr de Valera – little more than a geographical expression.
>
> England has given us the chance to do this. She should have
> given it earlier – but could she, before the war? What made it
> possible for Ulster to come to terms with us – what made it
> impossible for Ulstermen to maintain their previous attitude –
> was the action of those Irish Nationalists who went to the war
> ... What Willy Redmond saw as his goal – what he gave his life
> for gladly – was the unity of Ireland. What Mr de Valera and his
> friends have done and continue to do is to make that ideal ten
> times more difficult of attainment.
>
> Personally, I prefer infinitely for Ireland the position of a free

State in the British Empire to that of a small independent State, such as Denmark is to-day. Many nationalist Irishmen will agree with me in this – especially those who realise the conditions under which Denmark, for instance exists to-day ... Many will disagree. But the essential fact is that we can hope to unite Ireland on the former ideal – on the latter never.[22]

## CONCLUSION: PARTITIONING IRELAND

Neither Irishness nor Britishness were mutually exclusive identities. Irish nationalists were conscious that they were members of an Irish nation separate from the people of Great Britain. Irish unionists were conscious that they belonged to a Britannic national and imperial community that composed the United Kingdom of Great Britain and Ireland but extended beyond the British Isles; this identity included an Irish national consciousness but not one which sought separation or self-government from Britain. Both nationalists and unionists possessed an Irish idenity of varying intensities. The fundamental difference between them was that unionists possessed a Britannic identity. It was the link with the Crown which allowed unionists to possess a strong dual British–Irish identity and which made a Britannic identity problematic for some nationalists. The concept of British subjectship meant that everyone in the Empire was born into subjection and owed allegiance to the Crown. This provided a legal or statist definiton of Britishness. For unionists, however, it also represented an emotional attachment built over the years since the Anglo-Irish Union of 1801.

For nationalists of the Redmondite variety, allowing Ireland to take her place within the empire offered a potential bridge to common Irishness with unionists. Redmond hoped that the common sacrifice of Irish nationalists and unionists on the field of battle would have a seminal nation-building effect in the longer process of creating a common sense of Irishness. That sacrifice could also, with the granting of Home Rule, be a seminal experience binding Irishmen with Englishmen, Scotsmen, Canadians, Australians, New Zealanders and South Africans. Redmondite imperialism was aspirational; it was something to be acquired, slowly, if at all, as in South Africa which also had a difficult relationship with the imperial centre. The link with the Crown, however, allowed a people to be both British and something else in terms of their national or imperial allegiance. Pearse's republicanism was not similarily inclusive. Republicanism meant an Irish identity would be Irish only. An Irish citizen in an Irish republic automatically severed the Britannic duality of the link with the Crown. It ended the potential for an Irish nationalist to possess at least the legal fiction of an imperial patriotism. Furthermore, the blood sacrifice of the Rising contrasted with the blood sacrifice of the Somme. By his sacrifice, Pearse made the dream of an independent sovereign republic possible. But it also made the partition of Ireland permanent.

## CHAPTER NINE

# Remembering and Forgetting P.H. Pearse

## ROISÍN HIGGINS

Patrick Pearse was a person enormously changed by death. He anticipated the transformation and wrote to his mother in the days before his execution, 'this is the death I should have asked for if God had given me the choice of all deaths – to die a soldier's death for Ireland and for freedom'.[1] Pearse was executed by firing squad on 3 May 1916. He was someone whom W.B. Yeats recorded as 'a man made dangerous by the Vertigo of Self-Sacrifice'.[2] But Pearse said of himself from his hermitage that he shared with hermits two qualities: that he was poor and that he was merry, 'I am visibly poor, but I am merry only in an esoteric or secret sense, exhibiting to the outer world an austerity of look and speech more befitting my habitation than my heart'.[3] Few people knew this secret sense of Pearse and his other-worldly persona became an important feature of his life after death. On the one-hundredth anniversary of his birth the *Irish Times* asked, 'For what is he remembered?' and answered, 'As with other great figures of the past, often for our own self-esteem. We like to keep the memory of our heroes green and fresh. But we will seldom read what they wrote and said, and only fitfully follow their example.'[4]

Whatever the complexities and richness of his life, Pearse is most remembered for the week before his death. He was the Commander-in-Chief of the Irish Volunteers in the GPO during a rising which generally captured the imagination of Irish people if not their initial hearts. He also drafted the Proclamation of the Republic and, apart from James Connolly, was the only leader of Easter Week to leave extensive political writings. Therefore Pearse emerged as the central historical figure of the Easter Rising. It was Pearse who was recorded as the First President of the Republic, a matter which was challenged by Tom Clarke's widow Kathleen. She wrote in 1966 to Eamon Martin, a member of the commemoration committee set up to organise the fiftieth anniversary of the Easter Rising:

I think it is a dreadful thing for people ... to be trying to rob Tom Clarke of the one honour conferred on him by his comrades and if Pearse signed [himself President⁵] without authority (as it seems to me he did) I feel he is beneath contempt ... Surely Pearse should have been satisfied with the honour of Commander-in-Chief when he knew as much about commanding as my dog.[6]

Kathleen Clarke had a good case as her husband was a respected Fenian whose position as President would certainly have been in line with IRB thinking. However, as Charles Townshend has pointed out, the general lack of concern with Clarke's claim tells its own story.[7] In 1966 when the matter was brought to the attention of the Taoiseach, Seán Lemass, he sought the advice of Jack Lynch who replied that in his formative years and still, Pearse was the name he most associated with the Rising and he believed this was true of most of his generation and successive ones.[8] Despite Kathleen Clarke's best efforts, Pearse remained as the figure in the public mind who represented both civil and military authority during the Rising.

9.1
Commemorative
postcard. Courtesy
Pearse Museum.

IRISH REBELLION, MAY 1916

P. H. PEARSE.
Commandant-General of the Army of the Irish Republic),
Executed May 3rd, 1916.
One of the signatories of the "Irish Republic Proclamation."

Easter week 1916 was a military failure that has been reread as a great historical success. The execution of the leaders caught the popular imagination and subsequent events reframed the Rising as the pivotal action in a revolution which eventually led to independence for twenty-six counties in Ireland. Partition, the disputed Treaty with Britain and the civil war which followed meant that all subsequent events would be tainted by the memory of division. Therefore the Easter Rising came to hold an almost unrivalled place in the national story. In the early history of the Irish Free State, Sinn Féin and Fianna Fáil were most comfortable claiming the Rising as their inheritance though Cumman na nGaedheal, Fine Gael and Labour would not (and politically could not) concede ownership of the event to their political rivals.

The first formal military commemoration of the Rising took place in 1924 under the Cumann na nGaedheal government but, although invitations were issued to all the relatives of the executed leaders, only Michael Mallin's widow attended.[9] On the tenth anniversary of the Easter Rising, Eamon de Valera and Seán Lemass participated in an unofficial commemoration which was organised by Republicans in Glasnevin cemetery. Ten years later, as members of the government, they understood the importance of claiming the inheritance of the Rising for Fianna Fáil: the significance was underlined by the fact that 1936 was also the year that the IRA was declared an illegal organisation.[10] Pearse was used to symbolise an unbroken tradition of Republicanism and consequently to communicate the authority and legitimacy of Éamon de Valera. The coalition government under John A. Costello also recognised the power of the Rising and when the Republic of Ireland was officially realised in 1949 its launch took place at Easter. Indeed, as Diarmaid Ferriter has noted, commemoration of the Rising was divisive throughout the 1930s and 1940s and tedium rather than consensus marked celebrations in the two decades that followed.[11] Pearse and the Rising were used in party-building by Fianna Fáil and in efforts at state-building by all parties. By the 1970s the conflict in Northern Ireland increased the struggle over who had the right to claim the legacy of Pearse and the Rising, and northern Republicans were accused of politicising historical memory for violent ends. The memory of Pearse, of course, has always been political.[12]

Evocations of Pearse conveyed a clearly readable narrative of Irish history which represented both Irishness and independence. His place in Irish history was firmly set by his involvement in a signature historical event. As a result he became a figure onto whom was projected the hopes and disappointments of the nation. As confidence in the nation ebbed and flowed, so did Pearse's reputation. At times of uncertainty he was looked to as the surety of the Republican cause. Pearse was a figure who could be used as a measure against which the state was held up for criticism. However, by the 1970s he was also a figure who became implicated in the failures of the independent state and in the attempted destruction of its northern counterpart. Pearse inhabited a curious position in which he was used to criticise both romantic nationalism and anti-nationalism.

## PEARSE AS ICON

In the twenty-first century icons are most commonly understood as the small pictograms on computer screens that have been developed to assist the user. They are representations of what lies beyond the click of a mouse: a simplified image of an intricate computer tool. In the broader culture, also, icons operate as symbols representing complex systems of meaning, their sophistication concealed within their simplicity.

The most famous western artist of icons in the twentieth century was Andy Warhol, whose mass-produced images of famous people and consumer goods created an art that was indistinguishable from commercialism. Warhol's life as well as his art demonstrated the power of packaging a product. Like other Pop artists, he understood that in the age of mass media the images we remember are those which most closely resemble a sign and are simple, clear and repetitious.[13] Edward Carson was marketed, Alvin Jackson has written, 'with much the same vigour as was applied to Sunlight Soap, or to Dunville's whiskey' using the full range of Edwardian technology from film to postcards.[14] It was James Craig who choreographed Carson's political actions between 1912 and 1914 and succeeded in turning the Dubliner into an instantly recognisable symbol of Ulster resolve.[15] Carson's image became detached from the reality of his life and so it was free to serve the interests of different strands of unionism long after his death.

While he lived, Pearse did his own packaging. In his writing he placed himself in the company of Irish political martyrs and outlined how his sacrifice should be understood. Pearse choreographed his own role and followed his own script. What he could not have anticipated was just how successful this would be. After his death Pearse's image was a commodity to be reproduced on coins, stamps, posters and banners as he became the iconic representation of the revolutionary period. The technology of the early twentieth century was also used in his promotion. Photography was available but the images

9.2 Mrs
Margaret Pearse
lying in state.
City Hall, 1932.
Courtesy Pearse
Museum.

were not abundant. One photograph of Pearse taken *circa* 1912 has become his enduring image; shorthand, not for his life but for the idealised Republic he proclaimed under the portico of the GPO on 24 April 1916. Flags, songs and graves have been used to mark Republican memory but Pearse, in many ways, became its embodiment. Those who appealed to his image indicated that they were working for the Republic for which he had died.

Icons, in their strictest sense, are representations of the divine. In the figure of Pearse, the human and the divine for long appeared to be in confluence. This was, in part, of his own making. Fr Francis Shaw's seminal essay on the canon of Irish history published in 1972 (though written in 1966) was vociferous in its criticism of the way in which Pearse 'consistently and deliberately and without reservation … equate[d] the patriot and the patriot-people with Christ', which, Shaw argued, was in conflict with the whole Christian tradition.[16] The messianic message of Pearse's writing is laid out in his discussions of the 'New Testament' of Irish history in which the Four Gospels are written by Tone, Davis, Lalor and Mitchel. His writings are littered with references which juxtapose Christ and hero: 'a Man cannot save his people unless his people have some manhood. A Man, even if he be a Man-God, will live and die in vain for all who are voluntary slaves. Christ cannot save you if you want to be damned: much less can any earthly hero'.[17] Pearse's own death mimicked that of Emmet, whom he said had died 'that his people might live, even as Christ died'.[18]

Pearse's religiosity was underlined by the fact that he was believed to have spent his last hours in communion with the Virgin Mary and a representation of this scene appeared in advanced Nationalist propaganda posters in the year of his death.[19] He had also spent some of his final days writing to his own mother, Margaret. While in the Arbour Hill Detention Barracks he composed a poem in response to her request that he write something that would give her words to describe her son. In 'A Mother Speaks', Pearse's sacrifice is compared to that of Christ and his mother's with the Mother of God, and includes the entreaty, 'Dear Mary, I have shared thy sorrow/And soon shall share thy joy'.[20] He also wrote reassuring her, 'People will say hard things of us now, but we shall be remembered by posterity and blessed by unborn generations. You too will be blessed because you were my mother.'[21] Mrs Pearse in turn became entwined in the popular imagination with the mother of the nation; as an Irish incarnation of the Mother of God. On her death the *Irish Press* wrote:

> Ireland is bereaved by the death of Mrs Pearse; she was a national figure, honoured and loved. Wherever she appeared men felt the near presence of the inviolate tradition of nationhood. Party

divisions dropped away. She was the mother of Ireland's purest martyr since Emmet. She represented nationhood itself; for it was from her that Padraic and Willie drew their heroic inspiration.[22]

Of course party divisions did not drop away. Mrs Pearse had opposed the Treaty and become a founding member of Fianna Fáil. Nevertheless, the Pearses were looked to as a holy family by some in Ireland. When opening the Pearse Museum in 1979 the President, Patrick Hillery, noted that it was not often that a museum was dedicated to the memory of a family: 'But then the Pearses were no ordinary family. They stand enshrined in Irish history, remembered and revered.'[23] This depiction of Pearse as a devoted and religious son perfectly suited him to being the iconic representation of the Catholic Irish state and his life was used as a moral exemplar as effectively as his death was used to underpin a political tradition.

For some the role of the Christ-like Pearse had been clearly laid out at a young age, but clarity was not universal. Eamonn McCann remembered in *War and an Irish Town*, 'One learned quite literally at one's mother's knee that Christ died for the human race, and Patrick Pearse for the Irish section of it'.[24] However John A. Murphy wrote in the *Irish Times* in 1979 that, when asked to write about Pearse for five minutes, some of his students wrote that he was a priest who helped the IRA against the English, others (with some irony) got him confused with Daniel O'Connell and one described him (presumably because he had a turn in his eye) like Padre Pio with stigmata.[25]

## PEARSE AS MYTH

There was general opposition to icons in the early Christian Church because their popularity depended, to a large degree, on the belief in their miraculous powers. However, an early defender of icons declared that in venerating an icon, one worships the prototype represented there rather than the icon itself.[26] It is certainly true that Pearse came to be seen as an 'original' or 'archetypal' Republican, but it is much more problematic to determine exactly what prototype the icon of Pearse represents.

Pearse had drawn very little difference between the human, the divine and the mythical in depictions of himself, Cúchulainn and Christ. In his after-life it is the mythical Pearse which has been the most powerful. A myth is a story through which ideas are conveyed; it is transhuman and transcends time. Myth is not the same as fiction; indeed myth is seen to carry a truth much more powerful than fact.[27] The mythical Pearse was used to convey a story which was greater than his individual life. Therefore, who Pearse was and what he came to represent were not the same thing. Pearse's sacrifice could easily be translated into epic grandeur using the cultural markers of Celtic mythology and Christian tradition. He became a figure who embodied the nation and its culture: a figure who had died in order that these things might live.

Easter 1916 carried its own myths and Pearse, as the central figure of the Rising, was also associated with what that event had come to represent. The Proclamation of the Republic operated as an organising document which gave meaning, cohesion and intention to the chaos of Easter week. At the opening of the National Museum Exhibition in 1966, Patrick Hillery described the Proclamation as symbolising 'the central moment of the whole'.[28] It provided co-ordinates for the future reading of the event. Therefore, the Rising came to encapsulate the idea that the Irish nation had been continuously struggling against a giant oppressor for hundreds of years. It appeared to confirm that Ireland was a nation with inalienable rights and underlined the poetic destiny of that nation. The Proclamation drew legitimacy from this version of the past and also marked a break with it. It came to be seen as a Declaration of Independence and therefore was the central event in the origin myth of the mythical Republic which was much easier to commemorate than the birth of the real state.

As the idealised Republic was continuously deferred, Pearse simultaneously represented the lost glory of the past and the anticipated

9.3 Senator Margaret Pearse and Eamon de Valera at a commemorative event. Courtesy Pearse Museum.

glory of the future. Marc Bloch has written of this process of reorganising the past to suit present needs: 'Through the very fact of their respect for the past, people came to reconstruct it as they considered it ought to have been.'[29] The same may be said of Pearse. He was constructed in such a way that he might carry the myth of the Republic: that he might continue to convey its meaning. This goes some way to explaining why Ruth Dudley Edwards's biography of 1977 caused such a stir.[30] The book was not an assault on Pearse but it was read as such. On one level apart from Connolly, no other rebel leader had been subjected to such a full-scale re-evaluation and none had been evaluated so personally.[31] Edwards's book was also interpreted as part of a larger Revisionist project which was seen as anti-nationalist. However, part of the reaction to Edwards's biography was due to the fact that Pearse had come to symbolise something much larger than himself: for many people in Ireland he represented both moral and political integrity. Therefore, in arguing that Pearse had become involved in the Easter Rising because of the social, sexual and financial failures in his personal life, Edwards was, in effect, saying that the myths Ireland lived by were socially, sexually and financially flawed and this, unsurprisingly, hit a very raw nerve in Ireland of the 1970s. The mind of Pearse became an area of historical study[32] and many in the population responded as if it was the national psyche which was being raided.

## REMEMBERING PEARSE

There are few statues to the memory of Pearse in Ireland; yet, he is located in multiple places. His homes in Dublin and Galway and the school he ran in Rathfarnham have been preserved. Great Brunswick Street, the location of James Pearse's business and of the family home, was renamed Pearse Street in 1920 (though the change was not implemented until 1924).[33] A bust of Pearse was installed in Leinster House in 1937 and a plaque to Patrick and Willie Pearse was unveiled at their former home in 1952. Ideas of locating other memorials to Pearse in Dublin were floated but did not materialise. The Department of the Taoiseach raised the possibility of a memorial to Patrick and William on the site of the Crampton Memorial on Pearse Street in Dublin in the 1960s, but nothing came of the suggestion.[34] In the periodic calls for Nelson to be removed from his Pillar in O'Connell Street, Pearse's name was regularly mentioned. A correspondent to the *Sunday Press* suggested that 'Pearse's Pillar' would be 'most fitting and we could then proudly tell foreign visitors that there is a statue of one of the men that faced the might of an empire and struck a blow for Ireland's freedom'.[35] As Minister of Finance in

1964, Jim Ryan also expressed an interest in replacing Nelson with Pearse at the top of the Pillar,[36] however, any pursuit of this plan was scuppered by the blowing up of the Pillar in March 1966.[37] Pearse has been memorialised, instead, in the naming of streets, railway stations, GAA clubs, sports stadiums and in the names of community organisations in Ireland and beyond. He is commemorated in scholarships and prizes by Irish-language groups and educationalists. On the one hundredth anniversary of his birth £50,000 was set aside by the Department of Education to cover the expenditure of scholarships and publications.[38] Pearse may not have been often set in bronze or stone, but he has become ubiquitous on the Irish landscape.

Pearse is also remembered whenever the Easter Rising is commemorated. Despite the inconsistencies in scale in remembering the Rising throughout the twentieth century, commemorative events tended to conform to the more general pattern of Irish Republican ceremonies of mass, parades, speeches and the gathering of people at the graves of the dead. Added to this, events involving the memory of the Rising also had as their focus the reading of the Proclamation. This last act invoked the memory of Pearse, not just because he had been the main author of the document, but also because he was the person who read it aloud in public.

The act into which so much was subsequently invested had inauspicious origins. One witness recalled:

> There was very little noise in the street – practically silent. The crowd numbered about 200 and I'm sure that many of them didn't recognise the significance of what Pearse was saying. His voice didn't carry too well and it was difficult to hear him.
>
> He had the document of the Proclamation in his hand, standing between the columns of the G. P. O., in the middle, on what I judged to be a chair.
>
> But there was no reaction … when he had finished the crowd melted.[39]

The reading of the Proclamation may have been somewhat flat but the utterance itself was performative. This is a mode expression which brings into being a new state or reality (for example, 'I now pronounce you husband and wife'.[40]) The power of the statement comes from the investment in its authority; it operates as a 'consensual fiction'. The survival of this authority requires that it be asserted repeatedly.[41] The Republic did not automatically come into being just because Pearse declared it so. However, in retrospect, it came to be believed that once the Republic had been proclaimed nothing less could be acceptable. The commemorative reading of the Proclamation confirms this status. Pearse's actions were re-enacted every time the

Proclamation was read. Moreover, for some, the repeated reading serves to suggest that the Republic of Ireland is that which Pearse proclaimed (thus commemorations of Easter 1916 are understood more and more as a form of Independence Day). For those who reject this, the reading of the Proclamation nevertheless confirms that the Republic exists elsewhere and somewhere (in the future). Therefore, even among those who disagree over the politics of subsequent events, Pearse's reading of the Proclamation is seen as a critical moment in the inauguration of a Republic.

The Proclamation, like the Solemn League and Covenant (signed in 1912 by unionists demonstrating their opposition to Home Rule) would become in itself an important material symbol of identity. A replica of the Covenant was given to everyone who signed it and many had it framed and hung on their wall. In a similar way, one thousand copies of the Proclamation were printed in Liberty Hall by men who had been helping in the work of printing the *Workers' Republic*. As they did not have sufficient type to set the entire document, the Proclamation was set and printed in two parts.[42] Copies were pasted to pillars, walls and shop fronts around the centre of Dublin and Seán T. Ó Ceallaigh also posted three copies to his fiancé, his mother and the Secretary of the Archbishop of Dublin, for safe keeping. Only the one sent to his mother arrived and few versions of this first print run have survived.[43] However, copies of the Proclamation have subsequently been mass-produced and disseminated and it too has been hung on the walls of many Irish homes.

Cultural nationalism deploys its ideas through commodified symbols which are readable and replicable; through what some might call kitsch.[44] This is often seen as a worthless form of mechanised art that clutters homes, has no aesthetic value and trades in cheap sentiments. It may be said of the mass production of images of Pearse and the Proclamation that, that which was once revolutionary had been turned into kitsch and literally domesticated.[45] Richard Temple has explained the importance of the symbolic depth of icons:

> The pictorial language of icons is primarily symbolic. Literal and narrative values are secondary. An icon is a mystical commentary that goes beyond the face value of the historical event. If this is lost, if the image becomes merely narrative or sentimental and decorative, it is no longer an icon, since it is no longer an image of the divine expressed in the physical world.[46]

In a similar way, once images of Pearse and the Proclamation ceased to have a transformative effect – once they became merely narrative or sentimental – then they became empty icons. However, when at odds with the dominant culture, kitsch can also represent a stylised articulation of resistance in the domestic sphere. And, as David Lloyd has argued, the meaning and memory concealed within the imagery can be redeployed; indeed can experience sudden mobility.[47]

This was the case in Northern Ireland where Catholic and nationalist imagery was used to express and reinforce a separate identity within the state. These images were cultural manifestations of a political relationship and the politicisation of the cultural. Therefore within the context of the conflict, Pearse and the Proclamation were not meaningless, sentimental or nostalgic (even if some felt they fed a delusion). They were instead examples of the way in which myths operate out of time and can be adapted for new political circumstances. Pearse had come to represent both the ideological aspiration of the Republic and the figure of Christ-like sacrifice which galvanised earthly suffering with Irish unity as the promised after-life. The hunger strikers of the early 1980s drew on the traditions of both Christianity and Irish Republicanism in framing their campaign for political status within prisons. The nationalist population understood these references and the pages of death notices in the *Irish News* for Bobby Sands in May 1981 quoted, among others, the words of Pearse over the grave of O'Donovan Rossa and the biblically influenced 'No greater love can a man have than to lay his life down for his country'.[48]

9.4 Mrs Margaret Pearse in New York 1924. Courtesy Pearse Museum.

The personal sacrifices and brutal acts of northern Republicans were made sense of with reference to a much larger struggle. The historical and 'timeless' message of Pearse was used to interpret local and private suffering. The most intimate bodily humiliations were given historical rationalisation but were nevertheless rooted in the dark reality of a particular time and place. One participant in the 'no wash' campaign in the Maze prison (which at one point led to prisoners wiping their faeces on their cell walls) remembered:

> But when it came to it, I saw putting shit on the wall as an aspect of the struggle I was part of. At the time words and ideas

about pride, dignity and principles were a large part of the
vocabulary and thinking. I believe we were influenced by the
images of past Republican heroes but as our struggle was going
on in different circumstances, we had to use what methods we
had. Putting shit on the walls was one such method and we had
to come to terms with it in that light.[49]

Pearse and other secular martyrs were reached towards as a way of
comprehending and explaining a world in which individuals were literally surrounded in 'shit'. Yet it was also understood that the example of Easter 1916 was not static and could be utilised in different
ways in different circumstances. In order to be of continued significance, Pearse had to be adapted and adaptable.

Pearse became someone who was remembered in deeds – the
reading of the Proclamation and paramilitary violence – as well as in
the rhetorical rhythm of the southern state. He was a figure who was
used to stabilize and destabilize Irish politics: his myth, studiously
promoted, could not be controlled easily.

### FORGETTING PEARSE

The redeployment of Pearse as a symbol of military resolve and
Republican sacrifice in Northern Ireland complicated his memory.
However, a re-evaluation of Pearse had been taking place before the
breakdown of civil order in the north. The esteem in which Pearse
had been held in the Irish mind had been elevated to the point of
unsustainability. John Coakley wrote of him that 'the extravagances
of his disciples' claims regarding his greatness virtually guaranteed
that, sooner or later, Pearse would be brought crashing from the
pedestal on which he had been placed'.[50]

In fact, the removal of Pearse from his pedestal was gradual at
first. The release of archives and private papers in the 1960s allowed
professional historians to cast a more informed critical eye over the
events of Easter 1916, and that decade saw the moving away from
hagiographical treatments of Pearse and a reassessment of the cen-
trality of his role in the Rising.[51] The fiftieth anniversary of Easter
1916 saw the publication of a mixture of historical work, some of
which reinforced a traditional view of the Rising, while others also
offered new appraisals.[52] Moreover, although Pearse was used to promote the jubilee,[53] he was not an unproblematic figure in 1966. The
*Kilkenny People*, in discussing the difficulty of getting people to come
to a meeting to discuss plans for the commemoration noted:

  It is easy to understand, of course, the reluctance of many nationally minded people to attend a meeting which might possibly

have consisted of a series of long, boring, hypocritical speeches. People regard with considerable suspicion the high-blown utterances of many public men, and everyone is aware of the futility of talking about 'what Pearse would have thought if he was alive to-day'.[54]

Pearse was unassailable as the logo of the commemoration but he had become something of an abstract. The national project had changed in the Republic in the 1960s. The emphasis was on industrial development and the modernisation of the economy. Even the Christian Brothers (who tirelessly promoted Pearse) explained to their young readers in their publication, *Our Boys*: 'No! Love of county is not just emotion, not merely extravagant speeches; it is a common sense, down-to-earth, unselfish and willing work for the good of the Nation. Our ancestors shed their blood for Ireland; let us take off our coats and shed our sweat for her.'[55] As Taoiseach, Seán Lemass was keen to emphasise the value of practical patriotism. Regarding the commemoration, Lemass simultaneously invoked and moved beyond Pearse. He wrote: '"If our deed", said Pearse, "has not been sufficient to win freedom then our children will win it by a better deed". The deeds that are required of Irishmen today are of a different kind dictated by a different phase of history'.[56] The difficulty was in re-reading Pearse to accommodate this different phase. He continued, of course, as the most reassuring image the state could produce. But he had also become implicated in the 'long boring speeches' of public men and, for many, it was Pearse's co-insurrectionist who provided a more comprehensive and challenging blueprint.

James Connolly emerged as the most clearly realised figure of the jubilee. His life and political writings resonated in the difficult economic circumstances and strike action of the mid-1960s. It was in this context that Bernadine Truden, who chronicled the 1966 commemoration for the *Boston Globe*, noted that, at Tomás MacAnna's pageant in Croke Park, 'the greatest cheers came, not for any of the marching men, but for the strikers of 1913, when they burst onto the field with their placards. And the loudest boos were not for the red-coats, with their muskets and their cannons, but for the baton charge by the police that helped to break the strike!'[57] Connolly appeared as the more radical figure fifty years after the Rising. From 1938 his name had been given to a club in Britain which aimed to work for complete Irish independence and to promote Connolly's work. This grew to become the Connolly Association and, in 1966, the government had been keen to avoid their appropriation of the Easter Rising commemoration in Britain. A committee had been formed in London with 'the discreet but active assistance'[58] of the Irish Embassy and, despite a lack of enthusiasm about a parade to Trafalgar Square, it was felt that a meeting should be held there 'since not to do so would be to surrender the tradition of such meetings to organisations such as Clann na hEireann or the Connolly Association'.[59] In Ireland, the IRA had been taking a significant move to the Left in the 1960s and Connolly was the obvious bridge between nationalism and socialism. It was indeed this combination which had made Connolly a less likely icon of the Irish revolution than Pearse. However, it also meant that Connolly was not so implicated in the failures of the independent state. None of this is to say that Pearse had become unimportant but he was, to some extent, the victim of his own myth's success.

Pearse had become the other-worldly icon of the revolution: revered but not read. However, by the 1970s his image was shaken by the conflict in Northern Ireland and, J.J. Lee suggested, he was in danger of falling victim to mindless condemnation having been long the victim of mindless adulation.[60] Ruth Dudley Edwards's biography was the first significant academic assessment of Pearse's life and charted a course between these extremes. She wrote later that, although the book's reception was generally positive, quite a few people took serious exception to her view that the Provisional IRA were the true heirs of Pearse and to her assertion that Pearse was turned on exclusively by young male beauty.[61] Both were difficult ideas for some to digest about the First President of the Republic. The Provisionals were a proscribed organisation and homosexual sex was not decriminalised in the Republic of Ireland until 1993. Pearse had been understood as a priestly figure and Edwards's conviction that he had sublimated his sexual desires in his work did not dispel the sense of unease surrounding the supposition. Towards the end of the twentieth century, Ireland became more tolerant of homosexuality but the sexuality of priests was no longer assumed to be innocent. Therefore the personal life of Pearse, out of context, became a less secure touchstone of the Republic.

In the final decades of the twentieth century Pearse's public actions and private thoughts appeared to have problematic implications for his myth. Moreover, the economic difficulties of the 1980s created disenchantment in and with the Republic. Fintan O'Toole wrote that 1916 had inured the country to failure, 'befuddled us so that we don't know the difference between an inept tragedy of errors and a solid achievement'. He argued that a shrine to the divine Pearse was one that had been prayed at for too long: 'If Pearse is Christ, give us Barabbas.'[62] The government hardly knew what to do by the 75th anniversary of the Rising in 1991 and so did very little. Not everyone was happy with this official reticence and an independent commemoration committee sought to 'Reclaim the spirit of Easter 1916'. It asserted that the 'ideals of the Rising are an embarrassment to those in control of wealth and power in our country today. Social equality and national freedom are regarded as subversive concepts. To speak of 1916 is seen as a challenge to the whole set-up of this state'.[63]

The mythical Republic inaugurated by Pearse had always represented a challenge to the actual Republic fashioned by those who had lived on. The southern state had attempted to knit Pearse and the Rising into its fabric. However Pearse had not lived long enough to become again a constitutionalist and the radicalism of his ideas continued to be available to those who attempted to subvert the messages of the state. By the twenty-first century, however, Pearse has been reinstated as a centrepiece of official commemoration. Hanging in the office of the former Taoiseach, Pearse's portrait represented Bertie Ahern's apparently simple faith in Irish history. Ireland is now a country of political and cultural consumers. Irishness and independence are devalued currencies in a globalised economy, though images of Pearse allow people to think otherwise. Pearse can therefore be employed safely because what he represents has so little meaning in contemporary Ireland. He is a marker of what once was, not what might be.

CONCLUSION

Patrick Pearse was a figure who was at times impossible to criticise and, at others, very difficult to praise. An idea of him resonated vividly for the Irish population and yet the reality of his life was often obscure. Indeed, Pearse's enduring visual image – a profile – denies natural asymmetries and suggests a one-dimensional figure. However, for much of the Irish population, the one certainty about Pearse was his sincerity regarding the final task he undertook, and he became an underwriter for the integrity of those who claimed to act in his name. The difficulty, however, lay in the fact that many in Ireland held sincerely different views and so Pearse was called on as guarantor of more than one political position.

At the end of her biography Ruth Dudley Edwards suggested that Pearse had two major failings: that he was disappointed in the response of his countrymen to the vision he put before them and that he never questioned his own judgement; that he wrote, acted and died for people who did not exist.[64] However Pearse's flaws in life were the key to his immortality in after-life. In writing, acting and dying as he did, he willed the people of his imagination into existence. Those who invoked Pearse after he died became proof that he had died for people who did exist (in the future). That the death of Pearse and his fellow rebels in 1916 somehow helped to bring about a new reality was the thing that made the Pearse myth so compelling in Ireland; and also what made it so threatening to those who wanted to stabilise that new reality.

Patrick Pearse was not a one-dimensional figure. He was a complex mixture of Irish and English, modern and old-fashioned, assertive and self-conscious, public and private. The myth he became could barely accommodate these contradictions and indeed was strained under the recognition that he was human. On the ninetieth anniversary of the Easter Rising there were calls from across the political spectrum to return to the words of the Proclamation and to see it as a template for a free and inclusive Ireland.[65] Mary McAleese, as President of Ireland, concluded her remarks at the opening of a conference on the Rising, held in Cork, 'Yet their deaths rise far above the clamour – their voices, insistent still' before entreating the audience to enjoy the conference 'and the rows it will surely rise'.[66] The insistent voice of Pearse is that found in his own writings. When myths fall away the human being is the reward.

Language, Literature and Education
Teanga, Litríocht agus Oideachas

CHAPTER TEN

# The Imagined Community of Pearse's Short Stories

## ANGELA BOURKE

Between 1905 and 1915, Patrick Pearse published ten literary short stories in Irish, which have featured on school and university curricula ever since, despite being dismissed repeatedly by critics as naïve, sentimental or one-dimensional. Most of them appeared first in the the Gaelic League's bilingual weekly newspaper *An Claidheamh Soluis agus Fáinne an Lae*; all are set in Irish-speaking Conamara, in a place called Ros na gCaorach, and all but one ('An Mháthair') feature child protagonists or narrators. Most of the women characters are widows, and there are few adult males.[1] Philip O'Leary has surveyed the critical responses to these stories and has offered the most discerning reading of them to date, as insights into the shaping of Pearse's mind, noting that 'Successful or not, his creation of an idealized Irish-speaking West was a fully conscious aesthetic strategy'.[2] While perceiving Pearse's project as deliberately Utopian, however, O'Leary ends by reading the stories as 'the quiet acts of faith of a man who would make himself a political messiah'.[3]

This chapter will argue that Pearse's ten stories were less 'quiet acts of faith' than a sustained and deliberate use of the print medium to create what Benedict Anderson has famously termed an 'imagined community': a sense of common culture, heritage and destiny, fostered among people who might never meet face to face. For Anderson, a newspaper in the age of nation-building could create an image of the world in the private spaces of a reader's mind, just as fiction does. The very ephemerality of newspapers meant that the sense of strangers all reading the same edition at the same time offered continual reassurance to readers 'that the imagined world is visibly rooted in everyday life'. This, Anderson suggests, led to 'that remarkable confidence of community and anonymity which is the hallmark of modern nations'.[4] I shall attempt to show that Pearse's Utopian imagining had very precise aims, grounded equally in his

enlightened, holistic approach to education and in his experience as
a working journalist, alert at all times to the requirements and possibilities of print in the building of national identity.

As editor of *An Claidheamh Soluis* for six years from 1903, and as
a contributor thereafter, Pearse used its fiction pages to inspire and
motivate both the marginally literate Irish speakers of the impoverished western seaboard and the young town- and city-dwellers who
were learning Irish in classes run by the Gaelic League, to imagine
and create a new 'Irish Ireland'.  Whatever their mystic appeal, his
stories are clearly designed at a practical level to counteract the
images of deficiency, destitution and violence that dominated
accounts of the 'congested districts' of the western seaboard at the
turn of the twentieth century.  Gaeltacht areas suffered from real
problems of poverty, disease – especially tuberculosis – and emigration, but negative stereotypes hampered their economic development, discouraged tourists and made the flight of young people away
from them – often to conditions equally, if not more, impoverished
– seem inevitable.  Pearse's stories, by contrast, show a sturdy and
courteous Irish-speaking people, poor in material goods but rich in
social and intellectual capital.  Inhabiting a sunlit landscape where
they can be self-sufficient in practical, spiritual and intellectual matters, the community he depicts is bound by strong internal ties but
maintains cautious connections with an Irish-identified metropolis,
welcomes sensitive visitors and has much to teach them.  Pearse's stories invited his readers, and those who heard his stories read aloud,
to aspire to an organic way of life that would combine twentieth-century standards of literacy and hygiene with the oral modes and practical skills of traditional education.  As illustrations of his educational theory, set out in *The Murder Machine* and elsewhere, they offered
a vision of vernacular education and its relation to literacy that bears
comparison with the child-centred models of his contemporaries
Maria Montessori and Rudolf Steiner.

Pearse's first four stories were published under a pen-name in *An
Claidheamh Soluis* in 1905 and 1906, and collected in 1907 as
*Íosagán agus Sgéalta Eile*. Two more stories appeared in *An
Claidheamh Soluis* the same year, but the last four were completed
much more slowly, while he was occupied with the running of his
school for boys and with the increasingly militarism of the nationalist movement.  Months before the Rising and Pearse's execution by
firing squad, the Dundalgan Press had brought out six stories as *An
Mháthair agus Sgéalta Eile*.  It had taken some time to find a publisher, for by then, as he wrote to W.P. Ryan on 18 March 1915, 'Gaels
[were] putting their money into guns'.[5]  Three of the stories in this
second collection were new, while a fourth was his 1907 story

'Brighid na Gaoithe', reworked and expanded as 'An Bhean Chaointe'.

Barely a year after Pearse's death, his mother and sister's campaign to ensure both his status as a Gaelic martyr and his primacy among the dead heroes paid off in the publication of the *Collected Works of Padraic H. Pearse: Plays, Stories, Poems.*[6] Translations of the stories into a kind of Kiltartanese accounted for over half the contents of the volume, which would find its way into many thousands of homes and would remain on their (often uncrowded) shelves for generations.   Unlike the English versions of the plays and poems, which were Pearse's own, the new translations of the stories were by Joseph Campbell.[7] That they were translations, however, and the work of a hand other than Pearse's own, would have been clear only to those readers sophisticated or dedicated enough to read the Publisher's Note through to the end.   Through these English versions, as well as through the reading of the originals in schools, Eoghainín na nÉan, Íosagán and Sean-Mhaitias, and the mysterious figure of the Deargadaol, became as familiar to Irish people in the twentieth century as Charles Dickens's Little Nell and Oliver Twist.   And as the emerging Irish nation constructed its new identity, the stories' position, midway between the two official languages, joined with their author's status as martyr to complicate their reception and interpretation and give them something of the status of sacred texts prescribed for children while piously ignored by adults.   To appreciate their force at the time of their writing and first publication, therefore, it will be necessary to reach behind that mythologising.

10.1 Mrs Pearse by Seán O'Sullivan 1931. Courtesy Pearse Museum.

The fictional Ros na gCaorach ('Sheep Headland'), where Pearse's stories are set, is closely modelled on Ros Muc ('Pig Headland'), some 40 km west of Galway city, an area of outstanding natural beauty and equally noticeable poverty at the beginning of the twentieth century.   When Pearse first came there, aged 23, in April 1903, he had already been a sort of tourist in the Aran islands, and on Gaelic League expeditions to the Irish-speaking districts west of Galway city, but he immediately gained an individual, privileged access to the heart of this Irish-speaking community and met young people who shared his dreams, for he came to Ros Muc alone, as an examiner for the Gaelic League. The local schoolmaster, 35-year-old Pádraig Ó Conghaile (Patrick Connolly), had begun to teach adults to read and write their own language and had introduced *An Claidheamh Soluis* as reading material. The paper often advertised work for teachers of Irish – far better paid than casual labouring – and Colm Ó Gaora, born in Ros Muc in 1887, relates in his autobiography, *Mise*, how twelve young men, himself included, subscribed two-and-sixpence each to pay the expenses of an examiner, in order to gain the necessary Gaelic League certification.[8] Ros Muc was 'out of the tourist track',[9] and the weather was fine, so Pearse saw the place at its best. He stayed two nights longer than planned, before taking a horse-drawn car to Galway to catch the Dublin train. The following June he was back, in time for the traditional St John's Eve bonfires.[10]

In the first decade of the twentieth century Conamara had a seriously bad press. The terrain was difficult, with dozens of small islands, a coast broken by numerous sea inlets, and land that alternated between bog, bare rock and lakes, producing food only when carefully cultivated by hand, and then in meagre quantities. A prosperous shopkeeper class controlled access to markets and ensured that the poor remained poor and available to work for little money. The population had been swelled by economic migrants from farther inland, when failure of the potato crop twenty years earlier caused widespread destitution, and the fury of the Land War that followed in 1879-82 took the authorities by surprise. In January 1880, when members of the RIC attempted to carry out evictions in Carraroe, across a narrow stretch of water from Ros Muc, a reported 3,000 angry tenants kept several of them besieged in a house from Friday to Monday. Faction-fighting was still a recognised way of settling scores, and a significant proportion of the population spoke no English.

Several commentators travelled through Conamara in the last years of the nineteenth century and the early years of the twentieth, writing reports and recommending policy to government for the alleviation of distress and the avoidance of unrest. Among them was the Jesuit priest Thomas Finlay, UCD Professor of Economics and editor of the *New Ireland Review*, who visited Carna on behalf of the Manchester Relief Committee. His important essay about economic conditions there was published in April 1898, just as the Spanish-American war drove food prices even higher and brought severe hardship to those already struggling to survive.[11] It was followed two months later by an essay on Garomna by the secretary of the same committee.[12] Charles R. Browne MD conducted ethnographic surveys in Garomna and Leitir Meallán, and later in Carna and

Maighinis ('Mweenish'), for the Anthropometric Laboratories of Trinity College, Dublin, and published his findings in 1902, with many statistics and a number of photographs, as part of a ten-year series in the *Proceedings of the Royal Irish Academy*.

Of Garomna Island, south of Ros Muc, the Secretary of the Manchester Relief Committee wrote in 1898:

> Approaching the island from the direction of Carraroe boatslip, the visitor is struck with the appalling desolation of the scene. From the water's edge, across the whole island, the space seems occupied by bare rocks, those on the shore being washed white by the action of the sea. The peaty soil, if ever deposited, has long since been washed away from the greater part of the surface. A perfect maze of granite walls, bounding the holdings and their innumerable subdivisions, hides out all view of vegetation or of land. There are no trees or shrubs on Gorumna, and were it not for the almost numberless cabins that dot the face of the island, one could hardly believe the place inhabited, it appears so utterly uninhabitable.
>
> ... The average dwelling consists of one room only, and here the entire family and live stock are housed. [194–5]

Dr Browne described living conditions in Carna, 20 km farther west:

> As a rule the dwellings are primitive ... Whenever possible they are built on a flat of bare rock to afford a sound dry floor; if this is not available the floor is flagged, and there is a paved causeway around them. The older houses consist simply of one room and are built of dry stone and plastered inside. In some cases the wall is only raised to a certain height all round, the gables being built of turf; they have no chimney, the hearth being built against the gable wall and the smoke escaping through a hole in the roof, through which the ridge pole passes. Glazed windows are often absent, their place being taken by a hole in the wall closed by wooden shutters.

And later:

> As might be expected under such circumstances, domestic cleanliness and comfort are not at a very high level, and the sanitary condition of the houses leaves much to be desired ...[13]

Another account tells of big pigs lying stretched in front of the fire in one house, like tired dogs after a day's work.

The 1901 census supplies details of houses and households for all of these areas, including Ros Muc. Almost all the houses were built of local stone and thatched with sedge from nearby lake shores;

almost all were third-class houses, with one, two or three rooms. It goes without saying that almost none had indoor plumbing.

Colm Ó Gaora gives an account of the place and the time:

> Chuala mé ag mo mháthair mhóir nach raibh ach teach a hathar agus trí theach eile sa bpobal a raibh doirse adhmaid ortha nuair a bhí sí ina cailín óg. Corr-theach a rabh air ach aon doras amháin san am sin. Ghnídhidís mapaí tuighe agus chuiridís sa doras san oidhche iad. D'fheilidís in áit comhlaidh iad. Is beag teach a rabh simléar ó thalamh ann le n-a linn.

> I heard my grandmother say that when she was a young girl, only her father's house and three others in the parish had wooden doors. Very few houses had more than one door. They used to make mats out of straw and stuff them into the doorways at night. They served instead of doors. Hardly any house had a chimney built from the ground up in her time.[14]

He remembers the thatched houses:

> Ní rabh ach trí theach ceann slinne sa leath-phobal seo le mo chuimhne-se. A mhalrait de scéal atá anois ann. Dá seastá ar an gcnocán is áirde sa bparráiste agus breathnughadh thart ar na tighthe beaga ceann cíbe seo, bhéarfá an leabhar do mba dúradáin iad a shíolruigh nó a d'fhás aníos an an gcíb a bhí mór-thimcheall ortha.

> There were only three slate-roofed houses in this half-parish in my day. It's very different now. If you stood on the highest little hill in the parish and looked around at these small houses, all thatched with sedge, you'd swear they were little specks that had bred there, or grown up out of the sedge around them.[15]

The Irish-speaking people of Conamara were widely admired as splendid physical types, but they bore the serious stigma of a place notorious for poverty, danger and dirt, and stigma, as Erving Goffman writes, reduces life chances.[16] But Pearse was a press man, and in story after story from 1905 he set about replacing that stigmatised and stigmatising image with an idea of community designed to revitalise and invigorate the Irish-speaking west, encouraging like-minded tourists to visit and helping to stem emigration while kindling the imagination of the metropolis. The opening passage of his story 'Na Bóithre' gives a sense of how he saw his newspaper working to connect the revival movement in towns and cities with the Gaeltacht:

Ní raibh d'ainm ná de shloinne againn ar an bhfear céanna ach fear Bhaile Átha Cliath. Is é a deireadh Peaitín Pháraic linn gur fear scríofa páipéir nuaíochta é. Léadh Peaitín an páipéar Gaeilge a thagadh go dtí an mháistreás gach seachtain, agus is beag ní nach raibh ar eolas aige, mar bhíodh cur síos ar an bpáipéar sin ar imeachtaí an Domhain Thiar agus ar imeachtaí an Domhain Thoir, agus ní bhíodh teora leis an méid feasa a bhíodh ag Peaitín le tabhairt dúinn gach Domhnach ag geata an tséipéil.

The only name or surname we had for that man was the man from Dublin. Peaitín Pháraic used to tell us he was a newspaper writer. Peaitín used to read the Irish-language paper that came to the schoolmistress every week, and there was little he didn't know, for that paper used to tell of the doings of the Western World and the Eastern World, and there was no limit to the knowledge Peaitín had for us every Sunday at the chapel gate.

The references to the Western World and the Eastern World are borrowed from the oral tradition of heroic storytelling and are capitalised in the text lest the point be missed. Before literacy became general, it was not uncommon for one person in a community to read a newspaper aloud to an audience of eager listeners.[17]

The Midland Great Western Railway opened its 'Balfour' line from Galway to Clifden on 1 July 1895, but in Pearse's first summer of 1903 it instituted a 'Tourist Express' train direct from Dublin to Clifden.[18] With coaches painted in a special blue-and-white livery, the Tourist Express included the rare luxury of a dining car. It left Dublin at 12.00 noon, arriving in Clifden at 5.00 p.m., so Pearse could eat lunch on the train, and, if it ran on time, get to Maam Cross by about 4.00 p.m., from where a 'post-car' would take him the 15 km south to Ros Muc. He visited the area every summer from then on, and encouraged others to do the same. By 1910 he had had a single-storey house in vernacular style built over-looking Loch Oiriúlach, where he often brought pupils from St Enda's to stay.

10.2 Patrick Pearse on a rocking horse. Courtesy Pearse Museum.

The first story Pearse published was 'An Sagart' ('The Priest'),[19] which appeared in *An Claidheamh Soluis* in February 1905, almost two years after he took up the editorship. The pen-name above which it appeared, 'Colm Ó Conaire', managed both to distance the story

from the hand of the Dublin-based editor and to suggest a provenance
in far-off Conamara. The plot derives from a time in Pearse's own
middle-class Dublin childhood when, at the age of 10 or so, he used
to dress up in his mother's long white nightdress and pretend to be a
priest, saying mass in the bedroom he shared with his brother Willie,
enlisting Willie to ring the bell and move the big book from side to
side of the altar, and his two sisters to form the congregation.[20] The
action sits awkwardly in the vernacular architecture of Conamara,
however, where the poorest houses had at most one bedroom separate from the living area, with very little furniture, and where the
catholic liturgy would have had little of the magnificence to be found
in the fashionable St Andrew's church in Dublin, where the Pearse
family worshipped.

The child Páraic in this story, whose mother is a widow, who eats
porridge for his dinner and who has no shoes, is definitely poor. He
lives with his mother, his little sister and his infant brother ('a
dheartháirín beag bídeach') in a small house you can see in the val-
ley below as you walk westwards from An Gort Mór to Inbhear: the
geography is real and clearly directed at potential visitors to
Conamara, who will quickly learn that this family is clean. As the
story opens, Páraic, now aged 8, stands naked in a tub of water, his
wet skin glowing in the firelight and his curly hair glistening, while
his mother scrubs and scours him all over, slapping him gently when
he squeals and then kissing him on his sweet little red mouth
('[b]éilín beag dearg … milis'). The narrator looks on as the boy's
mother tells him the story of her son's priestly escapades a year earlier. This remarkable image has caused some unease among late
twentieth-century commentators, but Pearse's 1905 readers, whether
in Dublin or in Conamara, may have found it more reassuring than
disturbing, with its subliminal reminder of the ubiquitous Pears soap
posters of the time. The Pears posters were highly influential in raising standards of personal hygiene, and many of them showed naked
children at bath time.

In the second story, 'Eoghainín na nÉan', the mother of the
doomed, mystical Eoghainín – another young widow, apparently –
deals with worry about her son by cleaning:

> Chuaigh sí isteach go buartha. Ghlan sí an bord is na
> cathaoireacha. Nigh sí na scálaí is na miasa. Rug sí ar an scuab
> agus scuab sí an t-urlár. Scól sí an túlán agus na corcáin.
> Dheasaigh sí an lampa agus chroch ar an mballa é. Chuir sí tuil-
> leadh móna ar an tine. Rinne sí céad rud eile nar ghá di a
> dhéanamh. Ansin shuigh sí os comhair na tine ag smaoineamh
> di féin.

She went indoors, troubled. She cleaned the table and the chairs. She washed the bowls and dishes. She took up the sweeping brush and swept the floor. She scalded the kettle and the cooking pots. She trimmed the lamp and hung it on the wall. She put more turf on the fire. She did a hundred other things that she didn't need to do. Then she sat down in front of the fire to think.[21]

And the theme recurs in later stories: in 'An Mháthair' the young woman who hopes to see the Virgin Mary on Christmas Eve sweeps the floor of her house and cleans the chairs before retiring for the night.[22] In 'An Gadaí', when the young boy confesses his sin to the priest, his penance is to scrub his little sister's doll's house weekly, until she is well enough to do it herself.[23] In the longest of the stories, 'An Bhean Chaointe', the old woman whose son has been dead for twenty years has just washed and dried his suit of homespun *báinín* tweed when the young narrator meets her.[24]

'An Sagart' introduces other themes that will recur. There is no father in Páraic's household: he died, we are told, before Taimín, the baby, was born, and although that, according to the story's internal chronology, cannot have been all that long ago, neither mother nor children seem troubled by grief, even when Páraic's behaviour gives cause for concern. Three of the four earliest stories feature priests instead, as benign, enabling figures in the children's lives and as trusted confidants of worried mothers. In 'Eoghainín na nÉan' the priest is unnamed, but using first names only for an tAthair Seán in 'Íosagán' and an tAthair Rónán in 'An Sagart' (he will appear again in

10.3 William Pearse and Patrick Pearse. Produced as a commemorative card after their deaths by Mrs Margaret Pearse. Courtesy Pearse Museum.

'Na Bóithre') suggests young men – curates, perhaps – who do not stand on their dignity. 'Rónán', as a name especially associated with the Irish-speaking Aran Islands, and not yet fashionable elsewhere, hints that this priest may even be (unusually in the real Ireland of the time) a native speaker of Irish.

Pearse may have been hoping to accomplish a number of things through his stories' odd demographic. By depicting families without adult males, he avoided the technical difficulty of describing aspects of the culture or using registers of the language, with which he himself was unfamiliar, but he also edited out the kind of characters whom *Punch* cartoons regularly caricatured as ape-like and who might have put his readers off visiting Conamara. *Punch* stereotyped adult west-of-Ireland males as the kind of men who had kept the police captive in Carraroe, but the families Pearse portrays belong securely in Victorian popular fiction: gentle young widows, poor but honest, with one, two or at most three children. This stands in strong contrast to the households documented in the 1901 census, with their eight, ten and more children, as well as miscellaneous in-laws, lodgers and 'servants', even in some very poor houses.

The children in Pearse's stories make their own amusement, with the help of traditional songs, stories, rhymes and riddles in Irish, many of which are quoted in the text (but he may not have known that 'Fromsó Framsó', which the children play in 'An Sagart', was originally a game played by adults at wakes).[25] Like Pearse himself, his young characters take a keen and informed interest in natural history. Eoghainín's observations of the swallows are exact and ornithologically accurate. In 'An Gadaí', Antaine Ó Mainnín gets into trouble when the boys on their way home from school decide to go and watch the schoolmaster's bees swarming; at the end of the story his shy gifts to the same master's gracious daughter are taken from nature: a half-dozen duck-eggs; a handful of bilberries; a bunch of edible seaweed.

Toys in these stories are especially interesting: in 'Bairbre' (1906), Gaelic Leaguers would have learned the damage they might do by sending expensive gifts to children in the Gaeltacht. Brídín, aged about 4, is inseparable from Bairbre, her half-blind, bald, home-made second-hand doll, until the postman (agent of the metropolis) arrives with a large parcel sent by a lady from Dublin who had visited the area to learn Irish. The kind of banter that ensues makes it clear that such parcels are rare indeed. The new doll is factory-made, beautifully dressed and very glamorous, with eyes that open and close. Brídín precociously names her Niamh Chinn Óir, after the fairy queen in the story she has heard from Stiofán na Scéalta, the local storyteller. The story in question, 'Oisín i dTír na nÓg', would probably have been better known to learners of Irish than to children in Conamara, through County Clare poet Mícheál Coimín's *Laoi Oisín ar Thír na nÓg*, 'Oisín's song about the Land of Youth' (1750), which had inspired W.B. Yeats's 'The Wanderings of Oisín' (1889), among other reworkings. It is worth noting that in that tale Niamh is the seductive creature who leads Oisín to turn his back on the life he had been leading, and on the values of his own people. Shortly after writing 'Bairbre', however, Pearse began to relent somewhat in the matter of toys. In November 1903 he had become godfather to Sighle Bairéad, daughter of Stiofán Bairéad, an active and committed Gaelic Leaguer. At Christmas 1906 he sent her a toy tea-set, which she still owned in 1980.[26] A year later, in early January, he wrote to her father:

> Seo bronntanas beag atá mé a chur chugat le tabhairt do Shighle. Fá Nodlaig badh cheart dom é chur chugaibh, acht níorbh' fhéidir liom é fhághail i n-am. I nGleannta Aontruim a rinneadh an teach agus an trosgán. Tá an trosgán ro-mhór le cur isteach sa teach go héasgaidh, acht ní féidir trosgán de dhéantús Gaedhealach fhághail níos lugha ...

> Enclosed is a small gift which I am sending for Sighle. It should have arrived for Christmas but I could not secure it in time. It was made in the Glens of Antrim, both the house and the furniture. The furniture may be a little big to place in the house, but it is not possible to get smaller furniture of Irish manufacture ...[27]

'An Gadaí' (1915) is about just such a doll's house as Pearse mentions here, and about a doll that Antoine steals to give to his sick little sister. The doll's house stands under a rosebush in the teacher's garden (ordinary people in these stories do not have gardens or rosebushes). It is made of wood, painted white below and red above; it has a little green door and a glass window downstairs, with two more windows above, and it has furniture: tables, chairs, beds, dishes and other things. The fiction is untroubled by problems of scale, and the doll that sits in the doorway will be big enough for the sick child to hold in her arms. Pearse discourages his readers from kowtowing to the gentry, but presents the middle-class standards represented by schoolteachers as admirable and desirable.

The children's capacity for enjoyment in these stories is closely allied to their intelligence and alertness – as in the case of the boys who observe the bees – and to the education they receive from their families in the skills and techniques of work. When young Cóilín is kept from school in 'An Bhean Chaointe', he will miss his lessons, but the story shows how much he will learn that day about his environment and about his community's history, leaving the reader in no

10.4 Pearse's
cottage, Ros
Muc. Courtesy
Pearse Museum.

doubt that the boy will easily make up what he has missed at school.
It is time to rethatch the house, and Cóilin's father wants him to walk
to a lake several miles away, where a neighbour is cutting sedge, and
bring home a load of it with a donkey and cart. On the way to the
lake the boy meets the distracted old woman Muirne, who is looking
for her son, and on his way home shelters from the rain in her house.
Cóilin knows the names of people and places for miles around his
home, and is completely safe among them. He stops on his way to
admire an eagle sunning itself on a high rock, but he also knows the
times of the trains arriving at the nearest station. The following winter, while mending a sail by the fireside, his father tells the story that
explains old Muirne's behaviour; Cóilín's mother and sisters (like the
women at the opening of 'An Mháthair') are making homespun
cloth, while his brother lies on the floor reading a book but stopping
from time to time to tickle the narrator's bare feet. Literacy and oral
storytelling go hand-in-hand in this description, as do local history,
cosy family life and prodigious self-sufficiency – even if the children
are barefoot.

The stories become more technically complex from the earliest,
with their omniscient adult narrators, to those published in *An
Mháthair agus Scéalta Eile*. Reading them in sequence, we can
observe Pearse conscientiously filling out his cast of characters and
establishing links between them, as the same minor characters occur
in story after story. The earliest stories dealt with children – mostly
boys – and one old man, seanMhaitias; 'Bríd na nAmhrán' featured
an old woman, revered by her community (even by small boys) as a
superlative singer, while another old woman, and a complete nuclear
family, are described in 'Brighid na Gaoithe', which would become
'An Bhean Chaointe'. 'An Mháthair' daringly ventures into an

evening gathering of women, characterised by oral storytelling, respect for old age and profound spirituality, and even explores the inner agony of a childless married woman.

With 'An Deargadaol' Pearse begins to explore the dark side of community life. Often accused of anti-clericalism, he was no supporter of the authoritarian, disdainful, complacent parish priests who figure in so much contemporary commentary. Most of his stories give mainstream Catholicism a central role in traditional life, but with the priest as helper and advocate of his people. In 'An Bhean Chaointe' the parish priest travels to Dublin on the distraught mother's behalf, to intercede for her son with the authorities, and when he returns, unsuccessful, he tells his bad news while holding her two hands. The priest in 'An Deargadaol' is different: his curse has made the woman of the title, whose nickname likens her to the devil's coach-horse beetle – one of three cursed creatures, according to folklore – an outcast from her community. This story, which Colm Ó Gaora insists is based on an incident at mass in Ros Muc during Pearse's first visit there, finds a remarkable parallel in Patrick MacGill's *The Rat Pit*, set in County Donegal in the same period.[28] There, a woman known as 'the beansho' has been condemned publicly by the priest for bearing a child out of wedlock and is shunned by all the parishioners as a result. As in Pearse's story, however, it is this woman who comes to the aid of a little girl in distress and danger. Pearse, of course, makes no mention of what the Deargadaol's sin may have been.

10.5 Pearse family sitting room in St Enda's, *c.* 1960s/70s. Courtesy Pearse Museum.

'Na Bóithre' is a sort of Cinderella story, without the prince, and the only one to feature a girl as an autonomous central character. Nora has to stay at home to look after the baby while her parents and brother go to the party given by 'fear Bhaile Átha Cliath', but she rebels. Rehearsing the indignities of her life as a girl, and imagining a life free of care on the open road, she cuts off her hair, dresses in her brother's clothes and sets off in the dark, abandoning the baby. When she meets the priest on his way home from the party, she lies about who she is and then feels so guilty that spectres seem to pursue her, and she falls in a faint in the woods near Loch Oiriúlach, during which she sees a vision of Christ about to be crucified. Her own father finds her and carries her home, where she lies ill for a month. When she recovers she has discovered a new affection for her family, including the baby, and determines never to leave home again. The message of this story seems to be that while girls are capable of pluck and imagination, they seek adventure and independence at their peril.

Pearse's fictions observed one of the cardinal rules of periodical publication: stories should reflect the season in which they appear. 'Íosagán', which would become the title story of his first collection and which is the first story in *Gearrscéalta an Phiarsaigh*, was written for the Christmas 1906 issue of *An Claidheamh Soluis*. His own lack of acquaintance with Ros Muc in winter may have been the reason for the story's summer setting, or it may be that for the readers he hoped to reach, it was always summer in Conamara. 'Bríd na nAmhrán', about a traditional singer who dies after walking all the way to Dublin to compete in the Oireachtas, was published in the week when that annual event took place, in August 1907, ten years after it began. Remarkable here is the way the story depicts the revival festival, with its formal competitions, platforms and adjudicators, as centrally important to practitioners of a style of singing more usually associated with intimate domestic environments and with audiences who knew each other personally. With 'An Mháthair', published in *An Claidheamh Soluis* in Christmas 1913, Pearse seems again to be emphasising the independence of Conamara people from material concerns, at a time when Christmas in the English-speaking world was becoming increasingly commercial. His story pivots on the same custom as Máirtín Ó Direáin's World War II poem, 'Cuireadh do Mhuire', when candles burn in every window on Christmas Eve to welcome the Virgin Mary and her infant.

But the religious life Pearse depicts, like so much else in these stories, is highly selective. There is no mention of holy wells or 'patterns', or anything that might challenge the authority of the priest in religious observance. The women in 'An Mháthair' refer to oral traditions about the Virgin Mary, but Máire's mortifications of the flesh seem to be derived from the teachings of the Breton St Louis Grignion de Montfort (1673–1716), whose *Treatise on True Devotion to the Blessed Virgin* was 'rediscovered' in 1842 and became a central text in the new wave of Marian devotion in the late nineteenth century. This kind of devotion was profoundly different from the vernacular spirituality of the Gaeltacht, as expressed in religious songs and stories, and was especially popular in urban areas, among English-speaking people of some formal education.[29]

The same selectivity is apparent in 'Eoghainín na nÉan'. Although it owes much to Oscar Wilde's 'The Happy Prince' and to J.M. Barrie's *Peter Pan* (a hugely popular play when Pearse was writing, though not yet a book), 'Eoghainín' is essentially the same story as W.B. Yeats's 1886 poem 'The Stolen Child', itself a version of, or response to, a very commonly told legend type, about a child taken by the fairies. Such legends, which usually feature a changeling left instead of the stolen child, may often be read as code for narratives of tuberculosis, as Sir William Wilde noted in his commentary on the census of 1851.[30] Pearse's story about a little boy who seems to be turning his back on family and culture to fly away with the wild migrating swallows is clearly about TB too, but what is most striking in it is that there are no fairies. This is all the more strange when we consider the prevalence of fairy-belief legend in all parts of Ireland until quite recently, and Pearse's demonstrated reverence for other aspects of oral tradition. But the burning to death as a fairy changeling in 1895 of Bridget Cleary had attracted very negative publicity and had reverberated in international newspapers for months, with disastrous consequences for the credibility of the Home Rule campaign.[31] Stories about fairies smacked of superstition, which both challenged Catholicism and left Irish people open to the charges of primitive ignorance and barbarity that were commonplace in *Punch* and other periodicals, and in popular works like Charles Kingsley's *The Water Babies*. Pearse clearly wanted no such stigma to attach to his imagined community.

CHAPTER ELEVEN

# The battle before us now is a Battle of Words: Pearse and Postcolonial Theory[1]

## RÓISÍN NÍ GHAIRBHÍ

The theoretical negotiations of postcolonial studies are concerned with the ethics of representation and with the practical political and economic ends to which these are put.[2]

We who speak here tonight are the voice of one of the ancient indestructible things of the world. We are the voice of an idea which is older than any empire and will outlive any empire.[3]

Practitioners working within the burgeoning area of critical research now known as postcolonial studies or postcolonial theory seek to draw attention to occluded voices and texts ('the subaltern'; 'postcolonial literature') and concern themselves with mapping tensions between the colonised 'margins' and colonial 'centre'. Those using postcolonial theory to read, write and cite texts also tend to interest themselves in the various challenges faced by those seeking to readdress the historic marginalisation of a colonised culture, being wary, for example, of overly essentialist approaches. Máirín Nic Eoin notes that the marginalised status of Irish-language literature was also the result of historic colonialism and urged Irish-language critics to harness aspects of postcolonial theory in order to provide a fresh context for the study of their own literature.[4] A postcolonial framework is implicit, though underdeveloped in much critical work on the literature of the revival period, and further work remains to be done. Máire Ní Fhlathúin discusses the 'anti-colonial modernism' of some of Pearse's creative writing showing how a postcolonial approach can reconfigure his writings' interest as literature.[5] This chapter will use various critical approaches which are particularly associated with postcolonial theory in order to provide fresh insights into the creative writings of Patrick Pearse in both Irish and English.

It will be shown *inter alia* that Pearse himself anticipated much of the thinking associated with pre-eminent postcolonial theorists of the second part of the twentieth century.[6]

Scholars familiar with the Irish language have provided the most useful contextualisation of Pearse's creative *oeuvre* to date. Desmond Ryan, Séamas Ó Buachalla, Ciarán Ó Coigligh, Aisling Ní Dhonnchadha, Máire Ní Fhlathúin, Philip O'Leary, Cathal Ó HÁinle, Regina Uí Chollatáin and Caitríona Ó Torna have all provided important insights into Pearse's writings.[7] Notwithstanding the fact that Pearse's creative writings in English (particularly his dramatic works) aroused considerable interest at their first publication and performance, critical commentary has, with notable exceptions,[8] focused predominantly on his role as a moderniser within Irish-language literature. But is the role played by Pearse as a stylistic innovator during the Gaelic Revival the best framework by which we might judge the functions, forms and domains of his writing?

11.1 Mrs Margaret Pearse *c.* 1920s/30s. Courtesy Pearse Museum.

## MISE ÉIRE, THE CULTURAL CONTEXT

The views of some commentators have sometimes been overly influenced by the literary and political mores of their era. For Eugene McCabe, Pearse's famous poem 'Mise Éire' expressed an archaic nationalism which was crude and dangerous. Recalling his first hearing of 'Mise Éire' in 1993 at a time when the 'Troubles' still provided a cultural backdrop to political comment McCabe wondered if there was

> a word to descibe that kind of emotion? Nationalism? Tribalism? Atavism (the father of a great grandfather, from Avus a grandfather, resemblance to a remote ancestor, a reversion to the primitive, an obscure sense of belonging), whatever it means it's something we should be wary of); it can make wise men think and do very unwise things.[9]

McCabe's reading of 'Mise Éire', which views the poem's evoking of past culture as arbitrary and emotive, is predicated on a paradigm which has cultural value accrue in an evolutionary progression from archaism to modernity. A similar binary opposition between the possibilities inherent in an historic native culture and a culture that is deemed to offer the prospect of economic progress is found in Eavan Boland's reply to Pearse's poem, also called 'Mise Éire': I won't go back ... my nation displaced into old dactyls'.[10] The subaltern hero-ine of Boland's poem finds resolution to her cultural conflict in America and in the English language: she joins their centre and cap-italism is her cue.

Joe Cleary has commented positively on the role played by post-colonial theory in questioning critical approaches which he deemed overly in thrall to modernisation discourse.[11] Pearse himself stated that his own society's attachment to the idea of modernity had caused it to lose much that was valuable.[12] The critiques of 'Mise Éire' by McCabe and Boland cited above could suggest that Pearse sought a simple and naïve return to a native culture that had become an anachronism. Such was not the case. Stuart Hall attests that the colonial act engenders a form of culture involving 'different but related forms of relationship, interconnection, and discontinuity'.[13] Pearse's sophisticated understanding of the broken and disparate nature of surviving native culture is related memorably in his unfin-ished fable 'An Choill'/The Wood:

> And I used to call upon him in the loneliness of the Wood, but he never came to me, and I would realise he had been dead for hundreds of years and that he would never walk that Wood again, and that there was nothing alive after him on earth but a few of his thoughts and a few of his words and some memory of a few of his deeds. I have put together all that I gathered of his thoughts and his words and his exploits from the wise ones of the Wood. I do not say that I have woven the story properly.[14]

Pearse was vigilant against essentialist readings of culture, and as var-ious critics have noted, he consistently emphasised that a simple return to a precolonised Gaelic culture was neither possible nor desirable.[15] Writing about Gaelic literature in 1913 he voiced his aspi-ration that 'the old truths will find new mouths, the old sorrows and ecstasies new interpretation'.[16]

Cleary believes that cultural readings in the field of Irish Studies which are informed by postcolonial theory tend to have a wider focus since they take into account the capitalistic (imperialist) con-text which has been a formative influence on society.[17] Certainly cap-italist/imperialist imperatives were the predominant context for the marginalisation of Gaelic culture. Pearse himself believed that an inherent tension between political economy and the alternative worldview of native Gaelic culture provided the main challenge for those seeking a revival of Gaelic culture:

Be certain that in political economy there is no way of life either
for a man or a people ... Ye men and peoples, burn your books
on rent theories and land values and go back to your sagas.[18]

Pearse had earlier asserted that his idea of a Gaelic nation had come
from his childhood experiences of a residual (though living) Gaelic
culture and literature which he had witnessed through his elderly
Aunt Margaret's songs and recitations; indeed it is probable that he
first heard the Cailleach Bhéarra and Cúchulainn mentioned in 'Mise
Éire' through the personal witness of his aunt.[19] In the light of this
information and given Pearse's own stated views on culture, it is
unsurprising that a dichotomy between the mechanics of the market-
place and the organic call of native culture provides the poetic impe-
tus – and personally felt emotion – of 'Mise Éire':

Mór mo ghlór
Mé do rug Cúchulainn cródha
Mór mo náire
Mo chlann féin do dhíol a máthair.


Great my glory
It was I who bore the brave Cúchulainn.
Great my shame
My own children sold their mother.


## 'MISE ÉIRE', THE POLITICAL AND CULTURAL CONTEXT

A further context for 'Mise Éire' emerges when the contemporary
political and cultural structures to which Pearse was responding are
examined. 'Mise Éire' was first published in Pearse's political paper
*An Barr Buadh* on 30 March 1912. Thus the political events of
spring 1912 as reported in that paper form the immediate context
for the poem. As debate on the merit of the Home Rule bill intensified, the idea of 'sell out' or the 'díol' of 'Mise Éire' became a constant theme in the various editions of *An Barr Buadh*. The editors
and writers of the newspaper were described as 'a small group of
Gaels who value their fathers and who would be ashamed to sell
their native right'; they would not 'sell the native right of Gaels for
that thing called Home Rule'. Pearse contended that 'Most of the
Gaels of our time have been bought by foreigners... One of them
sold himself for a farm; another for a place in the service of the King
of England'.[20] The emphasis in 'Mise Éire' on the duties required by
familial ties and the espousal of Irish sovereignty inherent in the
poem's proud declamation of the dignity of an historic nation

(which Pearse had witnessed personally through his maternal relations) contrasted with, and could be read as a counterpoint to, the conciliatory tone of speeches made by John Redmond that same spring. As concern mounted over some of the terms contained in the Home Rule bill Redmond emphasised Ireland's ties to 'that great sisterhood of nations, the British Empire'.[21] It is noteworthy that Redmond contended in a parliamentary debate that his own stance was equivalent to that of Parnell. The monument in Parnell's honour, which was unveiled (by Redmond) in October 1911, provides a further meta-context for 'Mise Éire'. As well as Parnell's famous edict that 'no man should set the bounds to the march of a nation', an Irish-language coda was added to the monument which can almost be read as a summary of the sentiments of 'Mise Éire': 'Go Soirbhighe Dia Éire dá clainn' [May God prosper Ireland for her children].

Was Pearse evoking the ghost of Parnell in 'Mise Éire'? Joseph McGarrity later recalled Pearse's deep upset at Redmond's 'betrayal'.[22] It is worth noting in a *Barr Buadh* article published on 16 March 1912 Pearse had stated that Redmond needed to become bolder in his demands in order to be like Parnell; on the 23 March another article ('An nDíolfar Éire?' [Will Ireland be sold?]) had recalled what Pearse viewed as the selling out of Parnell. The original longer ver-

11.2 *An Macaomh*, 1913. Courtesy Pearse Museum.

sion of 'Mise Éire' specifically mourned the death of those who had been a source of hope for the speaker/Éire ('D'éag an dream inar chuireas dóchas' [Those I placed my hope in died). If Parnell was a lost leader, by 1912 the nationalist Parliamentary leaders were middle-aged men, and, as Éamonn Ceannt noted in another *Barr Buadh* article, the radical old Fenians were passing away rapidly. Ceannt wondered if it was not time for young men to move.[23] *An Barr Buadh* was a newspaper for and by a new generation of radicalised young men. The contrasts in 'Mise Éire' (the Cailleach Bhéarra epitomising hereditary pride, the family who 'sold' (out) and the radical young men towards whom the poem is directed) can be seen to reflect Pearse's reading of the tensions in contemporary nationalist politics. Meanwhile, it is clear from this brief examination of 'Mise Éire' that underlying intertextual references and immediate historical contexts provide a more reliable allusive framework for analysing the views expressed in Pearse's writings than does speculative discussion on his psychological motives. Regarding references to a 'cult of boyhood', Pearse himself referred to how both the Táin and the Fenian Cycle emphasised the potential inherent in youth.[24] Meanwhile his imaginative use of literary forms like poetry (and also letters and fables) to convey his political message in his political newspaper deserves further scrutiny.

## THE INTERTEXTUAL APPROACH

Pearse used an intertextual approach in order to connect with a historic culture in a way which avoided pastiche. The ability to capture the essence of an evolving story with an arresting image can be seen in 'Mise Éire', in which immediate political allusions provide the freshness in the poem's meaning. In Pearse's poem the voice is that of a betrayed mother and not the deserted lover of the Aisling genre. Though 'Éire' asserts that her children have now sold her, she has not lost her pride and the emotion evoked still calls on filial affection: the poem has a performative element. A similar performative function is held by the Mother Ireland voice of the 1916 Proclamation.[25] The stately rhythm and metre in 'Mise Éire' echoes that of 'An Chailleach Bhéarra', the medieval Irish lyric which provided one of the poem's motifs and a figure who also featured in the folk poetry of the County Meath of Pearse's Aunt Margaret's youth.[26] Meanwhile sixteenth- and seventeenth-century poetic references to the hereditary duties of Clanna Baoiscne and Clanna Morna are recalled in 'Mise Éire's contrasting allusion to 'clann' sell-out. In 'Mise Éire' the marginalised national literature of the townlands of Aunt Margaret's youth is restored to the modern domain of print journalism: Boland's vague 'old dactyls' still have currency. It is clear that Pearse developed the 'mother' voice of 'Mise Éire' both as a consequence of his own experience of Gaelic culture and as a conscious strategy of anti-colonial writing. In his 1916 pamphlet *The Sovereign People* Pearse wrote that

> A nation is bound together by natural ties, ties mystic and spiritual and ties human and kindly, an empire is at best held together by ties of human interest and at worst by brute force. The nation is the family at large, an empire is a commercial corporation at large.[27]

It is noteworthy that most of Pearse's creative and discursive writings are framed by family stories and have family and community memory and an emphasis on individual humanity and freedom as their moral compass. Pearse's (uncollected) essays on culture and nationality in *An Claidheamh Soluis agus Fáinne an Lae* and his 1916 series of pamphlets on identity and political morality provide important foundation texts for studies in postcolonial theory.

Pearse engaged with the recovery and popularisation of the occluded literature of an historic Gaelic nation in an energetic and imaginative manner. His 1908 account of 'The Veiled Woman of the Battlefield', an inspirational figure representing literature, provides a foundation fable for postcolonial theory.[28] While a member of the Coiste Ceantair of the Gaelic League, Pearse suggested the League hold a series of concerts and lectures and can thus be seen as the primary instigator of the widening of the Gaelic League's remit to the wider public sphere. He was an active member of the Gaelic League's Publications' Committee during a period when that committee oversaw the publication and marketing of various literary works and language aids, many of which secured a huge readership.[29] He also published scholarly editions of texts from the Fenian Cycle during his editorship of the weekly newspaper *An Claidheamh Soluis*.[30]

Pearse's drama 'Macghníomhartha Chúchulainn' was a sensitive dramatic enactment of what can be deemed the subaltern literary texts of the Ulster Cycle which had only recently come to public attention in scholarly editions.[31] He theorised his reimagining of the canon of Irish and European Literature in his talk/article 'Some

11.3
Commemorative postcard featuring the *Coming of Fionn* and the *The Boy Deeds of Cú Chulainn* pageant of 1909. Courtesy Pearse Museum.

Sgoil éanna,
Rát Feaṗnáin.

éamonn builḟin i n-a "Cairḃre" i "The Coming of Fionn," Máṗta 1909.

Feaṗgur ó Dúnlaing i n-a "Cúċulainn" i "Mac-Gníoṁaṗtaiḃ Cúċulainn," Meiṫeaṁ 1909.

Donnċaḋ Mac Finn i n-a "Fionn" i "The Coming of Fionn," Máṗta 1909.

St. Enda's College, Rathfarnham :
(1) Eamonn Bulfin as "Cairbre" in "The Coming of Fionn," March 1909 ; (2) Frank Dowling as "Cuchulainn" in the Cuchulainn Pageant, June 1909 ; (3) Denis Gwynn as "Fionn" in "The Coming of Fionn," March 1909.

Aspects of Irish Literature' and in a series later published as 'The Murder Machine', a series which itself anticipates Ngugi Wa Thiongo's critique of an imposed and unrepresentative curriculum. Pearse's radical re-imagining of Gaelic literature envisaged Diarmuid and Gráinne as an early novel,[32] the Ulster Cycle as a tragedy,[33] Cúchulainn as a prototype of Christ[34] and Deirdre as a version of Ibsen's Hedda Gabler.[35] Meanwhile his *Dánta Gríosuigthe Gaedheal* (Songs of the Irish Rebels) published in the *Irish Review* in 1913 gathered together a selection of sixteenth- and seventeenth-century Gaelic texts and translations of what are now canonical poems. He also published material recalled from his aunt and material collected from the Oireachtas prize-winning gardener at St Enda's (Mícheál Mac Ruaidhrí) in *An Macaomh*, the school journal. His famous tracts on political theory and nationality sold as penny pamphlets and the collection called *An tAithriseoir*, which Pearse co-edited, was an easily affordable collection of Irish-language poems which soon sold out its first edition.[36] It is worth noting that Pearse's literary, critical and political writings frequently found an audience which included those 'subalterns' discussed in the texts themselves at a time when other writers (Yeats and Synge, for example) showed little interest in reaching such a readership. Pearse's conscious mapping of a marginalised literature is reflected in his discussion of 'the "secret songs" of the dispossessed Irish' in the essay *Ghosts*, a phrase which anticipates Gayatri Spivak's famous discussion of the subaltern voice.[37] He published at least 300 Gaelic songs in *An Claidheamh Soluis* during his editorship of that paper.[38] Pearse's relationship with his aunt recalls that of the poet Michael Hartnett with his Gaelic grandmother ('I loved her from the day she died ... She was a language seldom spoken'). Both writers felt compelled by their personal witness of an unbroken, though imperfectly preserved, literary tradition to remake and renew that tradition for the future.

## DRAMA

Pearse's radical ideas for developing a native strand of drama has been underexamined. In a 1906 article in *An Claidheamh Soluis* he advised prospective practitioners of Gaelic drama

> first, to study the art of the Irish traditional reciter; and secondly, to pay an occasional visit to the Abbey Theatre ... the one puts the student in touch with Ireland while the other puts him in touch with the best contemporary ideas.[39]

His plays *Íosagán* and *The Master* were advertised as 'miracle plays'.

Later productions of his own drama show further proof of Pearse's conscious fusing of modern theatrical forms with native literary modes. He also found both imaginative settings and prestigious new domains for the new drama.  When Douglas Hyde's *An Naomh ar Iarraidh* and Standish O'Grady's *The Coming of Fionn* were staged at St Enda's a glittering array of city intelligentsia attended and following Pearse's astute publicising, the plays were reported upon in the *Irish Independent*, the *London Sphere*, the *Leader*, the *Nation* and *Sinn Féin*.[40]  The work song 'Ding Dong Dideáró' was incorporated into Pearse's production of his *Macghníomhartha Chúchulainn*, which was performed in the grounds of St Enda's in 1909; it was later performed  also at Castlebellingham Feis.  Pearse noted that he had

> kept close to the Táin even at the risk of what some people
> might call dramatic effect, but in this matter I have greater trust
> in the instinct of the unknown shapers of our epic than in the
> instinct of any modern.[41]

'Caoineadh na dTrí Muire' was sung in Pearse's Passion Play in 1911: one of the several plays to be performed at the Abbey.  His pageant *The Defence of the Ford*, which also drew on the Táin, was performed  at Jones' Road/Croke Park in 1913.[42]

Pearse's blending of modern dramatic forms with the idiom, themes  and modes of native literature can be compared to Ngugi Wa Thiongo's discussion of his own attempt to forge a postcolonial theatre. Both writers also sought out imaginative new spaces in which to site their new drama.[43] The hybrid cultural form of drama envisaged and developed by Pearse is also similar to the idea of syncretic theatre as described by Christopher Balme.[44] Pearse's lecture on the Kerry folk 'play' *Dúlaing Óg agus an Leannán Sí*, which was performed on a bill with *Íosagan* and *The Master* in the Irish Theatre, Hardewicke Street, in May 1915, provides further proof of his abiding interest in developing a native strand of drama.[45] Meanwhile his late play *The Singer*, which has a young man of the west reawaken nationalism by his songs, and which echoes both the Aisling and Yeat's *Cathleen Ni Houlihan* in form, reminds us that Pearse himself sited his political *credo* in subaltern culture.

## PROSE

A central tenet of postcolonial theory is the idea of struggle between the centre and the margins, an idea first developed by Jacques Derrida in a different context. This analytical framework, which features in Edward Said's *Orientalism* and Homi Babha's *The Location of*

11.4
*An Barr Buadh*,
April 1912.
Courtesy Pearse
Museum.

*Culture*, can also prove a useful critical approach for engaging with other aspects of Pearse's creative work. In the short story 'Na Bóithre' the voice of the metropolitan visitor is sublimated to that of the local Conamara country people. Anglo-Irish novels of the nineteenth century tended to have a metropolitan narrator who reported on the peasantry. Pearse's short stories follow the stylistic innovation of the short story by beginning *in medias res*, but because the subject matter and frame of reference for the characters also echo folk culture, it follows that Ros na gCaorach/Ros Muc are presented on their own terms. The country evoked is familiar, a local organic community; the antithesis of the 'strange country' which Daniel Corkery detected in the 'national' Anglo-Irish novels of the nineteenth century.[46] But in 'Na Bóithre' the locals interest themselves in international news, which is alluded to as 'Scéalta ón Domhan Thiar agus ón Domhan Thoir' (Stories from the Western and Eastern worlds) that is, in terminology reminiscent of the heroic tales of the manuscripts and folklore: the margins are the centre.

It is often contended that Pearse's short stories generally fail to
engage with the social, political and psychological issues which he
himself had proclaimed as the remit of a modern Gaelic literature. It
is worth noting in this regard that Pearse's characters are all marginalised in various ways. Nóra of 'Na Bóithre' has a mental breakdown
when she tries to stand up to the patriarchal mores of her rural community. A traveller and a 'woman who sinned' feature in 'An
Deargadaol'. The central character of 'An Bhean Chaointe' goes
insane when her son dies while incarcerated by the colonial authorities, provoking memories of colonial injustice and renewed desire
for independence within the narrator's family. Indeed, when we
become aware that Pearse later participated in a deputation to the
local government which sought financial assistance in raising awareness of the reasons for the widespread problem of consumption in
Ros Muc, the perceived sentimentality of Eoghainín's death may
need to be recast as a sympathetic exploration of pressing contemporary social issues framed in an idiom sympathetic to its subaltern subjects. The visions of Nóra, Máire and Eoghainín take place within
narratives which are for the most part grounded in realism. This narrative device can be likened to the style of present-day writers like
Milan Kundera and Gabriel García Marquez, whose use of magic
realism allows marginalised groups or ideas to be voiced within an
otherwise conventional style. Aisling Ní Dhonnchadha's assertion
that Pearse's short stories are of minor importance only, is perhaps
founded on the premise that a linear evolution of literature from folk
to modern forms is desirable.[47] Pearse attested that he had heard the
seeds of his stories from the people of Ros Muc: the stories should
therefore be read as adaptations incorporating folk elements whose
interest may perhaps lie chiefly in the progressive nature of their
hybrid form. Ciaran Ó Coigligh's edition of Pearse's Irish-language
poetry also shows Pearse to have adapted material from oral culture.[48]

### POSTCOLONIAL STUDIES: THE INTERNATIONAL CONTEXT

While Pearse's affinity with Gaelic literature was founded on emotion,
his own negotiation of identity was theorised in a sophisticated manner which encompassed a comparative aspect. For Pearse, the Gaelic
Revival could be theorised on an international plane and he attended
the Eisteddfod and Mod na hAlban from an early stage. His use of the
term 'Empire' when discussing Ireland's cultural and political position
consistently envisaged a dialectic which opposed the word of the
colonised to that of the coloniser calling for a 'briathar-chath' or 'battle of words' in 1912.[49] He sited his own nationalism in an international framework.[50] Among topics discussed by guest lecturers to St

Enda's were the cultural and social awakening of the Indian people and the language question in Georgia. During Pearse's own life his play *An Rí* was produced as part of a double bill with Rabindranath Tagore's *The Post Office* in the Abbey. In 1915 Tagore produced *An Rí* as *The King* in Bengal.[51] David Lloyd's vision for Irish postcolonial studies is relevant:

> Irish postcolonial studies is dedicated to the work of retrieving the different rhythms of historically marginalised cultures and to the alternative conceptions of culture and of social relations that account for their virtual occlusion from written history. But it is no less dedicated to the imagining out of that knowledge different alternative projects that will convert the damage of history into the terms for future survival.[52]

A critical approach which is guided by the notion that literary merit is reliant on modernity and which does not allow for the socio-cultural structures underlying texts, creates a limited viewpoint for appraising Pearse's work. A postcolonial reading of Pearse's *oeuvre* is instructive both for those involved in postcolonial studies and those interested in the influence and outlook of Pearse himself. The imaginative and evocative use of an immigrant voice to read 'Mise Éire' in the film *Aimhirghin* reminds us, as hopefully this chapter has also, that Pearse's work, far from being insular and atavistic, both embodies and embraces his vision of identity and culture as fluid, evolving and perennially renewable.

CHAPTER ELEVEN

# *An Cath atá romhainn anois is geall le Briatharchath é:* Pádraic Mac Piarais agus Léann an Iarchoilíneachais[1]

## RÓISÍN NÍ GHAIRBHÍ

The theoretical negotiations of postcolonial studies are concerned with the ethics of representation and with the practical political and economic ends to which these are put.[2]

We who speak here tonight are the voice of one of the ancient indestructible things of the world. We are the voice of an idea which is older than any empire and will outlive any empire.[3]

Cuireann léamha iarchoilíneacha ar an litríocht spéis i gcultúr na 'ngnáthdhaoine' ('na híochtaráin') agus sa sracadh idir 'imeall' agus 'lár'; ceistíonn siad an chanóin agus déanann cúram de na gaistí – an t-eisintiúlachas, mar shampla – a bhíonn roimh scríbhneoirí ar mian leo urlabhra bharántúil agus athghradam a bhaint amach dá gcultúir dhúchais mhionlaithe. Mheabhraigh Máirín Nic Eoin dúinn go luíonn litríocht na Gaeilge, litríocht ar dioscúrsa pobail mhionlaithe í, go heiseamláireach leis an saghas sin litríochta a bhíonn faoi mheas ag teoiriceoirí iarchoilíneacha agus mhol do lucht critice na Gaeilge dul i gcomhghuaillíocht chruthaitheach le bealaí scagtha léann an iarchoilíneachais.[4] Tá cosúlachtaí áirithe idir cuid den chur chuige a úsáidtear le plé le litríocht na hAthbheochana in Éirinn agus an cur chuige a bhíonn ag criticeoirí iarchoilíneacha. Pléann Máire Ní Fhlathúin an nua-aoiseachas frithchoilíneach a bhraith sí i gcuid de scríbhinní an Phiarsaigh agus na léargais mhalartacha a sholáthraíonn cur chuige iarchoilíneach ar fhiúntas liteartha shaothar Mhic Phiarais.[5]

San alt seo bainfear earraíocht as modhanna léirmhínithe a bhaineann le teoiricí iarchoilíneacha éagsúla chun léargais nua a sholáthar do chuid de shaothar agus d'obair an Phiarsaigh, i mBéarla agus i nGaeilge. Taispeánfar *inter alia* gur réamhaithris iad na múnlaí litríochta agus na léamha cultúrtha a d'fhorbair an Piarsach ar chuid dá mbeadh le rá ag scríbhneoirí aitheanta léann an iarchoilíneachais sa dara leath den bhfichiú haois.[6]

Tráchtairí le Gaeilge is fearr atá tar éis comhthéacsú a dhéanamh ar thogra cruthaitheach an Phiarsaigh agus i measc na gcriticeoirí atá tar éis léargais thábhachtacha a sholáthar tá Desmond Ryan, Séamas Ó Buachalla, Aisling Ní Dhonnchadha, Máire Ní Fhlathúin, Philip O'Leary, Ciarán Ó Coigligh, Cathal Ó Háinle, Regina Uí Chollatáin agus Caitríona Ó Torna.[7] Ainneoin na hairde a tharraing cuid dá shaothar Béarla, go háirithe a shaothar drámatúil, tráth a chumtha is a chéadléirithe, is gnách fós – cé is moite do roinnt bheag eisceachtaí[8] – gur i gcomhthéacs fhorbairt nualitríocht na Gaeilge amháin a aithnítear an Piarsach mar scríbhneoir ceannródaíoch. Ach an amhlaidh gurb é tábhacht an Phiarsaigh mar nuálaí stíle i litríocht na Gaeilge i rith na hAthbheochana Gaelaí, an tslat tomhais is fearr chun léargas a fháil ar mhúnlaí, ar fheidhmeanna agus ar fhearainn chruthaitheacha an scríbhneora?

### 'MISE ÉIRE': AN COMHTHÉACS CULTÚRTHA

Bíonn breithiúnas cuid eile de na léirmheastóirí faoi anáil chlaonta litearetha agus polaitiúla a gcúlra féin. Ba léir suaitheadh polaitiúil na ré comhaimseartha ag imirt tionchair ar bhreithiúnas Eugene McCabe is é ag meabhrú dó féin sa bhliain 1993 an chéad uair dar chuala sé 'Mise Éire':

> Is there a word to descibe that kind of emotion? Nationalism? Tribalism? Atavism (the father of a great grandfather, from Avus a grandfather, resemblance to a remote ancestor, a reversion to the primitive, an obscure sense of belonging), whatever it means it's something we should be wary of; it can make wise men think and do very unwise things.[9]

Níor léir do McCabe aon chóras ar leith bheith ag baint leis an meabhrú dúchais atá le fáil sa dán. Tá a luacháil ar 'Mise Éire' fréamhaithe i bparaidím a aithníonn fiúntas an chultúir mar ghluaiseacht ón tseanfhaiseantacht go dtí an nua-aimsearthacht. Léamh den sórt céanna a thug ar Eavan Boland an caitheamh i ndiaidh saol cúng seanfhaiseanta a shamhlú le bunteachtaireachtaí litearetha an Phiarsaigh i ndán cáiliúil dá cuid a 'fhreagraíonn' 'Mise Éire', agus a bhfuil an teideal céanna air. De réir léamh Bholand, bíonn rogha dhénártha idir an dul siar agus an dul chun cinn le déanamh i dtír iarchoilíneach agus is é an córas caipitlíoch a shainíonn fiúntas an chultúir. 'I won't go back … my nation displaced into old dactyls.'[10]

Aimsíonn íochtarán 'Mise Éire' Bholand féin slánú i Meiriceá agus sa Bhéarla.

In aiste a foilsíodh sa bhliain 2003 thug Joe Cleary moladh do chur chuige léann an iarchoilíneachais toisc go gceistíonn teoiriceoirí an réimse sin dioscúrsaí atá faoi róchuing, dar leis, ag nóisean an nua-aoisithe.[11] Ar an dála céanna dhearbhaigh Mac Piarais go sonrach go raibh sochaí a linne féin faoi ró-gheasa ag soiscéal an nua-aoisithe.[12] Tugann breithiúnais Bholand agus McCabe ar 'Mise Éire' le fios gur ag iarraidh filleadh scun scan ar chultúr mionlaithe caite a bhí an Piarsach. Ní fíor sin. Tá ráite ag an tráchtaire Stuart Hall gur ghin an gníomh coilíneach múnla eile den chultúr a bhí ilchineálach neamh-leanúnach.[13] Faightear achoimre ar thuiscintí sofaisticiúla an Phiarsaigh ar nádúr smidiríneach an chultúir Ghaelaigh sa bhfáidhscéal neamhchríochnaithe 'An Choill', a foilsíodh sa bhliain 1914:

> Agus do ghlaodhainn air i n-uaigneas na Coille, acht ní thigeadh chugham, agus do thuiginn go raibh sé marbh leis na céadtaibh bliadhan agus nach siubhlóchadh sé an Choill sin go deo arís, agus nach raibh beo ina dhiaidh ar an talamh ach beagán dá smuaintibh agus beagán dá bhriathraibh agus cuimhne éigin ar bheagán dá ghníomharthaibh. Do thiomsuigheas le chéile ar chnuasuigheas dá smuaintibh agus dá bhriathraibh agus dá imeachtaibh ó lucht eolais na Coille. Ní abraim gur fhigheas an scéal le chéile ina cheart.[14]

Is é fírinne an scéil go mbíodh Mac Piarais go síoraí ar an airdeall faoi bhaol an eisintiúlachais. Faoi mar atá criticeoirí éagsúla tar éis a thuairisc bhí sé go láidir den tuairim nach bhféadfaí litríocht na cosmhuintire a bhrú scun scan mar eisleamláir don nua-litríocht.[15] Dhearbhaigh sé go sonrach sa bhliain 1913 a dhóchas go mbainfí athbhrí as seanmhúnlaí na litríochta: ' … the old truths will find new mouths, the old sorrows and ecstasies new interpretation'.[16]

Áitíonn Cleary go mbaineann leathnú peirspictíochta leis na léamha iarchoilíneacha atá á ndéanamh i réimse Léann na hÉireann mar go gcuirtear san áireamh iontu an comhthéacs caipitlíoch – arb ionann é agus an comhthéacs impiriúlach – a mhúnlaíonn an tsochaí.[17] Go stairiúil ba é an córas caipitlíoch a d'fhág litríocht na Gaeilge imeallaithe. D'aithin an Piarsach féin an choimhlint idir an caipitleachas impiriúlach agus an cultúr dúchais mar chroílár an dúshláin a bhain le hathshealbhú na féiniúlachta Gaelaí:

> Be certain that in political economy there is no way of life either for a man or a people … Ye men and peoples, burn your books on rent theories and land values and go back to your sagas.[18]

Ní haon ionadh, i bhfianaise ráiteas cáiliúil thuas an Phiarsaigh faoin
eacnamaíocht pholaitiúil, agus i bhfianaise fhréamhadh a dhúile féin
i gcoincheap an náisiúin Ghaelaigh i seanchas oidhreachtúil a mhuin-
tire féin, go dtarraingítear codarsnacht in 'Mise Éire' idir meicníocht
leamh an mhargaidh agus glaoch misteach an dúchais ghlórmhair:

> Mór mo ghlóir;
> Mé do rug Cú Chulainn cródha.
> Mór mo náir
> Mo chlann féin do dhíol a máthair.[19]

## 'MISE ÉIRE': COMHTHÉACS POLAITIÚIL AGUS CULTÚRTHA

Foilsíodh 'Mise Éire' den chéad uair i nuachtán polaitiúil an
Phiarsaigh, *An Barr Buadh*, ar 30 Márta 1912. Is iad imeachtaí
polaitiúla an earraigh sin, faoi mar a pléadh iad in *An Barrr Buadh*,
garchomhthéacs 'Mise Éire'. Agus ceist *home rule* faoi phlé, bhí
eagráin éagsúla *An Barr Buadh* breac le tagairtí do 'dhíol'. B'ionann
lucht eagair agus scríbh an nuachtáin agus 'drong bheag de Ghaelaibh
len-ar ionmhuin a n-athardha agus le n-ar scorn a gceart dúchais do
dhíol', dream a mhaígh nach 'ndíolfaidís ceart dúchais Gaedheal ar an
ní ar a dtugtar Home Rule'. Mhaígh an Piarsach go raibh 'Gaedhil na
haimsire seo agus a bhformhór ceannaithe ag Gallaibh ... Do dhíol
duine acu é féin ar fheirm talún, duine eile ar bheart i seirbhís Ríogh
Shasana ...[20] Seasann béim 'Mise Éire' ar dhualgais oidhreachtúla na
clainne agus ar shaoirse shinseartha na hÉireann i gcodarsnacht le tuin
óráidí John Redmond earrach céanna seo na bliana 1912, óráidí a
bhéimnigh gaol na hÉireann le himpireacht na Breataine. Thug
Redmond le fios gurbh ionann tuairim Pharnell agus a thuairim féin,
agus dhearbhaigh a mhian go mbeadh Éire mar chuid de 'that great
sisterhood of nations that makes up the British Empire'.[21] Anuas ar
ráiteas cáiliúil Pharnell nach bhféadfaí stop a chur le máirseáil
náisiúin, bhí focail eile greanta ar an leac ómóis do Pharnell a
nochtadh don phobal (ag Redmond) i nDeireadh Fomhair na bliana
1911, focail ar geall le hachoimre ar bhunteachtaireacht 'Mise Éire'
iad: 'Go soirbhighe Dia Éire dá clainn.' An ag dúiseacht taibhse
Pharnell a bhí an Piarsach in 'Mise Éire'? Dhearbhaigh Joe McGarrity
gur ghoill 'tréas' Redmond go mór ar Mhac Piarais.[22] Ar eagrán 16
Márta bhí impithe ag an bPiarsach ar Redmond bheith ina 'Pharnell'
agus tarraingíodh anuas cás tuarnaimh Pharnell go sonrach san alt 'An
nDíolfar Éire?' a foilsíodh in *An Barr Buadh* ar 23 Márta 1912.

Tá dearbhghaol oidhreachtúil an Phiarsaigh le hiarsmaí thraidisiún neamhbhriste litríochta Gaeilge rianaithe agam cheana: de
Ghaeltacht na Mí agus de chúlra léannta muintir a mháthar.[23] Go

comhfhiosach córasach a chuaigh an Piarsach i mbun an cultúr iars-
mach seo a athréimniú. Seans gurbh iad na giotaí amhrán i nGaeilge
agus i mBéarla 'a chuala sé óna sheanaintín Margaret Brady' a thug
air trácht ar 'the "secret songs" of the dispossessed Irish' san aiste
*Ghosts*, mar shampla, cur síos a mheabhraíonn díospóireachtaí na
freacnairce ag tráchtairí iarchoilíneacha mar Gayatri Spivak faoi
fhearainn labhartha na n-íochtarán agus faoin stair cheilte.[24]
D'fhoilsigh sé féin thart ar thrí chéad amhrán le linn a thréimhse
eagarthóireachta ar an bpáipéar céanna. Is díol spéise na cosúlachtaí
idir teagmháil an fhile Michael Hartnett leis an nGaeilge trína
mháthair chríonna siúd ('I loved her from the day she died … She
was a language seldom spoken') agus teagmháil Mhic Phiarais leis na
Brádaigh. Is mar gheall ar a leath-theagmháil le traidisiún smiotaithe
a thóg an bheirt scríbhneoirí orthu féin eolas a chur ar an traidisiún
liteartha chun an bhearna a bhraitheadar i ndíoscúrsa na litríochta
(agus ina bpearsantachtaí féin) a atógáil arís, agus a chraobh-
scaoileadh. Fearacht Hartnett (agus Nuala Ní Dhomhnaill) lenár linn
féin, bhain an Piarsach leas as an idirthéacsúlacht chun a ráitis féin a
shníomh mar chuid de dhioscúrsa leanúnach dúchais gan titim i
ngaiste na haithrise.

In ionad cloí le trópanna na n-aislingí fáithchiallacha, filltear ar
íomháineachas dánta polaitiúla ón tséú agus ón tseachtú haois déag,
ar chuir an Piarsach oiread dúile iontu; dánta a bhéimnigh ársacht an
náisiúin Ghaelaigh trí thrácht ar dhualgais Chlanna Mórna agus
Chlanna Bhaoiscne agus trí ghinealach na nGael a rianadh siar go dtí
Milesius. Dearbhaítear oineach na hÉireann sa rithim mhaorga agus
san fhoclaíocht spárálach a mheabhraíonn filíocht na Meán-
Ghaeilge, leithéid na bunlirice 'An Chailleach Bhéarra' agus dánta
faoin gCailleach a bhí i mbéaloideas chontae na Midhe le linn óige
Aunt Margaret.[25] I ndán an Phiarsaigh tá Éire críon caite. Ach fearacht na Caillí, tá cuimhne aici ar mhianach a hóige. Agus a mbíonn
de phlé ann faoi dhúil an Phiarsaigh i gCú Chulainn, tá tábhacht ag
baint leis an bhfíric gurbh í Aunt Margaret a chéadrug Cú Chulainn
cróga i samhlaíocht an Phiarsaigh.

## CUR CHUIGE IDIRTHÉACSÚIL

Ach eolas a chur ar litríocht na Gaeilge, thuigfí do Bholand gurb é atá i
'Mise Éire' ná seandaictil shaíocht smionagarach náisiún na mbailte
fearann á n-athlonnú i bhfearann slán an chló. Is é an comhthéacs nua
a rianaíodh thuas a bhaineann geit fhreacnairceach an iriseora as
Cailleach Bhéarra 'Mise Éire'. In 'Mise Éire', máthair thréigthe is ea
Éire seachas leannán tréigthe na n-aislingí. Má chuireann sí tréigean
dualgas i leith a clainne, fós féin is máthair shíorghrách shíoruaibhreach

í: tá feidhm achtaithe ag an dán. Díol spéise gur guth na máthar gríosaithí seachas guth an leannáin thréigthe a fhaightear freisin i bhForógra na Poblachta.²⁶ Tugann leagan amach 'Mise Éire' slí don stair mar a sheachadtar í go hórgánach áitiúil (íochtaránach), mar gur guth máthar ag labhairt lena clann atá sa dán. Tá gach dealramh ar an scéal gur chothaigh an Piarsach an guth máithriúil seo mar straitéis chomhfhiosach. Scríobh sé san aiste *The Sovereign People*:

> A nation is bound together by natural ties, ties mystic and spiritual and ties human and kindly; an empire is at best held together by ties of human interest and at worst by brute force. The nation is the family in large, an empire is a commercial corporation in large.²⁷

I bhfianaise an ráitis thuas, is suntasach an ní é go raibh cuid mhaith d'insintí cruthaitheacha an Phiarsaigh fréamhaithe i gcruinneshamhail an teaghlaigh agus gurb é cuimhne na muintire atá mar fhráma tagartha agus moráltachta acu.²⁸ Is léir ón tagairt thuas féin go bhfuil ábhar oiriúnach in aistí an Phiarsaigh d'aon díolaim ar théacsanna bunaithe na scríbhneoireachta iarchoilíní. Áirítear anseo na haistí neamh-chnuasaithe ar cheisteanna cultúir agus náisiúnachta a foilsíodh in *An Claidheamh Soluis* agus aistí polaitiúla na sraithe *Tracts for the Times*.

Cuireann bonn idirthéacsúil a chuid scríbhinní eolas níos cruinne ar fáil seachas léamha a ghintear ag tuairimíocht faoina chlaontaí pearsanta. Thagair an Piarsach in *An Barr Buadh* don tslí ar leagadh béim ar mhoitíf dhánaíocht na hóige sa Táin agus san Fhiannaíocht.²⁹ Ach proifíl aoise na gcinnirí náisiúnacha parlaiminte agus an tslí ar mheas an Piarsach go raibh ag teip orthu seasamh láidir a thógáil a thabhairt sa mheá, tuigtear béim an Phiarsaigh in 'Mise Éire' agus i ndánta eile ar an gclann/an óige. Fir mheánaosta ab ea cinnirí an Pháirtí Éireannaigh agus an 'All for Ireland League' faoi 1912 agus mar a luadh in alt le hÉamonn Ceannt in eagrán 16 Márta de *An Barr Buadh* bhí na seanFhíníní ag fáil bháis go tiubh: ' … tá taobh eile den scéal ar óganacha na hÉireann … nach mithid dhíbh-se bheith ag corruighe?'³⁰ Nuachtán ógfhear ab ea *An Barr Buadh*; mar sin freagraíonn codarsnachtaí 'Mise Éire' (An Chailleach Bhéarra, an chlann do dhíol agus an ghlúin óg léitheoirí a rabhthas ag díriú orthu) agus béim an Phiarsaigh ar an óige i saothair eile do dheighilt aoise agus dearcaidh i saol polaitiúil na linne.

Tá ábhar fabhalscéil do lucht Iarchoilíneachais sa trácht a rinne Mac Piarais ar 'The Veiled Woman of the Battlefield', arbh ionann í, dar leis agus spiorad na litríochta. Ghlac an Piarsach ról fuinniúil samhlaitheach sna hiarrachtaí a bhí ar siúl ag Conradh na Gaeilge litríocht cheilte an bhéaloidis agus na n-eagrán speisialaithe litríochta

a chur faoi bhráid pobail leathain. Ba é a chéadmhol do Choiste
Ceantair Chonradh na Gaeilge gur cheart sraith phoiblí léachtaí agus
ceolchoirmeacha a chur ar siúl, gníomh a chuir bonn faoi láithreacht
an Chonartha sa phobal mór.[31] Bhí sé mar bhall de Choiste na
gClódhanna nuair a d'éirigh leis an gCoiste sin na mílte leabhar
Gaeilge agus leaganacha cóirithe de shaothair litríochta éagsúla a
dhíol le 'gnáthphobal'.[32] D'fhoilsigh sé a eagráin féin de théacsanna
Fiannaíochta in *An Claidheamh Soluis*.[33] Faoi mar a mheabhraíonn
Philip O'Leary dúinn, ba bheag saineolaí ar an Rúraíocht a bhí ann i
mblianta tosaigh an fhichiú haois tráth ar cuireadh eagráin
údárásacha le chéile de chuid den ábhar den chéad uair. Ba gheall le
litríocht cheilte an t-ábhar a chóirigh Mac Piarais agus a chuir sé faoi
bhráid pobail níos leithne ar bhealach tuisceanach trí leithéid a dhráma *Macghníomhartha Chúchulainn*. Mhol sé athshamhlaithe ar
chanóin na litríochta Éireannaí agus Eorpaí san alt 'Some Aspects of
Irish Literature' agus sa tsraith ar a dtugtar 'The Murder Machine'
(ina bhfuil réamhaithris freisin ar léamha Ngugi Wa Thiongo ar chu-
raclam atá deoranta ón gcultúr dúchais). Agus é ag tarraingt ar
thaighde na freacnaice, ba chorráistiúil radacach cuid dá raibh á
áiteamh ag an bPiarsach. Luaigh sé scéal Dhiarmada agus Ghráinne
mar luathúrscéal,[34] thagair do scéalta na Rúraíochta mar a bheadh
drámaí trágóideacha[35] ar Chú Chulainn mar shlánaitheoir de shliocht
diaga a raibh a scéal mar réamhinsint ar íobairt Íosa Críost;[36] agus
shamhlaigh Deirdre mar ábhar Hedda Gabler Ibsen.[37] Chuimsigh an
tsraith *Dánta Gríosuigthe Gaedheal* a chuir an Piarsach ar fáil, maille
le haistriúcháin agus nótaí eolais in *The Irish Review* sa bhliain 1913,
dánta ón seú/seachtú haois atá 'canónda' anois ach gur bheag eolas
an phobail orthu ag tosach an fhichiú haois. D'fhoilsigh sé seanchas
agus amhráin a mheabhraigh sé óna aintín agus ó bhuaiteoir
Oireachtais a d'oibrigh mar gharraíodóir i Scoil Éanna in *The Irish
Review* agus in *An Macaomh*. Mar chomheagarthóir ar an leabhar *An
tAithriseoir* chuir an Piarsach díolaim de dhánta Gaeilge ar fáil saor
in aisce do ghnáthlucht léite.[38] Ar chostas pingine a díoladh a phaim-
fléid pholaitiúla cháiliúla. Is suntasach an rud é gur shantaigh – agus
gur aimsigh – an Piarsach pobal leathan léitheoireachta, pobal a
chuimsigh na 'híochtaráin' a bhí faoi thrácht ina shaothar féin tráth
ar theip ar, nó nár suim le cuid de scríbhneoirí eile na ré (Yeats agus
Synge, mar shampla) a leithéid a dhéanamh.

## DRÁMA

Is beag aitheantas a thugann tráchtairí ar stair na drámaíochta
Gaeilge don scagadh cáiréiseach a dhein an Piarsach ar na múnlaí is
fearr a d'oirfeadh do dhrámaíocht Ghaelach a bheadh dúchasach

agus nua-aoiseach araon. In alt in *An Claidheamh Soluis* sa bhliain 1906 mhol an Piarsach d'aisteoirí agus do bhainisteoirí stáitse:

> ... first, to study the art of the Irish traditional reciter; and secondly, to pay an occasional visit to the Abbey Theatre ... the one puts the student in touch with Ireland while the other puts him in touch with the best contemporary ideas.[39]

Go comhfhiosach a chuaigh an Piarsach i mbun an chomhnasctha seo idir foirmeacha dúchais na drámaíochta agus na hamharclannaíochta nua-aimseartha. Faoin teideal 'Miracle plays' a fógraíodh *Íosagán* agus *The Master* sa bhliain 1906. Aimsíodh fearainn nua ghradamúla do shnáth seo na drámaíochta dúchais. Nuair a stáitsíodh na drámaí dúchais *An Naomh ar Iarraidh* le Dúbhglas de Híde agus *The Coming of Fionn* le Standish O'Grady i Scoil Éanna, bhí cuid de mhóruaisle shaol cultúrtha na cathrach i láthair ag ceann de na léirithe: de bharr poiblíocht an Phiarsaigh deineadh tuairisc ar na drámaí san *Irish Independent*, sa *London Sphere*, sa *Freeman's Journal*, sa *Leader*, sa *Nation* agus i *Sinn Fein*.[40] Bhí cóiriú ar amhrán saothair ('Ding Dong Didearó') mar chuid den dráma *Macghníomhartha Chúchulainn* a léiríodh ar thailte Scoil Éanna sa bhliain 1909 agus dúirt an Piarsach faoi:

> I have kept close to the Táin even at the risk of what some people might call dramatic effect, but in this matter I have greater trust in the instinct of the unknown shapers of our epic than in the instinct of any modern.[41]

Léiríodh an dráma ina dhiaidh sin arís ag Feis Bhaile an Ghearlánaigh. Chuir Mac Piarais sleachta as 'Caoineadh na dTrí Muire' sa léiriú clúiteach a deineadh dá dhráma Páise sa bhliain 1911. Mar ghlóir-réim, seachas mar dhráma traidisiúnta, a staitsíodh an dara dráma uaidh a tharraing ar an Táin, *The Defence of the Ford*, a cuireadh ar siúl i bPáirc an Chrócaigh/Jones's Road sa bhliain 1913.[42] Tá an cónascadh seo a rinne an Piarsach idir leagan amach na drámaíochta nua-aimseartha agus fearainn agus foirmeacha na n-ealaíon dúchais ag teacht le léamha an scríbhneora cháiliúil Ngugi Wa Thiongo ar mhúnlaí inmhianaithe na drámaíochta iarchoilíní.[43] Freagraíonn sé freisin don athchódú ar mhúnlaí dúchais a dtugann Christopher Balme '*syncretic theatre*' air.[44] Is léir ó léacht a thug an Piarsach faoi mhúnlaí dúchasacha na drámaíochta Gaeilge tráth ar léiríodh an dráma dúchais *Dúlaing Óg agus an Leannán Sí* i dteannta *Íosagán* agus *The Master* san Amharclann Ghaelach, Sr. Hardewicke, i mBealtaine na bliana 1915 go raibh taighde leanúnach ar siúl aige ar na féidearthachtaí a bhain le drámaíocht dhúchasach Ghaelach.[45] Tá *credo* polaitiúil an Phiarsaigh (agus an bunús íochtaránach ar dóigh

leis féin bheith leis an g*credo* sin) le fáil sa dráma 'The Singer' (1915)
áit a ngríosaíonn amhráin fir óig san iarthar a chomhaosaigh le héirí
amach i ndráma a mheabhraíonn idir fhoirm na hAislinge agus
Chathleen Ní Houlihan Yeats.

## PRÓS

Smaoineamh lárnach de chuid léann an iarchoilíneachais is ea an sracadh idir an chumhacht impiriúil agus an ceantar nó duine a imeal-
laíodh ag gníomh an choilínithe. Tá an leagan amach seo, a for-
braíodh ar dtús i gcomhthéacs eile ag Jacques Derrida le fáil mar
bhunchloch argóintí lucht teoirice an iarchoilíneachais, léithéid
Edward Said in *Orientalism* (1978) a aithnítear go minic mar théacs
bunaidh an réimse, agus Homi Bhabha in *The Location of Culture*
(1994). Ach an fráma coincheapúil seo a earcú soiléirítear sainfhoráis
a bhain an Piarsach amach i seánraí eile freisin – sa ghearrscéalaíocht,
mar shampla. Sa scéal 'Na Bóithre' déanann an Piarsach imeallú ar
ghuth an 'reacaire' chathairlonnaithe (an cuairteoir ó Bhaile Átha
Cliath/an carachtar a sheasann dó féin) agus fágtar an urlabhra faoi
mhuintir Ros na gCaorach – pobal imeallaithe Conamarach. In
úrscéalta 'náisiúnacha' an naoú céad déag, ba ghnách urlabhraí
d'aicme 'ghradamúil' ag tuairisciú ar an gcosmhuintir. Cloíonn
gearrscéalta an Phiarsaigh le coinbhinsiúin na gearrscéalaíochta léim
isteach san eachtraíocht *in medias res*. Ach toisc gur de ghuth an
bhéaloidis a labhraítear, cuireann an reacaireacht Ros na
gCaorach/Ros Muc – agus Éire – in iúl mar cheantar a fheidhmíonn
ina chomhthéacs slán féin. Tír aithnid mhuinteartha í seachas an 'tír
choimhthíoch' a bhraith Daniel Corkery in úrscéalta Angla-Éirean-
nacha, mar gur mhinic, dar leis, tráchtaire deoranta mar reacaire
iontu.[46] Nuair a mhaígh Synge nár úsáid sé ach réim focal ar leith sa
léiriú a rinne sé ar mhuintir an Iarthair in *The Playboy of the Western
World* bhí sé ag tabhairt le fios go raibh muintir an Iarthair ar deighilt
ó dhioscúrsa an mheitreapailis. Ach nuair a léitear amach an nuacht
ón iasacht ón nuachtán sa scéal *Na Bóithre*, 'Scéalta ón Domhan
Thiar is ón Domhan Thoir' atá i gceist, faoi mar a bhíodh in *An
Claidheamh Soluis* sa saol fíor: léarscáiliú a bhain feidhm as
frásaíocht na scéalta gaisce agus a d'fhág go raibh Conamara agus
Éire sa lár.

Dearbhaítear go minic nár chás le gearrscéalta an Phiarsaigh ar an
mórgóir na ceisteanna síceolaíochta, polaitíochta agus sóisialta a
luaigh an Piarsach féin mar ghnó na nualitríochta Gaeilge. Ach féach
gur daoine imeallaithe iad formhór na gcarachtar i ngearrscéalta an
Phiarsaigh. Cailín a mbíonn briseadh síos aici nuair a dhéanann sí iarracht cur i gcoinne chultúr patrarcach na linne í Nóra i 'Na Bóithre'.

Faightear fear siúil agus bean 'a rinne peaca' sa scéal 'An Deargadaol' agus bean atá as a meabhair sa scéal 'An Bhean Chaointe'. Tarlaíonn físeanna Mháire, Nóra agus Eoghainín na nÉan i scéalta a bhfuil a mbunús fréamhaithe sa réalachas. Mheabhródh modh reacaireachta seo an Phiarsaigh, a chuimsíonn eachtraí atá neamhspleách ar mhúnlaí réadúla insintí an láir, an réalachas draíochtúil a úsáidtear mar straitéis reacaireachta sa lá atá inniu ann ag leithéidí Gabriel Garçia Marquez agus Milan Kundera chun malairt gutha a chur ar fáil do dhaoine nó do thuairimí imeallaithe. Ach láithreacht an Phiarsaigh ar thoscaireacht a dhein achainí ar mhaoiniú scéimeanna leathadh eolais faoi na galair scamhóg, a bhí go rábach i gConamara sa bhliain 1908, a mheabhrú, tuigfear go bhfuil idir raidiceacht agus chomhthuiscint ag baint le scéal 'simplí' bhás Eoghainín.[47] D'fhéadfaí a áiteamh gur bhunaigh Aisling Ní Dhonnchadha a breithiúnas siúd ar ghearrscéalta an Phiarsaigh (gur den 'mhionghléas' iad ) ar an gcoincheap gur ann do, agus gur inmhianaithe an rud é, éabhlóid líneach na nualitríochta ón mbéaloideas i dtreo foirmeacha a chomhlíonann critéir áirithe nua-aoiseacha.[48]Ach féach gur dhearbhaigh Mac Piarais féin gur scéalta iad a chuala sé ó mhuintir Ros Muc féin: dá bhrí sin is ceart gur mar nuachóiriú ar scéalta béaloideasa nó mar scéalta hibrideacha ba chóir feidhm agus fearann na scéalta a mheas. Léiríonn eagrán Chiaráin Uí Choigligh de shaothar fileata an Phiarsaigh gur athleaganacha de dhánta a bhí ar fáil fós sa bhéaloideas cuid de dhánta an Phiarsaigh freisin.

## STAIDÉAR IARCHOILÍNEACH: COMHTHÉACS IDIRNÁISIÚNTA

Freagraíonn úsáid an téarma 'Empire' ag an bPiarsach don chontrárthacht chórasach a tharraingíonn scríbhneoirí iarchoilíneacha idir tacar ráitis an choilíní agus freagra an duine choilínithe, contrárthacht a shuítear i gcomhthéacs teoiriciúil ar léarscáil idirnáisiúnta.[49] Scríobh sé féin i dtaobh 'briathar-chath'.[50] Shuigh sé a náisiúnachas féin i gcomhthéacs scor impireacht na Breataine.[51] D'fhéach Mac Piarais ar athbheochan na Gaeilge mar chúis a raibh toise domhanda ag baint léi. Chuaigh sé chuig an Eisteddfod agus chuig Mod na hAlban mar theachtaire an Chonartha. I measc ábhar cainte léachtóirí a tháinig chuig Scoil Éanna bhí ceist teanga mhuintir na Seoirsia agus téarnamh cultúrtha agus sóisialta mhuintir na hIndia.[52] Le linn shaolré an Phiarsaigh féin léiríodh leagan dá dhráma 'An Rí' i dteannta *The Post Office* leis an scríbhneoir Indiach Rabindranath Tagore. Sa bhliain 1915 léiríodh leagan de 'An Rí' i mBengal na hIndia.[53] An méid a scríobh David Lloyd faoi fhís Léann an Iarchoilíneachais in Éirinn, is léir faoi seo gurbh é ab fhís do shaothar an Phiarsaigh chomh maith:

Irish Postcolonial studies is dedicated to the work of retrieving the different rhythms of historically marginalised cultures and to the alternative conceptions of culture and of social relations that account for their virtual occlusion from written history. But it is no less dedicated to imagining out of that different knowledge the alternative projects that will convert the damage of history into the terms for future survival.[54]

Nuair is é nóisean an nua-aoisithe a bhíonn mar chrann stiúrtha na léirmheastóireachta agus go háirithe nuair nach dtuigtear an cúlra soch-chultúrtha as ar fáisceadh an saothar, bíonn na slata tomhais a chuirtear ar fáil do shaothar an Phiarsaigh easnamhach místuama. Dearcadh forásach ilchultúrtha a spreag Mac Piarais seachas aon súil siar aonrach. Léiríonn an casadh samhlaíoch a baineadh as 'Mise Éire' don scannán *Aimhirghin* (inimirceach ag léamh 'Mise Éire') gur tacar éigríochta fós líon na mínithe is féidir a bhaint as a shaothar. Is saibhride léann an iarchoilíneachais agus ár n-eolas ar an bPiarsach araon ach leas a bhaint as lionsa iarchoilíneach chun athscrúdú a dhéanamh ar a shaol agus ar a shaothar.

# 'An Heroic Poet who didn't amass Riches':[1] P.H. Pearse and Máirtín Ó Direáin

## EOGHAN Ó hANLUAIN

It is probably true to say that it was apparent from Máirtín Ó Direáin's writing from the anthology *Ó Mórna agus Dánta eile* (1957) onwards, that he was deliberately fostering special style conventions in vocabulary, similes and metaphors to deal with particular patterns of his imagination and thought.

Words like 'cleacht' (practise) and 'glac' (take) come to mind immediately, for instance, in the case of vocabulary, considering how attracted he was by the proverbial construction of Irish, so that often the full meaning and effect of a poem was dependent on the reader's understanding of the meaning and function of the proverb. Or it appears that the poem is built on an established old saying which he tries to implement in a new way, or at least to weave it into the fabric of his own creation.

It was noted that what he was doing was laying a pattern of words which had long-term Irish literature and vocabulary acceptance, as well as the native fluency of his dialect, on his poetic concerns. Some of his poems would lead you to believe that it was the old saying itself, and whatever particular magic it played on him, that inspired the poem in him in the first instance.

He boldly, unapologetically let it be known in the preface of *Ó Mórna agus Dánta eile* that he intended to take out of the corners 'a number of words with the rust and dust of idleness on them that have not been put out of the corners yet and needed to be put out, so that they would be lights of joy in our presence. I intend to put some of them out of the corners, provided that God grants me the life and ability to do it.'[2]

This was, of course, what he did, and it is interesting to take a discerning look at samples of his work method, as in the poem

'Deireadh Oileáin' [End of an Island]:

> Life's beginning is everywhere
> Declining quickly every day,
> Men and time usually cohabiting
> Which foretells its death early.

> Tá an saol *céadra* i ngach áit
> Ag meath go mear gach lá,
> Fir is an cian ag *céadladh* de ghnáth
> A thuarann go luath a bhás.[3]

The two words 'céadra' [beginning] and 'céadladh' [cohabiting] are
to be found on the same page of Dinneen's Dictionary. A very good
example of the 'putting out of the corners' is how nicely they correlate with the construction of that poem so that his rummagings
over the language are a creative act in themselves, a style which
Pearse himself practised from time to time. In the same way, the three
words 'cadar' [hermaphrodite], 'cadhal' [skin] and 'cachtúil'
[servile], which Ó Direáin uses resourcefully in 'Ó Mórna', are to be
found on another page of Dinneen.

Another example of the way he came on an expression which suited him well in the poem 'Mar chaitheamar an choinneal' [As we
burned out the candle] is 'cléirigh an tréis' [the clerks of treason]:

> If it wasn't in tragic Kinsale
> That our way of life was ruined,
> Was it the wise leaders
> Or *the clerks of treason* who betrayed?

> Murar i gCionn tSáile an léin
> A cuireadh ár gcleacht ó rath,
> Arbh iad na cinnirí críonna
> Nó *cléirigh an tréis* a d'fheall?[4]

Indeed, he used this expression again in 'Smaointe dóite ar
sheancheist' [Bitter thoughts on an old question]:

> Who betrayed all of us
> Who were hoping our day would come?
> It is not enough to say the *treason of the clerks*,
> As clerks think of themselves.

> Cé d'fheall orainn go léir,
> Bhí ag dréim go dtiocfadh ár lá?
> Ní leor *tréas na gcléireach* a rá,

Mar bíonn cléirigh gar dóibh féin.[5]

It is probable that he effectively borrowed it from the title of Julien Benda's famous book *La Trahison des Clercs* [The Betrayal of the Intellectuals] or indirectly from a verse of William Empson's poem 'Just a smack at Auden':

> What was said by Marx, boys, what did it perpend?
> No good being sparks, boys, waiting for the end
> *Treason of the clerks,* boys, curtains that descend,
> Lights becoming dark, boys, waiting for the end.[6]

On the other hand 'La Trahison des Clercs' was the title of a noteworthy editorial in *Feasta* (January 1950) attacking the bias against Irish in University College Dublin.

    However, he never hesitated to allow a word or a turn of phrase which was lodged in his ear, and was also part of his 'courting with the old poem' henceforth, to run freely, a word which created rhythm in him, which awakened and fostered in him that melodious music which was the true native music of his poetry, music which imposes partnership on the reader.

    It must have been while Ó Direáin was at school that Pearse's writings, or at least some of them, were presented to him for the first time and he read them with fervour after that. I conclude that Pearse's stories and poems made a great impression on him. Many years later when he was recalling his family heading to Sunday mass, it is Pearse's description which he thinks about as a finishing touch to his own account:

12.1 Mrs Pearse and Thomas Warren arriving at the Dáil in 1922. Courtesy Pearse Museum.

> But in my time they used to go east early. Mass was in Youghal church, Youghal chapel. I'd say that it was six miles from us at any rate and there was a hillock in the road, a few hillocks in the road, and on a hot Summer day, the month of June now, for example, it was very hard on them going east then ... But I always noticed that the old people were the first over. Perhaps, indeed, they thought that they needed to start in time ... and the people used to walk east to mass ... And they used to be, as Pearse said in 'seanMhaitias', 'one by one and in little groups'.[7]

It is very obvious from certain of Pearse's poems and stories that they influenced some of Ó Direáin's poems. Pearse had a romantic view of Conamara, or that is what can be read from some of his stories and poems, in the same way as can be read from Ó Direáin's early poems about Árainn. In his delightful booklet *Conamara* (1954), Seán Mac Giollarnáth (1880–1970) says:

> There is a spot in Cois Fharraige behind a line of trees that stands between it and the sea. The line was so thin forty years ago that the trees only broke the glistening surface of the bay. Trees are always pleasing to behold, and very often the sea delights the eye, but trees and sea in proximity are doubly attractive and are exhilarating to the mind. Once on this spot I accompanied an Piarsach walking towards the trees and the sea. As was usual with him he seemed inclined to silence, but suddenly he spoke: 'We could have here a little Gaelic kingdom of our own.' It had for years been like this with him; in the midst of the most pleasantly distracting surroundings his thoughts were of an Irish-speaking nation.

Let us look at another of Ó Direáin's references to the same Pearse:

> Another little story about Pearse, may God have mercy on him. If I wasn't at the school, I saw the students. It was my privilege, that at least one of them was a dear friend of mine, Piaras Béaslaí. And Piaras was telling me a story once, about the detective Daniel Hoey [Daniel Hoey, +1919]. I'm not sure that some of Michael Collins' men did not catch your man later. But he was well on the alert … against this Hoey man and they knew well, they knew him well and they knew … that he was after them. But Pearse and Piaras Béaslaí were going home from a meeting one night and this man was following them and keeping an eye on them for a long time and Piaras Béaslaí said to Pearse, he said: 'That man is following us for a long time.' 'What man?', said Pearse. 'Is it that you don't know him?', he said. 'He is following you for half a year!' 'I never heard of him', said Pearse, 'I don't know the man at all.' Pearse had no interest in him, it didn't matter how many detectives were after him. He had something to do and he probably didn't care. But what Piaras Béaslaí meant was that Pearse was no revolutionary like Dan Breen [1894–1980] or Tom Barry [1897–1980]. He wouldn't be long following them, I'd say![8]

The following is another example of Ó Direáin's high regard for Pearse, and his defence of him as a writer. He is describing him in a poem of his own in 'An Sméis' [The Leer]:

> On his voice, I sensed his kind,
> The kind that practise the little lie,
> That it is clear that their jeering laughter is enough
> To put the naïve likes of me from the door.

If naïve itself, not blind,
And I have no need of *extended sight*
Over distance of space, the leering smile
To see on his mouth, and the surly expression.

Ar a ghlór do bhraitheas a shórt,
An sórt gur nós acu an mionéitheach,
Gur follas a ngáire cnáide is leor
Chun mo leithéid shaonta a chur ó dhoras.

Más saonta féin ní dall,
Is níor chall dom *síneadh radhairc*
Thar achar spáis, chun draothadh na sméise
A fheiceáil ar a bhéal, is smulc sách.[9]

'extended vision'. Colm Cille said, or he is credited with, 'my
vision I stretch over seas', when he was saying goodbye to
Ireland. As a result of that, Pearse was attacked by some of the
Munster authors at that time. It was they who were the ascendancy. It is not that I have anything against them, the creatures,
now or at that time, but they had the dominance, they had the
ability at that time! And they attacked Pearse vehemently when
he said that the white roads, I don't remember now exactly the
thing, but that 'the roads [were] stretching' … far away from
him. In spite of what Colm Cille said about the vision, 'my
vision I stretch over seas', and in spite also of that which we
have, and that which we often have … 'My pasture was
stretched with his pasture and we swapped them' … But a pasture would be 'stretched' with another pasture when they were
like this – together. Therefore that is correct in Irish, to be
stretched, and the road to be stretching from you also. That is
correct in Irish.[10]

This talk shows how devoted Ó Direáin was to Pearse's writing and
the loyalty and respect he had for that work. It might be well to mention two poems here about the Easter Rising and its aftermath by Ó
Direáin. The two poems are very closely linked. In truth, they are
reproductions of each other, 'Mná na hAiséirí' [Women of the
Rising] and 'Ár Laochra' [Our Heroes], and in truth again, both
would fit suitably into the fine anthology of poets of the era *Nine-
Sixteen. An Anthology* (1935), which Edna C. Fitzhenry collected:

Let us bow humbly to the band of daughters
Who stood unyielding in the righteous fight
To take the right of our race from foreigners,

Who bequeathed their devotion, their feminine heritage,
Gave their hearts' loyalty lovingly to Ireland.

The band of daughters were ready to stand
When this city lit up for a period with valour
When Easter's intoxication captured its main street for a week,
When our lions went to battle with foreigners,
When they called on the living and the dead to follow them.

Umhlaímis go humhal don bhuíon iníonda
A sheas gan feacadh sa spéirling fhíorga
Chun ceart ár gcine a bhaint de dhanair,
Thiomnaigh a ndúthracht, a ndúchas banda,
Thug dílse a gcroí go dil do Bhanba.

Bhí an bhuíon iníonda i dtreo chun seasaimh
Nuair a las an chathair seo seal den ghaisce,
Nuair a ghabh meisce Chásca a príomhshráid seachtain,
Nuair a chuaigh ár leoin chun gleo le Galla,
Nuair a ghairm ar a gcúl na beo is na mairbh.[11]

There is a clear reference here 'When they called on the living and the dead to follow them' to the words of Pearse at the start of the Easter Proclamation, 'In the name of God and of the dead generations'.

In 'Ár Laochra' [Our Heroes] Ó Direáin resorts to history again, enriching his own rhetoric and praising those of the Rising, but this time he draws upon the history of literature:

Your drunkenness of valour
Your victory
Your prize
Without a stain on your chalk uniforms
*And the word is wedged in the throat*
The person who would say if it were left to bleach
That there would be mildew with time.

Bhur meisce ghaisce,
Bhur mbua agaibh,
Bhur nduais agaibh,
Gan smál ar bhur n-éide chailce,
*Is dingtear an focal i mbráid*
An té déarfadh dá bhfágtaí ar tuar
Go ndéanfadh grán dubh le haimsir.[12]

Again here, Ó Direáin weaves Aogán Ó Rathaille's violent saying
deftly into the body of his own poem:

> Thou wave below, of highest repute, loud-voiced,
> The senses of my head are overpowered with thy bellowing;
> Were help to come again to fair Erin,
> *I would thrust thy discordant clamour down thy throat.*

> A thonn so thíos is aoirde céim go hárd,
> Meabhair mo chinn claoidhte ót bhéiceach tá;
> Cabhair dá dtigheadh arís go hÉirinn bháin
> *Do ghlam nach binn do dhingfinn féin it bhrághaid.*[13]

It is thought that the anthology *Ár Ré Dhearóil* is Máirtín Ó Direáin's
best work. It is there, in any case, that his last poem which I refer to
is to be found, 'Éire ina bhfuil romhainn' [Ireland in the coming
times] which is relevant here. We often read in Máirtín Ó Direáin's
work the disappointment of the person who was
deceived innocently and who looks back torment-
ed on the heaven he thinks, that went astray on
him. But he is also a person who looks unyielding-
ly on the fragments of the revolution that didn't
happen during his lifetime, the complete contrast
between the pettiness of life in Ireland, as it is,
according to himself, and the idealism that is being
wasted, like the host 'that fell from the hands of
the powerful' and is 'being gnawed at by the mice'.

The title 'Éire ina bhfuil romhainn' [Ireland in
the coming times][14] is indeed a translation of the
title of an early Yeats's poem, 'To Ireland in the
Coming Times', but accordingly Ó Direáin bap-
tised his own poem with contempt. If it be the
case, that Yeats's poem is visionary, which is
demonstrated by the hope and the sentimentality
of it, it is the hopeless bitterness which drives Ó
Direáin's poem:

12.2 Patrick and
William Pearse
aeridheacht, St
Enda's, *c.* 1914.
Courtesy Pearse
Museum.

> The person who bared his sword high
> In your part at the Easter of flames,
> If he thought that he freed you from too much shame,
> Who cares, because he was only a naïve man
> And an heroic poet who didn't amass riches,
> And who left only glory behind him;
> You will be obliged to sell his glory,
> As you had to before his coming
> To be a slave for every churl over there,

And if you are given a prostitute's respect again
Be a really great prostitute,
And sell his glory and give as much as possible,
To every churl over to demand,
Betray yet his wish and take to yourself
A new spouse and a love to bed,
Because you are no longer the spouse of Eoghan or Conn,
Pearse's spouse or the love of the heroes,
But if the love must be consummated,
I plead with you, lover of the Fianna
Not to bond with them without an abundance of dollars.


An té a nocht a chlaíomh go hard
I do pháirt um Cháisc na lasrach,
Má shíl gur shaor tú ón iomad náire
Nach cuma, óir ní raibh ann ach fear saonta
Is file laochta nár cruinníodh leis stór,
Is nár fhág ina dhiaidh ach glóir;
Cuirfear iallach ort a ghlóir a dhíol,
Faoi mar ab éigean duit roimh a theacht
A bheith i do thráill ag gach bodach anall,
Is má thugtar meas méirdrí arís ort
Bí i do mhéirdrigh mhóir dáiríre,
Is díol a ghlóir is tabhair a sháith
Do gach bodach aniar chun éilimh,
Reic fós a mhian is beir i do threo
Céile nua is a stór chun leapan,
Mar ní tú feasta céile Choinn ná Eoghain,
Céile an Phiarsaigh ná rún na laoch,
Ach más éigean an cumann a chur i gcrích
Agraim thú a shearc na bhFiann,
Gan ceangal leo gan raidhse dollar.[15]

Apart from that direct reference to the poem 'I didn't amass gold' by
Pearse, the direct reference is also to the common theme of prostitution
in eighteenth-century poetry:

Long though thou hast been, O majestic, gentle-mannered Erin,
A fair nursing-mother with hospitality and true knowledge;
Henceforth shalt thou be an unwilling handmaid to every with-
    ered band,
While every foreign churl shall have sucked thy breasts.

Cé fada dhuit, 'Éire mhaordha mhín-nósmhar,
It bhanaltrain tséimh le féile is fíor-eolus,
Beir feasta aca it mhéirdrigh fé gach críon-chóisir
'S gach ladrann caethach d'éis do chlí-dheolta.[16]

(Aodhagán Ó Rathaille)

But Ó Direáin also counts Pearse alongside Conn and Eoghan, raising him to the high, noble rank of those old heroes.

Ó Direáin himself was loyal to the ideals which were the result of the founding of the Irish state, but like many of his generation, he felt that it went astray in some way. Out of this discord, out of this tension, between the ideals which appeared to Ó Direáin's generation and the use that was being made during his lifetime of those same ideals, adapting them to the politics of the time, it was out of this that he created some of his most powerful poems.

12.3 Bust of Patrick Pearse by Oliver Shepherd 1936. Courtesy Pearse Museum.

# 'File Laochta nár cruinníodh leis Stór':[1] An Piarsach agus Máirtín Ó Direáin

## EOGHAN Ó hANLUAIN

Is dóigh liom gur fíor a rá go raibh sé le haithint ar scríbhneoireacht Mháirtín Uí Dhireáin ón gcnuasach *Ó Mórna agus Dánta eile* (1957) amach, go raibh nósmhaireachtaí speisialta stíle ó thaobh foclóra agus samhlacha á gcothú d'aon oghaim aige le freastal ar chlaonta ar leith a shamhlaíochta agus a mhachnaimh. Chuimhneodh duine láithreach ar fhocail ar nós 'cleacht' agus 'glac', cuirim i gcás, ó thaobh an fhoclóra, agus a thugtha agus a bhí sé do dhul seanfhoclach na Gaeilge, sa chaoi gur minic brí agus éifeacht iomlán dáin ag brath ar thuiscint an léitheora do chiall agus feidhm an tseanfhocail, nó go mbraitear go dtógtar an dán ar sheanrá bunaithe, a fhéachann sé lena chur i bhfeidhm ar bhealach nua, nó ar a laghad a shníomh isteach in inneach a dhéantúis féin.

Bhí sé le tabhairt faoi deara gurbh é a bhí ar bun aige, gréas focal, a raibh faomhadh fadaimseartha litríocht nó foclóireacht na Gaeilge aige, é sin, chomh maith le líofacht dúchais a chanúna, a leagan ar chúraimí coitianta a aigne, pátrúin áirithe á gcur ar léamh ar leith a mheoin agus ar a bhraistintí fileata. Shílfeá ar dhánta áirithe dá chuid gurbh é an seanrá féin agus cibé draíocht ar leith a d'imir sé air, gurbh é seo a bhog an dán ann an chéad uair.

Thug sé le fios go dána, neamhleithscéalach i réamhrá *Ó Mórna agus Dánta eile* go raibh ar aigne aige 'focla go leor a bhfuil meirg is deannach an díomhaointis orthu nár cuireadh as na cúinní fós, agus níor mhiste a gcur ionas go mba lóchrainn aitis inár bhfianaise iad. Tá rún agamsa roinnt acu a chur as na cúinní ach Dia tuilleadh saoil agus cumais a thabhairt dom chuige'.[2]

Rud a rinne sé ar ndóigh, agus is spéisiúil breathnú go grinn ar shamplaí dá mhodh oibre, a leithéid seo sa dán 'Deireadh Oileáin':

Tá an saol *céadra* i ngach áit
Ag meath go mear gach lá,

Fir is an cian ag *céadladh* de ghnáth
A thuarann go luath a bhás.[3]

An dá fhocal úd 'céadra' agus 'céadladh', tá siad le fáil ar an leathanach céanna d'fhoclóir an Duinnínigh. Sampla an-mhaith den 'chur as na cúinní' iad, a dheise a thagann siad le dul an dáin úd sa chaoi gur gníomh cruthaitheach ann féin a chuid ransaithe ar fud na teanga, nós a chleacht an Piarsach féin, ó uair go chéile. Sa tslí chéanna, tá na trí fhocal 'cadar', 'cadhal', agus 'cachtúil' a chuireann an Direánach chun tairbhe go seiftiúil in 'Ó Mórna' le fáil ar leathanach eile den Duinníneach.

Sampla eile den chaoi ar tháinig sé ar leagan cainte a d'fheil go binn dó sa dán 'Mar chaitheamar an choinneal', is ea 'cléirigh an tréis':

Murar i gCionn tSáile an léin
A cuireadh ár gcleacht ó rath,
Arbh iad na cinnirí críonna
Nó *cléirigh an tréis* a d'fheall?[4]

Leagan é 'cléirigh an tréis' a d'úsáid sé arís ar ndóigh in 'Smaointe dóite ar sheancheist':

Cé d'fheall orainn go léir,
Bhí ag dréim go dtiocfadh ár lá?
Ní leor *tréas na gcléireach* a rá,
Mar bíonn cléirigh gar dóibh féin.[5]

Is dóichí gur go díreach ó theideal leabhar cáiliúil Julien Benda *La Trahison des Clercs* (The Betrayal of the Intellectuals) a thóg sé ar iasacht go héifeachtúil é, nó go hindíreach ó dhán William Empson, 'Just a smack at Auden':

What was said by Marx, boys, what did it perpend?
No good being sparks, boys, waiting for the end
*Treason of the clerks,* boys, curtains that descend,
Lights becoming dark, boys, waiting for the end.[6]

Ar an lámh eile, ba é 'La Trahison des Clercs' an ceannteideal a bhí ar eagarfhocal suntasach in *Feasta* (Eanáir 1950) ag tabhairt faoi leatrom an Choláiste Ollscoile, Baile Átha Cliath, ar an nGaeilge.

Níor leasc leis riamh, áfach, ligean a thabhairt d'fhocal nó do leagan cainte a lonnaigh ar an gcluais istigh aige agus ar chuid dá 'shuirí le seandán' feasta é, focal a thuismigh rithim ann, a dhúisigh agus a chothaigh ann an ceol taidhiúir sin arb é fíorcheol dúchais a chuid filíochta é, ceol a bhrúnn páirtíocht ar an léitheoir.

Ní foláir nó gur ar scoil dó a cuireadh scríbhinní an Phiarsaigh nó

cuid díobh ina láthair an chéad uair agus gur léigh sé le díograis ina
dhiaidh sin iad. Déanaim amach go ndeachaigh scéalta agus dánta an
Phiarsaigh i gcion go mór air. Na blianta ina dhiaidh sin agus é ag
cuimhneamh ar a mhuintir ag triall ar aifreann an Domhnaigh is é cur
síos an Phiarsaigh a ritheann leis mar bhailchríoch ar a chuntas féin:

> Ach le mo linnse bhídís ag dul soir go moch. Bhíodh aifreann i
> dteach phobail Eochaille, séipéal Eochaille. Déarfainn go raibh
> sé sin sé mhíle uainn ar chuma ar bith nó cúig mhíle agus bhí
> aird sa mbóthar, cúpla aird sa mbóthar, agus lá te samhraidh, mí
> Meithimh anois, cuir i gcás, bhí sé an-dian orthu a gabháil soir
> ansin. ... Ach thugainn faoi deara i gcónaí gurb iad na sean-
> daoine na chéad daoine a bhíodh thoir. B'fhéidir, ar ndóigh, gur
> cheapadar nárbh fholáir dóibh tosaí in am. ... agus shiúladh na
> daoine soir go dtí an t-aifreann. Agus bhídis mar adeir an
> Piarsach in seanMhaitias, 'ina nduine, is ina nduine is ina mion-
> dreamannaí'.[7]

Is ríléir ar dhánta agus ar scéalta áirithe eile leis an bPiarsach go raibh
anáil acu ar dhánta leis an Diréanach. Bhí dearcadh rómánsúil ag an
bPiarsach ar Chonamara, nó sin atá le léamh ar chuid dá scéalta agus
dá dhánta ar nós mar atá le léamh ar chuid de dhánta tosaigh Uí
Dhireáin i dtaobh Árann. Deir Seán Mac Giollarnáth (1880-1970)
ina leabhrán gleoite, *Conamara* (1954):

> There is a spot in Cois Fharraige behind a line of trees that
> stands between it and the sea. The line was so thin forty years
> ago that the trees only broke the glistening surface of the bay.
> Trees are always pleasing to behold, and very often the sea
> delights the eye, but trees and sea in proximity are doubly
> attractive and are exhilarating to the mind. Once on this spot I
> accompanied an Piarsach walking towards the trees and the sea.
> As was usual with him he seemed inclined to silence, but sud-
> denly he spoke: 'We could have here a little Gaelic kingdom of
> our own'. It had for years been like this with him; in the midst
> of the most pleasantly distracting surroundings his thoughts
> were of an Irish-speaking nation.

Féachaimis ar cheann eile de thagairtí an Direánaigh don Phiarsach
céanna:

> Scéal beag eile faoin bPiarsach, go ndéana Dia trócaire air. Mura
> raibh mé ag an scoil chonaic mé na scoláirí. Bhí sé de phribhléid
> agam go raibh duine amháin, ar a laghad, ina chara ionúin
> agam, is é sin Piaras Béaslaí. Agus bhí Piaras Béaslaí ag inseacht
> dom scéil, uair amháin, faoin mbleachtaire Daniel Hoey [Daniel

Hoey, +1919]. Níl a fhios agam nár rug cuid d'fhir Mhíchíl Uí Choileáin ar mo dhuine níos deireanaí. Ach bhí siad san airdeall go mór ... ar an bhfear seo Hoey agus bhí a fhios acu go maith, bhí aithne mhaith air agus bhí a fhios acu ... go raibh sé ina ndiaidh. Ach bhí an Piarsach agus Piaras Béaslaí ag dul abhaile oíche éigin ó chruinniú agus bhí an fear seo ina ndiaidh á leanacht agus ag coinneáil súil orthu ar feadh i bhfad agus dúirt Piaras Béaslaí leis an bPiarsach, a deir sé: 'Tá an fear sin ár leanúint le fada.' 'Cén fear?' a deir an Piarsach. 'An mó nach bhfuil aithne agat air?' a deir sé. 'Tá sé sin do leanachtsa le leathbhliain!' 'Níor chuala trácht riamh air', arsa an Piarsach, 'níl aithne ar bith agam ar an bhfear'. Ní raibh aon spéis ag an bPiarsach ann, ba chuma cé mhéid bleachtairí a bhí ina dhiaidh. Bhí sé ag déanamh rud áirithe agus is dóigh go mba chuma leis. Ach séard a bhí i gceist ag Piaras Béaslaí nárbh aon réabhlóidí é an Piarsach ar mhodh Dan Breen [1894–1980] ná Tom Barry [1897–1980]. Ní bheadh sé i bhfad á leanacht siúd, déarfainn![8]

Sampla eile d'ardmheas an Direánaigh ar an bPiarsach, agus a chosaint air mar scríbhneoir, an méid seo a leanas. Ag cur síos dó ar dhán dá chuid féin atá sé in 'An Sméis':

Ar a ghlór do bhraitheas a shórt,
An sórt gur nós acu an mionéitheach,
Gur follas a ngáire cnáide is leor
Chun mo leithéid shaonta a chur ó dhoras.

Más saonta féin ní dall,
Is níor chall dom *síneadh radhairc*
Thar achar spáis, chun draothadh na sméise
A fheiceáil ar a bhéal, is smulc sách.[9]

'síneadh radhairc'. Dúirt Colm Cille nó cuirtear ina leith, 'mo radharc tar sáil sínim' nuair a bhí sé ag fágáil slán ag Éirinn. Dá bhrí sin, tugadh faoin bPiarsach, cuid de údair na Mumhan san am. B'iad siúd a bhí i gcinseal. Ní hé go bhfuil tada agamsa ina gcoinne, na créatúir, anois ná an uair sin, ach is acu a bhí an cinseal, is acu a bhí an cumas san am sin! Agus thugadar go dian faoin bPiarsach nuair a dúirt sé go raibh na bóithrí bána, ní cuimhin liom anois áirithe an rud, ach go raibh 'na bóithrí ag síneadh' ... i bhfad uaidh. D'ainneoin an rud a dúirt Colm Cille faoin radharc, 'mo radharc tar sáil sínim', agus d'ainneoin, freisin, an rud atá againn féin agus a bhí go minic againn. ... 'Bhí mo bhuailese sínte lena bhuaile siúd agus rinne muid iomlaoid' ...

Ach bheadh buaile 'sínte' le buaile eile nuair a bheidís mar seo – le chéile. Dá bhrí sin tá sé sin ceart sa Ghaeilge, a bheith sínte agus an bóthar a bheith ag síneadh uait freisin. Tá sé sin ceart sa Ghaeilge.[10]

Léiríonn an chaint seo a dhíograisí agus a bhí an Direánach i leith scríbhneoireacht an Phiarsaigh agus an dílseacht agus an urraim a bhí aige don saothar sin. Níor mhiste dhá dhán leis an Direánach a bhaineann le hÉirí Amach na Cásca agus ar lean dó a lua anseo. Tá dlúthbhaint ag an dá dhán le chéile. Le fírinne is macasamhla a chéile iad, 'Mná na hAiséirí' agus 'Ár Laochra', agus le fírinne arís, thoillfidís araon go feiliúnach sa díolaim bhreá d'fhilí na linne, *Nine-Sixteen. An Anthology* (1935), a thiomsaigh Edna C. Fitzhenry:

> Umhlaímis go humhal don bhuíon iníonda
> A sheas gan feacadh sa spéirling fhíorga
> Chun ceart ár gcine a bhaint de dhanair,
> Thiomnaigh a ndúthracht, a ndúchas banda,
> Thug dílse a gcroí go dil do Bhanba.
>
> Bhí an bhuíon iníonda i dtreo chun seasaimh
> Nuair a las an chathair seo seal den ghaisce,
> Nuair a ghabh meisce Chásca a príomhshráid seachtain,
> Nuair a chuaigh ár leoin chun gleo le Galla,
> Nuair a ghairm ar a gcúl na beo is na mairbh.[11]

Tá tagairt léir anseo in 'Nuair a ghairm ar a gcúl na beo is na mairbh', d'fhocla an Phiarsaigh ag tús Fhorógra na Cásca, 'In the name of God and of the dead generations'.

In 'Ár Laochra' téann an Direánach i muinín na staire arís ag saibhriú a reitrice féin agus é ag moladh lucht an Éirí Amach, ach gurb í stair na litríochta an uair seo a tharraingíonn sé chuige:

> Bhur meisce ghaisce,
> Bhur mbua agaibh,
> Bhur nduais agaibh,
> Gan smál ar bhur n-éide chailce,
> *Is dingtear an focal i mbráid*
> An té déarfadh dá bhfágtaí ar tuar
> Go ndéanfadh grán dubh le haimsir.[12]

Arís anseo, is cumasach mar a shníomhann an Direánach ráiteas foréigneach Aogáin Uí Rathaille:

> A thonn so thíos is aoirde céim go hárd,
> Meabhair mo chinn claoidhte ót bhéiceach tá;
> Cabhair dá dtigheadh arís go hÉirinn bháin

*Do ghlam nach binn do dhingfinn féin it bhrághaid.*[13]

go conláisteach, éifeachtúil isteach i gcorp a dháin féin.

Tuairimítear gurb é an díolaim *Ár Ré Dhearóil*, buaicshaothar Mháirtín Uí Dhireáin. Is ansin, ar aon chaoi, atá an dán is deireanaí dá chuid, a bhaineann le hábhar anseo, a dtráchtfaidh mé air, 'Éire ina bhfuil romhainn'. Léimid ar shaothar Uí Dhireáin go mion minic díomá an té ar baineadh dalladh púicín na soineantachta de, agus a fhéachann siar go cráite ar an bhflaitheas, dar leis, a chuaigh amú air. Ach is duine é, chomh maith, a fhéachann gan stríocadh ar smionagar na réabhlóide nár tháinig ann di lena linnsean, an ghlanchontrárthacht idir suarachas an tsaoil in Éirinn, mar atá, dar leis-sean, agus an t-idéalachas atá á ídiú, ar nós na habhlainne 'a thit as lámha na dtréan' agus atá 'á creimeadh ag na lucha'.

Is aistriúchán é an teideal 'Éire ina bhfuil romhainn',[14] ar ndóigh, ar theideal dhán luath Yeats 'To Ireland in the Coming Times', ach is le seanbhlas a bhaist an Direánach a dhán féin dá réir. Sa chás gur dán aislingeach é dán Yeats, arb é an dóchas agus an maoithneachas a sheolann é, is é an searbhas éadóchasach a thiomáineann dán an Direánaigh:

> An té a nocht a chlaíomh go hard
> I do pháirt um Cháisc na lasrach,
> Má shíl gur shaor tú ón iomad náire
> Nach cuma, óir ní raibh ann ach fear saonta
> Is file laochta nár cruinníodh leis stór,
> Is nár fhág ina dhiaidh ach glóir;
> Cuirfear iallach ort a ghlóir a dhíol,
> Faoi mar ab éigean duit roimh a theacht
> A bheith i do thráill ag gach bodach anall,
> Is má thugtar meas méirdrí arís ort
> Bí i do mhéirdrigh mhóir dáiríre,
> Is díol a ghlóir is tabhair a sháith
> Do gach bodach aniar chun éilimh,
> Reic fós a mhian is beir i do threo
> Céile nua is a stór chun leapan,
> Mar ní tú feasta céile Choinn ná Eoghain,
> Céile an Phiarsaigh ná rún na laoch,
> Ach más éigean an cumann a chur i gcrích
> Agraim thú a shearc na bhFiann,
> Gan ceangal leo gan raidhse dollar.[15]

Taobh amuigh den tagairt ghlandíreach don dán 'Níor cruinníodh liomsa ór' leis an bPiarsach, tá an tagairt lomdíreach chomh maith do théama coitianta an striapachais i bhfilíocht an ochtú haois déag:

Cé fada dhuit, 'Éire mhaordha mhín-nósmhar,
It bhanaltrain tséimh le féile is fíor-eolus,
Beir feasta aca it mhéirdrigh fé gach críon-chóisir
'S gach ladrann caethach d'éis do chlí-dheolta.[16]
(Aodhagán Ó Rathaille)

Ach chomh maith leis seo áiríonn an Direánach an Piarsach i dteann-ta Choinn agus Eoghain, á ardú go céim ard uasal na seanlaochra úd.

Thug an Direánach féin a dhílseacht do na hidéil ba siocair le bunú an Stáit dúchais ach ar nós go leor dá ghlúin bhraith sé go ndeachthas ar seachrán ar chuma éigin. As an imreas, as an teannas seo idir na hidéil a facthas do ghlúin Uí Dhireáin agus an caitheamh a bhíothas, lena linn féin, á chur sna hidéil chéanna sin, á n-oiriúnú do pholaitíocht na huaire, as seo a chum sé cuid de na dánta is cumasaí dá chuid.

## CHAPTER THIRTEEN

# Exploiting the Past:
# Pearse as Editor and Interpreter of
# Fiannaíocht *Literature*

## CAOIMHÍN BREATNACH

A nalysis of Pearse's editing and interpretation of texts of Irish literature from the *fiannaíocht* tradition indicates that he was subjec-
tive in his use of sources and that he was apparently influenced both
by previous works on that tradition and by nationalist sentiments. The
views of Pearse and other commentators on this material appear to be
somewhat one-sided and do not adequately reflect its complex nature.
Pearse's edition of the tale *Bruidhean Chaorthainn*, which literally
means 'The Hostel of the Rowan Tree',[1] and his version of an episode
from another *fiannaíocht* text, *Cath Fionntrágha*, will be examined in
this light.[2]

### PEARSE'S EDITION OF *BRUIDHEAN CHAORTHAINN*

As is the norm with *fiannaíocht* and other traditional literary Irish
tales, we have no information regarding the author, place or time of
composition of *Bruidhean Chaorthainn*. The language of the text and
the date of the earliest manuscript witness indicate that it was written some time between 1200 and 1600. The original version does
not survive and all the surviving manuscripts were written between
the seventeenth and nineteenth centuries. Aspects of the transmission
of the tale will be discussed in more detail below. The following is a
brief summary of the tale. A force of foreigners called Lochlannaigh
invades Ireland. News of their arrival reaches the high-king, Cormac
mac Airt, and he summons Fionn and the fianna to resist them. A battle is fought in which Fionn and the fianna rout the Lochlannaigh.
The king of the Lochlannaigh and his two eldest sons are killed. At
the end of the battle the king of Lochlann's youngest son is spared
and he plots to avenge the defeat of his fellow countrymen and, in
particular, the killing of his father and brothers. He succeeds in

entrapping Fionn and some of the fianna in an enchanted hostel and intends to kill these and the rest of the fianna with a newly recruited army he has brought to Ireland. This leads to several conflicts between various members of the fianna and their opponents. Fionn and his comrades are eventually freed from the hostel and the tale concludes with another battle in which the fianna again rout their enemy.

In Pearse's edition of *Bruidhean Chaorthainn* it is stated in the introduction that his interest in the tale was first aroused as a schoolboy when he read an English translation by P.W. Joyce in *Old Celtic Romances*.[3] Joyce's version of *Bruidhean Chaorthainn* is purportedly a translation based on three manuscripts now housed in the Royal Irish Academy and written in 1733, 1766 and 1841.[4] The purpose of *Old Celtic Romances* was to make various Irish texts available in English translation. None of the original Irish texts was published in the volume. For Joyce, Fionn mac Cumhaill was a great Irish hero whom he idolised to such an extent that he even disapproved of any unfavourable portrayal of him in the literature. In a note on Fionn and the fianna, he remarks, using somewhat anachronistic military terminology:

> The Fena or 'Fena of Erin' were a sort of militia or standing army, permanently maintained by the monarch for the support of the throne, and regularly trained to military service. They attained their greatest glory in the reign of Cormac Mac Airt ... Each province had its own militia under its own captain, but all were under the command of one general-in-chief. Their most renowned commander was Finn the son of Cumal ... commander-in-chief of the Fena under king Cormac Mac Airt; brave, wise, and far-seeing, a man of supreme military ability ... Like many great commanders, he had a little of the tyrant in his character, and was unforgiving to those who injured him. But in the story of Dermat and Grania, he is drawn in too unfavourable a light.[5]

It will be seen below that Joyce's idolisation of Fionn blinded him to the fact that *Bruidhean Chaorthainn* is a tale in which Fionn could hardly be described as 'wise, and far-seeing' or 'a man of supreme military ability'. So intent was he on idolising Fionn and the fianna, however, that in several instances where emphasis is placed on their heroic valour, Joyce adds his own personal embellishments to the narrative. Another instance in which Joyce's text is a figment of his own imagination and which would seem to reflect nationalist sentiments on his part occurs at the beginning of the tale. The leader of the foreigners says to his people that he wishes to take control of

Ireland, a country which his people had previously subdued and laid under tribute. Joyce's version has him state: 'yet they held it not long; for the men of Erin arose and expelled our army, regaining their ancient freedom'.[6] There is no mention in the original Irish text of 'the men of Ireland regaining their ancient freedom'.[7]

In addition to the stated influence of Joyce's version of the tale, Pearse also expressed the view that *Bruidhean Chaorthainn* was one of the finest tales ever written while Irish was dominant. The tale was to be regarded among the principal tales of Ireland, according to Pearse, not because of the story itself but because of the way it portrays noble thoughts, true heroism, true kindness and close comradeship among friends. Pearse singles out §§21–6 of his edition for special mention and says that it would be difficult to find anything to surpass these passages in the literature of Europe in terms of the beautiful thoughts and the mellifluous speech expressed in them.[8] The fol-

13.1 Denis Gwynn as Fionn in *The Coming of Fionn*, March 1909. Courtesy Pearse Museum.

lowing is a summary of this section of *Bruidhean Chaorthainn*. Fionn and the other members of the fianna in the enchanted hostel realise that they are trapped and fear that they are soon to be killed. Meanwhile, another group of the fianna become worried on account of not hearing from Fionn and the others for some time and two of them, a son and foster-son of Fionn, decide to go to the hostel. When they arrive, it is decided that Fionn's foster-son should defend a ford near the hostel while the son goes to seek help. Fionn's foster-son then encounters one of the enemy leaders and his warrior-band at the ford. He manages to kill a hundred warriors and after a heroic struggle with the enemy leader, is eventually beheaded by him. The enemy leader subsequently encounters Fionn's son who discovers that he is carrying the decapitated head of the foster-son with him. He kisses the foster-son's head three times, engages the enemy leader in battle and eventually beheads him. He then returns to the place where the corpse of the foster-son lies, sows his head back on, buries him and then takes the enemy leader's head in triumph to Fionn in the hostel.

His high estimation of this section and his remarks about the tale in general suggest that the main reason for Pearse's interest in *Bruidhean Chaorthainn* was the portrayal, as he saw it, of Fionn and the fianna as a closely united force of impeccable warriors without any internal enmity or rancour heroically defending Ireland in armed conflict against foreign invaders.

It would seem to be the case that the aspects of *Bruidhean*

*Chaorthainn* which appealed to Pearse also had a bearing on the text he presented to his readers. Pearse's edition, published in 1908 (and which has not been superseded in print) is very much an edition of its time. Many texts in Irish were published from manuscript sources for the first time and made accessible to a wider audience at the end of the nineteenth and the beginning of the twentieth centuries. As this was very much a pioneering stage, however, one cannot expect the rigorous standards of modern textual scholarship to have been applied to editions of that period. Furthermore, as the cataloguing of the many collections of Irish manuscripts was still in its infancy, editors were not aware of all the extant sources. Pearse's edition of *Bruidhean Chaorthainn* is a case in point in that he cites twenty-eight copies of the text which were known to him.[9] Versions of the tale have since been edited in an unpublished MA thesis by Breandán Ó Cróinín, who points out that there are, in fact, over ninety extant manuscript copies of the text.[10]

A critical edition of any literary tale must take account of all the extant manuscript witnesses and the textual changes which occurred in the course of that tale's transmission. In Pearse's time, however, it was often the case that the manuscripts forming the basis for edited texts were chosen at the personal whim of editors. The earliest extant version of *Bruidhean Chaorthainn* is stated by Pearse to have been written in 1603.[11] Without explaining why, however, he based his edition primarily on a manuscript written in 1844 and incorporated some readings from two eighteenth-century manuscripts.[12] The manuscript written in 1844 is said to have been in the possession of Pearse's friend Pádraig Ó Cearmada but is, unfortunately, no longer extant.[13]

There are some textual differences between Pearse's edited text and the extant manuscript versions. It is difficult to decide whether these differences are due to editorial intervention by Pearse himself or whether they were found in his late manuscript source, which is now lost. Although there is uncertainty as to their origin, there can be no doubt that these differences point to a conscious decision on Pearse's part to present a version of *Bruidhean Chaorthainn* of his own personal choosing to his readers. One may bear in mind in this regard the aspects of the tale which appealed to Pearse discussed above.

One of the differences occurs in a passage concerning a member of the fianna who is named Conán Maol or 'Bare Conán'. Conán was so named because he became stuck to the floor in the enchanted hostel and had to be pulled from it, thereby leaving his skin stuck to the ground. In Pearse's edition Conán loses the skin of his heels, the back of his head and his shoulder-blades.[14] In most of the manuscript versions, however (including two of the three manuscripts used by Pearse for his edition), Conán also loses the skin of his buttocks. Among the shortcomings of Irish texts published in Pearse's time was the frequent indulgence in bowdlerisation on the part of editors. In many cases, editors did not even acknowledge any alteration of text. As some scribes were also prone to alter or omit material they regarded as indelicate, it may be the case that the scribe of the third manuscript used by Pearse omitted the reference to Conán's buttocks. It remains the case nevertheless that Pearse made an editorial decision, either by following a particular manuscript version or by altering the manuscript evidence, to omit this section of text in his edition. Joyce clearly was of one mind with Pearse in this regard because in his version of the tale there is no mention whatsoever of this episode.[15]

We may here compare Pearse's edited version of sections of text relating to another member of the fianna, namely, Diarmaid ó Duibhne. The first instance occurs when the aforementioned Conán Maol, trapped in the enchanted hostel, asks Diarmaid to bring him food and drink. Diarmaid says that Conán's request is inappropriate, given the plight of the fianna. Conán taunts Diarmaid in response and says that if a woman had made the request, Diarmaid would have no hesitation in carrying it out. This is the basic text of all the manuscripts (including the two surviving manuscripts used by Pearse in his edition). In Pearse's edited text, however, *cara dlúth nó duine gaolmhar* 'close friend or relative' is found instead of *bean* 'woman'.[16] Diarmaid then has to go off and find food and drink. When he returns to the hostel, he has to make a hole in the roof in order to pour the drink down into Conán's mouth. He fails to hit the mark in his first attempt and Conán again taunts him by saying that if a woman was beneath him he would be deadly accurate. Some later scribes clearly felt that this item of text was indelicate and omitted it. In Pearse's edition, *cara dlúth nó duine gaolmhar* is again found instead of *bean*.[17] It would seem to be the case, therefore, that in his edited version of these sections of text relating to Conán Maol and Diarmaid, Pearse decided that any material which was not in keeping with his idealised view of the fianna was to be either excluded or modified.

13.2 Desmond Carney as Giolla na Naomh in An Rí, June 1912. Courtesy Pearse Museum.

## THE INFLUENCE OF GEOFFREY KEATING'S PORTRAYAL OF FIONN
## AND THE FIANNA

An idealised view of Fionn and the fianna would also seem to account for the failure of Joyce and Pearse, among others, to take into consideration a central aspect of the narrative of *Bruidhean Chaorthainn*. In this regard we may turn to a matter which has had an important bearing on the transmission of *fiannaíocht* texts and which has greatly influenced the views of some writers on this material. In an article he wrote on the fianna, Pearse refers to their portrayal as an army defending Ireland on behalf of high-kings and diligently guarding the harbours of Ireland against foreign invaders and points out that this is how the fianna were described by Geoffrey Keating in the seventeenth century.[18] The work by Keating referred to by Pearse is *Foras Feasa ar Éirinn,* a narrative history of Ireland down to the time of the arrival of the Anglo-Normans which is based on historical and traditional sources and which was compiled around the 1630s.[19] It instantly became very popular in Irish manuscript tradition and was widely accepted as an authoritative historical source. Keating also provided, on occasion, his own versions of traditional tales and such was the influence of his work that some scribes modified their copies of the same tales on the basis of Keating's versions.[20]

The view that one of the primary functions of Fionn and the fianna was to defend Ireland on behalf of high-kings, in particular the king Cormac mac Airt, against foreign invaders intent on violating her sovereignty is one which owes much to the influence of Keating. The latter, however, had a very idealistic view of Fionn and the fianna and examination of fiannaíocht sources presents us with a much more complex situation. In many of these sources, Fionn and Cormac mac Airt are, in fact, portrayed as bitter enemies.

Another aspect of Keating's portrayal of Fionn and the fianna not in keeping with all the sources is their role as guardians of Ireland's harbours against foreign invaders. *Bruidhean Chaorthainn* illustrates how this view has become so embedded in people's minds that, ironically, it has gone unnoticed that a central aspect of this tale is Fionn's remissness in this regard. When the Lochlannaigh arrive in Ireland they come ashore unchallenged at a harbour in Ulster and begin to plunder the country. Fionn and the fianna only become aware of this when they are informed by the king, Cormac mac Airt. The fianna are victorious in the first battle but this is followed by a series of errors of judgement on the part of Fionn, whose negligence and naïvety are the ultimate cause of the need to defeat the Lochlannaigh for a second time. The only Lochlannach survivor of the first battle is the king's youngest son. Fionn errs first of all in taking the son under his protection. He then allows him into his household and even crowns him king of Lochlann. After he has spent a long time in their company, members of the fianna warn Fionn about the danger of allowing their enemy to become so intimately associated with them and it is then decided that the king of Lochlann's association with the fianna should be brought to an end and that he should be given his own lands in Ireland. This too is a mistake compounded by Fionn's decision to allow him his own choice of land in whichever province he wishes. The newly crowned king chooses a district which is said to comprise Caonraighe (anglicised Kenry) in County Limerick, on the south side of the Shannon and a district of corresponding size on the north of the Shannon. As stated in the text, these districts were chosen by the king in order to give him access to the expansive harbour between both territories and, tellingly, it is added that this harbour was not normally guarded. Unsurprisingly, it is the king's intention to exploit this situation to his own advantage by bringing many of his followers and allies to Ireland via this unguarded harbour. It is clear, therefore, that although Fionn and the fianna engage in battle with foreigners in *Bruidhean Chaorthainn*, they are not portrayed as guardians of Ireland's harbours. Fionn, in fact, actually invites invasion by naïvely giving control of one of Ireland's main harbours to his enemy.

Mention has been made above of the influence of Geoffrey Keating's *Foras Feasa ar Éirinn*, on whose authority some scribes modified their copies of traditional tales. In several copies of *Bruidhean Chaorthainn* written after the circulation of *Foras Feasa ar Éirinn*, certain scribes, presumably accustomed to a portrayal such as Keating's of Fionn and the fianna as guardians of Ireland's harbours, found it strange that, in this tale, the king of Lochlann should have been given control of the Shannon harbour by Fionn. Consequently, various attempts were made to reconcile the discrepancy. In certain copies, such as that found in Royal Irish Academy MS 3 B 8, written in the early nineteenth century, the original text is modified by means of an explanation that Fionn guarded all the harbours of Ireland with the sole exception of Caonraighe. In Pearse's edition, it is explained that Fionn guarded the harbours and ports of Ireland but that his attention was focused mainly on the harbours in the north.[21] These are clearly later additions and represent somewhat desperate attempts to reconcile the contradictory evidence of different sources as the idea that Fionn guarded all the harbours of Ireland with the sole exception of Caonraighe or, even more implausibly, that his attention was focused on northern harbours, is radically undermined by the fact that at the beginning of the tale, as noted above, the Lochlannaigh arrive in Ireland on the coast of Ulster and are unchallenged by Fionn and the fianna.

Another failing on Fionn's part in *Bruidhean Chaorthainn* occurs after his enemy has eventually settled his army secretly in Ireland. While hunting, Fionn encounters the king of Lochlann but fails to recognise who he is. He is reproached by a member of the fianna who points out that it is more important for Fionn to be able to recognise his enemies than his friends. Following this, Fionn is compromised into visiting the enchanted hostel in which the king of Lochlann intends to kill him and it is now that the full consequences of Fionn's earlier mistakes are revealed as the fianna are forced into several conflicts with foreign enemies. The tale then concludes with the second battle between the opposing forces. Fionn and the fianna are victorious again and only a few foreigners manage to return to their ships. There is no mention of any leniency being shown to the enemy and it would seem that the intended message was that this is what should have happened after the first battle. A central theme of the tale would seem to be, therefore, that one's enemy should never be trusted.

*Bruidhean Chaorthainn* is a tale which has undergone significant modification in the course of its transmission and is one example of a fiannaíocht text which presents the reader with a somewhat more complex picture of Fionn and the fianna than that portrayed by Keating, Joyce and Pearse.

### PEARSE'S TEXT AND INTERPRETATION OF A PASSAGE FROM *CATH FIONNTRÁGHA*

Manuscript transmission is a matter which must also be taken into consideration in the case of a second fiannaíocht tale alluded to by Pearse, namely, *Cath Fionntrágha* or 'The Battle of Ventry'. As mentioned at the beginning of this chapter, Pearse cites a section of this tale in an article written in *An Barr Buadh*. The purpose of this article was to encourage the youth of Ireland to take a more active part in the defence of their nation. Pearse argues that although traditional Irish tales are not historical sources *per se*, they are historically important in that they provide an insight into the minds of those who produced them. Tales such as *Táin Bó Cúailnge* and *Cath Fionntrágha*, according to Pearse, provide an insight into the Gaelic mind at the time of their composition and they reflect a prevailing attitude that it was incumbent upon young people especially to defend the honour of their race. By way of illustration, he presents a passage of text from *Cath Fionntrágha* which portrays young boys dying heroically in defence of Ireland. Pearse does not cite his source for his version of the text and examination of the extant manuscript witnesses to *Cath Fionntrágha* shows it to be more in keeping with a

version found in some eighteenth and nineteenth century manuscripts. This later version represents a substantial modification of the
earliest extant version, written in the fifteenth century.[22] As may have
been the case with *Bruidhean Chaorthainn*, editorial intervention on
the part of Pearse is another matter which should be taken into consideration in assessing his version of the text from *Cath Fionntrágha*.
Examination of the earlier version of the episode suggests an alternative interpretation of its original import. I give below Pearse's version
of the text [translations here and below are my own]:

> Léightear i gCath Finntrágha, an tan do ghabh Rí an Domhain
> cuan agus caladh-phort i gcuan Finntrágha, agus an uair ba
> chlos fó cheithre háirdibh Éireann scéala na n-olc do bhí sé
> d'imirt ar Fhiannaibh Finn, gur labhair Fiachra Foltleabhar, rí
> Uladh, go ndubhairt: 'Truagh liom,' ar sé, 'méid an éigin i
> bhfuilid fir Éireann agus gan mo bheith féin inchatha.' Agus ní
> raibh de chlainn ag an rígh sin acht aon mhac amháin i gceann
> a thrí mbliadhan déag. 'Maith do-ghéantá-sa,' ar an mac, .i.
> 'ógbhadh Uladh do chur liom-sa chuca ó nach inchatha thú
> féin.' 'Ná habair sin,' ar an rí, 'óir ní hinchomhraic leanbh trí
> mbliadhan déag.' Agus do thuig an rí nárbh' áil leis an mac gan
> dul go Fiannaibh Éireann. 'Gabhtar an mac,' ar sé. Do gabhadh
> leo é agus do cuireadh i seomra fó iadhadh é agus dhá mhac
> déag de mhacaibh ríogh agus ró-fhlath Uladh leis. 'A óga,' ar sé,
> 'is maith do-ghéanadh sibh-se teacht liom-sa go Fiannaibh Éir-
> eann, óir gion go bhfuil bhur n-aire le ríghe Uladh do badh
> mhaith dhíbh clú do bhur rochtain féin.' Do chuaidh an
> comhrádh sin fó na maccaibh agus an tan do chodail an rí do
> chuadar-san fó theach na séad go dtugadar sciath agus claidh-
> eamh agus dhá chraoisigh gacha macaoimh leo as, go dtángadar
> rómpa go comh-dhíreach go rángadar Finntráigh. Agus do
> chuadar do chomhrac leis na hallmhurachaibh agus fó theacht
> do dhoirche na hoidhche ba chomh-thuitim do'n bhuidhin óig
> il-dhealbhaigh sin ar an tráigh.[23]

[It is read in *Cath Finntrágha* that when the King of the World
put into port in Ventry harbour and that when tidings of the evils
that he was inflicting on Fionn's fianna were heard all over
Ireland, Fiachra Foltleabhar, the king of Ulster, spoke and said:
'I think it unfortunate,' said he, 'that the men of Ireland are in
such a plight and that I myself am incapable of battle.' That
king's only offspring was a thirteen-year-old son. 'You would do
well,' said the son, 'to send the youths of Ulster with me to them
since you yourself are incapable of battle.' 'Do not say that,' said
the king, 'for a thirteen-year-old child is not capable of battle.'

The king was aware that the son was intent on going to the fianna of Ireland. 'Let the son be seized!' he said. He was seized by them and locked in a room together with twelve of the sons of the kings and great princes of Ulster. 'O youths!' said he, 'you would do well to come with me to the fianna of Ireland for although you do not expect to assume the kingship of Ulster it would be good for you to enhance your reputation.' That speech moved the sons and when the king was asleep they went to the house in which valuable objects were stored and took from it a shield, a sword and two spears each and proceeded directly until they reached Ventry. They went to fight with the foreigners and when darkness of night fell, that beautiful young band had died on the strand.]

Before discussing this passage in more detail, a few brief remarks may be made about the tale in general, especially because another short-coming of Pearse's version is that it is taken in isolation without any consideration of the text as a whole. *Cath Fionntrágha* is essentially a tale about a battle between Fionn and the fianna and an army of foreigners who have arrived in Ireland at Ventry. The tale was clear-ly not written by an author who simply wished to portray Fionn and the fianna as heroic defenders of Ireland on behalf of the high-king against an unjustified invasion. In point of fact, Fionn himself is the cause of the invasion as the army has arrived in Ireland to take revenge on him for eloping with both the wife and daughter of the king of France. Furthermore, Fionn was in a position to elope with these women because the earliest version of the text states that he was in military service with the king of France, having been banished from Ireland.[24] Mention of Fionn's banishment from Ireland did not appeal to those accustomed to his portrayal as a heroic defender of Ireland and is omitted in some later manuscript versions. Also note-worthy in this regard is a subsequent passage in which one of the fianna goes to seek help from Cormac mac Airt, the high-king of Ireland, because of the straitened circumstances of his companions in the conflict. Cormac expresses delight on hearing this news and points out that Fionn has passed many wrong judgements on him and his people and concludes by saying that he would prefer the foreign-ers, rather than Fionn, to be victorious.[25] Such sentiments did not find favour with certain later scribes. Thus, in some copies there is no mention of Cormac's preference for the foreigners while in oth-ers, for instance, Royal Irish Academy MS 23 B 15 written in 1824, the original text is completely twisted around by having the messen-ger say to Cormac that if Fionn loses the battle he will lose the king-ship of Ireland.

We may now compare the version of the episode from *Cath Fionntrágha* cited by Pearse with the earliest extant version.[26] A key aspect of the earliest version of this episode is the emphasis placed on the fact that the son of the king of Ulster is his only son and heir. Because of this, strenuous efforts are made, not only by his father but also by Fionn, to prevent him from participating in the battle. He has to be locked up because he refuses to obey the wise counsel of his father. In Pearse's version, the king's son encourages the other boys to join the battle by telling them that they will become famous for having done so. The following section, however, in which the king's son threatens the other boys if they do not comply with his wishes, has been omitted at this point:

> '*ocus* is cubhais dam-sa fós,' ar sé, 'nach racha proinn nó toma-ltas am bél-sa coidhchí ar ulcaibh rib-si innas co fhuiger-sa bás *ocus* co ngéba rí eachtrann ríghi Uladh tar éis m'athar-sa *ocus* co ruca ainbreatha oraibh-si.'[27]

> ['and I swear moreover,' said he, 'that neither refection nor food will ever pass my lips to spite you so that I may die and a foreign king will assume the kingship of Ulster after my own father and pass wrong judgements on you.']

It seems plausible to suggest that the point being made here in the earliest version is that the other boys could not be any worse off under foreign rule because the son himself is passing a wrong judge-ment on them, and forcing them to disobey the wishes of the king of Ulster.

There is no indication in the next section of Pearse's text, in which the boys escape and come to Ventry, that the participation of the boys in the battle met with any further disapproval. In the earliest and many other versions, however, Fionn refuses to allow the boys to take part in the battle, pointing out that it would be a grave matter to allow the king of Ulster's only son and heir to so do:

> 'Mo-chean-sa bar tacht *ocus* bar torrachtain,' ar Finn, '*ocus* gidheadh,' ar sé, 'dobadh scél mór énmac h'athar-sa do leigean dochum na n-allmurach *ocus* gan adhbhar rígh d'Ulltachaibh acht sé.'[28]

> ['Welcome is your coming and arrival,' said Fionn, 'and be that as it may,' said he, 'it would be a tragic event to let the only son of your father go against the foreigners because he is the only heir of the king of the Ulstermen.']

The son again displays great obstinacy and such is his determination to engage in battle that Fionn is forced to order members of the *fianna* to restrain and bind him.[29] The fianna encounter such difficulty in restraining him that his twelve young companions go unnoticed to fight a foreign warrior and are quickly killed and beheaded.[30] The son's refusal to accept the wishes of both his father and Fionn has now resulted in the deaths of his twelve young companions but, nevertheless, he remains obdurate. In another section of the narrative omitted in Pearse's abridged version, the king's son again indulges in threats to get his way. He warns the fianna that if he is not allowed to avenge his companions on the foreigner he will die of anger and shame. Were that to happen, he says, the fianna and the Ulstermen would be enemies for ever afterwards and his falling at the hands of the foreigner would be of little consequence compared to this.[31] The boy's actions now have further disastrous consequences in that the fianna are placed in a dilemma. They are forced into choosing what for them is the lesser of two evils and release him. He and the foreigner then engage in battle with one another and both are eventually killed in the encounter.[32]

The earliest version of this episode, therefore, presents us with a somewhat more complex scenario than that suggested by Pearse's version. It can be reasonably argued that it was not intended in the earliest version to portray the boys' participation in the battle as an instance of youthful self-sacrifice in noble defence of their country, but rather as a disastrous incident brought about by reckless folly and threats on the part of the king's son who ignored the counsel, not only of his father, but also of Fionn. It was regarded as a matter of great importance that the king of Ulster would be left without an heir because of the son's actions. The king's son is ultimately allowed to engage in battle because the only alternative is future enmity between Ulstermen and the fianna. There is therefore no impression of unity of purpose among opponents of the foreigners in the earliest version. This episode is one of many in the earliest extant version of *Cath Fionntrágha* which reflect the complexities of political and social life at the time of its writing in the fifteenth century.[33]

### CONCLUSION

The discussion above illustrates the extent to which an editor can influence a reader's understanding of a particular text. It has also been seen that, in the course of a lengthy transmission, a text can undergo important modifications. Changing political and cultural circumstances are some of the contributory factors to such changes.

As a textual editor, Pearse was in keeping with the editorial conventions of his time. Many of those conventions would now be deemed unacceptable, however. If there is to be a proper understanding of fiannaíocht literature and its transmission, it is essential that this extensive corpus of material be made available in modern critical editions. Editorial work of a similar nature is also a desideratum for numerous other wide-ranging sources from Old to Modern Irish. Until this is done, much of Irish literature will remain accessible only in manuscript and long outdated editions and the latter will continue to form the basis for inadequate and misleading analysis.

CHAPTER FOURTEEN

# Masculinity and Citizenship: Boyhood and Nationhood at St Enda's

## ELAINE SISSON

Oliver Sheppard's famous bronze statue of the dying Cúchulainn occupies a central position in the window of the General Post Office (GPO). The statue, which was modelled between 1911 and 1912, became a memorial to the 1916 Rising when it was installed in the GPO in 1935. Although finished in 1912 it was not until after the revolutionary events of the next few years that representations of the heroic and martyred Cúchulainn gained public emotional and political currency. By 1935 the figures of Patrick Pearse and Cúchulainn were undeniably linked in the nationalist imagination to the extent that Cúchulainn's bravery in the face of death was mapped on to Pearse's final moments.

14.1 Oliver Sheppard statue of Cúchulainn in the GPO.

The association of Pearse with Cúchulainn within the public imagination in the early years of the state merely reinforced an earlier literary and visual connection between the two figures which had been much in evidence at St Enda's, Pearse's school for boys, established in 1908. The figure of the boy-hero was borrowed by Pearse from mythology as the foundation for a modern Celtic masculine identity for the boys at the school. The leadership qualities of the warrior-hero were combined with the scholarly attributes of Celtic Christian masculinity to produce a contemporary prototype of nationalist male identity. Pearse drew on pre-Christian sources for the model of the warrior-poet, embodied in the character of Cúchulainn, woven into a Christian model of the scholar-saint, exemplified by the life of St Colmcille, to produce a modern nationalist figure: the revolutionary boy-citizen. Pagan culture provided masculine role models from bardic literature who were versed in the military arts and who were accomplished athletes and scholars. Early Christian Ireland contributed the role of the artist-scholar-saint and the sentimentalised figure of Íosagán in Pearse's short stories, which represented emotional sensitivity and a sacramentalised spirituality. In light of this understanding, it is fair to assert Pearse's vision of a modern *macaomh* with that of a boy-citizen who combined the courage and physical passion of Cúchulainn with the strength of character and humility of Íosagán.

## CÚCHULAINN AT ST ENDA'S

St Enda's boys were a regular fixture in Dublin's social and cultural life in the early years of the twentieth century and were considered as emblematic of the potential of Irish manhood. The authority of the St Enda's boys as an imaginative symbol for Ireland, past and present, is evident in the many ways in which St Enda's was understood as a type of national spectacle. Between 1908 and 1912 the boys performed in seven different plays at the Abbey Theatre and numerous others in the school; they also acted in at least six open-air pageants of Irish history at St Enda's, Jones Road and feiseanna around the country. In addition, postcards of the school were sold and circulated, sporting events at which the boys played were well attended, and generally, the St Enda's boys were considered to be actively living many of the ideals promoted by cultural nationalism.[1]

St Enda's provided a training ground for the teasing out of a new definition of Irish masculinity. Elsewhere I have outlined the influence of early Christian culture on Pearse's model of contemporary boyhood. This chapter is confined to addressing the particular cultural and visual influences of the figure of Cúchulainn at St Enda's.[2] Pearse was interested in the way in which imperialist understandings of history, mythology, popular literature and male chivalry had proved an inspirational mix for generations of English schoolboys. The figure of Cúchulainn offered Pearse a role model who was a potent combination of heroic martyr, athlete, warrior, poet with moral courage and strength of character: in fact the very epitome of late Victorian masculinity in circulation within the English public school system. This chapter argues that the success of Cúchulainn as a role model was not confined to the reappropriation of Ireland's heroic past, but was directly linked to reinforcing contemporary cultural codes of masculinity.

It is important to recognise that Cúchulainn was not merely understood to be a mythological or historic figure; he was so embedded into the curriculum that he operated as a figure of continuity between the past and the present. Padraic Ó Conaire, a pupil at the school, recalls that from the outset 'we understood that it was Pearse's goal to make every student a Cúchulainn, for Cúchulainn

14.2 Fragment of a motto painted in uncial lettering by the Morrow Brothers over the fanlight of Cullenswood House. The words were said to have been spoken by Cúchulainn and translate as ' I care not though I were to live but one day and one night provided my fame and my deeds live after me'. Courtesy Pearse Museum.

was his exemplar'.[3] Every morning Pearse told a tale from the Cúchulainn saga to the assembled schoolboys and teachers. Desmond Ryan comments on how the boys joked among themselves that the Hound of Ulster was an 'important if invisible' member of staff.[4] Cúchulainn's presence at St Enda's throughout that first year was visualised in a number of different forms.  In Cullenswood House, the first site of St Enda's from 1908 to 1910, the Morrow Brothers' fresco of the boy-hero taking arms dominated the front hall, for Pearse thought: 'it would be a noble thing to set [it] somewhere where every boy that entered the school might see it'.[5] Around the mural was an inscription in uncial lettering of Cúchulainn's famous choice between life and fame: 'I care not though I live but one day and one night if only my names and deeds live after me'. The detailed panel showed a figure with an uplifted shield and spear ready for battle.[6]

The use of exercise books and Modh Díreach teaching charts illustrated with the figure of Cúchulainn further reinforced the daily visual connection to the heroic past.[7]

At the end of the first highly successful year, the school held a prize day and open-air pageant which told the story of how the boy-hero Setanta took arms and became known as Cúchulainn.  The pageant made public the connection between Cúchulainn and St Enda's, a relationship which had already been sealed within the everyday life of the school.  Pearse's stated desire was that the end-of-year pageant would consolidate the boys' devotion to Cúchulainn and 'crown our first year's work with something worthy and symbolic'.[8]  His wish was that the students would 'leave St Enda's under the spell of their most beloved hero, the Macaomh', who was, he argued not only 'the greatest figure' in Irish epic but 'in the epic of the world'.[9]

## CÚCHULAINN AND LITERARY REVIVALISM

At the time of the 1909 St Enda's pageant, the story of Cúchulainn had moved from its place as a dusty myth to a central position within the nationalist imagination. The publication of Standish O'Grady's *History of Ireland* between 1879 and 1880 marked the emergence of Cúchulainn in the publishing market. Following the success of O'Grady's second volume, subtitled 'Cúchulainn and his contemporaries', a number of popular editions of stories from the Ulster Cycle appeared in print. Eleanor Hull published an edited collection, *The Cúchulainn Saga in Irish Literature*, in 1898, which included Kuno Meyer's seminal translation of *The Wooing of Emer*.  Hull, a friend of Pearse, shared his conviction that there should be versions of Irish myths and legends suitable for children and had written to him pursuing the possibility of publishing a series of such texts through the networks of the Gaelic League.[10] Subsequently Hull was responsible for the editing and publication of a number of children's texts, in particular an edition of *Cúchulainn The Hound of Ulster* in 1909, which was beautifully illustrated by Stephen Reid. Lady Gregory had published her first popular editions of Cúchulainn stories as early as 1902.[11]

14.3 *Modh Díreach Teaching Chart*, Dundalgan Press, *c.* 1909. Courtesy Pearse Museum.

As to what Cúchulainn represented in this context, it can be argued that Cúchulainn, far from being considered an historical figure, provided comment on discrete but connected contemporary debates on masculinity, citizenship and adolescence.  Furthermore, the popularisation of the Cúchulainn stories created a new market for Irish national popular culture. The repackaging of myth and legend in new visual and popular forms as a means of expressing national feeling had considerable currency throughout Europe at this time, as is evidenced in the popular cultural revivals of other emergent nations, especially in Norway, which gained its independence from Sweden in 1905.  There was evidence of much cross-fertilisation of ideas and influence from Scandanavia within the fashionable pan-Celtic movements of the 1890s and 1900s.[12] Cúchulainn functioned as more than an example of heroic masculinity from the past; he provided a blueprint for a contemporary vision of a modern active, scholarly, athletic, Celticised

male citizen-in-waiting. The life of Cúchulainn offered a template
for the transition from boyhood to adolescence to manhood within
an Irish context. Obviously the life of Christ also offers such a template and there are several connections between the two figures.
Christ however, no matter how hard an ardent nationalist tried,
could never be claimed as Irish. What Cúchulainn represents is a
potent mix of Irishness, manliness and heroism. Furthermore, like
Pearse's stories of the boy-Jesus Íosagán, tales of the boy Setanta illustrated the sense of purpose, destiny and honourable simplicity which
were so heavily promoted at St Enda's. Unlike Íosagán, who remains
a child, Setanta grows into the adolescent Cúchulainn, who is physi-
cally brave and morally courageous. There is little evidence of the
adult life and death of Cúchulainn being promoted, visualised or
studied at the school with the same energy as his boyhood and adolescence.


## HYPER-MASCULINITY AND AUTHENTICITY

Christian codes of behaviour, as embodied in Íosagán, are organised
around the principles of humility, passivity, humanity and intuition
while the warrior rules of masculinity delineate a world of physical
prowess, honour, duty, courage and chivalry. Within the school these
discourses of pagan maleness co-exist with discourses on Christian
manliness, and provide the substance of the contemporary Celtic
boy-citizen: the macaomh. However, the models of Christian
Celticism on offer were largely constructed within the discourse of
the infant (boy-Jesus); the feminised (the artist-aesthete saint) and the
domestic (the Holy family).[13] The struggle to articulate an 'authentic'
Irish masculinity which combined potency with physicality was
not going to be found within the Christian tradition. Ashis Nandy
suggests that part of the assertion of political and intellectual independence is that colonised cultures often indulge in rhetoric of
hyper-masculinity.[14] Hyper-masculinity is a state where the values of
traditional masculinity – rationality, strength, order, dominance – are
grossly intensified and the femininity is denigrated or rejected. The
pagan world of Cúchulainn is a world without women, even as mothers, and where boys and men are emotionally nurtured within the
bardic system of patronage. The fear of being 'feminised' or 'domesticated' is eradicated because there is no femininity. The mythological male figures of Irish legend suggest that there is an unmediated
'true' masculine identity which can be recouped from history and
imported into the present tempered only by the 'civilising' virtues of
Christian compassion.

Pearse's desire for an authentic masculinity could be seen as a part of his preoccupation with ancient Ireland as a better place to live. However his concerns about true manliness reflect many ideas in circulation within the late nineteenth and early twentieth centuries about the domesticating and taming influences of femininity. Eamhain Macha, Pearse's fantasy playground, where the boys of the Fianna Éireann lived together, is a version of a larger contemporary society which privileges male power, but in this case it was Irish rather than imperial power which held sway. Far from being caught in past reveries of mythological manhood, Pearse's desire to recapture a sense of male authenticity is adapted from the debates then circulating within the rhetoric of imperial heroism. What Pearse succeeds in doing effectively, is to import the language and ideology of imperial patriotism, heroism and chivalric masculinity and to reshape it in a language which, while using the ideology of Edwardian masculinity, manages to suggest that Irish manhood is natural, ahistoric and, by predating English versions of maleness, is more authentic. He achieves this mostly by the appropriation of Cúchulainn, whose brand of Irish masculinity, he asserts, is on display at St Enda's. This is evidenced by Pearse's comments on a hurling match which took place at St Enda's in 1910, where he imagines seeing Cúchulainn playing alongside the boys.[15] The physicality and speed of hurling coupled with its resonance within the stories of Setanta's boyhood led Pearse to consider it a more authentically masculine game. More acutely however, it was the fact that Pearse considered himself to be witnessing the unbroken continuum of history where the boys of St Enda's were hurling on the playing fields of ancient Ireland.

Other observers also commented on the special relationship between the St Enda's boys and the heroes of Irish legend, focusing on the curricular emphasis on the heroic. W.P. Ryan, whose son Desmond was a pupil at the school, records his emotions on viewing a St Enda's pageant based on life in Eamhain Macha. He suggests that the tableau was so convincing that he, along with the entire audience, was able to suspend disbelief and imagine himself part of 'heroic antiquity'. It was easy, he recalls, to imagine the boys of St Enda's in Tara or Eamhain Macha. Expressing his opinion that 'the heroic spirit had entered into the boys' hearts and minds' during the play, he suggested that even after the performance had ended he recognised that 'the evening's life and spirit were not something isolated' and that whatever spirit the boys had displayed was part of a 'natural continuation' of what they were learning in school. Further, he suggested that 'Cúchulainn and [his] heroic kin had become part of the mental life of the teachers and the taught'.[16] Sean O'Casey, not known for sentimental indulgence, was moved by the spectacle of the St Enda's

boys in a Cúchulainn pageant in Jones Road in June 1913.  He
described it 'in colour, form, dignity of movement and vigour of
speech' as 'the loveliest thing that had ever patterned the green sward
of the playing field of Jones Road'.[17]  Again, as was expressed by
many commentators on St Enda's over the years, there was the feeling that the boys were not merely re-enacting the past but were link-
ing the audience to history by embodying the past in the present.  As
an unnamed reviewer commented in the Gaelic League newspaper,
*An Claidheamh Soluis agus Fáinne an Lae*, the St Enda's productions
were praised for blending the ancient and modern Ireland but 'the
blending is so happy and natural that no-one can distinguish which
is exactly the old and which the new'.[18]

## MODERNITY AND PHOTOGRAPHIC TIME

The tension between the old and new, between tradition and modernity, is one which is felt in all embryonic nationalisms.[19] The tensions
within nationalism between concepts of preservation and tradition
and those of modernisation inevitably produce dualities within
debates on cultural and political identity.  Walter Benjamin has commented that the mapping of progress depends on systematically
inventing images of 'archaic time' to identify what is historically new,
while at the same time  emphasising its continuing and on-going links
with an imaginatively constructed 'authentic' past.[20] The inspirational shadow of Cúchulainn at St Enda's can therefore be understood not merely to be a way of talking about the antiquity and value
of Ireland's past but also as a means of envisaging the transformation
of a current state of affairs.  What the figure of Cúchulainn provides
for St Enda's is a narrative of continuity between the authentic past
and revolutionary future.

   One of the ways in which the past can be reimagined and recon-
structed is through the technology of photography.  The photograph
had existed in various forms since the middle of the nineteenth century but it was not until late in that century that technological
advances in exposure and development times of photographic plates
and the design of  more mobile and less cumbersome cameras resulted
in a more democratic access to the photograph.  The explosion of
interest in photography in the late nineteenth and early twentieth
centuries was only partly to do with ease of access to the newly available technology through freelance photographers and photographic
studios.  More significantly, 'having one's portrait done' was a visual
means of documenting the newly emergent middle classes.[21] It is no
coincidence that early photographic studio portraits emulate and echo
the conventions of fine art portrait painting; a means of representation

to which most people would never have access. Benedict Anderson has persuasively argued that it is within the demographic of such newly aspirational urban, literate middle classes that national culture takes hold as a mass cultural movement.[22] For example, in Ireland it was the popularity of the Gaelic League within urban centres which ensured its success regardless of its importance elsewhere.

The vogue among middle-class nationally minded urbanites for photographs and photographic postcards was capitalised upon by Pearse. He issued a number of photographic postcards as a means of raising funds for the school. While some of the images are merely illustrative – showing the grounds and classrooms of St Enda's – others are more ideologically rich. Images of the boys dressed in the clothes of ancient Ireland – as warriors, saints and heroes – were, on the one hand a means of demonstrating the rich cultural life of the school, but, on the other hand were a visual shorthand to suggest that the current pupils and the heroes of ancient Ireland existed within the same narrative. Martin Heidegger has observed that the modern age *is* the age of representation and that photography is the technological apparatus of modernity: 'The conquest of the world as picture ... is what distinguishes the essence of the modern age'.[23] How better to isolate a single moment and present it as a visual link between the past and the present than to produce a fixed image which can also be mass-produced? Photographic images produced by St Enda's of Cúchulainn as a boy illustrate how the photograph is a powerful way to demonstrate the collision of history and temporality. The recording of an historical event (both an event from history and an historical story) illustrates how modernity, through the apparatus of technology, can be used to fix a version of the past more potently and more precisely than ballad-singing or story-telling.

A 1909 studio photograph of the pupil Frank Dowling is a case in point. Dowling played the lead in a St Enda's production of *The Boy Deeds of Cúchulainn*. Pearse described him as embodying 'in face and figure and manner' his personal ideal of Cúchulainn, who was, he suggested, one 'of the comeliest of the boys of Éire'.[24] Distilled in the figure of Cúchulainn was 'a boy's aloofness and a boy's mystery ... a boy's earnestness ... and a boy's irresponsible gaiety'. For Pearse, Cúchulainn was not a fictional mythological hero, he was a flesh and blood boy who had been touched by something akin to divinity. It was only in Cúchulainn's 'strange moments of exaltation' when the 'hero-light shone above his head' like the Christ-child's halo, that, according to Pearse, his peers recognised Cúchulainn as an heroic 'radiant figure'.[25] The framing of Dowling is quite low as if his figure is weighed down by the blackness of the backdrop. The picture is

14.4 Side profile of
Frank Dowling.
Courtesy Pearse
Museum.

posed as if to suggest that 'Cúchulainn' is unaware of the
presence of the camera as he contemplates the solemnity of
his destiny. The stylised photograph of the studio differs
from the other illustrative images of the life of the school in
circulation. All photographs, staged or not, involve the
comprehension of the viewer of what is seen (as opposed to
what is meant). Any image may be said to have a denotative
and a connotative meaning: what is observed and what is
communicated. Alan Sekula has observed that 'any mean-
ingful encounter with a photograph must necessarily occur
at the level of connotation'.[26] The connotative meanings of
the image of Frank Dowling as Cúchulainn, the quint-essen-
tial boy of Ireland, have far greater resonance than that of
a mere image from a play which took place in the school.
The photograph is not merely a denotative image of a boy-actor posing as a mythical hero, nor is it a connotative image of the importance of Cúchulainn for a generation of schoolboys: the image suggests that a St Enda's boy and Cúchulainn are one and the same
thing. Photographs are never simply records of temporal and spatial
events: they are themselves historical documents and the complexities of the event they represent are matched by the complexities of
viewing or consuming the image. According to the anthropologist
Elizabeth Edwards: 'The photograph by its very nature is

14.5 Patrick Pearse, *c.*
1909. Courtesy Pearse
Museum.

of the past. Yet it is also of the present … the *there-then*
becomes the *here-now*'.[27] Comparing the photograph of
Frank Dowling to the now almost iconic profile photograph of Pearse invites connections between the two.
Although Pearse famously disliked having his photograph
taken head on due to a slight cast in his eye, the photograph nevertheless echoes the connotative meanings
attached to Dowling as Cúchulainn. Pearse is unselfconscious, purposeful, resolved: like Dowling/Cúchulainn he
faces an unknown future. It is perhaps this visual resonance between these two images at this time that is later
fixed on to Sheppard's bronze.

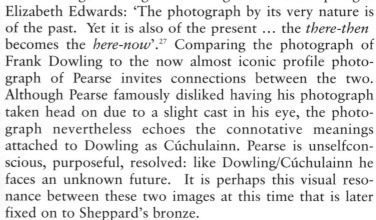

CONCLUSION

The potency of Oliver Sheppard's statue of Cúchulainn in post-
Revolutionary Ireland effectively erased other possible representations of the hero. The art historians John Turpin and Belinda Loftus
have both commented on the post-1916 popular and commercial
appropriation of Sheppard's image of Cúchulainn from army medals
to business trophies, which have little to do with his status as nation-

alist hero.[28] Even the appropriation of the image of Cúchulainn by loyalist paramilitaries as the 'ancient defender of Ulster from Irish attacks over 2,000 years ago' owes much to Sheppard's bronze. The loyalist mural reproduced the familiar stance of Sheppard's dying Cúchulainn with head bowed – albeit with the added colour of a Union Jack and a shield emblazoned with the Red Hand of Ulster.

Within nationalist iconography as a whole the figure of Cúchulainn seems to stand alone as a male icon. Belinda Loftus's extensive work on nationalist iconography does not unearth any comparable male figure.[29] After the establishment of the nation state, there seems to have been little or no attempt to configure Ireland as a boy or young man within the nationalist imagination. Many of the popular images of Cúchulainn currently in circulation owe much to Sheppard's model, suggesting that Sheppard's bronze has become the definitive representation of the macaomh. With the exception of Sheppard's enduring Cúchulainn, the image of the boy or young man seems to have disappeared almost completely from nationalist iconography after 1916. While never a particularly predominant visual signifier within nationalism, the figure of the boy, aside from that of Cúchulainn, did have currency in Irish Ireland before 1916. An earlier piece of work by Sheppard called *Inis Fáil* included a young boy and was shown at the

14.6. Loyalist mural featuring Cúchulainn, 1994.

Art Oireachtas in 1906.  Although written some ten years before the
events of 1916, Pearse's reading of the Sheppard artwork anticipates
the fusion of the themes of martyrdom, masculinity and heroism which
mark Pearse's later work and deeds. Pearse reviewed the exhibition for
*An Claidheamh Soluis* and was entranced by Sheppard's 'group in
bronzed plaster'.[30] Describing the artist as 'the greatest poet and one
of the most creative minds in Ireland today', he singled out for praise
Sheppard's depiction of a young boy featured in the plaster frieze.
Sheppard's statue, *Inis Fáil*, or 'The Isle of Destiny', is an allegorical
rendition of Ireland and the figure of a 'little tender lad' had tremendous resonance for Pearse. In *An Claidheamh Soluis* he remarked on
the beauty and boyishness of the child, singling out Sheppard's eye for
contour and delicacy.  For Pearse, the boy symbolised the future of
Ireland and he praised Sheppard for communicating so eloquently 'the
hesitation of a child confronted with a mighty task' but with the added
dimension of also expressing the child's 'growing of a great resolve'.[31]

While the revolutionary boy-hero seems to have faded from
nationalist iconography after 1916, it was not only Pearse who used
the figure of the boy to promote ideals of nation.  It would be overly
simplistic to suggest that the imaginative investment in the icon of
the boy died with Pearse.  Instead, the image of Ireland as mother
seems have been secured as *the* definitive image of nationalist Ireland
in the immediate years after the Rising.  The allegorical symbol of the
mother has always had currency in nationalist discourse but after
1916 the prevailing mood secured the fusion of religious discourse
and national martyrdom which privileged images of Ireland as a
grieving mother.  Belinda Loftus argues that the popular visual and
figurative acquaintance with icons of the Virgin Mary made it easy to
map one image of a bereaved mother on to another.

The adolescent Cúchulainn, situated within the transitional stage
between boyhood and manhood, may be seen as mirroring actual
political and social events.  No longer a child but still not a fully
matured adult, Cúchulainn, along with the other adolescent boys of
Pearse's dramas, increasingly represents that transitional state
between empire and independence.  It can be argued that the disap-
pearance of the figure of the boy-warrior in nationalist iconography –
most particularly visualisations of Cúchulainn – in the years after
1916 is explained by its failure to function as a unifying image of
nationhood.  The boy-warrior served as a potent symbol of potential
manhood and of citizenship, but the war of independence and the
civil war fractured political and national allegiances to the extent that
such an image no longer represented a shared ideal of citizenship.
This also perhaps explains how the image of the mother was secured
as the representative image of Ireland since the mother gives birth to

all the children of the nation. In years of civil war the question which may have lingered around the figure of the boy-warrior was: whose child was he? Whose legacy did he represent? If Republican thought suggested that the nation had still to be fully established then the boy-warrior, as a symbol of a shared future reality, became an unstable image which exposed ideological fracture as opposed to ideological certainty. Similarly, if the state of nationhood has been achieved then the use of a symbol which suggests that nationhood is promised, but deferred, becomes redundant and so the image of Cúchulainn no longer holds currency within pro-Treaty nationalism. Since neither nationhood nor manhood can ever fully be owned or possessed the symbol of the macaomh occupies an unstable position within any ortho-doxy as he functions as a reminder that nationhood/manhood is contin-ually deferred and always in process. The image of the boy-warrior functions most powerfully as a pre-revolutionary symbol precisely because he embodies the promise of what has not yet been achieved and so wields an imaginative power about what is yet possible. For these reasons Cúchulainn found expression within St Enda's as a symbol of revolutionary potential and of male power.

## CHAPTER FIFTEEN

# Radicalising the Classroom: Pearse, Pedagogy of Progressivism

## BRENDAN WALSH

This chapter seeks to describe aspects of the educational thought and work of Patrick Pearse. In doing so it suggests that his work was characteristic of later progressive educational thinkers and that his conceptualisation of school as an agent of political and cultural control was perceptive and forward-looking and locates him within the radical education tradition. It suggests that his conceptualisation of schooling as an agent of political and cultural resistance anticipated the work of later radical thinkers such as Henry Giroux and Paulo Freire and has generally remained unacknowledged.

### PEARSE AND PEDAGOGY: THE LONG SILENCE

Pearse's militant separatism has tended to overshadow the educational work to which he dedicated his adult life. He has been described alternately as fascistic and naïve, and charged with endorsing 'the development of close, intimate or erotic relationships between pupils and their teachers'.[1] In 1966 Eavan Boland noted that his educational achievements had become the casualty of a 'well-bred distaste',[2] and Elaine Sisson observed that he remains so contentious that to admit to writing on him, 'presupposes that the idea is either to debunk the myths of martyrdom or to reinforce him as an icon of the past'[3] while his educational work has been described as a 'startling success' by Raymond Porter.[4] Between 1903 and 1908 Pearse dedicated much of his writing to education in *An Claidheamh Soluis agus Fáinne an Lae*, the mouthpiece of the Gaelic League; between 1910 and 1912 he oversaw St Ita's school for girls and between 1908 and 1916 he operated St Enda's, which remained open until 1935.

The relationship between Pearse's advocacy of physical force and the development of sectarian conflict in Northern Ireland understandably tended to overshadow discussions about his legacy. Academics, with exceptions, have tended to ignore Pearse's pedagogic writings, possibly assuming that they represented little more than musings on Irish-language acquisition, were parochial, or bore the stigma of republican militancy. Finally, it is possible that Pearse became so readily identified

15.1 Annual prize-giving day, with Pearse seated towards the right and Douglas Hyde seated (in profile) wearing a cloth cap, *c.* 1914. Courtesy Pearse Museum.

with the troubled history of Irish in schools that today the Irish public regard him and the language in much the same way; they like the idea, but do not know very much.

## THE COLONIAL CLASSROOM: SCHOOLING AND IRISH

Pearse founded St Enda's in 1908 at a time when the education system was wholly examination-driven and informed by colonial assumptions about the relationship between Ireland and England. School History examinations for 1906 ask, for example: 'How did the Whigs and Tories of Queen Anne's reign differ?'; 'Give as fully as you can an account of the British surrender at Saratoga or at Yorktown'; 'Give a brief account of Farifax's campaign in Kent and Essex during the Second Civil War'; 'Distinguish three Dukes of Norfolk during the Tudor period, and write a short account of two of them'.[5] C.S. (Todd) Andrews, a past pupil of St Enda's, which he 'loathed', recalled that Dublin was 'totally Anglicised ... an English city ... our nursery rhymes were English and we knew all about Dick Whittington, Robin Hood and Alice in Wonderland, but we never heard of Fionn or Cúchulainn ... at school ... Irish was never mentioned'.[6] Roger Casement recalled that at Ballymena Academy he was taught 'nothing about Ireland ... I don't think the word was ever mentioned in a single class of the school'.[7]

Pearse believed that vernacular language was a principle characteristic of nationhood, reflecting a sense of 'otherness' or separateness. By controlling the school curriculum, texts and mechanisms of evaluation

15.2 Halla Mór,
St Enda's.
Courtesy Pearse
Museum.

throughout the nineteenth century a succession of governments had contributed to the decline of the language through hostility or indifference. Since the Tudor period the language had been understood as a barrier, first to proselytism and later to political compliance, and while by the early twentieth century this conception had faded, Pearse and the Revivalist movement considered it an inherent token of nationhood. For Pearse, it was appropriate that the classroom, which for so long had been used as a vehicle for eradicating the language, should become the site of its Renaissance. Government attitudes toward the language during the preceding eighty years are, perhaps, best illustrated by the anomaly of English-only speaking inspectors visiting all Irish-speaking schools, causing Micheál O'Guiheen, for example, to recall that, in his youth, an inspector who visited the Great Blasket island, 'hadn't a word of Irish ... but to our misfortune he had plenty of English'.[8]

Pearse argued that since the sixteenth century schooling had been used first as a means of proselytism and later as a means of political assimilation. Emile Durkheim's observation that schooling was the systematic socialisation of the young had been grasped much earlier by the Tudor and Elizabethan administrations that founded parish and diocesan schools to encourage English speech and habit. Pearse held that, from that time, schooling in Ireland had become a political act, aimed at fostering a compliant, Protestant, English-speaking people. The later omission of Irish language, literature and history from the school curriculum represented the imposition of a silence or systemic absence generated by a dominant elite.

The national school system was founded in 1831 but Irish was not permitted until 1879. It was excluded from Intermediate (secondary) schools under the provisions of the Intermediate Education Act (1878), only being introduced after pressure from antiquarians like Edward Hudson, former owner of the Hermitage, which housed St Enda's between 1916 and 1935. Celtic, as it was then known, did not carry the same marks as other languages. The Preparatory Grade examination was worth 500 marks while the remaining grades were worth 600. However, French and German were worth 700 in all grades while English, Latin and Greek merited 1,200 marks. Students were only permitted to study Irish in the senior classes at National school, which removed formal school support at the early stages for Irish-speaking children, while also preventing English speakers from acquiring Irish at the earliest possible stage in school. Ultimately it reinforced the notion that the language was neither practical nor culturally significant. Although the success of the Gaelic League in the late nineteenth century resulted in a remarkable take-up of Irish in schools, students opting to study the language selected it from a list of so-called 'extra' subjects that included French, Latin, German, Greek, Italian and Spanish. In 1904–5 the number of students taking Irish at Intermediate level rose from 2,527 to 3,218. Ranking the languages in order of number of candidates illustrates the strong position of Irish: French (9,156); Latin (4,029); Irish (3,218); German (1,101); Greek (1,081); Italian (34) and Spanish (10).[9] Of twenty-seven subjects in the honours category, Irish was placed sixth on the list in terms of the number of students opting to study it. In 1906 the numbers taking Irish at Intermediate level rose to 4,087, an increase of 869 on the previous year. Of the seven languages listed in the Report of the Commissioners of Education for the year, only French had a larger enrolment (1,290).[10]

In the same year the government announced that it intended to discontinue paying fees for extra subjects, including Irish. The cost of maintaining this subject through results fees (remuneration to schools based on examination success) had increased from £1,000 to £12,000 in four years due wholly to the increased interest in the language, yet this represented a mere .01 per cent of the educational budget for one year; less than half the salary cost of the Dublin Office of the Commissioners of National Education.[11] Pearse and the League were not wholly misguided in suspecting the government's commitment to the language in schools. The Commissioners accepted the Treasury's decision and reminded the public that they had, it should be remembered, sanctioned bilingual teaching in Irish-speaking districts. However, they had also appended the proviso that such 'instruction (was) utilised in teaching … English'.[12]

## ST ENDA'S: A RADICAL DEPARTURE

Pearse resented the emphasis upon terminal examination and what he considered a very limited curriculum, complaining in 1912 that 'the same textbooks are being read tonight in every secondary school ... in Ireland. Two of Hawthorne's *Tanglewood Tales* ... a few poems in English' being the entire literary corpus for 'three-quarters' of the country's pupils.[13] He famously condemned the system as a 'murder machine' dedicated to cramming; it was unimaginative, underfunded and unsympathetic to the aspirations of cultural nationalists. Seeing it as an *instrumentum regni*, he recognised, long before the development of theories of education as resistance, that it could be subverted by a system in opposition, a network of Irish-Ireland schools, informed by the tenets of Gaelic revivalism. This early conceptualisation of school as a means of resistance – an act of defiance – had antecedents in the nonconformist movements of the early nineteenth century, members of which, excluded from Oxford and Cambridge, founded the new 'red-brick' universities and so disrupted the machinery that ensured the maintenance of the social elite. Pearse described his project as challenging the existing education system of Ireland, telling an American audience in 1914 that 'the whole experiment of Irishising education in Ireland must stand or fall with St Enda's'.[14]

## SCHOOLING IN DEMOCRACY

St Enda's was radical in its purpose and operation. It was to be a 'boy-republic'; a schooling in democracy. Eton and Harrow prepared boys for the mantle and administration of Empire, St Enda's would encourage its subversion; if Waterloo was won on the playing fields of Eton, Ireland's heroes would train on the hurling fields of St Enda's.[15] While ostensibly a bilingual school, Pearse encouraged the boys to make Irish the first language and responded to questions in English by asking 'Céard e seo?' The experiment was radical in 1908, politically potent and deliberate at a time when post addressed in Irish could be returned-to-sender by the General Post Office. Again, the 'boy republic' was radical in its inclusive and democratic operation. The election of leaders from among the boys to act as a student council was intended to democratise the school experience. In 1913 a senior pupil named James Rowan suggested that cricket become the school summer sport, claiming that the sons of 'modern patriots' played the game, although others argued, in the pages of the school magazine, that it was an 'English' pastime.[16] Pearse referred the decision to the council, which called for a school vote. St Enda's electing

15.3 1967 reunion of former St Enda's pupils who fought in the 1916 Rising. *Standing, left to right*: Éamonn Bulfin, Conor McGinley, Desmond Ryan, Fintan Murphy. *Front row, left to right*: Brian Joyce, Frank Burke, Major General Joseph Sweeney. Courtesy Pearse Museum.

to play cricket would result in certain public embarrassment and it is testament to Pearse's democratic instinct and integrity as an educator that he was prepared to take such a risk.

The student council is characteristic of radical and progressive schools. The Moot (council meeting) at which students voted also operated at Dartington Hall in England. The school's founder, William Curry, was much influenced by Bertrand Russell, whose writings on schooling are often significantly similar to those of Pearse. Pearse, for example, believed that schooling in Ireland was intended to 'tame' the people, designed 'by our masters ... to make us willing or at least manageable slaves'.[17] Russell held that 'almost all education [was] aimed at strengthening some group ... it is this motive ... which determines the subjects taught, the knowledge offered and the knowledge withheld'.[18] Pearse wrote of the education system as 'shaping and moulding' and Russell described education as moulding children to 'unnatural shapes'.[19] Pearse held that education in Ireland was a 'state controlled institution ... which produces articles necessary to the progress ... of the state',[20] and Russell, that education systems were designed for 'the maintenance of the existing order'.[21] Pearse believed that the teacher was becoming popularly regarded as an official whose task it was to assist pupils' 'earning capacity later on',[22] while Russell mused that too often teaching was regarded as helping pupils to make money or achieve 'a good position'.[23] Later A.S. Neill would place the student council at the heart of the radically progressive Summerhill School. It

was not until the 1998 Education Act that student councils were provided for in Irish legislation.

## SCHOOLING AS FOSTERAGE

Democratic participation was only one radical characteristic of
Pearse's educational paradigm. He was immersed in the romanticism
of the late nineteenth century child-centred movement, but he
emphasised the significance of the relationship between teacher and
learner, rather than the experience of the learner alone. Searching for
an appropriate metaphor for this relationship Pearse turned to the
Gaelic notion of fosterage. The laws governing the practice were
complicated but it is possible, given Pearse's regular use of the
National Library in Dublin, that he was familiar with the code in
some detail. *Seanchus Mór* (The Ancient Laws of Ireland) had been
published in Dublin in 1869 and the library at St Enda's contained a
1901 edition by Robert Atkinson.

Fosterage entailed the interchanging of children, usually between
noble families, so that they might learn the arts of oratory, tribal law,
rhetoric and military skills. Usually the process served to ensure
peace between powerful families or tribes (*tuath*). The practice survived in different guises until the Middle Ages, when it was common
for youths who displayed unusual ability, or belonged to well-con-
nected or ambitious families, to be placed under the guardianship of
a mentor who could assist their development. Pearse employed the
notion as a metaphor for the ideal teacher–pupil relationship. He
knew that the term was historically oblique and joked about 'How
blue Dr Hyde, Mr Yeats and Mr MacNeill would look if their friends

15.4 St Enda's
drill class in
Cullenswood
House, pre-1910.
Courtesy Pearse
Museum.

informed them that they were about to send their children to be fostered',[24] but the notion is not very dissimilar from the contemporary understanding of the teacher as acting *in loco parentis*; an understanding that remains at the heart of teaching.

In turning to the Gaelic model of fosterage, and the notion of learning as craft rather than process, Pearse identified the significance of learning as a transaction; a deeply human activity in which the learner is encouraged, not simply to become learned, but good, in other words, education was a moral activity.[25] Against the scramble for results fees, the process whereby Intermediate schools were awarded extra remuneration based upon examination results, Pearse set the ideal of the learning transaction as free from prescribed texts, set curricula and terminal examinations, a radical vision in 1908.

## A PROGRESSIVE CURRICULUM AT ST ENDA'S

Throughout the first half of the twentieth century progressive educators such as William Curry and A.S. Neill insisted upon the place of the arts in schooling. School plays, the pupils' endeavours in *An Scoláire* and the musical evenings held at the Hermitage, sometimes with the girls from St Ita's, testify to the importance Pearse placed on the arts as imperative to an enlightened understanding of education. Theatre at the Hermitage was intended to be culturally significant and often received attention in the national press, particularly when transported to the fledgling Abbey Theatre. Dramatic productions were an important part of life at the school. In February 1909 Pearse decided that the feast day of St Enda (21 March) should be celebrated by the performance of two plays at the school; Douglas Hyde's *An Naomh ar Iarraidh* (The Lost Saint) and *The Coming of Fionn* by Standish O'Grady.

The plays were performed in March and were praised in *An Claidheamh Soluis agus Fáinne an Lae*, the pupils 'played as if they were perfectly at home in the ways of the Fianna, as if captured by the spirit of the ancient heroes'.[26] *Sinn Féin* recorded that 'the performance of *An Naomh ar Iarraidh* gave one the impression that the play could never be better produced'.[27] Such press coverage provided St Enda's with valuable publicity. More than one hundred people attended on the evening of 20 March. The performance on the following night was watched by a 'brilliant literary audience' including Eoin MacNeill, W.B. Yeats, D.P. Moran and Padraig Colum'.[28] Encouraged by their success, Pearse proposed an end-of-term pageant based on the boyhood deeds of Cúchulainn. The pageant was performed in the school grounds on 22 June 1909 before an audience of 500 guests.

Pearse planned to stage his own play *Iosagán* and Padraig Colum's *The Destruction of the Hostel* at Christmas 1909. *Iosagán* was staged again at St Enda's on St Bridget's Day, 1910. During the Easter Week of May 1911 the pupils performed Pearse's *A Passion Play*. His contemporary and occasional visitor to St Enda's, Máire Nic Shiubhlaigh, recalled that the quality of the performance 'created something of a minor sensation in Dublin' and believed it to be 'probably the first really serious piece of Gaelic dramatic writing produced'.[29] These performances made considerable demands on the time of Pearse and his staff. The commitment and willingness of his brother William, Thomas MacDonagh, deputy Headmaster, and the wider staff meant that, in a short time, the school acquired a reputation for competent performance. Nic Shiubhlaigh recalled that the results achieved 'were remarkable' and that 'the acting was of a high standard'.[30]

15.5 Thomas MacDonagh. Commemorative postcard. Courtesy Pearse Museum.

While Pearse argued for a re-conceptualisation of the teacher–pupil relationship, he also urged changes in teaching methodology, all of which became characteristic of radical educators and, in time, of mainstream schooling. He was particularly innovative in the area of language acquisition, arguing for the use of Irish (or the designated language) in conversation with pupils and during extra-curricular activities. He encouraged the involvement of pupils in correcting their peers' work in class, described the use of corporal punishment for mistakes as 'the very acme of stupid and purposeless folly' and encouraged pupils to learn by doing, particularly in the sciences.[31] The 1897 Commission on Practical and Manual Instruction (Belmore Commission) had encouraged a more child-centred and practical approach to science teaching. While lack of funding meant that the Commission's recommendations remained little more than aspirational for most schools, Pearse strove to provide a fully equipped science laboratory. He was particularly keen to encourage the natural sciences and employed the services of David Houston, Professor of Zoology at Trinity College and Biology at the College of Surgeons, Dublin, to teach on a part-time basis at St Enda's, where his sons Cyril and Walter were enrolled. Houston's habit of giving lessons in the grounds of the Hermitage earned him the

IRISH REBELLION, MAY 1916.

THOMAS MacDONAGH
(Commandant of Bishop Street Area),
Executed May 3rd, 1916.

nickname 'creeping-out'. The pupils of St Enda's and St Ita's were addressed by a number of the most prominent Revivalists of the period including: Douglas Hyde; Countess Markievicz; Roger Casement; Maud Gonne McBride; Eoin MacNeill and Standish O'Grady.[32] These lectures reflected a key aspect of Pearse's founding philosophy; St Enda's would be the new Eamhain Macha and its boys would sit at the feet of the 'heroes and seers and scholars' of early twentieth century Ireland.[33]

Pearse was convinced that his schools should have an appropriate physical location. He conceptualised school in quasi-monastic terms as a type of retreat where children could engage in learning without being troubled by the coercion of state examinations. In so doing, he prefigured aspects of Michael Oakeshott's thinking on the nature and purpose of schooling.[34] He actively sought to locate St Enda's in a place apart, moving to the Hermitage because at Cullenswood House the city was too near and the hills too far, as stated in *An Macoamh* in 1910. St Enda, he mused, had 'fared across thirty miles of stormy sea to find a rocky home in Aran'.[35] Cognisant of the need to find a worthy home for his school, he was always conscious of the influence of place, environment and architecture upon a child's experience of school, and hoped that the environs of the Hermitage would expose the boys to those 'elemental forces' of life and nature. Of course the Hermitage had significant historical associations. Edward Hudson, who bought the house in 1786, had been on friendly terms with his neighbour, the lawyer John Curran. Curran was a member of the Irish Parliament between 1783 and 1797; had supported Catholic emancipation and defended a number of the United Irishmen after the failed rebellion of 1803. His daughter Sarah had been secretly engaged to Robert Emmet (1778–1803). They had often met in the grounds of the Hermitage and Pearse once mused that it was 'the sprit of Emmet that led me to these hillsides … I came out to Rathfarnham in the wake of Emmet'.[36]

## ST ENDA'S AND THE EASTER RISING

If, as the past pupil Denis Gwynn suggested, Pearse used his school 'as the instrument to provide himself with a band of young politicians who would follow him to the scaffold', he must have been very disappointed.[37] Less than twenty past pupils were involved in the Rising and the number may have been as low as twelve. At least four were members of the Irish Republican Brotherhood before Pearse. It was inevitable that some would become involved and Pearse was, perhaps, only one influence amidst the developing culture of republican separatism. Countless insurgents, who had no contact with St

Enda's or Pearse were caught up in the climate of the time, although some keenly felt his influence. St Enda's pupil Joseph Sweeney, for example, recorded that he 'came very much under the influence of Pearse, as most of the older boys did … we were committed completely to the idea of separation, the old Wolfe Tone definition of freedom'.[38] Upon leaving school, Sweeney studied engineering at University College Dublin, and Pearse swore him into the IRB in 1915. The group of past pupils who were to take part in the Rising, as part of 'E' Co. 4th Battalion, or 'Pearse's Own', assembled at the Yellow House, a public house adjacent to Rathfarnham Castle, on Easter Monday morning before leaving for their respective posts, despite the efforts of Eoin MacNeill to dissuade them.[39]

The number of past pupils who took part in the Rising is uncertain. Mrs Margaret Pearse insisted that it was no more than 'sixteen or seventeen'.[40] Writing in 1918, Frank Fahy, a past pupil of St Enda's, thought the number to be seventeen.[41] The eight who joined Pearse at the General Post Office (GPO) and were later interned at Frongoch Prison Camp in Wales were Eamon Bulfin, Joseph Sweeney, Frank Burke, Desmond Ryan, John Kilgallon, Fintan Murphy, Brian Joyce (Seoighe) and Joseph O'Connor. Micheál Mac Ruadhraí and Patrick Donnelly, both employees at the Hermitage, were also imprisoned at Frongoch. David Sears, who was a senior boy at St Enda's from 1914 to 1916, may also have taken part in the Rising. His early biographer Le Roux held that only twelve ex-pupils participated in the Rising.[42] In a letter to Mrs Pearse, penned from inside the GPO on Wednesday 26th April, Pearse assured his mother that the St Enda's boys who were with him were 'in excellent spirits'.[43] On 1st May these boys were taken to Richmond Barracks, as was William Pearse. Patrick was taken to Arbour Hill and believed that 'E' Co. 4th Battalion was also there. In his final letter to his mother on 3rd May he expressed his hope that 'the St Enda's boys [would] be safe'.[44]

Louis Le Roux insisted that Pearse knew that by teaching the boys the 'history of the Conquest' he would make them 'resolute and devoted men who should rapidly win rank as patriots'. [45] Clearly Pearse taught his pupils that duty to country, in any form, was a characteristic of good citizenship, although the models he placed before them, such as Tone and Emmet, were militant nationalists. Pearse had seen his pupils 'moved inexpressibly' by the story of Emmet or Anne Devlin and had found it 'legitimate' to make use of that reaction for 'educational purposes'.[46] Denis Gwynn's condemnation may be partly justified, but it is equally reasonable to suggest that the small number of past pupils that took part in the Rising suggests that Pearse's influence may have been less than previously imagined. The St

Enda's old boys who joined him at the GPO did so as adults and Pearse cannot justifiably be held accountable for their decision.

The influence teachers may exercise is not an uncomplicated issue. In Ireland the teaching body had a history of sedition dating back to the Wexford Rebellion and before that through the penal period. The Minutes of the Commissioners of National Education, 27 July 1916, recorded that allegations had been made that the Rising was fermented 'by the careful instilling of revolutionary principles in the teaching of many of our primary schools'. This was not an uncommon view, although the report of the following year, attested that: 'no evidence has been adduced which would warrant the conclusion that seditious teaching ... exists to any appreciable extent'.[47] Indeed, Denis Gwynn's decision to join the British armed forces at the outbreak of the First World War was, perhaps, eloquent testimony to the schooling in patriotism he received at St Enda's.

## CONCLUSION

A tangible legacy of Pearse's educational work is represented by the existence of a small number of schools that trace their origin to his endeavours at St Enda's and St Ita's. James O'Byrne, a former member of staff at St Enda's founded Ard Scoil Éanna in Crumlin, Dublin, in the late 1930s, where it continues to operate. Louise Gavan Duffy, who had offered to lease St Ita's in 1912, founded Scoil Bhríde in Dublin in 1917. Ms Margaret Pearse provided a permanent location for the school near Cullenswood House in the mid-1960s. The school holds the legacy of Pearse as 'part of (its) identity' and at present operates with an enrolment of 330 pupils.[48] A group of parents opened a gaelscoil in Cullenswood House in 1997 after a long restoration project. Lios na nÓg practises full immersion in the Irish language and the school staff and parents are conscious of, and respect, the legacy of Pearse.[49]

These are doubtless fitting memorials to Pearse's work, but the radical conceptualisation he introduced in understandings of the purpose and nature of schooling in pre-independent Ireland remain unclear. In recognising that schooling could operate as an agent of change, that it could become a vehicle for dissent, Pearse predates later conceptualisations of schooling as emancipatory. The realisation that curricular colonialism could be confronted and inverted *within* the school – the structure that historically had acted as its vehicle – represents a significant contribution to the field of educational inquiry.

Pearse's argument that the curriculum represented an act of political absorption was among the earliest contributions to the discourse concerning the relationship between curriculum and power. By insisting that the 'cultural script' of curriculum could be challenged and rewritten, Pearse identified schooling as a contested terrain, a reflection of the wider contemporaneous socio-political tension. His work was characterised by an instinct for progressivism, articulated in democratic participation in school, suspicion of prescribed methodology and the principles and practices described above. The integrity of his progressivism has traditionally received scant recognition and his perceptive and forward-looking understanding of schooling as an agent for the transmission of social and cultural dispositions by the political elite still has to be fully acknowledged. The radical educational paradigm did not exist when Pearse was writing. Given its evolution since the 1970s, a reappraisal of Pearse's educational thought and work is now appropriate.

# Notes
# Nótaí

## INTRODUCTION

1. Emmanuel Kehoe, 'Off Message', *Sunday Business Post*, 23 March 2008, p.5.
2. P.H. Pearse, 'The Individual', Editorial, *An Claidheamh Soluis agus Fáinne an Lae*, 1 September 1906, p.6.

## RÉAMHRÁ

1. Emmanuel Kehoe, 'Off Message', *Sunday Business Post*, 23 Márta 2008, lch.5.
2. Pádraic Mac Piarais, 'The Individual', Eagarfhocal, *An Claidheamh Soluis agus Fáinne an Lae*, 1 Meán Fómhair 1906, lch.6.

## CHAPTER ONE

1. Ruth Dudley Edwards, *Patrick Pearse. The Triumph of Failure* (London and Boston: Faber and Faber, 1977).
2. *Oxford Dictionary of National Biography*, http://www.oxforddnb.com/view/article/37840?docPos=5.
3. National Library of Ireland, Pearse Papers (hereafter cited as NLI PP), P7638 plus Ms 21406, Letter to Pearse, dated 27 January 1901.
4. National Archives of Ireland, Census 1901.
5. Patrick Pearse, unpublished autobiographical fragment, Pearse Museum, Rathfarnham, Dublin.
6. Letter to William O'Brien, dated 30 March 1912, Séamas Ó Buachalla (ed.), *The Letters of P. H. Pearse* (Gerrards Cross: Colin Smythe, 1980), p. 259.
7. NLI PP, Ms 33702, Speech delivered by Patrick Pearse in the USA in 1914.
8. Allen Library, Box 187, Copy of Court Martial and Execution of Pearse.
9. Michael Lennon Papers, in the author's possession (hereafter cited as LP), interview notes with Veale.
10. LP, interview notes with Eamon O'Neill(?) Conan & Sceilg. All of the men mentioned were executed after the Easter Rising.
11. NLI PP, Ms 33702, speech delivered by Patrick Pearse in the USA in 1914.
12. Ibid.
13. LP, interview notes with Veale.
14. Brian Crowley, '"His Father's Son": James and Patrick Pearse' in *Folk Life. Journal of Ethnological Studies*, Vol. 43, 2004–2005, pp. 71–88, pp. 80–2.
15. James Pearse, *A Reply to Professor Maguire's Pamphlet 'England's Duty to Ireland' as it Appears to an Englishman* (Dublin, 1886).
16. LP, interview notes with Liam O'Donnell.
17. Pearse, unpublished autobiographical fragment, Pearse Museum.
18. LP, interview notes with Veale.
19. The Scholastic Story of Padraic Pearse (Box 187, Allen Library); 'They were Schoolboys! The Pearse Brothers at the "Row"', in *Christian Brothers Westland Row, Centenary Record 1864–1964*, p. 43.
20. LP, letter to Michael Lennon from Omar Crowley, dated 19 April 1947.
21. Quoted in Edwards, *Patrick Pearse*, p. 16.

22. LP, letter from E.O Danluan [?] to Michael Lennon, dated 19 [?] 1947.

23. Jerome F. Cronin in *Irish Independent*, 2 April 1957; LP, interview notes with Staunton (Crown solicitor); LP, letter from Colm O' Loughlin to Michael Lennon, dated 13 May 1947; Edwards, *Patrick Pearse*, p. 16 and p. 47.

24. Jerome F. Cronin in *Irish Independent*, 2 April 1957.

25. LP, interview notes with Veale; LP, letter from J. A. Duffy to Michael Lennon, dated 30 September 1947; LP, interview notes with Lennon Snr; Eamon O'Neill, Conan & Sceilg.

26. LP, letter from Jimmy Whelan to Michael Lennon, dated 30 October 1945. See also, LP, letter from J. A. Duffy to Michael Lennon, dated 30 September 1947.

27. LP, interview notes with Veale, Eamon O'Neill, Conan & Sceilg and Eamonn O'Neill.

28. LP, letter from Wm. Val. Jackson to Michael Lennon, dated 19 [?] 1947.

29. LP, letter from J. A. Duffy to Michael Lennon, dated 30 September 1947.

30. Ibid.

31. LP, letter from Jimmy Whelan to Michael Lennon, dated 30 October 1945.

32. LP, letter from Colm O' Loughlin to Michael Lennon, dated 13 May 1947; LP, letter from Frank Fahey to Michael Lennon, dated 15 March 1948; LP, interview notes with Rd Foley; LP, interview notes with Bulmer Hobson; Jerome F. Cronin in *Irish Independent*, 27 March 1957.

33. LP, interview notes with Liam O' Donnell; National Library of Ireland, scrapbook of Frank Martin (hereafter cited as NLI FM), Ms 32695/1, 'Memories of Pearse' by M.H. in *The London Herald* [no date]; Pearse, unpublished autobiographical fragment, Pearse Museum.

34. LP, letter from Seamus Mullivan to Michael Lennon, dated 28 February 1947. See also LP, interview notes with Michael Dowling; LP, letter from Frank Fahey to Michael Lennon, dated 15 March 1948.

35. LP, letter from Colm O' Loughlin to Michael Lennon, dated 13 May 1947. See also, LP, letter from Hamill to Michael Lennon, dated 26 August 1946.

36. Pearse, unpublished autobiographical fragment, Pearse Museum.

37. Open letter to himself, dated 11 May 1912, in Ó Buachalla (ed.), *The Letters of P. H. Pearse*, pp. 264–5.

38. O'Neill quoted in, Edwards, *Patrick Pearse,* p. 14.

39. LP, interview notes with Kate Elizabeth Field (daughter of Henry Pearse).

40. LP, interview notes with J. J. O'Looney; LP, letter Torna (O Donehada) to Michael Lennon, dated 26 November 1946; LP, letter from Wm Val. Jackson to Michael Lennon, dated 19 [?] 1947.

41. LP, letter from Eoghan Ó Neachtain to Michael Lennon, dated 28 September 1947.

42. LP, letter from Justice Wm S. Black to Michael Lennon, dated 6 December 1946.

43. LP, interview notes with Eamonn O'Neill; LP, letter from Torna (O Donehada) to Michael Lennon, dated 26 November 1946; NLI, Ms 10883, Eoin MacNeill's memoirs; Edwards, *Patrick Pearse*, p. 26.

44. *Three Lectures on Gaelic Topics* reprinted in *Collected Works of Pádraic H. Pearse. Songs of the Irish Rebels and Specimens from an Irish anthology. Some aspects of Irish Literature: Three Lectures on Gaelic Topics* (Dublin, Cork, Belfast: Phoenix Publishing Co., Ltd, n.d.), pp. 218–21.

45. NLI PP, Ms 10833, Lecture invitation Pearse to speak on 'The Battle of Two Civilisations', letter dated 15 February 1901.

46. 'Letter to the Editor', dated 13 May 1899, Ó Buchalla, *Letters of P.H. Pearse*, pp. 8–9.

47. *An Claidheamh Soluis agus Fáinne an Lae,,* 19 November 1904, quoted in Edwards, *Patrick Pearse*, p. 72.

48. *An Claidheamh Soluis*, 7 January 1905, quoted in Edwards, *Patrick Pearse*, p. 71.

49. *An Claidheamh Soluis*, 27 August 1904, quoted in Edwards, *Patrick Pearse*, p. 70.

50. *An Claidheamh Soluis*, 26 November 1904, quoted in Edwards, *Patrick Pearse,* p. 72; Séamas Ó Buachalla (ed.), *An Piarsach sa Bheilg. P.H. Pearse in Belgium. P.H. Pearse in Belgïe,* (Dublin: An Gúm, 1998), pp. 111–12.

51. NLI, Ms 5049, Letter to Séamus Ó Ceallaigh, dated 26 December 1904.

52. Edwards, *Patrick Pearse*, p. 152.

53. LP, interview notes with Mrs Bradley.

54. LP, interview notes with Mrs Bradley; LP, interview notes with Veale; LP, interview notes with Justice Wm S. Black; LP, interview notes with Hobson.

55. Kilmainham Gaol Archive (hereafter cited as KGA), 23LRIP15/3, Letter of recommendation by Douglas Hyde, dated 2 October 1905. Also KGA 23LRIP15/4, Letter from Edmund Hogan.

56. The Bill proposed reforming Irish government through the transfer of eight departments to the control of a partly elected council which would have limited administrative powers.

57. *An Claidheamh Soluis,* 18 May 1907.
58. *An Claidheamh Soluis,* 16 December 1905.
59. Ibid.
60. *An Claidheamh Soluis,* 11 May 1907.
61. *An Claidheamh Soluis,* 7 September 1907.
62. *An Claidheamh Soluis,* 11 January 1908.
63. *An Claidheamh Soluis,* 7 September 1907.
64. LP, interview notes marked L C26.
65. *An Claidheamh Soluis,* 7 March 1908. See, also, *An Claidheamh Soluis agus Fáinne an Lae,* 24 April 1909; *An Claidheamh Soluis agus Fáinne an Lae,* 24 July 1909.
66. Letter to Cathal O'Shannon, dated January 1912, Ó Buachalla, *The Letters of P.H. Pearse,* p. 246.
67. Letter to Sean Mac Caoilte, dated 18 February 1912, Ó Buachalla, *The Letters of P. H. Pearse,* p. 255.
68. Letter to Sean T. Ó Ceallaigh, dated 17 February 1912, Ó Buachalla, *The Letters of P. H. Pearse,* p. 253.
69. *An Barr Buadh,* 5 April 1912, quoted in Edwards, *Patrick Pearse,* p. 159.
70. Quoted in Edwards, *Patrick Pearse,* 164. First meeting was 2 April 1912, Letter to Sean T. Ó Ceallaigh, dated 28 March 1912, Ó Buachalla, *The Letters of P. H. Pearse,* p. 257.
71. *An Barr Buadh,* 27 April 1912, quoted in Edwards, *Patrick Pearse,* p. 160.
72. Report on the address by Pearse to the Gaelic League in Carrick-on-Suir, 27 November 1912.
73. Open letter to himself, dated 11 May 1912, Ó Buachalla (ed.), *The Letters of P. H. Pearse,* pp. 264–5.
74. 'The Coming Revolution' in *An Claidheamh Soluis,* 8 November 1913.
75. Ibid.
76. LP, copy of article in *New York Evening Journal,* St Patrick's Day 1914.
77. 'How Does She Stand?', Emmet commemoration lecture in Brooklyn, 2 March 1914, in *Collected Works of Padraic H. Pearse. Political Writings and Speeches* (Dublin and London: Maunsel & Roberts Limited, 1922), pp. 64–75.
78. 'How Does She Stand?', Emmet commemoration lecture in New York 9 March 1914, in *Collected Works of Padraic H. Pearse. Political Writings and Speeches,* p. 87.
79. National Archives of Ireland, WS367 Joseph Gleeson.
80. Letters to McGarrity 1915–16, *passim,* in Ó Buachalla (ed.), *The Letters of P. H. Pearse.*
81. Letter to his legal executors, 25 November 1914, Ó Buachalla (ed.), *The Letters of P. H. Pearse,* pp. 335–7.
82. Edwards, *Patrick Pearse,* pp. 157–238.
83. Open letter to Douglas Hyde, dated 4 May 1912, Ó Buachalla (ed.), *The Letters of P. H. Pearse,* pp. 262–4.
84. LP, letter from Colm O Loughlin to Michael Lennon, dated 13 May 1947. See, also, LP, interview notes with Osborn Bergin; LP, interview notes with Alf White; LP, interview notes with Michael Dowling; LP, interview notes with Sean Ó Briain; LP, letter from Mrs Bradley to Michael Lennon, dated 22 February 1947; LP, Jerome F. Cronin in *Irish Independent,* 2 April 1957; 'How Does She Stand?', Emmet commemoration lecture in Brooklyn 2 March 1914, in *Collected Works of Padraic H. Pearse. Political Writings and Speeches,* pp. 64–75.
85. LP, interview notes with Rd Foley.

CHAPTER TWO

1. An earlier version of this article appeared as 'His Father's Son: James and Patrick Pearse' in *Folk Life, Journal of Ethnological Studies,* Vol. 43, 2004–5, pp. 71–88.
2. Patrick Pearse, unpublished autobiographical fragment, Pearse Museum, Rathfarnham, Dublin. PMSTE.2003.0946, pp. 14–15 (page references here and below are to the hand-written page numbers applied by Pearse to the manuscript).
3. Ruth Dudley Edwards, *Patrick Pearse. The Triumph of Failure* (Dublin: Poolbeg Press Ltd, 1990), p. 11.
4. National Library of Ireland, James Pearse Papers (hereafter cited as NLI JPP), Ms 21,082 James Pearse to Margaret Pearse (undated).
5. Pearse, unpublished autobiographical fragment, Pearse Museum, p. 7.
6. Pearse, unpublished autobiographical fragment, Pearse Museum, p. 6.
7. Richard Hoggart, *The Uses of Literacy. Aspects of working-class life with special reference to publications and entertainments* (London: Penguin Books, 1992), pp. 318–20.

8. Edward Royle, *Radicals, Secularists and Republicans, Popular Freethought in Britain, 1866–1915* (Manchester: Manchester University Press, 1980), p. 199.
9. Desmond Ryan, *Remembering Sion. A Chronicle of Storm and Quiet*, (London: Arthur Barker Ltd, 1934), p. 160.
10. Thomas D'Arcy McGee, *History of Ireland* (Glasgow: Cameron and Ferguson, n/d).
11. Edmund Ollier (ed.), *Cassell's History of the War between France and Germany, 1870–71. Vols I and II* (London: Cassell & Co. Ltd, n/d).
12. 'H.H.', *A Century of Dishonour. A Sketch of the United States Government's Dealings with the North American Tribes* (London: Chatto and Windus, 1881).
13. Flavius Josephus, *The Works of Flavius Josephus, The Learned and Authentic Jewish Historian, and Celebrated Warrior* (London: George Virtue, 1841).
14. Philo Judaeus, *The Works of Philo Judaeus,* (London: Henry G. Bohn, 1854).
15. Gerald Fitzgerald, *A Hebrew Grammar, for the use of the Students of the University of Dublin* (Dublin: R. E. Mercier, 1798).
16. Archbishop Justiniano of Cranganor and Carlos Vero, *The Inquisition and Judaism, A Sermon Addressed to Jewish Martyrs on the Occasion of an Auto-Da-Fé at Lisbon, 1705. Also a Reply to the Sermon* (London: J. Wertheimer, 1845).
17. Hypathia Bradlaugh Bonner, *Charles Bradlaugh, A Record of his Life and Work,* Vol. I, (London: T. Fisher Unwin, 1894).
18. Bradlaugh Papers, Bishopsgate Institute, London (hereafter cited as CBP), No. 1800 James Pearse to Hypathia Bradlaugh Bonner, 29 January 1891.
19. Royle, *Radicals, Secularists and Republicans,* p. 208.
20. Statistic quoted by Alistair Rowan in 'Irish Victorian Churches: Denominational Distinctions' in *Ireland: Art into History*, Raymond Gillespie and Brian P. Kennedy ed.(Dublin: Town House, 1994), p. 208.
21. In his autobiography Patrick only makes reference to one child dying in infancy. He does not seem to have been aware that his father had a fourth child by his first wife. Pearse, unpublished autobiographical fragment, Pearse Museum, p. 9.
22. NLI JP, Ms 21,082, correspondence of James and Margaret Pearse (no date).
23. Pearse, unpublished autobiographical fragment, Pearse Museum, pp. 41–2.
24. Mary Brigid Pearse, *The Home-Life of Patick Pearse, as told by himself, his family and friends* (Dublin: Browne and Nolan Limited, 1934), pp. 107–9.
25. *Exhibition of Irish Arts and Manufacturers 1882, Rotunda, Dublin. Complete Official Catalogue,* (Dublin: Irish Exhibition Company (Limited), 1882), p. 60.
26. Jeremy Williams, *A Companion to Architecture in Ireland, 1837–1921* (Dublin: Irish Academic Press, 1994), p. 127.
27. Thomas J. Duffy, 'Ecclesiastical Sculpture in the church of St Michael, Tipperary' in *Thought Lines 4, An Anthology of Research*, Paul Caffrey ed. (Dublin: National College of Art and Design, 2000), p. 59.
28. NLI JJP, Ms 21,1078, Account book, 1889–98.
29. Ignatius Fennessy, 'Patrick Pearse and the Four (of Five) Masters' in *Donegal Annual / Bliainiris Dhún na nGall. Journal of the County Donegal Historical Society,* No. 53, 2001, pp. 81–7.
30. James Pearse to Archdeacon Kinnane, P.P. of Fethard, 13 January 1883. Pearse Museum, PMSTE. 2003.0265.
31. NLI JP, Ms 21077 Fr Pius Devine to James Pearse, 26 December 1877.
32. CBP, No. 1117, Debenture issued by Charles Bradlaugh and Annie Besant, as the Freethought Publishing Co., for £50 lent by James Pearse of Dublin, 30 May 1884.
33. Brian Crowley, 'His Father's Son: James and Patrick Pearse' in *Folk Life, Journal of Ethnological Studies*, Vol. 43, 2004–5, pp. 81–2.
34. 'Humanitas', *The Follies of the Lord's Prayer*, (London: Freethought Publishing Company, 1883).
35. 'Humanitas', *Socialism, A Curse, being a reply to a lecture delivered by Edward B. Aveling D.Sc. entitled 'The Curse of Capitalism'* (London: Freethought Publishing Company, 1884).
36. Humanitas', *Is God the First Cause? Being also a reply to Father Burke's Theory of Science and Received Religion* (London: Freethought Publishing Company, 1883).
37. Unfortunately I have not been able to locate a copy of *Against Socialism*. However advertisements for it appear in the *Agnostic Journal* between 13 April and 11 May 1889 and *The Freethinker* between 14 April and 30 June 1889.
38. James Pearse, *A Reply to Professor Maguire's Pamphlet 'England's Duty to Ireland' as it Appears to an Englishman* (Dublin: M.H. Gill & Son, 1886).
39. Thomas Maguire, *England's Duty to Ireland as it appears to a Loyal Irish Roman Catholic,* (Dublin: William McGee, 1886).

40. Ibid., p. 20.
41. Ibid., p. 16.
42. Ryan, *Remembering Sion,* p. 102.
43. David Thornley, 'Patrick Pearse and the Pearse Family' in *Studies,* Autumn–Winter 1971, p. 338.
44. James Pearse, *England's Duty to Ireland as it appears to an Englishman,* p. 13.
45. Ibid., p. 39.
46. Ibid., p. 40.
47. Ibid., p. 27 and p. 31. 'Humanitas' also singles out Davitt for particular praise in *Charles Bradlaugh and the Irish Nation,* describing him as 'the greatest man of them all' (London: Freethought Publishing Company, 1885), p. 23.
48. *The Freeman's Journal,* 7 September 1900.
49. Patrick Pearse, unpublished autobiographical fragment, Pearse Museum.
50. Calendar of Wills and Probate, National Archives of Ireland.
51. Séamas Ó Buachalla, (ed.), *A Significant Irish Educationalist. The Educational Writings of P. H. Pearse* (Dublin and Cork: Mercier Press, 1980), pp. 321–2.
52. Edwards, *Patrick Pearse,* pp. 74-8.
53. Ibid., p. 158.
54. Thornley, 'Patrick Pearse and the Pearse Family', p. 346.
55. Louis Le Roux, *Life of Patrick Pearse* (Dublin: Talbot Press, 1932), pp. 40–1; This originally appeared in *An Barr Buadh,* Bealtaine 11, 1912, under the title 'Beart Litreach do Chuaidh Amugha IX. Chum Phádraicmhicphiarais', 'Ní fheadar an maith liom thú nó nach maith. Ní fheadar an maith le héinne thú. Tá a fhios agam gur gráin le n-a lán thú. … Táir ródhorcha ionnat féin, a Phiarsaigh. Ní dhéanann tú caidreamh le Gaedhealaibh. Séanann tú a gcomhluadar. An uair thagas tú ina measc tagann mar do bheadh néall dubh id'fhochair agus luigheann ortha. … An í an fhuil Shasanach úd ionnat is cionntach leis sin, ní fheadar? … Is dóigh liom go bhfuil dhá Phiarsach ann .i. fear gruamdha doineannta agus fear geal soineannta.'
56. James Pearse may have had an influence on the writing of these poeMs In the period just prior to the 1916 Rising, Pearse's mother asked him: 'to write something for me – as your father used to. He wrote such beautiful things when your Auntie Kate and Grandfather died'. Mary Brigid Pearse, *The Home-Life of Patrick Pearse,* p. 51. Both these poems by James Pearse survive in the Pearse Museum Collection (PMSTE.2003.0058 and PMSTE.2003.1194)
57. J.A. Shields, *Patrick Pearse - Irish Patriot* (Private Edition, 1937), p. 2.
58. *Leabhrán Cuimhneacháin arna Fhoilsiú ar Ócáid Bronnadh Eochar Scoil Éanna ar Uachtarán na hÉireann Eamon De Valera 23 Aibreán 1970.*
59. Pat Cooke, *Scéal Scoil Éanna. The Story of an Educational Adventure* (Dublin: Office of Public Works, 1986), p. 2.

CHAPTER THREE

1. Ruth Dudley Edwards, *Patrick Pearse. The Triumph of Failure,* (London: Faber and Faber, 2nd edition, 1979), p. 120.
2. Mary Brigid Pearse (ed.), *The Home-Life of Patrick Pearse,* (Dublin: Browne and Nolan, 1934), p. 147.
3. The Royal University of Ireland established by Charter in 1880 was the first university in Ireland to admit women, equally with men, to its examinations and degrees. Its degrees were conferred on women for the first time in 1884, when nine women gained the awards. The RUI was dissolved in 1908 with the establishment of the National University of Ireland.
4. Mary Hayden, 'My Recollections of Patrick Pearse' in Mary Brigid Pearse (ed.), *The Home-Life of Padraig Pearse,* p. 147.
5. National Library of Ireland, Mary Hayden Papers, Hayden Diary (hereafter cited as NLI Hayden Diary), 8 December 1897. The diary references in this chapter are from the years 1897–1903, Mss 16,676-16, 683.
6. Mary Colum, *Life and the Dream* (Dublin: Dolmen Press, revised edition, 1966), p. 96.
7. Mary M. Macken, 'Musings and Memories; Helena Concannon MA, D.Litt.' in *Studies,* Vol. XLII, No. 165, March 1953, p. 92.
8. Edwards, *Patrick Pearse,* p. 29.
9. NLI Hayden Diary, 29 March 1902.
10. Ibid., 30 March 1902.
11. Ibid., 31 March 1902.

12. Ibid., 21 April 1902.
13. Ibid., 21 May 1902.
14. National Library of Ireland, Patrick Pearse Papers (hereafter cited as NLI PP), Ms 21054 (4), Hayden to Pearse, 1 June [1907 ?]. Two letters here attributed to 1907 are undated. Internal and other evidence, and the fact that they are written on black-bordered notepaper suggests the year as 1907. Hayden's uncle, John Hayden, died on 25 April 1907. One of the letters is dated 1 June. The other was written around the same time. Both are from Manchester.
15. NLI PP, Ms 21054 (4), Hayden to Pearse, 27 December [1902].
16. NLI Hayden Diary, 1 January 1903.
17. Ibid., 7 January 1903.
18. Ibid., 28 January 1903.
19. Ibid., 7 February 1903.
20. Ibid.
21. Ibid., 1 March 1903.
22. NLI PP, Ms 21054(4), Hayden to Pearse, 7 March [1903].
23. Edwards, *Patrick Pearse*, p. 64.
24. Regina Uí Chollatáin, *An Claidheamh Soluis agus Fainne an Lae* (Dublin: Cois Life Teoranta, 2004), p. 90.
25. NLI Hayden Diary, 10 March 1903.
26. Ibid., 15 May 1903.
27. NLI PP, Ms 21054(4), Hayden to Pearse, 1 June [1907 ?].
28. P.H. Pearse, 'The Dead Bill and Ourselves', *An Claidheamh Soluis agus Fáinne an Lae*, 25 May 1907.
29. NLI PP, Ms 21054 (4), Hayden to Pearse, 1 June [1907 ?].
30. Hayden, 'My Recollections of Patrick Pearse', p.148.
31. Edwards, *Patrick Pearse*, p. 153.
32. NLI PP, Ms 21054 (4), Hayden to Pearse, 1 June [1907?].
33. Edwards, *Patrick Pearse*, p. 55.
34. Hayden had had an on-off, long drawn out engagement (about which in earlier years she had not been especially enthusiastic) to Arthur Conan, who had gone to live in South Africa, chiefly for health reasons. He died there in August 1903.
35. NLI PP, Ms 21054 (4), Hayden to Pearse, 1 June [1907 ?].
36. NLI PP, Ms 21054 (4), Hayden to Pearse, [no date].
37. NLI PP, Ms 21054 (4), Hayden to Pearse, [1907 ?].
38. NLI PP, Ms 21054 (4), Hayden to Pearse, 1 June [1907 ?].
39. Ibid.
40. NLI PP, Microfilm POS 7639, Hayden to Pearse [no date]
41. NLI PP, Ms 21050, Hayden to Pearse, 14 March 1905.
42. Mary Hayden, 'My Recollections of Patrick Pearse', p. 147.
43. NLI PP, Ms 21054 (4), Hayden to Pearse, [1907 ?].
44. Hayden, 'My Recollections of Patrick Pearse', p. 149.
45. University College Dublin Library, Special Collections, Curran Papers, Ms 25, Catholic Graduates and Undergraduates Association.
46. The Irish Universities Act, 1908, established two new universities: the National University of Ireland and the Queen's University of Belfast. The National University had three constituent colleges in Dublin, Cork and Galway.
47. Mary Hayden, 'Irish in the New University', *Freeman's Journal*, 28 December 1908, 5 February 1909; Pádraic Pearse, 'Irish Ireland and the University Question', *An Claidheamh Soluis*, 8 February 1908, 'A Question for the Senate', *An Claidheamh Soluis*, 2 January 1909.
48. Gaelic League, Annual Report 1909 (Dublin, 1909).
49. Hayden, 'My Recollections of Patrick Pearse', p.148.
50. Edwards, *Patrick Pearse*, p. 29.
51. Anne V. O'Connor and Susan M. Parkes, *Gladly Learn and Gladly Teach. Alexandra College and School 1866–1966* (Dublin: Blackwater, 1984), p. 58.
52. *An Claidheamh Soluis*, 29 May 1909.
53. *An Macaomh*, Vol. 1, No. 1, 1909, p. 85.
54. Máire Ní Aodáin, 'The Golden Mean' in *An Claidheamh Soluis*, 7 and 14 January 1905. M.Ní A. 'Living for Ireland' in *An Claidheamh Soluis*, 25 January 1908.
55. Hayden, 'My Recollections of Patrick Pearse', pp. 147–8.
56. NLI PP, Ms 21059, Hayden to Mrs Pearse, 11 June [1916].
57. Ibid.

58. Hayden, 'Women and the New Constitution. Hard Won Rights to be Lost', *Cork Examiner*, 29 June 1937.
59. Mary Hayden and G.A. Moonan, *A Short History of the Irish People* (Dublin: Educational Company of Ireland/Talbot Press, 2nd edition [n.d]), p. 548.
60. Hayden, 'My Recollections of Patrick Pearse', p. 150.

CHAPTER FOUR

1. Patrick Pearse, unpublished autobiographical fragment, Pearse Museum, Rathfarnham, Dublin. PMSTE.2003.0946, p.1. An edited version of the autobiography was incorporated by his sister Mary Brigid Pearse into *The Home-Life of Patrick Pearse* (Dublin: Browne and Nolan, 1934). Page references here and below are to the hand-written page numbers applied by Pearse to the manuscript.
2. There is an allusion in the manuscript (p. 2) to the November 1913 issue of his school magazine *An Macaomh*, and elsewhere a reference to his being 'in the midst of military plans and organisation' (p. 44). This places its composition sometime after he became a Director of Military Organisation for the Irish Volunteers in December 1914.
3. Samuel Beckett, 'Recent Irish Poetry' in *The Bookman*, No. 86, 1934, reprinted in Michael Smith (ed.), *The Lace Curtain: A Magazine of Poetry and Criticism* (Dublin: New Writers Press, 1971), p. 59.
4. A word search of some of his key political essays 1913–16 reveals the following frequencies of his use of the word 'generation': 'From a Hermitage' (1913) [9]; 'The Coming Revolution' (1913) [4]; 'Why We Want Recruits' (1915) [4]; 'Ghosts' (1915) [16]; 'The Separatist Idea' (1916) [2]; 'The Sovereign People' (1916) [1]; 'The Spirtual Nation' (1916) [3]. Seamus Deane has noted Pearse's use of the word as one of his stylistic clichés; see Seamus Deane, *Celtic Revivals: Essays in Modern Irish Literature* (London: Faber, 1985), p. 71.
5. Robert Wohl, *The Generation of 1914*, (London: Weidenfeld and Nicholson, 1980), p. 3.
6. Pearse, unpublished autobiographical fragment, Pearse Museum, p. 35.
7. Seamus Ó Buachalla (ed.), *A Significant Irish Educationalist: the educational writings of P.H. Pearse* (Cork: Mercier, 1980), p. 333.
8. Deane, *Celtic Revivals*, pp. 70-72.
9. Francis Shaw, 'The Canon of Irish history – A challenge' in *Studies*, Vol. LXI, No. 242, Summer, 1972, p. 123.
10. A.O.J. Cockshut, 'Victorian Thought' in A.C. Pollard (ed.), *The Victorians* (London: Sphere, 1970), p.17.
11. Kenneth Reddin, 'A Man called Pearse', *Studies*, Vol. XXXIV, No.134, June 1945, p. 245.
12. R.F. Foster, *The Irish Story: Telling Tales and Making it Up in Ireland*, (Oxford: Oxford University Press, 2002), p.11.
13. Geoffrey Keynes (ed.), *The Poetical Works of Rupert Brooke* (London: Faber, 1974), p. 20.
14. Wohl, *Generation of 1914*, p. 87.
15. Ó Buachalla, *A Significant Irish Educationalist*, p. 338.
16. Henry Frowde, *Poems of Tennyson* (Oxford: Oxford Editions, 1906), p. 450.
17. Patrick Pearse, 'The Sovereign People', reprinted in *Collected Works of Padraic H. Pearse: Political Writings and Speeches* (Dublin and London: Maunsel and Roberts Limited, 1922), pp. 367–8.
18. Thomas Hutchinson (ed.), *Shelley: Poetical Works* (Oxford: Oxford University Press, 1967), p. 641.
19. Rose Lovell-Smith, 'The Animals of Wonderland: Tenniel as Carroll's reader' in *Criticism*, Fall, Vol. 45, No. 4, 2003, pp. 383–416.
20. Pearse, 'From a Hermitage' in *Collected Works*, p. 166.
21. Paul Fussell, *The Great War and Modern Memory* (Oxford: Oxford University Press, 2000), p. 245.
22. Mark Girouard, *The Return to Camelot* (New Haven: Yale University Press, 1981), pp. 64, 136, 269–70.
23. Desmond Ryan, *Remembering Sion* (London: Arthur Blake, 1934), p. 111.
24. Ó Buachalla, *A Significant Irish Educationalist*, p. 342.
25. Pearse, 'From a Hermitage', November 1913, in *Political Writings*, pp. 185, 187.
26. Quoted in Brian Barton, *From Behind a Closed Door* (Belfast: Blackstaff, 2003), pp. 109–110.
27. Girouard, *The Return to Camelot*, p. 170.
28. Lytton Strachey, *Eminent Victorians* (New York: Putnam, 1918), p. 31.

29. Thomas Mann, *Death in Venice* (London: Penguin, 1970), pp.16 and 64.
30. Ó Buachalla, *A Significant Irish Educationalist*, p. 343.
31. Ruth Dudley Edwards, *Patrick Pearse: The Triumph of Failure* (London: Faber, 1979), p. 170.
32. Ryan, *Remembering Sion*, p. 111.
33. Mary Bridget Pearse, *The Home-Life of Patrick Pearse*, p. 138.
34. 'Cuimhní na bPiarsach: Memories of the Brothers Pearse' (booklet) (Dublin: Brothers Pearse Commemoration Committee, 1958), p. 10.
35. Louis Le Roux, *Life of Patrick Pearse*, translated into English by Desmond Ryan (Dublin: Talbot Press, 1932), pp. 40–41.
36. Karl E. Meyer, 'An Edwardian Warning', *World Policy Journal*, Vol. 17, no. 4, 2001 pp. 47–57.
37. Mary Brigid Pearse, *The Home Life of Patrick Pearse*, pp. 80; 83–84.
38. Ó Buachalla, *A Significant Irish Educationalist*, p. 343.
39. Ibid., p 324.
41. H.H. Munro, *The Collected Short Stories of Saki* (London: Wordsworth Editions, 1993), p. 9.
42. Wohl, *The Generation of 1914*, p. 87.
43. Ibid., p. 89.
44. Jackie Wullschlager, *Inventing Wonderland: The Lives and Fantasies of Lewis Carroll, Edward Lear, J.M. Barrie, Kenneth Grahame, and A.A. Milne* (London: Methuen, 1995), p. 146.
45. Elizabeth K. Helsinger, 'Ulysses to Penelope: Victorian Experiments in Autobiography', in George P. Landow (ed.), *Approaches to Victorian Autobiography*, (Ohio: Ohio University Press, 1979), p. 4.
46. Helsinger, *Approaches to Victorian Autobiography*, p. 19.
47. Ibid., p. 40.
48. Wullschlager, *Inventing Wonderland*, p. 23.
49. Elaine Sisson, *Pearse's Patriots: St Enda's and the Cult of Boyhood* (Cork: Cork University Press, 2004), p.137.
50. R.F. Foster, *Modern Ireland: 1600–1972*, (London: Allen Lane, 1988), p. 477.
51. Ryan, *Remembering Sion*, p. 141.

CHAPTER FIVE

1. Richard Ellmann, *James Joyce*, (Oxford: Oxford University Press, 1982), p. 3.
2. P.H. Pearse, 'Some Aspects of Irish Literature', in *Collected Works: Songs of the Irish Rebels*, (Dublin: The Phoenix Publishing Co. Ltd, 1924), p. 157.
3. Ernest Bloch outlined this theory most fully in his trilogy *The Principle of Hope* (Oxford: Basil Blackwell, 1986).
4. Patrick Pearse, *Collected Works of Pádraic H. Pearse. Political Writings and Speeches,* (Dublin and London: Maunsel & Roberts Limited, 1922), p. 25.
5. J.J. Horgan, *Parnell to Pearse* (Dublin: Browne and Nolan, 1948), p. 285.
6. Patrick Pearse, *An Macaomh* 2, 2 May 1913, p. 8.
7. Patrick Pearse, *Plays, Stories, Poems* (Dublin: 1924), p. 323.
8. Ibid., pp. 337–8.
9. Ellsworth Mason and Richard Ellmann (eds.), *The Critical Writings of James Joyce* (New York: Viking, 1959), p. 174.
10. Patrick Pearse, 'Réamhrá', *Íosagán agus Scéalta Eile* (Baile Átha Cliath: Connradh na Gaedhilge, 1907).
11. Patrick Pearse, 'Séadna and the future of Irish prose', *An Claidheamh Soluis agus Fáinne an Lae*, 24 September 1904, p. 8.
12. For the background to this antagonism, see Ruth Dudley Edwards, *Patrick Pearse. The Triumph of Failure* (London: Faber and Faber, 1979), pp. 94–8.
13. Patrick Pearse, 'About Literature', *An Claidheamh Soluis*, 26 June 1906, p. 7.
14. Patrick Pearse, ' Traditionalism', *An Claidheamh Soluis*, 9 June 1906, p. 7.
15. Pearse, *Plays, Stories, Poems*, p. 324.
16. Thomas Mc Donagh, 'Language and Literature in Ireland', *The Irish Review*, IV, March–April 1914, pp. 176–82.
17. Ashis Nandy, *The Intimate Enemy: Loss and Recovery of Self under Colonialism* (Oxford: Oxford University Press, 1983), *passim*.
18. The phrase was coined by journalist John Healy in his commentaries in *The Irish Times*.
19. Richard Sennett, *The Fall of the Public Man: On the Social Psychology of Capitalism* (New York: Vintage Books, 1978), p. 184.

## CHAPTER SIX

1. 'Life in Ireland, is in truth, very full and interesting just now. It is as if the history of a century were being crowded into a generation.' The title of this chapter is based on this reading of P.H. Pearse's article 'Gleo na gCath', *An Claidheamh Solius agus Fáinne an Lae*, 6 June 1903.
2. Patrick Pearse, 'Ulster', Editorial, *An Claidheamh Soluis*, 24 December 1904.
3. Regina Uí Chollatáin, *Iriseoirí Pinn na Gaeilge. An Cholúnaíocht Liteartha: critic iriseoireachta*. (Baile Átha Cliath: Cois Life, 2008), pp. 67–9; 82–5.
4. Julian Baggini, *Making Sense. Philosophy behind the headlines* (Oxford: Oxford University Press, 2002), p. 20.
5. Ruth Dudley Edwards, *Patrick Pearse. The Triumph of Failure* (Dublin: Poolbeg Press, 1990), pp. 64–110; Raymond J. Porter, *P.H. Pearse* (New York: Twayne Publishers Inc., 1973), pp. 36–65.
6. Philip O'Leary, *The Prose Literature of the Gaelic Revival 1881–1921. Ideology and Innovation* (Pennsylvania: Pennsylvania State University Press, 1994).
7. Proinsias Mac Aonghusa, *Ar Son na Gaeilge. Conradh na Gaeilge 1893–1993*, (Baile Átha Cliath: Conradh na Gaeilge, 1993); Donncha Ó Súilleabháin, *An Piarsach agus Conradh na Gaeilge* (Baile Átha Cliath: Clódhanna Teoranta, 1981).
8. Liam Mac Uistín, *An Ród seo Romham. Saol agus Saothar Phádraic Mhic Phiarais*. (Baile Átha Cliath: Comhar Teoranta, 2006), pp. 30–44; Regina Uí Chollatáin, *An Claidheamh Soluis agus Fáinne an Lae 1899–1932* (Baile Átha Cliath: Cois Life, 2004), pp. 90–116.
9. [Translation my own] 'D'fhág an oiliúint intinne a fuair sé mar dhlíodóir a lorg ar stíl scríbhneoireachta an Phiarsaigh agus ar an modh argóna a chleachtadh sé i gcúrsaí iriseoireachta sa Chlaidheamh Soluis.' Séamas Ó Buachalla, *Pádraig Mac Piarais agus Éire lena linn* (Baile Átha Cliath: Cló Mercier, 1979), p. 18.
10. John Horgan, Paul McNamara and John O' Sullivan, 'Irish Print and Broadcast Media. The political, economic, journalistic and professional context', in John Horgan, Barbara O'Connor and Helena Sheehan (eds), *Mapping Irish Media. Critical Explorations* (Dublin: UCD Press, 2007), p. 35.
11. Patrick Pearse, *The Separatist Idea*, 1 February 1916; *The Sovereign People*, 31 March 1916; see Regina Uí Chollatáin, 'P.H. Pearse deeply influenced by writings of James Fintan Lalor', *Laois Heritage Society Journal*, Volume 3 (Laois: Laois Heritage Society, 2006), pp. 24–35.
12. 'One of the greatest facts we have to face is that Irish has absolutely no chance to hold its own as a spoken language unless it also holds its own and makes good its position as a cultivated, that is, a read and written language. One of the chief objects in view in establishing a weekly paper in Irish was this – the creation of an Irish reading public, which is an absolute necessity if the League is to be maintained.' Patrick Pearse, 'Strengthen the Weak Points', Editorial, *An Claidheamh Soluis*, 11 August 1900, p. 8.
13. Liam Mac Mathúna, *Béarla sa Ghaeilge. Cabhair Choigríche: An Códmheascadh Gaeilge/Béarla i Litríocht na Gaeilge 1600–1900* (Baile Átha Cliath: An Clóchomhar Tta., 2007), pp. xi–xv, 266–8.
14. Jean-Christophe Penet, 'Thomas Davis, *The Nation* and the Irish Language', *Studies – An Irish Quarterly Review*, Autumn 2007, pp. 433–43.
15. [translation my own] 'Ba mhór idir meon intleachtóirí *fin-de-siècle* na hAthbheochana seo agus dearcadh na gnáthmhuintire a bhí ag glacadh chomh réidh sin leis an mBéarla go dtí sin, nach mór i gan fhios dóibh féin.' Mac Mathúna, *Béarla sa Ghaeilge*, p. 230.
16. O'Leary, *The Prose Literature of the Gaelic Revival*, pp. 15, 16.
17. Pearse, 'What is a national language?', Editorial, *An Claidheamh Soluis*, 28 January 1905.
18. [Translation my own] Tuigeann sé - rud nach dtuigeann cuid againn féin fós - gurab í an Ghaedhilg bun is an baránta is treise ag Náisiúntacht na hÉireann. Tuigeann sé, má mhaireann an Ghaedhilg go mairfidh Éire 'n-a náisiún.' Pearse, 'Cia shabhálfas an Ghaedhilg?', Editorial, *An Claidheamh Soluis*, 30 September 1905.
19. Pearse, 'Gleo na gCath', *An Claidheamh Soluis*, 20 August 1904.
20. Uí Chollatáin, *Iriseoirí Pinn na Gaeilge*, pp. 54, 231.
21. Edwards, *Patrick Pearse*, p. 343.
22. O'Leary, *The Prose Literature of the Gaelic Revival*, p. 129.
23. Pearse, 'A Plea for Brotherhood', Editorial, *An Claidheamh Soluis*, 28 July 1906.
24. Pearse, 'The Individual', Editorial, *An Claidheamh Soluis*, 1 September 1906.
25. Benedict Anderson, *Imagined Communities: Reflections on the Origin and Spread of Nationalism*, (London: Verso, 2006), pp. 45, 42–6.

26. Ibid., pp. 6–7.
27. See Mike Cormack 'Introduction: Studying Minority Language Media' in *Minority Language Media. Concepts, Critiques and Case Studies* (Clevedon: Multilingual Matters, 2007), p. 6.
28. Brian McNair, *Cultural Chaos. Journalism, news and power in a globalised world* (New York: Routledge, 2006), p. 205.
29. Ivor Kenny, *Talking to Ourselves: Conversations with editors of the Irish news media*, (Galway: Kenny's Bookshop and Art Gallery, 1994), p. 1.
30. David H. Weaver, 'Who are Journalists?', in Hugo de Burgh (ed.), *Making Journalists* (Routledge: London, 2005), p. 45.
31. Póilín Ní Chiaráin, 'Saol Iriseora' in Niall Comer (ed.), *Iriseoireacht na Gaeilge: Litearthacht, Litríocht nó Nuacht?* (Doire: Éigse Cholm Cille, 2006), p. 34.
32. Jean Aitchison, *Word Weavers. Newshounds and Wordsmiths* (Cambridge: Cambridge University Press, 2007), p. 12.
33. Pearse, 'The Bilingual Programme in Practice', Editorial, *An Claidheamh Soluis*, 1 October 1904.
34. Kenny, *Talking to Ourselves*.
35. Ibid., p. 285.
36. Pearse, 'The Dead Bill and Ourselves', Editorial, *An Claidheamh Soluis*, 25 May 1907.
37. Kenny, *Talking to Ourselves*, p. 147.
38. Patrick Pearse, 'By Way of Comment', *An Macaomh*, December 1909.
39. Kenny, *Talking to Ourselves*, p. 1.
40. [Translation my own] 'Tá aon rud amháin atá ar chumas gach éinne – a dhícheall', Pearse, 'Déanam ár ndícheall', Editorial, *An Claidheamh Soluis*, 5 January 1907.
41. Pearse, 'Next Week', Editorial, *An Claidheamh Soluis*, 9 May 1906.
42. 'Its analysis … is grounded in the belief that the relationship between the media and the communities they serve is a complex and subtle one, symbiotic and mutually revelatory. The media inform social and political change, as well as reflecting it…' John Horgan, *Irish Media. A Critical History since 1922* (London: Routledge, 2001), p. 2.
43. Iarfhlaith Watson, *Broadcasting in Irish. Minority language, radio, television and identity* (Dublin: Four Courts Press, 2003), p. 117.
44. Horgan, *Irish Media*, p. 2, pp. 28–55.
45. Pearse, 'Mellowness', Gleo na gCath, *An Claidheamh Soluis*, 31 October 1908.
46. Porter, *P. H. Pearse*, pp. 37–65.
47. James Fintan Lalor, First letter to *The Nation*, 19 April 1847.
48. Pearse, 'The New University: Irish essential for matriculation', Editorial, *An Claidheamh Soluis*, 22 August 1908.
49. [translation my own] 'Dá mbeadh Éire dealuighthe ar fad ó Shasana i gcás poilitidheachta i mbáireann, is dócha go mbeadh sí i n-a náisiún neamhspleádhach, acht ní bheadh sí i n-a náisiún Ghaedhealach óir an fhaid is do bheadh an Béarla n-a ghnáth-theangain ag Gaedhealaibh, pé saoirseacht a bheadh inti, ní bheadh i nÉirinn tar éis an tsaoghail ach náisiún Gallda', Pearse, 'Dá ríribh' Editorial, *An Claidheamh Soluis*, 6 February 1909.
50. Tomás Ó Néill, *Fiontán Ó Leathlobhair* (Baile Átha Cliath: Cló Morainn, 1962), p. 128.
51. 'Is maith an gníomh do rinnis an uair do chuiris Scoil Éanna ar bun. Is maith an gníomh do rinnis an uair do chuiris Scoil Íde ar bun. Mo chomhairle dhuit: tabhair aire do Sgoil Éanna agus do Sgoil Íde agus ná bac a thuilleadh le cúrsaibh politidheachta. Tá do dhóthain mhór ar d'aire. Caith uait an BARR BUADH, scaoil urchar le n-a fhear seann-ma, cuir deireadh leis an gCumann Nua úd gan ainm, agus déan go maith an rud do chuiris romhat le déanamh ceithre bliadhna ó shoin. Níor éirigh an dá thráigh riamh leis an ngobadán. Táir-se ag iarraidh freastail ar cheithre trághaibh. Ní éireochaid leat. Rud eile. Impidhim agus athchuingim ort gan a thuilleadh d'fhabhal-scéaltaibh do scríobhadh. Beir buaidh agus beannacht. Mise Iubhar Mac Riangabhra.' Pádraic Mac Piarais, 'Beart Litreach do Chuaidh Amudha. IX. 'Chum Phádraicmhicphiarais', *An Barr Buadh*, 11 Bealtaine 1912.
52. Marshall McLuhan, *Understanding Media. The Extensions of Man* (London: Routledge and Kegan Paul, 1964), p. 205.
53. Kenny, *Talking to Ourselves*, p. 263.
54. Pól Ó Muirí, *Magill*, February 2005.
55. Edwards, *Patrick Pearse*, p. 61.
56. Pearse, 'The Psychology of a Volunteer', Editoral, *An Claidheamh Soluis*, 3 January 1914.

## CHAPTER SEVEN

1. Ruth Dudley Edwards, *Patrick Pearse: the Triumph of Failure* (London: Victor Gallancz, 1977), pp. 6–7, 37–8, 99, 202.
2. 'National Education', *The Nation*, 3 December 1842; 'Propagandism', *The Nation*, 18 September 1843; 'The Present and the Future', *The Nation*, 21 October 1843.
3. 'Sismondi on Federalism', *The Nation*, 2 September 1843.
4. See P.C. Parr (ed.), *Carlyle's Lectures on Heroes, Hero-worship and the Heroic in History* (Oxford: Clarendon Press, 1910).
5. Charles Gavan Duffy, *Young Ireland: a Fragment of Irish History, 1840–1850* (London: Cassell, Petter, Galpin & Co., 1880); *Four Years of Irish History, 1845–1849* (London: Cassell, Petter, Galpin & Co., 1883).
6. John Mitchel, *The Last Conquest of Ireland (Perhaps)* (Glasgow: Cameron and Ferguson, 1876), pp. 136–7.
7. Patrick Pearse, 'Ghosts' in Desmond Ryan (ed.), *Collected Works of Padraic H. Pearse – Political Writings and Speeches* (Dublin: Phoenix Publishing Co., 1917–22), p. 231.
8. Patrick Maume, *The Long Gestation: Irish Nationalist Life 1891–1918* (Dublin: Gill and Macmillan, 1999), p. 164.
9. Pearse, 'Ghosts', *Political Writings*, p. 223.
10. Ibid., p. 225.
11. Ibid., pp. 241–5.
12. 'Robert Emmet and the Ireland of Today' New York, 2 March 1914, *Political Writings*, p. 66.
13. Pearse, 'Ghosts' *Political Writings*, p. 230.
14. Patrick Pearse, 'The Sovereign People', 31 March 1916, *Political Writings*, pp. 370–71.
15. Patrick Pearse, 'The Story of a Success' in Ryan (ed.), *Collected Works of Padraic H. Pearse*, p. 54.
16. Pearse, 'Robert Emmet and the Ireland of today', New York, 2 March 1914, *Political Writings*, pp. 64–75. For Emmet's influence on Pearse, see especially Marianne Elliott, *Robert Emmet: the Making of a Legend* (London: Profile Books, 2003), pp. 153–5, 178–9.
17. Patrick Pearse, 'Oration on T.W. Tone', Bodenstown, 22 June 1913, *Political Writings*, pp. 53–4.
18. Helen F. Mulvey, *Thomas Davis and Ireland: a Biographical Study* (Washington D.C.: Catholic University of America Press, 2003), pp. 205–27.
19. Thomas Davis, *Literary and Historical Essays* (Dublin: James Duffy, 1846), p. 232.
20. Thomas Davis, 'The Library of Ireland' in D. J. O'Donoghue (ed.), *Essays Literary and Historical by Thomas Davis* (Dundalk: Dundalgan Press, 1914), p. 355.
21. Pearse, 'The Spiritual Nation', *Political Writings*, pp. 304-5.
22. 'Our National Language', *The Nation*, 1 April 1843.
23. 'Our National Language', *The Nation*, 30 December 1843.
24. Pearse, 'The Spiritual Nation', *Political Writings*, pp. 303–4.
25. 'Education', *The Nation*, 18 February 1843.
26. Ibid.
27. Patrick Pearse, 'The Murder Machine' in Ryan (ed.), *Collected Works of Padraic H. Pearse*, pp. 16, 40–41.
28. Pearse, 'The Sovereign People', *Political Writings*, pp. 350–51.
29. *Workers' Republic*, 18 March 1916.
30. *Irish Felon*, 22 July 1848.
31. Pearse, 'The Sovereign People', *Political Writings*, p. 346.
32. Patrick Pearse, 'From a Hermitage, Part II' and 'Ghosts', *Political Writings*, pp. 168, 169, 235.
33. Mitchel, *Last Conquest*, pp. 217–20; Pearse, 'The Murder Machine', in Ryan (ed.), *Collected Works of Padraic H. Pearse*, p. 8.
34. James Quinn, 'John Mitchel and the Rejection of the Nineteenth Century', *Éire-Ireland*, XXXVIII, parts 3–4 (Fall/Winter 2003), pp. 90–108.
35. Pearse, 'The Murder Machine', in Ryan (ed.), *Collected Works of Padraic H. Pearse*, pp. 13–14.
36. John Mitchel, *Jail Journal* (Dublin: M.H. Gill & Son, 1913), pp. 91–2; Pearse, 'The Sovereign People', *Political Writings*, p. 368.
37. Desmond Ryan, 'The Man Called Pearse', in Ryan (ed.), *Collected Works of Padraic H. Pearse*, p. 169.
38. Desmond Ryan, *Remembering Sion: a Chronicle of Storm and Quiet* (London: Arthur Barker, 1934), pp. 12–4.
39. Pearse, 'The Sovereign People', *Political Writings*, p. 343.

40. Ibid., pp. 365–6.
41. Patrick Pearse, 'Peace and the Gael', December 1915, *Political Writings*, p. 218.
42. Patrick Pearse, 'From a Hermitage, Part IV', *Political Writings*, p. 209.
43. Ryan, 'The Man Called Pearse' in Ryan (ed.), *Collected Works of Padraic H. Pearse*, p. 188.
44. Seán Farrell Moran, *Patrick Pearse and the Politics of Redemption* (Washington D.C.: Catholic University of America Press, 1994), p. 284.
45. *Irish Volunteer*, 22 May 1915.
46. Patrick Pearse, 'O'Donovan Rossa Speech', 1 August 1915, *Political Writings*, p. 135.
47. Pearse, 'Ghosts', *Political Writings*, p. 226.
48. Pearse, 'The Sovereign People', *Political Writings*, p. 365.
49. Ryan, 'The Man Called Pearse' in Ryan (ed.), *Collected Works of Padraic H. Pearse*, p. 133.
50. 'The Tocsin of Ireland', *The Nation*, 29 July 1848. This article also appears in Charles Gavan Duffy, *My Life in Two Hemispheres*, 2 vols (London: T. F. Unwin, 1903), Vol. 1, p. 289, a work held in the St Enda's library.
51. Pearse, 'From a Hermitage, Part IV', *Political Writings*, pp. 194–5.
52. Ryan, 'The Man Called Pearse' in Ryan (ed.), *Collected Works of Padraic H. Pearse*, p. 147.
53. 'Proclamation of the Republic' (Dublin, 1916).
54. Thomas Paine, 'The Rights of Man, Part 1' in Michael Foot and Isaac Kramnick (eds), *The Thomas Paine Reader* (London: Penguin, 1987), p. 204; Karl Marx, 'The Eighteenth Brumaire of Louis Napoleon' in Karl Marx and Friedrich Engels, *Selected Works*, (London: Lawrence and Wishart, 1970), p. 96.
55. Piaras F. MacLochlain (ed.), *Last Words: Letters and Statements of the Leaders Executed After the Rising at Easter 1916* (Dublin: Kilmainham Jail Restoration Society, 1971), p. 19. These sentiments were echoed in his poem 'The Mother': 'They shall be spoken of among their people, / The generations shall remember them, / And call them blessed'.
56. MacLochlain, *Last Words*, p. 28.
57. Patrick Pearse, Preface to 'Ghosts', *Political Writings*, p. 221.
58. Ryan, *Remembering Sion*, p. 132.

CHAPTER EIGHT

1. John Hutchinson, *The Dynamics of Cultural Nationalism* (London: Allen and Unwin, 1987), p. 153.
2. Patrick Pearse, *The Collected Works of Padraic H. Pearse* (Dublin: Phoenix Publishing Co., 1918–1922), pp. 299–302.
3. Ibid., p. 343.
4. *Irish Freedom*, February 1913.
5. Pearse, *Collected Works*, p. 223.
6. Ibid., pp. 291–2.
7. Ibid., p. 268.
8. John E. Redmond, *The Justice of Home Rule,* (London: Irish Press Agency 1912), p. 13.
9. House of Commons Debates Vol XXXVII (Hansard, 15/4/12) Cols 144–6, 15 April 1912.
10. Ibid., Vol XXXVI Col 1490, 11 April 1912.
11. Redmond, *Justice of Home Rule*, p. 5.
12. *Freeman's Journal*, 7 September 1914.
13. University College Dublin Archives T.M. Kettle Papers LA34/399, 3 September 1916.
14. *Irish Times*, 31 August 1917.
15. Ibid.
16. Ibid.
17. *Belfast News Letter*, 11 July 1916.
18. Public Records Office of Northern Ireland, D627/436/30, Stronge to de Fellenburg Montgomary, 26 September 1918.
19. *Church of Ireland Gazette*, 11 May 1917.
20. *Freeman's Journal,* 19 June 1917.
21. *Freeman's Journal,* 22 June 1916.
22. *Freeman's Journal,* 26 November 1917.

## CHAPTER NINE

1. Pearse to his mother, 3 May 1916, in Piaras Mac Lochlainn, *Last Words: Letters and Statements of the Leaders Executed after the Rising at Easter 1916* (Dublin: Stationery Office, 1990), p. 33.
2. Charles Townshend, *Easter 1916: The Irish Rebellion* (London: Penguin, 2006), p. 309.
3. P.H. Pearse, 'From a Hermitage', in *The Collected Works of Padraic H. Pearse: Political Writings and Speeches* (Dublin and London: Maunsel and Roberts Ltd, 1922), p. 143.
4. *Irish Times*, 10 November 1979.
5. Pearse signed himself as 'Commander in Chief of the Forces of the Irish Republic, and President of the Provisional Government' in the 'Manifesto to the Citizens of Dublin', 25 April 1916, in Mac Lochlainn, *Last Words*, pp. 6–7.
6. National Archives of Ireland, Department of the Taoiseach (hereafter cited as NAI DT), 97/6/469, Kathleen Clarke to Éamon Martin, 29 March 1965. Kathleen Clarke did not hold Éamon Martin responsible and saw him as an ally in this issue. Clarke also raised the question of the Presidency in her memoir, *Revolutionary Woman: My Fight for Ireland's Freedom* (Dublin: O'Brien Press, 1997), p. 145 and p. 169.
7. Townshend, *Easter 1916*, p. 161.
8. NAI DT, 97/6/469, Jack Lynch to Seán Lemass, 19 May 1965.
9. Diarmaid Ferriter, 'Commemorating the Rising, 1922–65: "A Figurative Scramble for the Bones of the Patriot Dead"?', in Mary E. Daly and Margaret O'Callaghan (eds), *1916 in 1966: Commemorating the Easter Rising* (Dublin: Royal Irish Academy, 2007), p. 200.
10. Ibid., p. 202.
11. Ibid., p. 199.
12. For a discussion of the political use of Pearse's after-life see Shauna Gilligan, 'Image of a Patriot: The Popular and Scholarly Portrayal of Patrick Pearse, 1916–1991' (unpublished MA thesis, National University of Ireland, 1993).
13. Robert Hughes, *The Shock of the New: Art and the Century of Change* (London: Thames and Hudson, 2000), p. 346.
14. Alvin Jackson, 'Unionist Myths 1912–1985', *Past and Present*, 136, 1992, pp. 169–172.
15. Ibid.
16. Father Francis Shaw, S.J., 'The Canon of Irish History: A Challenge', *Studies: An Irish Quarterly Review*, Summer 1972, p. 123.
17. Pearse, 'From a Hermitage', in *Collected Works of Padraic H. Pearse: Political Writings and Speeches* (Dublin and London: Maunsel and Roberts Ltd, 1922), p. 169.
18. Patrick Pearse, 'How Does She Stand', in *The Collected Works of Padraic H. Pearse*, p. 69 and p. 71.
19. 'The Last Hours of Patrick Pearse', 1916 Propaganda Poster cited in Ben Novick, *Conceiving Revolution: Irish Nationalist Propaganda after the First World War* (Dublin: Four Courts, 2001), p. 140.
20. Mac Lochlainn, *Last Words*, p. 22.
21. Pearse to his mother, 1 May 1916, in Mac Lochlainn, *Last Words*, p. 19.
22. *Irish Press*, 23 April 1932, in Gilligan, 'Image of a Patriot', p. 32.
23. *Irish Times*, 12 November 1979.
24. Eamonn McCann, *War and an Irish Town* (London: Pluto Press, 1993), p. 65.
25. *Irish Times*, 15 November, 1979, in Gilligan, 'Image of a Patriot', p. 71.
26. Richard Temple, 'Icon', in Jane Turner (ed.), *The Dictionary of Art*, Volume XV (London: Macmillan, 1996), p. 75. The defender was Basil the Great (329–79).
27. See Richard Kearney, *Myth and Motherland, Field Day Pamphlet Number 5* (Derry: Field Day Theatre Company, 1984) and Jonathan F. Vance, *Death So Noble: Memory, Meaning and the First World War* (Vancouver: University of British Columbia Press, 2000).
28. National Archives of Ireland, Department of External Affairs (hereafter cited as NAI DEA), 2000/14/87, address by Dr P. J. Hillery, Minister for Industry and Commerce, on the occasion of his officially opening the 1916 Exhibition in the National Museum, Dublin, 12 April 1966.
29. Marc Bloc, *Feudal Society* (Chicago, IL: University of Chicago, Press, 1961), p. 102, in Vance, *Death So Noble*, p. 9.
30. Ruth Dudley Edwards, *Patrick Pearse: The Triumph of Failure* (London: Victor Gollancz, 1977).
31. Townshend, *Easter 1916*, p. 353.
32. William Irwin Thompson, *The Imagination of an Insurrection: Dublin 1916* (Oxford: Oxford University Press, 1967) and Seán Farrell Moran, 'Patrick Pearse and the European

Revolt against Reason', *Journal of the History of Ideas* (1989).

33. Katriona Byrne, *Pearse Street: A Study of the Past, A Vision for the Future* (Dublin: Dublin Civic Trust, 2001), p. 26.

34. See correspondence in the Department of the Taoiseach, NAI DT, S 16770 B/62, 1962 and S 16770 B/63, 1963.

35. *Sunday Press*, 21 May 1961.

36. NAI DT, S4523C/95, Cabinet meeting, 7 July 1964.

37. See Roisín Higgins, 'Sites of Memory and Memorial', in Daly and O'Callaghan (eds), *1916 in 1966*, pp. 273–279.

38. Dáil Éireann – Volume 311 – 21 February 1979, Written Answers – Pearse Commemoration Projects.

39. William Fallon in *Sunday Press*, 14 April 1963.

40. Performative, as explained by David Lloyd, involves the articulation of an apparently foundational statement through which an institutional reality is affected. Examples of the performative utterance are 'I now declare you husband and wife' and 'Let there be light'. The first draws on state/church power and the second on divine power. Each can only be effective if those involved recognise the authority of the institution which gives effect to the utterance. David Lloyd, *Critical Conditions: Field Day Essays, Ireland After History* (Cork: Cork University Press, 1999), p. 13 and p. 110. He uses the work of J.L. Austin, *How to Do Things with Words* (Cambridge MA: Harvard University Press, 1962).

41. Lloyd has written 'the performative is a consensual fiction that organizes a community and its relations of authority. It is no less subject to "iteration", the performative always being a citation of prior encoded utterance. Accordingly, we can say that it is only in its iteration that the authority of any institution is affirmed, each time anew, so that in fact the institution depends on its reiteration rather than on any actual founding moment'. Lloyd, *Ireland After History*, p. 110.

42. John O'Connor, *The 1916 Proclamation* (Dublin: Anvil Books, 2007), pp. 27–9.

43. Ibid., p. 32. For personal accounts of the Rising see Keith Jeffery (ed.), *The GPO and the Easter Rising* (Dublin: Irish Academic Press, 2006).

44. Lloyd, *Ireland after History*, pp. 89–100.

45. For a discussion of the way in which kitsch saturates everyday life see ibid., p. 90. Lloyd draws on the work of Franco Moretti, *The Way of the World: The Bildungsroman in European Culture* (London: Verso, 1991).

46. Temple, 'Icon', p. 76.

47. Lloyd, *Ireland After History*, p. 94.

48. *Irish News*, 6–8 May 1981.

49  Brian Campbell, Laurence McKeown and Felim O'Hagan (eds), *Nor Meekly Serve My Time: the H Block Struggle 1976–1981* (Belfast: Beyond the Pale, 1994), p. 42.

50. John Coakley, 'Patrick Pearse and the "Noble Lie" of Irish Nationalism', *Studies: An Irish Quarterly Review*, Vol. 72, No. 286, Summer 1983, p. 133.

51. For example see F.X. Martin, '1916 – Myth, fact and mystery', in *Studia Hibernia*, 7, 1967, pp. 7–124 and Maureen Wall, 'The Background of the Rising, from 1914 until the countermanding order on Easter Saturday 1916' and 'The plans and the countermand: the country and Dublin', in Kevin B. Nowlan (ed.), *The Making of 1916: studies in the history of the Rising* (Dublin: Stationery Office, 1969), pp. 157–97 and pp. 201–51.

52. For a discussion of historiography in the 1960s see Michael Laffan, 'Easter Week and the Historians', in Daly and O'Callaghan, *1916 in 1966*, pp. 323–42.

53. Pearse's image was used on the mountains of official and unofficial literature produced for the commemoration. His portrait appeared on the official commemorative coin, on the 5d stamp which would be used for internal letters, and the symbol 'An Claidheamh Solais' was the official badge of the commemoration – adopted in the hope that it would usurp the Easter Lily.

54. *Kilkenny People*, 4 February 1966.

55. 'Patriotism', *Our Boys*, March 1966. See Carole Holohan, 'More than Revival of Memories?: 1960s Youth and the 1916 Rising' in Daly and O'Callaghan (eds), *1916 in 1966*, p. 183.

56. Seán Lemass, 'The Meaning of the Commemoration', *Easter Commemoration Digest*, 1966.

57. Bernardine Truden, 'Recollections of the 50th Anniversary of the Easter Rising of 1916', pamphlet (Dublin: 1966). Collection of articles which were originally published in the *Boston Globe*.

58. NAI DEA, L.114/89, Memorandum, Department of External Affairs, 9 February 1966.

59. NAI DEA, L.114/89, Embassy in London to External Affairs, 19 July 1965. Clann na

hÉireann had been formed in 1964 and described itself as 'the only organisation in Britain catering for the Nationally-minded emigrant', *United Irishman*, May 1966.

60. J.J. Lee, 'A Jacobin after his Time', *Irish Press*, 21 April 1977. Review of Edwards, *Patrick Pearse*.

61. Ruth Dudley Edwards, 'Paving the way to hell', *Irish Times*, 3 July 2004. Review of Elaine Sisson, *Pearse's Patriots: St Enda's and the Cult of Boyhood* (Cork: Cork University Press, 2004).

62. Fintan O'Toole, '1916: the failure of failure', in Dermot Bolger, (ed.), *Letters from the New Island: 16 on 16 Irish Writers on the Easter Rising* (Dublin: Raven Arts Press, 1988), p. 42.

63. 75th Anniversary of the Easter Rising: Souvenir Programme: Concert, Parade and Pageant, Saturday 16th April 1991.

64. Edwards, *Patrick Pearse*, p. 343.

65. See '1916 – A View from 2006', remarks by Mary McAleese, President of Ireland, at the conference 'The Long Revolution: The 1916 Rising in Context', University College Cork (27 January 2006), and Speech by Gerry Adams, President of Sinn Féin to Sinn Féin árd fheis, RDS, Dublin (18 February 2006) (http://cain.ulst.ac.uk).

66. McAleese, '1916 – A view from 2006'.

## CHAPTER TEN

1. Throughout this essay, quotations from the stories and the spellings of titles and proper names are taken from the definitive scholarly edition by Cathal Ó Háinle: *Gearrscéalta an Phiarsaigh* (Baile Átha Cliath: Helicon, 1979, and reprints). An exception is the name of Loch Oiriúlach, spelled here as on Ordnance Survey Ireland Discovery Series map no. 45, at 38N, 92—94E; Pearse spells it in metathesised form as 'Eileabhrach'.

2. Philip O'Leary, *The Prose Literature of the Gaelic Revival, 1881–1921: Ideology and Innovation* (University Park, PN: Pennsylvania State University Press, 1994), pp. 118–30, at p. 122.

3. Ibid., p. 130.

4. Benedict Anderson, *Imagined Communities: Reflections on the Origin and Spread of Nationalism* (London: Verso, 1991 [1983]), pp. 33–6.

5. Séamas Ó Buachalla (ed.), *The Letters of P.H. Pearse* (Gerrards Cross: Colin Smythe, 1980), p. 490.

6. Pearse, Padraic, *Collected Works of Padraic H. Pearse: Plays, Stories, Poems* (Dublin: Phoenix, 1917), pp. 125–310. On p. vii the publisher thanks '*An Clodhanna Teoranta* [sic] for the permission accorded to Mrs Pearse to publish translations of *Íosagán, An Sagart, Bairbre, Eoganín na nÉan*'. Cf. Ruth Dudley Edwards, *Patrick Pearse: The Triumph of Failure* (London: Victor Gollancz, 1977 and reprints), Chapter 8, 'Aftermath', pp. 323–44.

7. *Plays, Stories, Poems*, 'Publisher's Note', p. vii. For Campbell, see Norah Saunders and A.A. Kelly, *Joseph Campbell, Poet and Nationalist 1879–1944: A Critical Biography* (Dublin: Wolfhound, 1988), and Eiléan Ní Chuilleanáin (ed.), *As I was among the captives: Joseph Campbell's Prison Diary, 1922–1923* (Cork: Cork University Press, 2001). After his release from internment in the Curragh Camp, Campbell emigrated to New York, where he remained until 1935.

8. Colm Ó Gaora, *Mise* (Baile Átha Cliath: Oifig an tSoláthair, 1943), pp. 38–9.

9. Pearse to Owen Clarke, 3.6.1910. *Letters*, p. 163.

10. Mrs M. Connolly, 'A Voice from the West' in Mary Brigid Pearse, *The Home Life of Pádraig Pearse, as Told by Himself, His Family and Friends* (Cork and Dublin: Mercier, 1979 [1934]), pp. 110–12.

11. Cf Ó Gaora, *Mise*, p.32.

12. T.A. Finlay, 'The Economics of Carna', *New Ireland Review* 9, no. 2, April 1898, pp. 65–77; E. Keogh, 'In Gorumna Island', *New Ireland Review* 9, no. 4, June 1898, pp. 177–200.

13. Charles R. Browne, MD, 'The Ethnography of Carna and Mweenish, in the Parish of Moyruss, Connemara', *PRIA* 22 (1900–2) p. 523–5. The paper was read at the Royal Irish Academy on 12 November 1900.

14. Ó Gaora, *Mise*, p. 15; translation mine. For woven mats used as hangings in doorways see E. Estyn Evans, *Irish Folk Ways* (London: Routledge, 1957), p. 206; for wattled smoke canopies used instead of chimneys, see ibid., pp. 62–5. Compare Browne's reference above to houses where smoke escaped through a hole in the roof; other commentators report that in many poor houses it was simply allowed to pass through the thatch.

15. Ó Gaora, *Mise*, p. 19, translation mine.

16. Erving Goffman, *Stigma: Notes on the Management of a Spoiled Identity* (Harmondsworth: Penguin, 1968 [1963]), p. 15.
17. Mary Carbery, *The Farm by Lough Gur* (Cork: Mercier, 1973 [1937]), pp. 27–8, describes a 'strong' farmer of the 1860s reading aloud every Sunday from the *Freeman's Journal* for his illiterate neighbours.
18. Arthur Balfour, Chief Secretary for Ireland, 1887–1891, introduced the Light Railways (Ireland) Act in 1889. Kevin O'Connor, *Ironing the Land: the Coming of the Railways to Ireland* (Dublin: Gill and Macmillan, 1999), pp. 86–7.
19. It was originally called 'An tÁbhar Sagairt', 'The Would-Be Priest', but this was ambiguous, being the normal term for a clerical student.
20. Mary Brigid Pearse (ed.), *The Home-life of Pádraig Pearse.*
21. *Gearrscéalta*, p. 73; translation mine.
22. Ibid., p. 86.
23. Ibid., p. 116.
24. Ibid., p. 120.
25. Nicholas Williams, *Cniogaide Cnagaide* (Baile Átha Cliath: An Clóchomhar, 1988), p. 385.
26. *Letters*, pp. 103–4.
27. *Letters*, pp. 116, 399–400.
28. Ó Gaora, *Mise*, p. 39. Cf. Patrick MacGill, *The Rat Pit* (Dingle: Brandon, 1983 [1915]), pp. 3–18.
29. For the contrast between these two kinds of spirituality, see Margaret MacCurtain, 'Fullness of Life: Defining Female Spirituality in Twentieth-Century Ireland' (1989), in her *Ariadne's Thread: Writing Women into Irish History* (Galway: Arlen House, 2008), pp. 175–210. See further, Angela Partridge [Bourke], *Caoineadh na dTrí Muire: Téama na Páise i bhFilíocht Bhéil na Gaeilge* (Baile Átha Cliath: An Clóchomhar, 1983), and Emmet Larkin, *The Historical Dimensions of Irish Catholicism* (Dublin: Four Courts, 1997 [1976]).
30. Sir William Wilde, *Census of Ireland Report, 1851* (1854), Part V, Vol. 1 (Dublin: 1856), p. 455 See also Angela Bourke, *The Burning of Bridget Cleary: A True Story* (London: Pimlico, 1999), pp. 29–38.
31. Bourke, *The Burning of Bridget Cleary.*

CHAPTER ELEVEN
(Translation Róisín Ní Ghairbhí)

1. I would like to acknowledge the support given to me by Dr Máirín Nic Eoin while writing this essay. I would also like to acknowledge encouragement and assistance given by my colleagues, particularly Ruán O'Donnell, Eoin Flannery, Angus Mitchell, Brian Crowley, Professor Tadhg Foley, and by the conveners of the conference, in particular Dr. Regina Uí Chollatáin.
2. Eoin Flannery, *External Association: Ireland, Empire and Postcolonial Theory*, Third Text, Volume. 19, Issue 5, September 2005, p. 453.
3. P. H. Pearse, 'Robert Emmet. An Address Delivered at the Emmet Celebration in the Aeolian Hall, New York, 9 March 1914. By the Late P.H. Pearse, Commander in Chief IRA.' Sheet conserved at Pearse Museum/Kilmainham Gaol.
4. Máirín Nic Eoin, *Trén bhFearann Breac*, (Baile Átha Cliath: Cois Life, 2005).
5. Máire Ní Fhlathúin, 'The Anti-colonial Modernism of Patrick Pearse', in H. Booth and N. Rigby (eds), *Modernism and Empire* (Manchester: Manchester University Press, 2000), pp.156–74.
6. As this essay is primarily an exploration of Pearse's writings, references to postcolonial theory will of necessity be at a simple level; a deeper discussion of salient themes and issues will be found in the works cited.
7. Desmond Ryan, *The Man Called Pearse* (Dublin: Maunsel and Co., 1919); Séamas Ó Buachalla, *Na Scríbhinní Liteartha le Pádraig Mac Piarais* (Baile Átha Cliath: Cló Mercier, 1979); *An Piarsach sa Bheilg* (Baile Átha Cliath: An Gúm, 1998); (ed.), *The Letters of P.H. Pearse*, (Gerrards Cross: Colin Smythe, 1980); Cathal Ó Háinle (ed.), *Gearrscéalta an Phiarsaigh*, (Baile Átha Cliath: Helicon/Cló Thalbóid, 1979); Ciarán Ó Coigligh, *Filíocht Ghaeilge Phádraic Mhic Phiarais* (Baile Átha Cliath: An Clóchomhar, 1981); Aisling Ní Dhonnchadha, *An Gearrscéal sa Ghaeilge 1898–1940* (Baile Átha Cliath: An Clóchomhar, 1981); Máire Ní Fhlathúin, 'The Anti-colonial Modernism of Patrick Pearse'; Ciarán Ó Coigligh, *Filíocht Ghaeilge Phádraig Mhic Phiarais* (Baile Átha Cliath: An Clóchomhar, 1981); Philip O'Leary, *Prose Literature of the Gaelic Revival 1881–1921, Ideology and*

*Innovation* (University Park, PN: Pennsylvania State University Press, 1994); Regina Uí Chollatáin, *An Claidheamh Soluis agus Fáinne an Lae, 1899–1932 : anailís ar phríomhnuachtán Gaeilge ré na hAthbheochana,* (Baile Átha Cliath: Cois Life, 2004); Caitríona Ó Torna, *Cruthú na Gaeltachta 1893–1922* (Baile Átha Cliath: Cois Life, 2005).

8. See Seamus Deane, 'Pearse, Writing and Chivalry' in *Celtic Revivals, Essays in Modern Irish Literature 1880–1980* (London: Faber and Faber, 1985), pp. 63–74 and James Moran, (ed.), *Four Irish Rebel Plays* (Dublin: Irish Academic Press, 2007).

9. Eugene McCabe, 'Introduction' in Dermot Bolger (ed.), *Pádraic Pearse, Rogha Dánta/Selected Poems* (Dublin: New Island, 2001), p. 7.

10. See Eavan Boland, 'Mise Éire', in *The Journey and Other Poems* (New York/Dublin: Carcanet/Arlen House, 1987), pp. 10–11.

11. Joe Cleary, 'Misplaced Ideas? Colonialism, Location and Dislocation in Irish Studies', in Clare Carroll and Patricia King (eds), *Ireland and Postcolonial Theory,* (Cork: Cork University Press, 2003), pp. 16–45.

12. P. H. Pearse, 'By way of comment', *An Macaomh,* May 1913, p. 8.

13. Stuart Hall, 'What was the Post Colonial?: Thinking at the Limit', in Iain Chambers and Linda Corti (eds), *The Post Colonial Question. Common Skies: Divided Horizons* (London: Routledge, 1996), pp. 252–3.

14. P. H. Pearse, 'An Choill'/ 'The Wood', *The Irish Review,* July/August 1914, p. 253.

15. *An Claidheamh Soluis agus Fáinne an Lae,* 2 June 1906; Ó Háinle, *Gearrscéalta an Phiarsaigh*: O'Leary, *The Prose Literature of the Gaelic Revival 1881–1922.*

16. Pearse, 'By way of comment', *An Macaomh,* May 1913, p. 8.

17. Joe Cleary, 'Misplaced Ideas? Colonialism, Location and Dislocation in Irish Studies', p. 21.

18. Pearse, 'By Way of Comment', *An Macaomh,* May 1913, p. 8.

19. Pearse's personal witness of and sophisticated interaction with Gaelic civilisation is discussed at length in Roisin Ní Ghairbhí, 'A people that did not exist?': Some Sources and Contexts for Patrick Pearse's Militant Nationalism', in Ruán O'Donnell, (ed.), *Among the Nations: The Impact of the 1916 Rising* (Dublin: Irish Academic Press, 2008), pp.161–86.

20. 'Chun Fuighligh Gaedheal an méid seo', *An Barr Buadh,* 16 Márta 1912 [translation my own].

21. John Redmond, *The Home Rule Bill* (1912), p. 47.

22. Joe McGarrity, 'Twenty Years Ago in America', *An Camán,* 31 March 1934, p. 13.

23. Eamonn Ceannt, 'Na Finíní', *An Barr Buadh,* 16 Márta 1912.

24. 'Chun Ógbhaidhe Éireann, *An Barr Buadh,* 4 Bealtaine 1912; 'Gríosadh', *An Barr Buadh* 11 Bealtaine 1912.

25. On the mother/child dialectic in the Proclamation see Richard Haslam http://social. chass.ncsu.edu/jouvert/v4i1/hasla.htm

26. See Róisín Ní Ghairbhí, 'A people that did not exist?'

27. P. H. Pearse, *The Sovereign People, Tracts for the Times* (Dublin: Whelan, 1916).

28. 'The Veiled Woman of the Battlefield', *An Claidheamh Soluis,* 3 March 1908.

29. Ruth Dudley Edwards, *Patrick Pearse. The Triumph of Failure* (London: Victor Gollancz, 1977), pp. 41–2.

30. Editions of 'Bodach an Chóta Lachtna', 'Bruidhean Chaorthainn' (and 'Toraidheacht Fhiacail Ríogh Gréag' under co-editorship) were published in *An Claidheamh Soluis.* Edwards, *Patrick Pearse,* pp. 89–90.

31. O'Leary, *The Prose Literature of the Gaelic Revival,* pp. 255–61.

32. 'Some Aspects of Irish Literature' in *Collected Works of Pádraic.H. Pearse. Songs of the Irish Rebels and Specimens from an Irish Anthology. Some aspects of Irish Literature: Three Lectures on Gaelic Topics* (Dublin, Cork, Belfast: Phoenix Publishing Co., n.d.), p. 142.

33. Ibid., pp. 156–7.

34. Ibid., p. 156.

35. *An Claidheamh Soluis,* 26 May 1906.

36. Tadhg Ó Donnchadha agus Pádraig Mac Piarais (eds), *An tAithriseoir,* Imleabhar 2. (Baile Átha Cliath, 1900, 1902, 1914).

37. P. H. Pearse, *Ghosts, Tracts for the Times* (Dublin: Whelan, 1916).

38. Uí Chollatáin, *An Claidheamh Soluis agus Fáinne an Lae 1899–1932,* p. 104.

39. 'Irish Acting', *An Claidheamh Soluis,* 7 July 1906.

40. *An Macaomh,* Meitheamh 1909, pp. 13–14, 86.

41. P.H. Pearse, 'By Way of Comment', *An Macaomh,* Summer 1909, p. 15.

42. Séamas Ó Buachalla, *Na Scríbhinní Gaeilge le Pádraig Mac Piarais* (Cork: Cló Mercier, 1979), p. 17.

43. Ngugi Wa Thiongo, *Decolonizing the Mind,* (London/Nairobi: Currey, 1986), p. 45.

44. Christopher B. Balme, *Decolonising the Stage: Theatrical Syncretism and Postcolonial Drama*, (Oxford: Clarendon Press, 1999), p. 6.
45. 'Fógra: Íosagán. A Miracle Play, Irish Theatre Hardwicke Street', 20–22 Bealtaine 1915. conserved at Kilmainham Gaol.
46. Daniel Corkery, *Synge and Anglo-Irish Literature*, (Cork: Cork University Press, 1931), pp. 7–8; see also Vera Kreilkamp, 'Fiction and Empire: The Irish Novel', in Kevin Kenny (ed.), *Ireland and the British Empire* (Oxford: Oxford University Press, 2004).
47. Aisling Ní Dhonnchadha, *An Gearrscéal sa Ghaeilge 1898–1940* (Baile Átha Cliath: An Clóchomhar, 1981), p. 69.
48. 'Consumption in Connemara: Deputation to the Local Government Board', *Irish Times*, 15 February 1908.
49. 'An cath atá romhainn anois is geall le briathar-chath é.' 'An Bhearna Bhaoghail', *An Barr Buadh*, 13 Márta 1912.
50. Ní Ghairbhí, 'A people that did not exist?'
51. 'A St Enda's Play in Bengal' *An Claidheamh Soluis*, 28 August 1915.
52. David Lloyd, 'After History: Historicism and Irish Postcolonial Studies', in Clare Carrol and Patricia King (eds.), *Ireland and Postcolonial Theory*, (Cork: Cork University Press, 2003), p. 62.

## CHAPTER ELEVEN

1. Is mian leis an údar buíochas a ghabháil leis an Dr Máirín Nic Eoin agus le comhghleacaithe Choláiste Phádraig as a gcuid tacaíochta leis seo. Buíochas freisin le Ruan O'Donnell, Eoin Flannery, Angus Mitchell, Brian Crowley, an tOllamh Tadhg Foley agus eagraithe na comhdhála, go háirithe an Dr Regina Uí Chollatáin as a spreagadh.
2. Eoin Flannery, 'External Association: Ireland, Empire and Postcolonial Theory', *Third Text*, 19, 5 (September 2005), lch. 453.
3. P.H. Pearse, 'Robert Emmet. An Address Delivered at the Emmet Celebration in The Aeolian Hall, New York, 9th March 1914. By The Late P.H. Pearse, Commander in Chief IRA.' Bileog ar coiméad i bPríosún Chill Mhaighneáin.
4. Máirín Nic Eoin, *Trén bhFearann Breac* (Baile Átha Cliath: Cois Life, 2005), lch. 44.
5. Máire Ní Fhlathúin, 'The Anti-colonial Modernism of Patrick Pearse', in Howard Booth and Nigel Rigby (eds), *Modernism and Empire* (Manchester: Manchester University Press, 2000), lgh. 156–74.
6. Ceal spáis coimrítear agus simplítear an plé ar theoiricí iarchoilíneacha san alt seo; is féidir eolas níos mine a fháil ach tarraingt ar na saothair a dtagraítear dóibh.
7. Desmond Ryan, *The Man called Pearse* (Dublin: Maunsel and Co., 1919); Séamas Ó Buachalla, *Na Scríbhinní Liteartha le Pádraig Mac Piarais* (Baile Átha Cliath/Corcaigh: Cló Mercier, 1979); *An Piarsach sa Bheilg* (Baile Atha Cliath: An Gúm, 1998); (ed.), *The Letters of P.H. Pearse with a foreward by F.S.L. Lyons* (Gerrards Cross: Colin Smythe, 1980); Aisling Ní Dhonnnchadha, *An Gearrscéal sa Ghaeilge 1898–1940* (Baile Átha Cliath: An Clóchomhar, 1981); Máire Ní Fhlathúin, 'The Anti-colonial Modernism of Patrick Pearse'; Ciarán Ó Coigligh, *Filíocht Ghaeilge Phádraig Mhic Phiarais* (Baile Átha Cliath: An Clóchomhar, 1981); Cathal Ó Háinle (eag.), *Gearrscéalta an Phiarsaigh* (Baile Átha Cliath: Cló Thalbóid, 1979, 1999); Philip O'Leary, *Prose Literature of the Gaelic Revival 1881–1921: Ideology and Innovation* (University Park, PN: Pennsylvania State University Press, 1994); Regina Uí Chollatáin, *An Claidheamh Soluis agus Fáinne an Lae 1899–1932* (Baile Átha Cliath: Cois Life, 2004); Caitríona Ó Torna, *Cruthú na Gaeltachta 1893–1922* (Baile Átha Cliath: Cois Life, 2005).
8. Seamus Deane, 'Pearse, Writing and Chivalry', in *Celtic Revivals. Essays in Modern Irish Literature 1880–1980* (London: Faber and Faber 1985), lgh. 63–74; James Moran (ed.), *Four Irish Rebel Plays* (Dublin: Irish Academic Press, 2007).
9. Eugene McCabe, 'Introduction', in Dermot Bolger (ed.), *Pádraic Pearse. Rogha Dánta/Selected Poems* (Dublin: New Island, 1993), lch. l.
10. Eavan Boland, 'Mise Éire', in *The Journey and other Poems* (New York/Dublin: Carcanet/Arlen House, 1987), lgh. 10–11.
11. Joe Cleary, 'Misplaced Ideas? Colonialism, Location and Dislocation in Irish Studies', in Clare Carroll and Patricia King (eds), *Ireland and Postcolonial Theory* (Cork: Cork University Press, 2003), lgh. 16–45.
12. Proinsias Mac Aonghusa agus Liam Ó Reagáin (eag.), 'The Murder Machine', *The Best of Pearse* (Dublin/Cork: Mercier Press, 1967), lch. 37.
13. Stuart Hall, 'What was the Post Colonial? Thinking at the Limit', in Iain Chambers and

Linda Corti (eds), *The Post Colonial Question: Common Skies, Divided Horizons* (London: Routledge, 1996), lgh. 252–3.

14. Pádraic Mac Piarais, 'An Choill', *Irish Review*, Iúil 1914, lch. 252.

15. Tá plé cuimsitheach déanta ar dhearcadh forásach an Phiarsaigh i dtaobh na litríochta in Philip O'Leary, *The Prose Literature of the Gaelic Revival 1881–1922.* Féach freisin réamhrá Chathail Uí Háinle ar *Gearrscéalta an Phiarsaigh* agus *An Claidheamh Soluis,* 2 Meitheamh 1906.

16. 'By way of comment', *An Macaomh*, Bealtaine 1913, lch. 8.

17. Cleary, 'Misplaced Ideas?', lch. 21.

18. 'By Way of Comment', *An Macaomh*, Bealtaine 1913, lch. 8.

19. Pádraic Mac Piarais, *The Complete Works of P.H. Pearse. Scríbhinní* (Baile Átha Cliath: Phoenix Publishing Co., g.d.), lch. 211.

20. 'Chun Fuighligh Gaedheal an méid seo', *An Barr Buadh*, 16 Márta 1912.

21. John Redmond, *The Home Rule Bill 1912*, lch. 47.

22. Joe McGarrity, 'Twenty Years Ago in America', *An Camán*, 31 Márta 1934, lch. 13.

23. Róisín Ní Ghairbhí, '"A people that did not exist?" Some Sources and Contexts for Patrick Pearse's Militant Nationalism', in Ruan O'Donnell (ed.), *Among the Nations: The Impact of the 1916 Rising* (Dublin: Irish Academic Press, 2008), lgh. 161–86.

24. P.H. Pearse, *Ghosts* (Tracts for the Times) (Dublin: Whelan, 1916).

25. Féach Ní Ghairbhí, *op. cit.*

26. Tá plé spéisiúil déanta ar léiriú na máthar i bhForógra na Pobachta ag Richard Haslam. Féach http://social.chass.ncsu.edu/jouvert/v4i1/hasla.htm.

27. P.H. Pearse, *The Sovereign People* (Tracts for the Times) (Dublin: Whelan, 1916).

28. Máire Ní Fhlathúin, 'The anti-colonial modernism of Patrick Pearse', in Howard J. Booth and Nigel Rigby (eds), *Modernism and Empire* (Manchester: Manchester University Press, 2000), lgh. 156–74.

29. 'Chun Ógbhaidhe Éireann, *An Barr Buadh*, 4 Bealtaine 1912; 'Gríosadh', *An Barr Buadh*, 11 Bealtaine 1912.

30. Éamonn Ceannt, 'Na Finíní', *An Barr Buadh*, 16 Márta 1912.

31. Ruth Dudley Edwards, *Patrick Pearse: The Triumph of Failure* (London: Victor Gollancz, 1977), lch. 21.

32. Dudley Edwards, *The Triumph of Failure*, lgh. 41–2.

33. Foilsíodh eagráin de 'Bodach an Chóta Lachtna', de 'Bruidhean Chaorthainn' (agus de 'Toraidheacht Fhiacail Ríogh Gréag' faoina chomheagarthóireacht) in *An Claidheamh Soluis*. Edwards, *The Triumph of Failure*, lgh. 89–90.

34. 'Some Aspects of Irish Literature', in *Collected Works of P.H. Pearse. Songs of the Irish Rebels and Specimens from an Irish Anthology. Some Aspects of Irish Literature. Three Lectures on Gaelic Topics* (Dublin: Pheonix Publishing Co., n.d., 1919), lch. 142.

35. Ibid., lgh. 156–7.

36. Ibid., lch. 156.

37. *An Claidheamh Soluis*, 26 Bealtaine 1906.

38. Tadhg Ó Donnchadha agus Pádraic Mac Piarais (eag.), *An tAithriseoir*, Imleabhar 2 (Baile Átha Cliath: 1900, 1902, 1914).

39. 'Irish Acting', *An Claidheamh Soluis*, 7 Iúil 1906.

40. *An Macaomh*, Meitheamh 1909, lgh. 13–14, 86.

41. P.H. Pearse, 'By Way of Comment', *An Macaomh,* samhradh 1909, lch. 15.

42. Luaite ag Séamas Ó Buachalla, *Na Scríbhinní Gaeilge le Pádraig Mac Piarais* (Corcaigh: Cló Mercier, 1979), lch. 17.

43. Ngugi Wa Thiongo, *Decolonising the Mind* (London/Nairobi: Currey, 1986), lch. 45.

44. Christopher B. Balme, *Decolonising the Stage: Theatrical Syncretism and Postcolonial Drama* (Oxford: Clarendon Press, 1999), lch. 6.

45. 'Fógra: Íosagán. A Miracle Play, Irish Theatre Hardwicke Street', 20–22 Bealtaine 1915. Ar coimeád i bPríosún Chill Mhaighneáin.

46. Daniel Corkery, *Synge and Anglo-Irish Literature* (Cork: Cork University Press, 1931), lgh. 7–8; Vera Kreilkamp, 'Fiction and Empire: The Irish Novel', in Kevin Kenny (ed.), *Ireland and the British Empire* (Oxford: Oxford University Press, 2004).

47. 'Consumption in Connemara: Deputation to the Local Government Board', *Irish Times*, 15 February 1908.

48. Aisling Ní Dhonnchadha, *An Gearrscéal sa Ghaeilge 1898–1940* (Baile Átha Cliath: An Clóchomhar, 1981), lch. 69.

49. Féach, mar shampla, 'Robert Emmet. An Address Delivered at the Emmet Celebration in The Aeolian Hall, New York, 9th March 1914 By The Late P.H. Pearse, Commander in Chief IRA'; and Ní Ghairbhí, op cit.

50. 'An cath atá romhainn anois is geall le briathar-chath é.'; 'An Bhearna Bhaoghail', *An Barr Buadh*, 13 Márta 1912.
51. Féach Ní Ghairbhí, op.cit.
52. *An Macaomh*, Nollaig 1909, lch. 50; Meadhon Samhraidh, 1909, lgh. 81–2; Nollaig 1910, lch. 71.
53. 'A St Enda's Play in Bengal', *An Claidheamh Soluis*, 28 Lúnasa 1915.
54. David Lloyd, 'After History: Historicism and Irish Postcolonial Studies', in Clare Carroll and Patricia King (eds), *Ireland and Postcolonial Theory* (Cork: Cork University Press, 2003), lch. 62.

## CHAPTER TWELVE
(Translation Regina Uí Chollatáin)

1. Máirtín Ó Direáin, 'Éire ina bhfuil romhainn', *Ár Ré Dhearóil*, Eoghan Ó hAnluain (eag.), *Máirtín Ó Direáin. Danta 1939–1979* (Baile Átha Cliath: An Clóchomhar Teoranta, 2004 [1980]), lch. 62.
2. Máirtín Ó Direáin, *Ó Mórna agus Dánta Eile* (Baile Átha Cliath: Cló Morainn, 1957), p. 15.
3. Eoghan Ó hAnluain (ed.), *Máirtín Ó Direáin. Dánta 1939–1979* (Baile Átha Cliath: An Clóchomhar Teoranta, 2004 [1980]), p. 62. [translation Regina Uí Chollatáin]
4. Ibid., p. 112. [translation Regina Uí Chollatáin]
5. Ibid., p. 194. [translation Regina Uí Chollatáin]
6. William Empson, 'Just a Smack at Auden' in Robert Skelton (ed.), *Poetry of the Thirties* (London: Penguin Books, 1964), lch. 64.
7. Eoghan Ó hAnluain, *Ón Ulán Ramhar Siar* (Baile Átha Cliath: An Clóchomhar Teoranta, 2002), p. 42. [translation Regina Uí Chollatáin]
8. Ibid., p. 126. [translation Regina Uí Chollatáin]
9. Ó hAnluain, *Máirtín Ó Direáin*, p. 61. [translation Regina Uí Chollatáin]
10. Ó hAnluain, *Ón Ulán Ramhar Siar*, p. 146.[translation Regina Uí Chollatáin]
11. Ó hAnluain, *Máirtín Ó Direáin*, p. 76. [translation Regina Uí Chollatáin]
12. Ibid., p. 94. [translation Regina Uí Chollatáin]
13. Aodhagán Ó Rathaille, 'An tan d'aistrigh go duibhneachaibh láimh le tonn tóime i gCiarraighe', in Patrick S. Dinneen and Tadhg O'Donoghue (eds), *Dánta Aodhagáin Uí Rathaille. The Poems of Egan O'Rahilly* (London: Irish Texts Society [2nd edn], 1911), pp. 28–9.
14. Ó hAnluain, *Máirtín Ó Direáin*, p. 111.
15. Ibid., p. 111. [Translation Regina Uí Chollatáin]
16. Ó Rathaille, 'Créachta Crích Fódla', in Dinneen and O'Donoghue (eds.), *The Poems of Egan O'Rahilly*, pp. 2–3. [Translation Regina Uí Chollatáin]

## CHAPTER TWELVE

1. Máirtín Ó Direáin, 'Éire ina bhfuil romhainn', *Ár Ré Dhearóil*, Eoghan Ó hAnluain (eag.), *Máirtín Ó Direáin. Danta 1939–1979* (Baile Átha Cliath: An Clóchomhar Teoranta, 2004 [1980]), p. 62.
2. Máirtín Ó Direáin, *Ó Mórna agus Dánta Eile* (Baile Átha Cliath: Cló Morainn, 1957), Ich. 15.
3. Eoghan Ó hAnluain (eag.), *Máirtín Ó Direáin. Dánta 1939–1979* (Baile Átha Cliath: An Clóchomhar Teoranta, 2004 [1980]), lch. 62.
4. Ibid., lch. 112.
5. Ibid., lch. 194.
6. William Empson, 'Just a Smack at Auden' in Robert Skelton (ed.), *Poetry of the Thirties* (London: Penguin Books, 1964), lch. 64.
7. Eoghan Ó hAnluain, *Ón Ulán Ramhar Siar* (Baile Átha Cliath: An Clóchomhar Teoranta, 2002), lch. 42.
8. Ibid., lch. 126.
9. Ó hAnluain, *Máirtín Ó Direáin*, lch. 61.
10. Ó hAnluain, *Ón Ulán Ramhar Siar*, lch. 146.
11. Ó hAnluain, *Máirtín Ó Direáin*, lch. 76.
12. Ibid., lch. 94.

13. Aodhagán Ó Rathaille, 'An tan d'aistrigh go duibhneachaibh láimh le tonn tóime i gCiarraighe', in Patrick S. Dinneen and Tadhg O'Donoghue (eds), *Dánta Aodhagáin Uí Rathaille. The Poems of Egan O'Rahilly* (London: Irish Texts Society [2nd edn], 1911), lgh. 28–9.
14. Ó hAnluain, *Máirtín Ó Direáin*, lch. 111.
15. Ibid., lch. 111.
16. Ó Rathaille, 'Créachta Crích Fódla', in Dinneen and O'Donoghue (eds), *Dánta Aodhagáin Uí Rathaille*, lgh. 2–3.

## CHAPTER THIRTEEN

1. Pádraic Mac Piarais (ed.), *Bruidhean Chaorthainn* (Baile Átha Cliath: Connradh na Gaedhilge, 1908).
2. Pádraic Mac Piarais, 'Gríosadh', *An Barr Buadh*, Imleabhar 1, uimhir 9 (11 Bealtaine, 1912), p. 1.
3. Pádraic Mac Piarais, *Bruidhean Chaorthainn*, p. i; Patrick W. Joyce, *Old Celtic Romances* (Dublin: Roberts Wholesale Books Ltd, n.d. [repr. of 3rd edn, 1907]).
4. Patrick W. Joyce, *Old Celtic Romances*, p. xiv.
5. Ibid., pp. 465–6.
6. Ibid., p. 178.
7. Cf., for example, Pádraic Mac Piarais, *Bruidhean Chaorthainn*, p. 2.
8. Ibid., p. viii.
9. Ibid., pp. i–ii.
10. Breandán Ó Cróinín, 'Bruidhean Chaorthuinn ón lámhscríbhinn is sine i Leabharlann Náisiúnta na hAlban' (unpublished MA thesis, NUI Maynooth, 1995).
11. Pádraic Mac Piarais, *Bruidhean Chaorthainn*, p. iii.
12. Ibid., pp. v-vii.
13. See Pádraic de Brún, *Lámhscríbhinní Gaeilge: Treoirliosta* (Baile Átha Cliath: Institiúid Ard-léinn Bhaile Átha Cliath, 1988), pp. 82, §376.
14. Pádraic Mac Piarais, *Bruidhean Chaorthainn*, p. 33.
15. Patrick W. Joyce, *Old Celtic Romances*, p. 216.
16. Pádraic Mac Piarais, *Bruidhean Chaorthainn*, p. 28.
17. Ibid., p. 30.
18. Pádraig Mac Piarais, 'An fhiann agus an fhiannaidheachd', *Irisleabhar na Gaedhilge* 10 (1900), pp. 532–8 (537).
19. David Comyn and Patrick S. Dinneen (eds), *Foras Feasa ar Éirinn le Séathrún Céitinn D.D.: The History of Ireland, by Geoffrey Keating, D.D.*, Vols IV, VII, IX, XV (London: Irish Texts Society, 1902–14).
20. See, for example, Caoimhín Mac Giolla Léith (ed.), *Oidheadh Chloinne hUisneach*, Vol. LVI(London: Irish Texts Society, vol. 56, 1993), p. 22 and Meidhbhín Ní Úrdail, 'Seachadadh *Cath Cluana Tarbh* sna lámhscríbhinní', *Léachtaí Cholm Cille* 34 (2004), pp. 179–215 (182–7).
21. Pádraic Mac Piarais, *Bruidhean Chaorthainn*, p. 7.
22. Cecile O'Rahilly (ed.), *Cath Finntrágha* (Dublin: Dublin Institute for Advanced Studies, 1962); Kuno Meyer (ed.), *Cath Finntrága* (Oxford: Anecdota Oxoniensia, 1885).
23. Pádraic Mac Piarais, 'Gríosadh', *An Barr Buadh* (cf. n. 2 above).
24. Cecile O'Rahilly, *Cath Finntrágha*, pp. 1–2, ll. 20–7.
25. Ibid., p. 24, ll. 740–55.
26. Ibid., pp. 19-23, ll. 569–720.
27. Ibid., p. 19, ll. 591–5.
28. Ibid., p. 21, ll. 634–7.
29. Ibid., p. 21, ll. 638–61.
30. Ibid., p. 21, ll. 661–4.
31. Ibid., p. 22, ll. 669–75.
32. Ibid., pp. 22–3, ll. 676–720.
33. These matters are discussed in more detail in Caoimhín Breatnach, 'The historical context of *Cath Fionntrágha*', *Éigse* 28 (1994–95), pp. 138–55 and *idem*, 'Cath Fionntrágha', *Léachtaí Cholm Cille* 25 (1995), pp. 128–43.

CHAPTER FOURTEEN

1. Elaine Sisson, *Pearse's Patriots: St Enda's and the Cult of Boyhood* (Cork: Cork University Press, 2004), pp. 6–20.
2. Elaine Sisson, 'Imperial Romanticism: Cúchulainn, Wagner and Heroism', *Pearse's Patriots*, pp. 78–98.
3. Pádraig Óg Ó Conaire, 'Cuimhní Scoil Éanna' [Memories of St Enda's] in David Sears (ed.), *Cuimhní na bPiarsach: Memories of the Brothers Pearse* (*The Cross*, May 1917, repr. Pearse Brothers Commemoration Committee, Dublin, 1966), p. 22.
4. Desmond Ryan, 'A Retrospect', *A Story of A Success: Being a record of St. Enda's College, September 1908 to Easter 1916* (Dublin and London: Maunsell and Co., Ltd, 1912), p. 90.
5. Patrick Pearse, 'Our Heritage of Chivalry', *An Claidheamh Soluis agus Fáinne an Lae*, 14 November 1908.
6. Desmond Ryan, 'Pearse, St Enda's College and the Hound of Ulster', *Threshold,.* Vol. 1. Autumn 1957, p. 55. The current whereabouts of the original panel is unknown although a copy of the uncial inscription was commissioned by Pat Cooke, then curator of the Pearse Museum, and installed in St Enda's, The Hermitage, Rathfarnham.
7. The Dundalgan Press in Dundalk published a series of three 'Cúchulainn Charts' for nouns, adjectives and verbs, as well as a Cúchulainn Reader and Primer for teaching Irish, all of which were in use at St Enda's.
8. Patrick Pearse, 'By Way of Comment', *An Macaomh*, Vol. 1, No. 1 (Midsummer, 1909).
9. Ibid.
10. National Library of Ireland, Pearse Papers, MS21,054 Folder 5, Letter from Eleanor Hull to Pearse, undated *c.* 1906.
11. Lady Augusta Gregory, *Cúchulainn of Muirthemne: The Story of the Men of the Red Branch of Ulster* (Dublin 1902, repr. Gerrard's Cross: Colin Smythe, 1970).
12. See Nicola Gordon Bowe (ed.), *Art and the National Dream: The Search for Vernacular Expression in Turn of the Century Design* (Dublin: Irish Academic Press, 1993). See also Widar Halen, *Dragons from the North* (Dublin and Bergen, 1995), which traces links between the aesthetics of Irish Celtic Revivalism and Scandanavian forms and style, pp. 7–12.
13. Sisson, *Pearse's Patriots*, pp. 40–55.
14. Ashis Nandy, *The Intimate Enemy: The Loss and Recovery of Self Under Colonialism* (Oxfordi: Oxford University Press, 1983), p. 10.
15. Pearse, 'By Way of Comment', *An Macaomh*, Vol. 1, No. 3, Christmas, 1910.
16. W.P. Ryan, quoted in *An Macaomh*, Vol. 1, No.1, Midsummer, 1909.
17. Sean O'Casey, 'In this Tent, the Republicans' in *Drums Under the Window* collected in *Autobiographies 1* (New York: Carroll and Graft, 1984), p. 618.
18. 'Fionn and his Contemporaries in Dublin', *An Claidheamh Soluis*, 27 March 1909.
19. Clifford Geertz, *The Interpretation of Cultures* (London: Hutchinson, 1975) and Partha Chatterjee, *Nationalist Thought and the Colonial World: A Derivative Discourse* (Minneapolis: University of Minnesota Press, 1993).
20. Walter Benjamin, 'The Work of Art in the Age of Mechanical Reproduction', in *Illuminations* (New York: Harcourt, Brace and World, 1968), pp. 217–51.
21. John Tagg, *The Burden of Representation: Essays on Photographies and Histories* (London: Macmillan Education, 1988).
22. Benedict Anderson, *Imagined Communities: Reflections on the Origin and Spread of Nationalism* (London: Verso, 1983).
23. Martin Heidegger, 'The Age of the World Picture' translated by William Lovitt, in *The Question Concerning Technology* (New York: Harper and Row, 1977), pp. 115–54.
24. Pearse, 'By Way of Comment', *An Macaomh*, Vol. I, No. 1, Midsummer, 1909.
25. Ibid.
26. Alan Sekula, 'On the Invention of Photographic Meaning' in Victor Burgin (ed.), *Thinking Photography* (London: Macmillan Education, 1982), p. 93.
27. Elizabeth Edwards, *Anthropology and Photography* (New Haven: Yale University Press, 1992), p. 7.
28. Belinda Loftus, 'In Search of a Useful Theory', *CIRCA*, No. 40, Summer 1988, and John Turpin, 'Cúchulainn Lives On', *CIRCA*, No. 69, Autumn 1994.
29. Belinda Loftus, *Mirrors: Mother Ireland and William III* (Dundrum: Picture Press, 1994) and *Mirrors: Orange and Green* (Dundrum: Picture Press, 1994).
30. Patrick Pearse, 'The National Salon: A Report on the Oireachtas Art Exhibition', *An Claidheamh Soluis*, 11 August 1906.

31. Patrick Pearse, 'The National Salon'. The initial plaster maquette for the statue 'Inis Fáil' was later cast in bronze and is now housed at Kilmainham Gaol after being exhibited for a time at the Hugh Lane Gallery in Dublin. The original plaster casting of 'Inis Fáil' was donated to the Pearse Museum in Rathfarnham by the National Museum some years ago.

CHAPTER FIFTEEN

1. David Limond, 'The Schoolmaster of all Ireland: The Progressive credentials of Patrick Henry Pearse 1879–1916', *History of Education Review*, vol. 34, no. 1, 2005 pp. 63–75.
2. Eavan Boland, 'Aspects of Patrick Pearse', *The Dublin Magazine*, No. 1, Vol. 5, Spring 1966 (Dublin: New Square Publications Limited, 1966).
3. Elaine Sisson, *Pearse's Patriots: St Enda's and the Cult of Boyhood* (Cork: Cork University Press, 2004), p. 2.
4. Raymond J. Porter, *P.H. Pearse* (New York: Twayne, 1973), Preface.
5. Intermediate Examinations Board, June 1906. (MS 21097/P7643.) Intermediate Board of Education, Dublin. National Library of Ireland.
6. C.S. Andrews, *Dublin Made Me* (Dublin: Lilliput Press, 2001), p. 42.
7. Geoffrey De Parminter, *Roger Casement* (London: Barker, 1936), p. 34.
8. Michael O'Guiheen, *A Pity Youth Does Not Last* (Oxford: Oxford University Press, 1982), p. 12.
9. Spanish, which only had ten candidates, three of whom failed, is excluded. See *Report of the Intermediate Education Board 1905* [Cd. 2944], H.C. 1906, Table IV. Intermediate Board of Education, Dublin. National Library of Ireland.
10. *Report of Intermediate Board, 1907*. Intermediate Board of Education, Dublin. National Library of Ireland.
11. See *The Seventy-Second Report of the Commissioners of National Education, 1905–6*, [3154], H.C. 1906. Commissioners of National Education, Dublin. National Library of Ireland. This calculation is based upon the 'Statement of Account', p. 105.
12. Ibid. This calculation is based upon the 'Statement of Account', p. 21.
13. Patrick Pearse, *The Murder Machine*, 'Of Freedom in Education'. All references to *The Murder Machine*, parts of which appeared in separate publications at different times, are from Seamas O'Buachalla (ed.), *A Significant Irish Educationalist: The Educational Writings of P.H. Pearse* (Dublin: Mercier Press, 1980).
14. *The Gaelic American*, 7 March 1914.
15. *An Scoláire*, 20 Márta 1913, p. 2. The school magazine of St Enda's. Pearse and various senior pupils maintained editorial control. While mainly a mouthpiece for Pearse's thoughts upon the school and its events, it also featured articles by pupils and staff.
16. *An Scoláire*, 20 April 1913, p. 6.
17. Pearse, *The Murder Machine*, 'Back to the Sagas', 1914.
18. Bertrand Russell, *Education and the Social Order* (London: Allen and Unwin, 1931), p. 160.
19. Bertrand Russell, *The Principles of Social Reconstruction* (London: Allen and Unwin, 1916), p. 102.
20. Pearse, *The Murder Machine*, 'An Ideal in Education' (originally published June 1914, in *Irish Review*).
21. Russell, *Principles of Social Reconstruction*, p. 104.
22. Pearse, *The Murder Machine*, 'An Ideal in Education.' 1914.
23. Russell, *Principles of Social Reconstruction*, p. 103.
24. Patrick Pearse, 'By Way of Comment', *An Macaomh*, Vol. 1, No. 2, December 1909.
25. Pearse, 'The Philosophy of Education' *An Claidheamh Soluis agus Fáinne an Lae*, 12 November 1904.
26. 'The Return of the Fianna', *An Claidheamh Soluis*, 27.3.1909, p. 11.
27. *Sinn Féin*, 27 March 1909.
28. Ibid.
29. Máire Nic Shiubhlaigh, *The Splendid Years* (Dublin: Duffy, 1955), p. 146.
30. Ibid.
31. Patrick Pearse, 'The Secondary School: Thoughts and Suggestions', *An Claidheamh Soluis*, 13 January 1906.
32. Douglas Hyde (1860–1949), Irish-language scholar, President of the Gaelic League and first President of Ireland. Countess Markievicz (1868–1927), republican activist and participant in the Easter Rising. Roger Casement (1864–1816) member of the Gaelic League, executed for his involvement in the Easter Rising. Maud Gonne (1866–1953) political

activist, founder of *Inghinidhe na hEireann* (Daughters of Ireland) in Dublin in 1900 and *Bean na hEireann* (Woman of Ireland), a journal espousing military separatism (1908), supported the anti-treaty forces during the Irish Civil War. Eoin MacNeill (1867–1945), nationalist, historian and Professor of Early Irish History at University College Dublin. Commander in Chief of the Irish Volunteers (founded November 1913), supporter of the 1921 Treaty and Minister for Education in the Free State. MacNeill's two sons attended St Enda's. James O'Grady (1846–1928), historian and antiquarian, author of *History of Ireland: The Heroic Period* (1878), founding figure of the Gaelic literary revival.

33. Pearse, 'By Way of Comment', *An Macaomh*, Christmas 1909.
34. Timothy Fuller (ed.), *The Voice of Liberal Learning* (New Haven: Yale University Press, 1989), *passim*.
35. National Library of Ireland, Pearse Papers, MS 21094.
36. Patrick Pearse, 'By Way of Comment', *An Macaomh*, Vol. I, No. 2, Christmas 1909. Robert Emmet, revolutionary and participant in the ill-fated United Irishmen rebellion, May 1803, executed in Dublin the following September.
37. See *Dublin Review*, Spring 1923. Desmond Ryan later wrote that 'Denis Gwynn's total lack of humour, political prepossessions and post-war disillusion colour his otherwise living portrait of Pearse'. See Desmond Ryan, *Remembering Sion* (London: Arthur Barker Ltd, 1934) p. 161. In 1931 Gywnn recalled Pearse's 'colossal egoism' and remarked that 'he came to see and live the day that was to come when he himself was to lead a rebellion in Dublin in the tradition of Robert Emmet's rising in 1803'. See Denis Gwynn, *The Life and Death of Roger Casement*, (London: Jonathan Cape, 1930), p. 395.
38. Kenneth Griffith and Timothy O'Grady (eds.), *Curious Journey, An Oral History of Ireland's Unfinished Revolution*, (London: Hutchinson, 1982), p. 37.
39. Seán O'Mahon, *Frongoch: University of Revolution* (Dublin: FDR Teoranta, 1987), p. 114.
40. Margaret Pearse, oral recording, Pearse Museum, Rathfarnham, Dublin.
41. Frank Fahy, *Memories of the Brothers Pearse* (Dublin, 1960), Archive Collection, Pearse Museum, St Enda's, Rathfarnham.
42. Louis N. Le Roux, *Patrick H. Pearse* (Dublin: Phoenix Publishing Co. Ltd, 1932), p. 176.
43. Pearse, 'Patrick Pearse to Mrs Pearse', 26 April 1916, in Séamas Ó Buachalla. (ed.), *The Letters of P.H. Pearse*, (Buckinghamshire: Colin Smythe Ltd., 1980), p. 346.
44. Ibid., 'Patrick Pearse to Mrs Pearse', 3 May 1916, p. 347.
45. Le Roux, *Patrick H. Pearse*, p. 120.
46. Pearse, 'Back to the Sagas', *The Murder Machine*, 1914.
47. *Report of the Commissioners of National Education in Ireland for 1915–16* [8372], H.C., 1917. Dublin: The Commissioners of National Education, National Library of Ireland.
48. Iseult Ní Chléirigh, Principal of Scoil Bhríde, interviewed by author, 16 March 2004.
49. Áine Ní Fhíthigh, Principal of Lios na nÓg, interviewed by author, 16 March 2004.

# Bibliography
# Leabharliosta

Aitchison, J. *Word Weavers: Newshounds and Wordsmiths* (Cambridge: Cambridge University Press, 2007).

Anderson, B. *Imagined Communities: Reflections on the Origin and Spread of Nationalism* (London: Verso, 1983).

Andrews, C.S. *Dublin Made Me* (Dublin: The Lilliput Press, 2001).

Baggini, J. *Making Sense: Philosophy Behind the Headlines* (Oxford: Oxford University Press, 2002).

Balme, C.B. *Decolonising the Stage: Theatrical Syncretism and Postcolonial Drama* (Oxford: Clarendon Press, 1999).

Barton, B. *From Behind a Closed Door* (Belfast: Blackstaff, 2003).

Beckett, S. 'Recent Irish poetry', *The Bookman*, no. 86 (1934), reprinted in M. Smith (ed.), *The Lace Curtain: A Magazine of Poetry and Criticism* (Dublin: New Writers Press, 1971).

Benjamin, W. *Illuminations* (New York: Harcourt, Brace and World, Inc., 1968).

Bloch, E. *The Principle of Hope* (Oxford: Basil Blackwell, 1986).

Bloch, M. *Feudal Society* (Chicago: University of Chicago Press, 1961).

Boland, E. 'Aspects of Patrick Pearse', *The Dublin Magazine*, 5, 1 (spring) (Dublin: New Square Publications Limited, 1966).

Boland, E. 'Mise Éire', in E. Boland, *The Journey and Other Poems* (New York/Dublin: Carcanet/Arlen House, 1987).

Bourke, A. *The Burning of Bridget Cleary: A True Story* (London: Pimlico, 1999).

Bradlaugh Bonner, H. *Charles Bradlaugh: A Record of his Life and Work*, vol. I, (London: T. Fisher Unwin, 1894).

Breatnach, C. 'The historical context of *Cath Fionntrágha*', *Éigse*, no. 28 (1994–95), pp. 138–55.

Breatnach, C. 'Cath Fionntrágha', *Léachtaí Cholm Cille*, no. 25 (1995), pp. 128–43.

Browne, C.R. 'The ethnography of Carna and Mweenish, in the parish of Moyruss, Connemara', *PRIA*, no. 22 (1900–2).

Byrne, K. *Pearse Street: A Study of the Past, A Vision for the Future* (Dublin: Dublin Civic Trust, 2001).

Campbell, B., McKeown L. and O'Hagan, F. (eds), *Nor Meekly Serve My Time: The H-Block Struggle 1976–1981* (Belfast: Beyond the Pale, 1994).

Carbery, M. *The Farm by Lough Gur* (Cork: Mercier Press, 1937).

Chatterjee, P. *Nationalist Thought and the Colonial World: A Derivative Discourse* (Minneapolis: University of Minnesota Press, 1993).

Christian Brothers, 'They were schoolboys! The Pearse brothers at the "Row"', *Christian Brothers Westland Row, Centenary Record 1864–1964* (n.d., n.p.).

Clarke, K. *Revolutionary Woman: My Fight for Ireland's Freedom* (Dublin: O'Brien Press, 1997).

Cleary, J. 'Misplaced ideas? Colonialism, location and dislocation in Irish Studies', in C. Carroll and P. King (eds), *Ireland and Postcolonial Theory* (Cork: Cork University Press, 2003).

Coakley, J. 'Patrick Pearse and the "noble lie" of Irish nationalism', *Studies: An Irish Quarterly Review*, 72, 286 (summer 1983).

Cockshut, A.O.J. 'Victorian thought', in A.C. Pollard (ed.), *The Victorians* (London: Sphere, 1970).

Colum, M. *Life and the Dream* (Dublin: Dolmen Press, 1966).

Comyn, D. and Dinneen, P. S. (eds), *Foras Feasa ar Éirinn, le Séathrún Céitinn, D.D.: The History of Ireland, by Geoffrey Keating, D.D.* (London: Irish Texts Society, vols. 4, 8, 9, 15, 1902–14).

Cooke, P. 'The Unrevised Stereotype: Thomas MacDonagh and the 1916 Rising', in *Graph*, second series, Issue 2 (1996), pp. 116–131.

Cooke, P. *Scéal Scoil Éanna: The Story of an Educational Adventure* (Dublin: Office of Public Works, 1986).

Corkery, D. *Synge and Anglo-Irish Literature* (Cork: Cork University Press, 1931).

Cormack, M. 'Introduction: studying minority language media', in M. Cormack, *Minority Language Media: Concepts, Critiques and Case Studies* (Clevedon: Multilingual Matters, 2007).

Crowley, B. 'His father's son: James and Patrick Pearse', in *Folk Life: Journal of Ethnological Studies*, vol. 43 (2004–5).

*Cuimhní na bPiarsach: Memories of the Brothers Pearse* (booklet) (Dublin: Brothers Pearse Commemoration Committee, 1958).

Davis, T. *Literary and Historical Essays* (Dublin: James Duffy, 1846).

Davis, T. 'The Library of Ireland', in D.J. O'Donoghue (ed.), *Essays Literary and Historical by Thomas Davis* (Dundalk: Dundalgan Press, 1914).

Deane, S. *Celtic Revivals: Essays in Modern Irish Literature* (London: Faber and Faber, 1985).

De Brún, P. *Lámhscríbhinní Gaeilge: Treoirliosta* (Baile Átha Cliath: Institiúid Ard-léinn Bhaile Átha Cliath, 1988).

De Parminter, G. *Roger Casement* (London: Barker, 1936).

Dinneen, P.S. and O'Donoghue, T. (eds), *Dánta Aodhagáin Uí Rathaille* [*The Poems of Egan O'Rahilly*], 2nd edition (London: Irish Texts Society, 1911).

Duffy, C.G. *Young Ireland: A Fragment of Irish History, 1840–1850* (London: Cassell, Petter, Galpin & Co., 1880).

Duffy, C.G. *Four Years of Irish History, 1845–1849* (London: Cassell, Petter, Galpin & Co., 1883).

Duffy, C.G. *My Life in Two Hemispheres*, 2 volumes (London, T.F. Unwin, 1903).

Duffy, T.J. 'Ecclesiastical sculpture in the Church of St Michael, Tipperary', in P. Caffrey (ed.), *Thought Lines 4: An Anthology of Research* (Dublin: National College of Art and Design, 2000).

Edwards, E. *Anthropology and Photography* (New Haven: Yale University Press, 1992).

Edwards, R.D. *Patrick Pearse: The Triumph of Failure* (London: Victor Gollancz, 1977).

Elliott, M. *Robert Emmet: The Making of a Legend* (London: Profile Books, 2003).

Ellmann, R. *James Joyce* (Oxford: Oxford University Press, 1982).

Evans, E.E. *Irish Folk Ways* (London: Routledge, 1957).

*Exhibition of Irish Arts and Manufacturers 1882, Rotunda, Dublin. Complete Official Catalogue* (Dublin: Irish Exhibition Company Limited, 1882).

Fahy, F. *Memories of the Brothers Pearse* (Dublin: Brother Pearse Commemoration Committee, 1960).

Fennessy, I. 'Patrick Pearse and the four (of five) masters', in *Donegal Annual/Bliainiris Dhún na nGall: Journal of the County Donegal Historical Society*, no. 53 (2001).

Ferriter, D. 'Commemorating the Rising, 1922–65: "A figurative scramble for the bones of the patriot dead?"', in M. E. Daly and M. O'Callaghan (eds), *1916 in 1966: Commemorating the Easter Rising* (Dublin: Royal Irish Academy, 2007).

Finlay, T.A. 'The Economics of Carna', *New Ireland Review*, IX, 2 (April 1898), pp. 65–77.

Flannery, E. 'External association: Ireland, empire and postcolonial theory', *Third Text*, 19, 5 (September 2005).

'Fógra: Íosagán: A Miracle Play, Irish Theatre Hardwicke Street', 20–22 Bealtaine 1915.

Foster, R.F. *Modern Ireland: 1600–1972* (London: Allen Lane, 1988).

Foster, R.F. *The Irish Story: Telling Tales and Making it Up in Ireland* (Oxford: Oxford University Press, 2002).

Frowde, H. *Poems of Tennyson* (Oxford: Oxford Editions, 1906).

Fuller, T. (ed.), *The Voice of Liberal Learning* (New Haven: Yale University Press, 1989).

Fussell, P. *The Great War and Modern Memory* (Oxford: Oxford University Press, 2000).

Geertz, C. *The Interpretation of Cultures* (London: Hutchinson, 1975).

Gilligan, S. 'Image of a patriot: the popular and scholarly portrayal of Patrick Pearse, 1916–1991' (unpublished MA thesis, National University of Ireland, 1993 ).

Girouard, M. *The Return to Camelot* (New Haven: Yale University Press, 1981).

Goffman, E. *Stigma: Notes on the Management of a Spoiled Identity* (Harmondsworth: Penguin, 1963).

Gordon Bowe, N. (ed.), *Art and the National Dream: The Search for Vernacular Expression in Turn of the Century Design* (Dublin: Irish Academic Press, 1993).

Gregory, A. *Cúchulainn of Muirthemne: The Story of the Men of the Red Branch of Ulster* (Gerrards Cross: Colin Smythe, 1970).

Griffith, K. and O'Grady, T. (eds), *Curious Journey: An Oral History of Ireland's Unfinished Revolution* (London: Hutchinson, 1982).

Gwynn, D. *The Life and Death of Roger Casement* (London: Jonathan Cape, 1930).

Halen, W. *Dragons from the North* (Bergen: West Norway Museum of Applied Art, 1995).

Hall, S. 'What was the post colonial? Thinking at the limit', in I. Chambers and L. Corti (eds), *The Post Colonial Question: Common Skies, Divided Horizons* (London: Routledge, 1996).

Hayden, M. and Moonan, G.A. *A Short History of the Irish People* (Dublin: Educational Company of Ireland/Talbot Press, n.d.).

Heidegger, M. 'The age of the world picture', translated by W. Lovitt, in M. Heidegger, *The Question Concerning Technology* (New York: Harper and Row, 1977).

Helsinger, E.K. 'Ulysses to Penelope: Victorian experiments in autobiography', in G.P. Landow (ed.), *Approaches to Victorian Autobiography* (Ohio: Ohio State University Press, 1979).

Higgins, R. 'Sites of memory and memorial', in M. E. Daly and M. O'Callaghan (eds), *1916 in 1966: Commemorating the Easter Rising* (Dublin: Royal Irish Academy, 2007).

Hoggart, R. *The Uses of Literacy: Aspects of Working-Class Life with Special Reference to Publications and Entertainments* (London: Penguin Books, 1992).

Holohan, C., 'More than a Revival of Memories?: 1960s Youth and the 1916 Rising', in M. E. Daly and M. O'Callaghan, *1916 in 1966: Commemorating the Easter Rising* (Dublin: Royal Irish Academy, 2007).

Horgan, J.J. *Parnell to Pearse* (Dublin: Browne and Nolan, 1948).

Horgan, J. *Irish Media: A Critical History Since 1922* (London: Routledge, 2001).

Horgan, J., McNamara P. and O'Sullivan, J. 'Irish print and broadcast media: The political, economic, journalistic and professional context', in J. Horgan, B. O'Connor and H. Sheehan (eds), *Mapping Irish Media: Critical Explorations* (Dublin: UCD Press, 2007).

Hughes, R. *The Shock of the New: Art and the Century of Change* (London: Thames and Hudson, 2000).

'Humanitas', *Charles Bradlaugh and the Irish Nation* (London: Freethought Publishing Company, 1885).

'Humanitas', *The Follies of the Lord's Prayer* (London: Freethought Publishing Company, 1883).

'Humanitas', *Is God the First Cause? Being Also a Reply to Father Burke's Theory of Science and Received Religion* (London: Freethought Publishing Company, 1883).

'Humanitas', *Socialism: A Curse, Being a Reply to a Lecture Delivered by Edward B. Aveling DSc. entitled 'The Curse of Capitalism'* (London: Freethought Publishing Company, 1884).

Hutchinson, J. *The Dynamics of Cultural Nationalism* (London: Allen and Unwin, 1987).

Hutchinson, T. (ed.), *Shelley: Poetical Works* (Oxford: Oxford University Press, 1967).

Jackson, A. 'Unionist Myths 1912–1985', *Past and Present*, 136 (1992).

Jeffery, K. (ed.), *The GPO and the Easter Rising* (Dublin: Irish Academic Press, 2006).

Joyce, P.W. *Old Celtic Romances* (Dublin: Roberts Wholesale Books Ltd, n.d. [reprint of 3rd edition, 1907]).

Kearney, R. *Myth and Motherland*, Field Day pamphlet number 5 (Derry: Field Day Theatre Company, 1984).

Kennedy, C. (ed.), *The Diaries of Mary Hayden 1878–1903*, vols I–V (Killala: Morrigan, 2005).

Kenny, I. *Talking to Ourselves: Conversations with Editors of the Irish News Media* (Galway: Kenny's Bookshop and Art Gallery, 1994).

Keogh, E. 'In Gorumna Island', *New Ireland Review*, IX, 4 (June 1898).

Keynes, G. (ed.), *The Poetical Works of Rupert Brooke* (London: Faber, 1974).

Kreilkamp, V. 'Fiction and empire: the Irish novel', in K. Kenny (ed.), *Ireland and the British Empire* (Oxford: Oxford University Press, 2004).

Laffan, M. 'Easter week and the historians', in M. E. Daly and M. O'Callaghan (eds), *1916 in 1966: Commemorating the Easter Rising* (Dublin: Royal Irish Academy, 2007).

Larkin, E. *The Historical Dimensions of Irish Catholicism* (Dublin: Four Courts Press, 1976).

*Leabhrán Cuimhneacháin arna Fhoilsiú ar Ócáid Bronnadh Eochar Scoil Éanna ar Uachtarán na hÉireann Éamon de Valera, 23 Aibreán 1970.*

Lemass, S. 'The meaning of the commemoration', *Easter Commemoration Digest* (Dublin: Sackville Press, 1966).

Le Roux, L. *Life of Patrick Pearse* (Dublin: The Talbot Press, 1932).

Limond, D. 'The schoolmaster of all Ireland: the progressive credentials of Patrick Henry Pearse 1879–1916', *History of Education Review*, 34, 1 (2005).

Lloyd, D. *Ireland After History (Critical Conditions)* (Field Day essay series) (Cork: Cork University Press, 1999).

Lloyd, D. 'After history: historicism and Irish postcolonial studies', in C. Carroll and P. King (eds), *Ireland and Postcolonial Theory* (Cork: Cork University Press, 2003).

Loftus, B. 'In search of a useful theory', *CIRCA*, 40 (summer 1988).

Loftus, B. *Mirrors: Mother Ireland and William III* (Dundrum: Picture Press, 1994).

Loftus, B. *Mirrors: Orange and Green* (Dundrum: Picture Press, 1994).

Lovell-Smith, R. 'The animals of Wonderland: Tenniel as Carroll's reader', *Criticism*, 45, 4 (fall 2003).

Mac Aonghusa, P. *Ar Son na Gaeilge: Conradh na Gaeilge 1893–1993* (Baile Átha Cliath: Conradh na Gaeilge, 1993).

MacCurtain, M. *Ariadne's Thread: Writing Women into Irish History* (Galway: Arlen House, 2008).

MacGill, P. *The Rat Pit* (Dingle: Brandon, 1983 [1915]).

Mac Giolla Léith, C. (ed.), *Oidheadh Chloinne hUisneach* (London: Irish Texts Society, vol. 56, 1993).

Macken, M. 'Musings and Memories; Helena Concannon, MA, DLitt', *Studies*, vol. XLII (March 1953), pp. 90–7.

MacLochlain, P.F. (ed.), *Last Words: Letters and Statements of the Leaders Executed After the Rising at Easter 1916* (Dublin: Kilmainham Jail Restoration Society, 1971).

Mac Mathúna, L. *Béarla sa Ghaeilge. Cabhair Choigríche: An Códmheascadh Gaeilge / Béarla i Litríocht na Gaeilge 1600–1900* (Baile Átha Cliath: An Clóchomhar, 2007).

Mac Piarais, P. 'An fhiann agus an fhiannaidheachd', *Irisleabhar na Gaedhilge*, uimh. 10 (1900), pp. 532–8.

Mac Piarais, P. (ed.), *Bruidhean Chaorthainn* (Baile Átha Cliath: Connradh na Gaedhilge, 1908).

Mac Piarais, P. 'Gríosadh', *An Barr Buadh*, Imleabhar 1, Uimhir 9 (11 Bealtaine 1912).

Mac Uistín, L. *An Ród seo Romham: Saol agus Saothar Phádraic Mhic Phiarais* (Baile Átha Cliath: Comhar Teoranta, 2006).

Maguire, T. *England's Duty to Ireland as it Appears to a Loyal Irish Roman Catholic* (Dublin: William McGee, 1886).

Mann, T. *Death in Venice* (London: Penguin, 1970).

Martin, F.X. '1916 – myth, fact and mystery', *Studia Hibernica*, no. 7 (1967), pp. 7–124.

Marx, K. 'The eighteenth brumaire of Louis Napoleon', in K. Marx and F. Engels, *Selected Works* (London: Lawrence and Wishart, 1970).

Mason, E. and Ellmann, R. (eds), *The Critical Writings of James Joyce* (New York: Viking, 1959).

Maume, P. *The Long Gestation: Irish Nationalist Life 1891–1918* (Dublin: Gill and Macmillan, 1999).

McCabe, E. 'Introduction', in D. Bolger (ed.), *Pádraic Pearse: Rogha Dánta/Selected Poems* (Dublin: New Island, 2001).

McCann, E. *War and an Irish Town* (London: Pluto Press, 1993).

McCartney, D. *UCD: A National Idea. The History of University College Dublin* (Dublin: Gill and Macmillan, 1999).

McDonagh, T. 'Language and literature in Ireland', *The Irish Review*, vol. IV (March–April 1914).

McGarrity, J. 'Twenty years ago in America', *An Camán*, 31 March 1934.

McLuhan, M. *Understanding Media: The Extensions of Man* (London: Routledge and Kegan Paul, 1964).

Meyer, K. (ed.), *Cath Finntrága* (Oxford: Anecdota Oxoniensia, 1885).

Meyer, K.E. 'An Edwardian warning', *World Policy Journal*, 17, 4 (2001).

Mitchel, J. *The Last Conquest of Ireland (Perhaps)* (Glasgow: Cameron and Ferguson, 1876).

Mitchel, J. *Jail Journal* (Dublin: M.H. Gill & Son, 1913).

Moran, J. (ed.), *Four Irish Rebel Plays* (Dublin: Irish Academic Press, 2007).

Moran, S.F. 'Patrick Pearse and the European revolt against reason', *Journal of the History of Ideas*, 50 (1989).

Moran, S.F. *Patrick Pearse and the Politics of Redemption* (Washington, DC: Catholic University of America Press, 1994).

Morrissey, T.J. *Towards a National University: William Delany SJ (1835–1924)* (Dublin: Wolfhound Press, 1983).

Mulvey, H.F. *Thomas Davis and Ireland: A Biographical Study* (Washington, DC: Catholic University of America Press, 2003).

Munro, H.H. *The Collected Short Stories of Saki* (London: Wordsworth Editions, 1993).

Nandy, A. *The Intimate Enemy: Loss and Recovery of Self under Colonialism* (Oxfordi: Oxford University Press, 1983).

Nic Eoin, M. *Trén bhFearann Breac* (Baile Átha Cliath: Cois Life, 2005).

Ní Chiaráin, P. 'Saol Iriseora', in N. Comer (ed.), *Iriseoireacht na Gaeilge: Liteartacht, Litríocht nó Nuacht?* (Doire: Éigse Cholm Cille, 2006).

Ní Chuilleanáin, E. (ed.), *'As I was among the captives'*: *Joseph Campbell's Prison Diary, 1922–1923* (Cork: Cork University Press, 2001).

Nic Shiubhlaigh, M. *The Splendid Years* (Dublin: Duffy, 1955).

Ní Dhonnchadha, A. *An Gearrscéal sa Ghaeilge 1898–1940* (Baile Átha Cliath: An Clóchomhar, 1981).

Ní Fhlathúin, M. 'The anti-colonial modernism of Patrick Pearse', in H. Booth and N. Rigby (eds), *Modernism and Empire* (Manchester: Manchester University Press, 2000).

Ní Ghairbhí, R. "A people that did not exist?" Some sources and contexts for Patrick Pearse's militant nationalism', in R. O'Donnell (ed.), *Among the Nations: The Impact of the 1916 Rising* (Dublin: Irish Academic Press, 2008).

Ní Úrdail, M. 'Seachadadh *Cath Cluana Tarbh* sna lámhscríbhinní', *Léachtaí Cholm Cille*, uimh. 34 (2004), pp. 179–215.

Novick, B. *Conceiving Revolution: Irish Nationalist Propaganda after the First World War* (Dublin: Four Courts Press, 2001).

Ó Buachalla, S. *Na Scríbhinní Gaeilge le Pádraig Mac Piarais* (Cork: Cló Mercier, 1979).

Ó Buachalla, S. *Pádraig Mac Piarais agus Éire Lena Linn* (Baile Átha Cliath: Cló Mercier, 1979).

Ó Buachalla, S. (ed.), *A Significant Irish Educationalist: The Educational Writings of P.H. Pearse* (Dublin and Cork: Mercier Press, 1980).

Ó Buachalla, S. (ed.), *The Letters of P.H. Pearse* (Gerrards Cross: Colin Smythe, 1980).

Ó Buachalla, S. (ed.), *An Piarsach sa Bheilg. P.H. Pearse in Belgium. P.H. Pearse in België* (Dublin: An Gúm, 1998).

O'Casey, S. 'In this tent, the republicans', in *Drums Under the Window* collected in *Autobiographies 1* (New York: Carroll and Graft, 1984).

Ó Coigligh, C. *Filíocht Ghaeilge Phádraic Mhic Phiarais* (Baile Átha Cliath: An Clóchomhar, 1981).

Ó Conaire, P. Óg 'Cuimhní Scoil Éanna' ['Memories of St Enda's'] in D. Sears (ed.), *Cuimhní na bPiarsach: Memories of the Brothers Pearse* (*The Cross*, May 1917), reprinted by Pearse Brothers Commemoration Committee, Dublin, 1966).

O'Connor, A.V. and Parkes, S.M. *Gladly Learn and Gladly Teach: Alexandra College and School 1866–1966* (Dublin: Blackwater, 1984).

O'Connor, J. *The 1916 Proclamation* (Dublin: Anvil Books, 2007).

O'Connor, K. *Ironing the Land: The Coming of the Railways to Ireland* (Dublin: Gill and Macmillan, 1999).

Ó Cróinín, B. 'Bruidhean Chaorthuinn ón lámhscríbhinn is sine i

Leabharlann Náisiúnta na hAlban', (unpublished MA thesis, NUI Maynooth, 1995).

Ó Direáin, M. 'Éire ina bhfuil romhainn', in *Ó Mórna agus Dánta Eile* (Baile Átha Cliath: Cló Morainn, 1957).

Ó Donnchadha, T. agus Mac Piarais, P. (eds), *An tAithriseoir*, iml. 2 (Baile Átha Cliath, 1900, 1902, 1914).

Ó Gaora, C. *Mise* (Baile Átha Cliath: Oifig an tSoláthair, 1943).

O'Guiheen, M. *A Pity Youth Does Not Last* (Oxford: Oxford University Press, 1982).

Ó Háinle, C. (ed.), *Gearrscéalta an Phiarsaigh* (Baile Átha Cliath: Helicon/Cló Thalbóid, 1979).

Ó hAnluain, E. *Ón Ulán Ramhar Siar* (Baile Átha Cliath: An Clóchomhar, 2002).

Ó hAnluain, E. (ed.), *Máirtín Ó Direáin: Dánta 1939–1979* (Baile Átha Cliath: An Clóchomhar, 2004).

O'Leary, P. *The Prose Literature of the Gaelic Revival, 1881–1921: Ideology and Innovation* (University Park, PN: Pennsylvania State University Press, 1994).

O'Mahon, S. *Frongoch: University of Revolution* (Dublin: FDR Teoranta, 1987).

Ó Néill, T. *Fiontán Ó Leathlobhair* (Baile Átha Cliath: Cló Morainn, 1962).

O'Rahilly, C. (ed.), *Cath Finntrágha* (Dublin: Dublin Institute for Advanced Studies, 1962).

Ó Súilleabháin, D. *An Piarsach agus Conradh na Gaeilge* (Baile Átha Cliath: Clódhanna Teoranta, 1981).

O'Toole, F. '1916: The failure of failure', in D. Bolger (ed.), *Letters from the New Island. 16 on 16: Irish Writers on the Easter Rising* (Dublin: Raven Arts Press, 1988).

Ó Torna, C. *Cruthú na Gaeltachta 1893–1922* (Baile Átha Cliath: Cois Life, 2005).

Padbury, J. 'Mary Hayden (1862–1942), historian and feminist', *History Ireland*, 15, 5 (September/October 2007), pp.10–11.

Padbury, J. 'Mary Hayden and women's admission to the university: the establishment of the National University of Ireland in 1908', *Dublin Historical Record*, 61, 1 (spring 2008), pp.78–86.

Paine, T. 'The Rights of Man, Part 1', in M. Foot and I. Kramnick (eds), *The Thomas Paine Reader* (London: Penguin, 1987).

Parr, P.C. (ed.), *Carlyle's Lectures on Heroes, Hero-worship and the Heroic in History* (Oxford: Clarendon Press, 1910).

Partridge [Bourke], A. *Caoineadh na dTrí Muire: Téama na Páise i bhFilíocht Bhéil na Gaeilge* (Baile Átha Cliath: An Clóchomhar, 1983).

Pearse, J. *A Reply to Professor Maguire's Pamphlet 'England's Duty to*

*Ireland' as it Appears to an Englishman* (Dublin: M.H. Gill & Son, 1886).

Pearse, M.B. *The Home Life of Patrick Pearse, as told by himself, his family and friends* (Dublin: Browne and Nolan Ltd, 1934).

Pearse, P.H. 'Unpublished autobiographical fragment', Pearse Museum, Rathfarnham, Dublin.

Pearse, P.H. 'Réamhrá', *Íosagán agus Scéalta Eile* (Baile Átha Cliath: Connradh na Gaedhilge, 1907).

Pearse, P.H. *Collected Works of Pádraic H. Pearse. Songs of the Irish Rebels and Specimens from an Irish Anthology. Some aspects of Irish Literature: Three Lectures on Gaelic Topics* (Dublin, Cork, Belfast: Phoenix Publishing Co. Ltd, n.d.).

Pearse, P.H. 'An Choill' ['The Wood'], *The Irish Review* (July/August 1914).

Pearse, P.H. *Collected Works of Padraic H. Pearse: Plays, Stories, Poems* (Dublin: Phoenix, 1917).

Pearse, P.H. *Collected Works of Padraic H. Pearse. Political Writings and Speeches* (Dublin and London: Maunsel & Roberts Ltd, 1922).

Penet, J.C. 'Thomas Davis, *The Nation* and the Irish language', *Studies – An Irish Quarterly Review* (autumn 2007).

Porter, R.J. *P.H. Pearse* (New York: Twayne Publishers Inc., 1973).

Quinn, J. 'John Mitchel and the rejection of the nineteenth Century', *Éire–Ireland*, 38, parts 3–4 (fall/winter 2003).

Reddin, K. 'A Man called Pearse', *Studies – An Irish Quarterly Review*, 34, 134 (June 1945).

Redmond, J.E. *The Justice of Home Rule* (London: Irish Press Agency, 1912).

Redmond, J. E. *The Home Rule Bill* (London/New York: Cassell and Co., 1912).

Rowan, A. 'Irish Victorian churches: denominational distinctions', in R. Gillespie and B.P. Kennedy (eds), *Ireland: Art into History* (Dublin: Town House, 1994).

Royle, E. *Radicals, Secularists and Republicans: Popular Freethought in Britain, 1866–1915* (Manchester: Manchester University Press, 1980).

Russell, B. *The Principles of Social Reconstruction* (London: Allen and Unwin, 1916).

Russell, B. *Education and the Social Order* (London: Allen and Unwin, 1931).

Ryan, D. 'A Retrospect', *A Story of A Success: Being a Record of St Enda's College, September 1908 to Easter 1916* (Dublin and London: Maunsel and Co. Ltd, 1912).

Ryan, D. *The Man Called Pearse* (Dublin: Maunsel and Co. Ltd, 1919).

Ryan, D. (ed.), *Collected Works of Pádraic H. Pearse* (Dublin: Phoenix Publishing Co., 1917–22).

Ryan, D. *Remembering Sion: A Chronicle of Storm and Quiet* (London: Arthur Barker Ltd, 1934).

Saunders, N. and Kelly, A.A. *Joseph Campbell, Poet and Nationalist 1879–1944: A Critical Biography* (Dublin: Wolfhound, 1988).

Sekula, A. 'On the invention of photographic meaning', in V. Burgin (ed.), *Thinking Photography* (London: Macmillan Education, 1982).

Sennett, R. *The Fall of the Public Man: On the Social Psychology of Capitalism* (New York: Vintage Books, 1978).

Shaw, F. 'The Canon of Irish history: a challenge', *Studies – An Irish Quarterly Review*, 61, 242 (summer 1972).

Shields, J.A. *Patrick Pearse: Irish Patriot* (Private edition, 1937).

Sisson, E. *Pearse's Patriots: St Enda's and the Cult of Boyhood* (Cork: Cork University Press, 2004).

Strachey, L. *Eminent Victorians* (New York: Putnam, 1918).

Tagg, J. *The Burden of Representation: Essays on Photographies and Histories* (London: Macmillan Education, 1988).

Temple, R. 'Icon', in J. Turner (ed.), *The Dictionary of Art*, volume XV (London: Macmillan, 1996).

Thompson, W.I. *The Imagination of an Insurrection: Dublin 1916* (Oxford: Oxford University Press, 1967).

Thornley, D. 'Patrick Pearse and the Pearse family', *Studies – An Irish Quarterly Review* (autumn/winter 1971).

Townshend, C. *Easter 1916: The Irish Rebellion* (London: Penguin, 2006).

Truden, B. *Recollections of the 50th Anniversary of the Easter Rising of 1916* (Dublin: [pamphlet], 1966).

Turpin, J. 'Cúchulainn Lives On', *CIRCA*, no. 69 (autumn 1994).

Uí Chollatáin, R. *An Claidheamh Soluis agus Fáinne an Lae 1899–1932* (Baile Átha Cliath: Cois Life, 2004).

Uí Chollatáin, R. 'P.H. Pearse deeply influenced by writings of James Fintan Lalor', *Laois Heritage Society Journal*, 3 (Laois: Laois Heritage Society, 2006).

Uí Chollatáin, R. *Iriseoirí Pinn na Gaeilge. An Cholúnaíocht Liteartha: Critic Iriseoireachta* (Baile Átha Cliath: Cois Life, 2008).

Vance, J.F. *Death So Noble: Memory, Meaning and the First World War* (Vancouver: University of British Columbia Press, 1997).

Wall, M. 'The background of the Rising, from 1914 until the countermanding order on Easter Saturday 1916', in K.B. Nowlan (ed.), *The Making of 1916: Studies in the History of the Rising* (Dublin: Stationery Office, 1969).

Wall, M. 'The plans and the countermand: The country and Dublin', in K.B. Nowlan (ed.), *The Making of 1916: Studies in the History of the Rising* (Dublin: Stationery Office, 1969).

Wa Thiongo, N. *Decolonizing the Mind* (London/Nairobi: Currey, 1986).

Watson, I. *Broadcasting in Irish: Minority Language, Radio, Television and Identity* (Dublin: Four Courts Press, 2003).

Weaver, D.H. 'Who are journalists?', in H. de Burgh (ed.), *Making Journalists* (London: Routledge, 2005).

Wilde, W. *Census of Ireland Report, 1851* (1854), Part V, Vol. 1 (Dublin: 1856).

Williams, J. *A Companion to Architecture in Ireland, 1837–1921* (Dublin: Irish Academic Press, 1994).

Williams, N. *Cniogaide Cnagaide* (Baile Átha Cliath: An Clóchomhar, 1988).

Wohl, R. *The Generation of 1914* (London: Weidenfeld and Nicholson, 1980).

Wullschlager, J. *Inventing Wonderland: The Lives and Fantasies of Lewis Carroll, Edward Lear, J.M. Barrie, Kenneth Grahame and A.A. Milne* (London: Methuen, 1995).

# Index
# Innéacs